OKANAGAN UNIV/COLLEGE LIBRARY

02802429

Sociological Theory

D0370724

CARIBOO COLLEGE
BRITISH COLUMBIA

Sociological Theory

Volume 2

From the 1920s to the 1960s

Richard Münch

Nelson-Hall Publishers
Chicago

Library of Congress Cataloging-in-Publication Data
(Revised for vol. 2)

Munch, Richard, 1945–
  Sociological theory.

  Includes bibliographical references and indexes.
  Contents: v. 1. From the 1850s to the 1920s–
v. 2. From the 1920s to the 1960s.
  1. Sociology–Philosophy. 2. Sociology–History.
HM24.M838 1993 301'.01 92-39833
ISBN 0-8304-1338-3 (v.2)
ISBN 0-8304-1394-4 (case contains three volumes)

Copyright © 1994 by Nelson-Hall Inc.
Reprinted 1994
All rights reserved. No part of this book may be reproduced in any form without permission in
writing from the publisher, except by a reviewer who wishes to quote brief passages in connection
with a review written for broadcast or for inclusion in a magazine or newspaper. For information
address Nelson-Hall Publishers, 111 North Canal Street, Chicago, Illinois 60606.

Manufactured in the United States of America

10 9 8 7 6 5 4 3 2

The paper used in this book meets the
minimum requirements of American
National Standard for Information
Sciences—Permanence of Paper for
Printed Library Materials, ANSI
Z39.48-1984.

CONTENTS

Preface   vii

Introduction to Volume 2   ix

PART ONE

The Structure of Social Action   1

1. Action Theory, Systems Theory, and Analytical
   Functionalism: Talcott Parsons   3

2. Empirical Functionalism: Robert K. Merton   119

3. Studies in Delinquent Subcultures: Albert J. Cohen
   and James F. Short, Jr., Walter B. Miller, Milton J. Yinger,
   Gresham M. Sykes, and David Matza   138

4. The Structure of Everyday Life: The Phenomenological
   Sociology of Peter L. Berger and Thomas Luckmann   144

5. The Social World as an Accomplishment of Social Practice:
   Harold Garfinkel's Studies in Ethnomethodology   173

PART TWO

The Politics of Social Action   187

6. The Functions of Social Conflict: Lewis A. Coser   189

7. A Theory of Domination and Conflict: Ralf Dahrendorf   201

PART THREE

The Economics of Social Action   **215**

  8. Social Exchange Theory: George C. Homans   217

  9. A Theory of Exchange and Power: Peter M. Blau   257

PART FOUR

The Symbolics of Social Action   **279**

10. The Development of Moral Consciousness: Jean Piaget   281

11. Symbolic Interactionism: Herbert Blumer   288

12. The Dramaturgy of Strategic Communication:
    Erving Goffman   306

    Bibliography   327

    Name Index   341

    Subject Index   345

Preface

THESE VOLUMES have been written for students, teachers, scholars, and researchers. They emerged from many years of lecturing and teaching courses in sociological theory. I am therefore very much indebted to the many students who joined my classes and served as critical examiners of my presentation of sociological theories. They forced me first of all to make the greatest effort to present the theories in a way that allows students to understand their message and to critically discuss them. The reluctance of many theorists to do this leaves the teacher of a course in sociological theory with an enormous task. The favorable response of my students over many years of preparing presentations of theories in a teachable form has encouraged me to compile the results of these years of teaching in a textbook, which I hope will receive the same favorable response from many students in many theory classes.

These volumes have been written with the intention of providing texts for teaching sociological theory that overcome the weaknesses of those available to date. I endeavor to be more comprehensive in covering the whole development of sociological theory, from classical origins to contemporary debates. I have attempted to be less biased toward certain national and paradigmatical traditions in order to allow sociological theory to be taught on an international and pluralistic level. I have tried to present theories in a more systematically structured way, by revealing their core and their distinctive statements in order to allow easier access to their message. The theories are presented much more in discourse, mutually throwing light on their more obscure aspects and on their erroneous aspects. I hope teachers will find the book as helpful for teaching sociological theory as I did the materials that eventually constituted the book.

These volumes have also been written for scholars. This work is not simply a history of social thought, but a reconstruction and continuation of sociological discourse with the aim of advancing our theoretical knowledge to a new level: constructing networks of theories by way of interparadigmatical and intertheoretical discourse. I hope that many of my colleagues will join this enterprise.

These volumes have also been written for researchers. The state of theoretical knowledge is presented in a systematically structured way, which I hope invites researchers to work with that knowledge and to relate empirical research to theoretical questions more than has been usual up to now. Their reluctance to do so was caused to a not inconsiderable degree by the often very confusing writing style of many theorists. I have tried very hard to improve upon that style of writing theory.

This project has been written with the support of many people: students, assistants, colleagues, friends and family. Without their help the book would not have come to light. Many thanks to all of them. Special thanks go to Neil Johnson for working on the English language of this book.

For their assistance with references, preparing name and subject indices, and with word processing work, I wish to thank Susanne Gabele, Renate Kolvenbach, Christian Lahusen, Karin Rhau and Willy Viehöver. Special thanks also go to Michael Opielka for valuable comments in the final stage of working on the manuscript.

INTRODUCTION TO VOLUME 2

THE PERIOD from the 1920s to the 1960s can be seen as one of consolidation and differentiation in sociological theory on a new level of development. First of all there is Talcott Parsons's great attempt at synthesis that originated in his years as a student in England and Germany from 1924 to 1926. In the 1950s, Parsons rose to the position of the dominant theorist, which he retained well into the 1960s. Also in the 1950s we see Robert K. Merton in the most influential position next to Parsons. They both contributed to what was labeled as "structural functionalism" at that time, though with different emphases. Whereas Parsons concentrated on so-called analytical and grand theory, Merton put more emphasis on empirical and middle-range theories.

The dominance of structural functionalism naturally provoked rebellious reactions by scholars who wanted to free themselves and others from its constrictions. The major argument against structural functionalism criticized what was said to be too great a preoccupation with understanding and explaining the structure of social action in its institutional order. Critics tried to pay more attention to subcultural variation, the structure of everyday life, the momentary ordering activities of actors in everyday situations, conflict, exchange, symbolic interaction, and social change. After its consolidation by structural functionalism, which also implied its unification and the leveling out of differences, sociological theory again differentiated into a plurality of paradigms on a new consolidated level of development in this process. Albert J. Cohen, James F. Short, Jr., Walter B. Miller, Milton Yinger, Gresham Sykes, and David Matza made contributions to understanding the subcultural varieties of social life beyond its structuration by its dominant values, norms, and institutions. The phenomenological sociology of Peter L. Berger and Thomas Luckmann enhanced our knowledge of the elementary structures of everyday life. Harold Garfinkel's studies in ethnomethodology turned the phenomenological approach toward greater emphasis on the momentary ordering activities of actors in everyday situations.

Lewis A. Coser and Ralf Dahrendorf pointed out the nature and significance of conflict in social life. George C. Homans and Peter M. Blau opened our eyes to the economic dynamics involved in any realm of social action. Herbert Blumer and Erving Goffman paved the way for studying the involvement of symbolic interpretation, self-presentation, framing, and identity management in social interaction. Beyond sociology in its pure sense we also have to acknowledge the contribution made by the Swiss psychologist Jean Piaget to understanding the development of moral consciousness within the social context of the human individual's life as part of the symbolics of social action. Though Piaget's work on this subject dates back to 1932, its recognition in sociology can be taken as part of sociological theory's differentiation after the breakdown of structural functionalism's reign.

We will reconstruct the outlined development within the framework of a four-fold action space that can be differentiated basically into four fields: the *economics of social action*, with the function of its opening and adaptation to varying situations; the *politics of social action*, with the function of its specification and orientation toward goal attainment; the *structure of social action*, with the function of its closing and integration in an ordered system; and the *symbolics of social action*, with the function of its generalization and latent pattern maintenance within a framework of meaning (see chapter 2, volume 1; Münch, 1987a, 1987b). I have ordered the various contributors to the consolidation and differentiation of sociological theory from the 1920s to the 1960s according to their primary concern with studying the nature of a specific field of social action within that action space. That primary concern is their home base from which they explore the other parts of the social world. I will elaborate how the contributors saw the nature of their field of primary concern and how they stretched out to the other fields in a more or less balanced or biased way.

PART ONE

The Structure of Social Action

ACTION THEORY, SYSTEMS THEORY, AND ANALYTICAL FUNCTIONALISM: TALCOTT PARSONS

TALCOTT PARSONS was born in 1902 and died in 1979 while visiting Germany to be honored on the fiftieth anniversary of receiving his doctorate from the University of Heidelberg. Visiting London and Heidelberg in the twenties and writing his doctoral dissertation on the spirit of capitalism in the works of Max Weber and Werner Sombart in 1927 made Parsons the major mediator between European and American social theory.

Parsons was a Harvard professor throughout his academic life and became the central figure around which theoretical debate centered in the 1950s and 1960s. Harvard University became a center of sociology after its program had been set up by Pitirim Sorokin (1889–1968), who had been appointed to the first chair in sociology in 1929. He taught sociological theory from a European perspective and was particularly interested in the macro-social transformations of society in their social and cultural change (Sorokin, 1927, 1928, 1937–1941, 1956). Sorokin was outranked by Parsons in the 1940s; Parsons was made chairman of the department in 1944. Parsons founded the department of social relations, which included sociology, psychology, and anthropology, two years later.

The third great Harvard sociologist was George C. Homans (1910–1989), who rebelled against Parsons's analytical functionalism with his attempt to reveal the psychological propositions that allow us to explain social behavior (Homans, 1961, 1974). Instead of following Parsons's work on conceptual schemes, as he put it, he tried to work out propositions for the explanation of social behavior (Homans, 1967). Homans's influence in the department was growing in the 1970s while Parsons's influence was declining. Homans ousted Parsons from his dominant position in the 1970s just as Parsons had ousted Sorokin in the 1940s.

From his first major work, *The Structure of Social Action,* published in 1937, to his last collection of essays, *Action Theory and the Human Condition*, published in 1978, Parsons was devoted to providing a theoretical framework for sociology that was supposed to serve as the focal point for synthesizing the accumulated theoretical knowledge. The major message of *The Structure of Social Action* is that the classical founders of social science presented in the book — economist Alfred Marshall and sociologists Vilfredo Pareto, Emile Durkheim, and Max Weber — had converged in overcoming the split between the two opposing paradigms of positivism and idealism. This was partly a statement of fact and partly a creative reconstruction of the classical works by Parsons himself. He demonstrated this convergence in a formally structured way, particularly by addressing the question of how the existence of social order can be explained in theoretical terms. In a whole series of publications following his first work, Parsons remained devoted to this fundamental program. In the following sections, I will give a formal reconstruction of the development of Parsons's work that criticizes, corrects, revises, and extends Parsons's contributions with the aim of carrying out that program beyond Parsons himself.

Social Order as a Central Problem in Sociological Theory

The question of social order has been a central problem for sociological theory since the beginning of sociology as a specific discipline defining its own subject matter with its own conceptual frame of reference in the late nineteenth and early twentieth centuries. Georg Simmel, a classic German sociologist who contributed to the development of sociology at that time, went to the heart of the problem in a question that he formulated in analogy to Immanuel Kant. Kant (1781/1964a), who was concerned about our knowledge of the world, had asked: How is objective knowledge possible? Simmel (1908: 21–30) now asked: How is society possible? His question seeks to establish how it is possible that people engage in interaction and, out of this interaction, form a society. The question implies the more specific question: How is social order possible? And what this means is: How is it possible that people can predict each others' actions in such a way that they can rely in their actions on confirmed expectations regarding the actions and expectations of other actors?

What Is Social Order? Four Examples

A social order exists to the extent that actors can establish confirmed expectations of others' actions and expectations. The actions of individuals are predictable; deviation of actions from predictions is the exception to the rule.

That which is contrary to order is called disorder, or "anomie," which means the lack of rules for action (from the Greek *nomos*, which means "law," and is turned to the contrary in a-nomie). Disorder, or anomie, is always a problem for actors because, being unable to establish firm expectations, they do not know how to act, and this leads to insecurity, hesitation, frustration, and withdrawal from interaction. Let us examine some examples.

Two students may agree to help each other in preparing their exams, that is, to exchange their knowledge. Student A is expected to give B his or her support in mathematics; B is expected to give his or her support to A in sociology. Now let us suppose that the sociology exam takes place this term and the mathematics exam next term. B supports A in sociology this term, but as the next term comes, A is too busy and has no time to support B in mathematics. This is a deviation from the agreement and from B's expectation. The more students experience such deviations from initial agreements, the more they doubt the reliability of other students. As a result, students refuse to engage in exchange of support and thus withdraw from interaction. Everybody retreats to studying alone; social interaction and the exchange of knowledge break down. Order exists when each actor can expect from other actors that they will act out agreements as they were originally established. Mutual trust is possible, and thus interaction runs smoothly. Reality as we know it lies between these two extremes of order and disorder and alternates between a higher and a lower level of trust and corresponding social exchange.

In another example, suppose there is one fellowship available for the most able student in empirical sociology. Several students are in competition with one another. It is announced that the student selected will be the one who provides the best confirmation for a theory by empirical data. It may be that several students succumb to the temptation to fake data, that is, to provide data they themselves have invented, or to withhold relevant data they possess so that other students in competition with them cannot use the data. In this case, any student who does not make use of faking and/or withholding data is placed at a disadvantage. This means that everybody is forced to make use of fraud (deceit) and force in order to realize his or her goals. Everybody fights with any available means. The results of action become completely unpredictable because they can always be counteracted by superior force and the more intelligent deceit of others. The consequence is a universal struggle for power. Unpredictability and disorder result from the fact that the power and deceit of one actor, which predominate at a given moment, may always be counteracted by the power and deceit of other actors.

In another example, five students may agree to form a group in order to prepare for an exam. To give a degree of reliability to their cooperation they must establish a certain cohesion and solidarity. But after working together for some time they recognize that all five students also have very close relationships to other students who expect their solidarity and who feel unfriendly toward the members of the exam study group. The other students say, "You're working in a group with Jack and Ann, and I can't stand them; what made you want to do that?" Thus, the study-group students are always in conflict with regard to their solidarity and to the norm they should follow. If they have their regular meetings on Friday evenings from six to eight, but are always under pressure from their friends to meet them in the café, their solidarity toward the exam group can no longer be guaranteed. There is no order of solidarity relationships within the group.

In a final example, two students, A and B, strike up a friendship. However, when student A realizes that B also spends quite a lot of time with C, D, and E — all of them people A does not like — A is disappointed with B and reacts angrily. For a different reason, B is equally angry; B expects A either to share in the friendship with the others or, failing that, at least to allow him or her to continue being friends with C, D, and E. Each accuses the other of not behaving like a real friend. In other words, they fail to understand one another. Each one has a different conception of the meaning of friendship. Thus, neither one can predict the actions of the other. What A perceives as being inconsistent with friendship is for B consistent with friendship, and vice versa.

We can conclude from our examples four different forms of order (and its opposite, disorder).

1. Each actor can expect/not expect other actors to act out what they have agreed upon when an exchange is made.
2. Each actor can expect/not expect that his or her action directed toward a certain goal will not always be in danger of being counteracted by the force and deceit of other actors.
3. Each actor can expect/not expect from other actors with whom he or she cooperates that they will not withold their solidarity in favor of other solidarity relationships when it matters most.
4. Each actor can expect/not expect that other actors attach the same meaning to the words (concepts, terms) they use in communication.

What we can derive from these examples is that actors must share common rules of exchange, competition, solidarity, and communication in order to keep their actions predictable. The next questions, then, are: How do such rules emerge? And how can they be maintained?

The Emergence and Maintenance of Social Order

Two divergent approaches to the explanation of the emergence and maintenance of social order are the positivistic and the idealistic approaches, each of which occurs in two different versions (Parsons, 1937/1968: chapters 2 and 3).

1. Positivistic Explanations of Action and Order

We can subdivide this category between positivistic explanations of action in general and then, as a derivative of this, positivistic explanations of social order.

1.1. Positivistic Explanations of Action

In the positivistic view, the action (A) of an individual is the result of his or her pursuing ends (E) by applying means (M) under certain conditions (C). For example, a student aims to pass an exam in sociology (E). Conditions affecting the student's preparation for the exam are the required reading, the fact that he or she is still unfamiliar with the literature, and the literature is on reserve in the college library (C). The means that the student applies, in order to attain the desired end, is to go to the college library and read the required literature for several hours each week of the term (M).

There are two ways in which action results from these factors: rational adaptation or natural selection.

1.1.1 Rational Adaptation

In rational adaptation, the actors make use of their knowledge of the relationship between conditions, means, and ends. Our student applies his or her knowledge that going to the library and reading the book selections is an appropriate means to the end "passing the exam" under the conditions that certain reading is required and he or she is relatively ignorant of sociology.

1.1.2 Natural Selection

In natural selection, actors pursue ends by applying means under certain conditions but without appropriate knowledge of the relationships between conditions, means, and ends. The consequence of this is that the only actions to succeed are those which are accidentally adapted to conditions. In our example, the system of examination in connection with required reading allows only those students to survive in the system who have acquired the relevant knowledge of sociology by reading in the library.

Explaining surviving types of behavior by natural selection derives from Darwin's (1888) theory of the evolution of living organisms. According to this theory evolution brings about the survival of those species that are adapted to the conditions of their environment.

1.2 The Positivistic Explanation of Order: Factual Order

In the positivistic view, order is the outcome of actors' mutually strategic action. They act strategically in the sense that they force each others' actions as external conditions to which they have to adapt in the same way as they must adapt to material things they cannot communicate with. In a soccer match, for example, a player in team A cannot ask a player in team B to give him the ball; the player must adapt to the situation and exert external constraints on opponents in order to gain possession of the ball. There are two types of order that may emerge under these conditions: accidental and compulsory.

1.2.1 Accidental Order

Accidental order emerges by chance and varies from situation to situation. If I go to the flea market with an old bike hoping to sell it to someone and to buy an old-fashioned dress, it is a matter of chance if I find a buyer for my bike and another person is at the market trying to sell an old-fashioned dress like the one I have been looking for. If a lot of people expect such good luck and go to the flea market, it becomes reasonably probable that there will be a chance to sell a bike and to buy an old-fashioned dress.

1.2.2 Compulsory Order

Compulsory order emerges out of the existence of stable external material conditions to which all actors have to adapt in the same way. The fact that a soccer match takes place on a marked-out playing field with goals at either end makes the actions of the teams predictable in a certain way and enables team members to adapt their actions to each other. In a more formal example, the existence of a central superordinate sanctioning power that has imposed fixed rules on actors and applies punishments for the violation of the rules makes it possible to predict behavior that complies to those rules. All actors have to adapt to the conditions set by the central sanctioning power.

Another type of compulsory order results from the inborn instinctual determination of behavior. For example, the instinctual disposition of parent animals to care for their offspring and of the members of animal groups to share food with their fellows and to defend their fellows against enemies provides for an order in their lives that is rooted in heredity. Its involuntary character makes it a special type of compulsory order. Inasmuch as human life is rooted in the same instinctual structures, it, too, involves order of this type.

1.2.3 The Hobbesian Problem of Order

Positivistic approaches to the question of order face what has been termed the Hobbesian problem of order. In his work *Leviathan* (Hobbes, 1651/1966), the British philosopher Thomas Hobbes made the observation that if actors are free to make their own choice of ends and means, they always come into conflict with one another; that is, what for one actor is a positive achievement in realizing an end causes corresponding harm to another actor seeking to realize his or her own ends. It is not possible for both actors to achieve their ends at the same time (e.g., when two sporting teams meet, only one can emerge as the winner). The question is, though, how can one ensure that one really does realize one's goals? Relying purely on force and fraud may help. Yet, if everyone relies on such force and fraud, they must also fear that they will be used by everyone else.

In this situation no predictable order exists. But Hobbes assumes that individuals recognize their situation and jump from the "natural state" to the state of civilization by concluding a mutual contract. They give over all their power to a superordinate entity (a ruler, a parliamentary body, an authority, the "leviathan"), which has the duty to impose binding rules of behavior and to apply negative sanctions against violations of the rules. Hobbes argues that it is economic calculation that opens individuals' eyes to the idea that a mutual contract gives them a better opportunity to optimize their ends than they would have if each person were to rely on his or her ability to use force and fraud. However, this is too optimistic a view of where economic calculation can lead.

The individuals in Hobbes's "state of nature" rely on force and fraud because they cannot trust each other to fulfill individual contracts. But the question is, what makes individuals believe other people will be faithful to the great social contract? It is this inconsistency in his argument that leads Hobbes to the solution that individuals must not have the right to retreat from the contract unless the superordinate authority ceases to provide for a stable order. Hobbes even resorts to the traditional position of subjecting the individual to the authority of God and thus inconsistently refutes his assumption that the human individual is free in his or her choice and is guided only by subjective reason. Thus Hobbes switches from the accidental to the compulsory solution to the problem of order. Positivism always oscillates between these two solutions: liberalism and authoritarianism. This is the so-called utilitarian dilemma. Utilitarianism is an approach that tries to conceive of order as the result of the spontaneous economic calculations of free individuals (mostly in a market), which is accidental order. The liberal position always has the retreat to the authoritarian position hovering in the background. That is, liberal positivists are inclined to put at least the supervision over the maintenance of rules in the hand of a central authority (the state, the government).

Another type of reasoning that dispenses with the idea of the voluntary creation of order and favors a compulsory order results from introducing an inborn instinct of sympathy for one's fellows. David Hume (1739/1978, 1777/1980) and Adam Smith (1759/1966) made such assumptions. Apart from the fact that this approach to explaining order drops the idea of voluntary human action, it also faces the problem that it covers only interaction between members of primordial groups but fails with regard to interaction that reaches beyond their boundaries. Sympathy for one's fellows very often involves antipathy and even hostility toward people outside one's group who are seen as potential enemies. Behavior determined by such inborn instincts proceeds very much according to the friend/enemy scheme of animal life. Whereas instinctual regulation secures order in primordial groups, it also creates disorder in large groups. The more human life involves interaction beyond the boundaries of primordial groups, the more the friend/enemy scheme becomes a major obstacle to the creation of new and complex types of order. This is the problem of developing societies. Their economic, political, and cultural growth multiplies interaction beyond primordial ties, yet the behavior of people in a developing society remains very much determined by the friend/enemy scheme. The rise and fall of dictatorial orders and severe struggles between hostile groups seems to be their fate for a long time. Their modernization proceeds between compulsory order and disorder.

The liberal position was developed particularly in Anglo-Saxon thought, for example, John Locke in the seventeenth century, David Hume and Adam Smith in the eighteenth century, and Jeremy Bentham and John Stuart Mill in the nineteenth century. Nowadays, the new political economy of social scientists like Milton Friedman, James Buchanan, James Coleman, and Gary Becker provides further examples of this view. The viewpoint of the external enforcement of an order was developed to a much greater extent in French nineteenth-century positivism, from Saint-Simon to Auguste Comte.

2. Idealistic Explanations of Action and Order

We may subdivide idealistic explanations into explanations of action and explanations of social order.

2.1 Idealistic Explanations of Action

In the idealistic view, actors derive the appropriate actions (A) under certain conditions (C) from ideas (I). Symbolic ideas applied to specific conditions result in specific actions. Two individuals who are in love with one another are able to derive the right actions under different conditions from the idea of love: they pay attention to each other, help each other, give each other presents on certain special days, and so on. The idea of equal opportunity tells us what to do in education: not to discriminate in handling admissions, paying attention to students, and conducting exams.

Idealistic explanations of action occur in two different versions: subsuming action under generally valid ideas and conforming in action to the existing, concrete norms of a life-world.

2.2.1 Application of Generally Valid Ideas

The conscious application of rationally justified and thus valid ideas to specific conditions is a version of idealism in which the individual always has to justify his or her actions with regard to generally valid ideas. Every action carried out in the education field has to be justified with regard to the idea of equal opportunity. Alternatively, a scientist who gives up a hypothesis because it has failed certain tests is applying to his or her action the idea that science is a search for truth.

2.1.2 Conforming to Concrete Norms

Conformity to concrete norms means that the individual actor is committed to the community in which he or she lives and which has a certain tradition of rules governing behavior. The mother who always gets up at seven in the morning to fix breakfast for her family without seeking other alternatives is conforming to the rules of this family's life-world. Everything we do as a matter of habit falls under this version of idealism.

2.2 The Idealistic Explanation of Order: Normative Order

In the idealistic view, order results either out of rational agreement or out of customs that are unconsciously taken for granted: ideal or conformistic order.

2.2.1 Ideal Order

Ideal order is an outcome of the rational justification of ideas that, as a result, can be assumed to be universally valid; that is to say, everyone who is endowed with reason would agree with these ideas. Generally valid ideas are those on which actors who are engaged in a discourse where nothing but the best argument counts would all agree. An argument is the product of a person tracing back the validity of a more specific idea to the validity of a more general idea. I might argue, for example, that if the idea of equal opportunity holds true, there must be no discrimination on the grounds of sex, race, or ethnic origin when it comes to the admission of students to a university. An order of this kind is an ideal order.

2.2.2 Conformistic Order

A conformistic order is the outcome of what actors commonly share and commonly take for granted. That is, they act on the basis of a consensus within a group that has its own tradition and life-world of self-evident norms. Within such a group, the members share a lot of common norms that they always apply in action. In this way their actions are completely predictable to the other members. A family, a student fraternity, a neighborhood, and a university department all have certain traditions on which the members can rely in action. That means order is based on the conformism of members of a group with regard to that group's norms. When father and the children get up at 7:30 A.M. in order to have breakfast at 7:40, they rely on mother's rule conformity. If a student group meets every Friday at 6:00 P.M., the members of the group can rely on the others to be at their meeting place so that they will not have wasted their time.

2.2.3 The Kantian Problem of Order

Immanuel Kant, the German philosopher, asked a question similar to Hobbes's in his own work (Kant, *Critique of Practical Reason*, 1788/1964b, for translation, see 1952b; *Perpetual Peace*, 1795/1964d, for translation, see 1972). However, he shifted the solution to the idealistic position. He demonstrated that whenever several actors live within the same limited space for action while pursuing their own ends independently, the realization of one actor's ends precludes the realization of the others' ends. The meaning of the solution he puts forward is that actors must reach beyond, or transcend, the limits of their own egoistic pursuit of ends and attain a position where they are guided by universal reason alone. This means that, in any action they wish to perform, actors must ask if this could be made a universal law, that is, a law everybody would agree upon if guided only by pure reason. Universal agreement on basic laws is Kant's solution to the problem of order. Such laws are categorically imperative: their validity is independent of changing means, conditions, or ends. In distinction to this, hypothetical imperatives are valid only with regard to such changing means, conditions, and ends. The basic categorical imperative is the rule: "So act that the maxim of your will could always hold at the same time as a principle establishing universal law" (Kant, 1788/1964b: 54; for translation, see 1952b: 302). But the question remains as to whether any concrete rule can be established in the way Kant describes. Kant's categorical imperative and any subsumed specific categorical norm remains rather too general to guide action concretely. It provides only the basis for an ideal order.

Thus, in order to become more concrete, idealism has to turn toward the other element in its view, namely toward conformism. Even Kant recommended the conformity of the individual to the norms that have been established by political authority according to the rule of their general validity. And after Kant, Hegel (1821/1964-1971) reconciled the universally valid law with the legal order of the state in the idea of the state, thus switching much more than Kant had done to the position of conformism. For Kant, the moral categorical imperative and the legal order are separated, the former providing the standard against which the latter, ever deviating, must be measured. For Hegel, universal morality and the legal order find their reconciliation in the idea of ethical practice (*Sittlichkeit*) as brought to expression in the state. This is the idealistic dilemma: on the one hand, rules are discussed that claim the validity of moral order, but, on the other hand, when concrete rules for action have to be established, they relapse into conformism. In present-day discussions, the idealistic position can be clearly recognized in the German philosopher Jürgen Habermas's theory of communicative action. In his view, order is the outcome of action being anchored in the interplay between communication in a life-world that is taken for granted and the rational justification of norms in discursive procedures; the criterion for the validity of norms is rationally achieved consensus.

However, we have to recognize that Kant himself also points the way toward a position that transcends, that is, reaches beyond, idealism. We can at least conclude from his work by inference that a concrete order must rely on the combination of categorical and hypothetical norms, which also means a combination of idealistic and positivistic factors. This leads to the concept of the interpenetration of those idealistic and positivistic factors and to the synthesis of positivism and idealism in voluntarism as intended (though the synthesis achieved is not perfect) in the work of Talcott Parsons.

3. The Voluntaristic Synthesis of Idealism and Positivism in the Explanation of Action and Order

3.1 Concrete Action and Order

Concrete action and order is always a result of the dominance of positivistic factors or of idealistic ones, or a mixture of the two. Let us again take a soccer match as an example. As long as the match is in progress, the teams apply force against each other in a strategic manner. They take the actions of their opponents as external conditions to which they have to adapt passively or actively. There is no communication. Nevertheless, there are rules that guide their actions. Fouls are prohibited, the ball must not cross the sidelines or goal lines, the aim is to score goals, and so on. The communicative basis of the rules of the game can easily be recognized when the referee stops the match because a rule has been violated. Sometimes the decision of the referee solicits communications from players and from the spectators arguing against or for the decision. And, to a certain extent, the discussion of the interpretation of the rules reaches beyond the match itself, leading to a public discourse on the question of whether certain rules can still be considered reasonable if they are measured against the general underlying idea of the game (e.g., regarding equality of opportunity among the competing teams). Thus, strategic aspects and communicative aspects are interlinked in the concrete performance of the soccer players. A zone of interlinkage of both aspects is the situation in which a concrete situation is defined as rule conforming or rule deviating by the referee.

3.2 Interpenetration

A specific form of mixed concrete action and order results from the interpenetration of idealistic and positivistic factors. Interpenetration means that both sides are existent in their own right but exert a formative influence on one another via their interlinkage in zones of interpenetration. The referee in the above example forms such a zone of interpenetration. He applies the rules of the game that are idealistic and communicative in character to concrete strategic actions in the match that can be explained in the positivistic view. The referee in his action transmits the communicative rules into the realm of strategic action, which is normatively shaped in this process. At the same time, the ongoing match leads to the realm of the rules being permeated by the strategic action of the teams insofar as the referee, for example, accepts a certain amount of roughness as it occurs during the match. He also transmits facts of the match in his report into deliberations on the rules, which may be changed as a result of such reports and the changes they reflect in how matches are played in reality.

3.3 Voluntaristic Order

What is the meaning of voluntarism? It must mean that action is not solely the result of chance or compulsion in the adaptation to conditions nor solely the result of a straightforward derivation from rules that are taken for granted or from objective reason, which impose themselves on the actor.

It must mean that action is the result of the interplay of positivistic and idealistic factors that the individual as actor has to handle and to relate to one another. Because the balance of the interpenetration of positivistic and idealistic factors is of first importance, the individual actor standing between these factors can maintain a certain autonomy and can thereby avoid becoming a victim of either external conditions or external ideas. He or she can play out one part against the other. This is the part of the individual that Freud called the "ego" in distinction to the "id" (biological drives as conditions) and to the "superego" (norms as external ideas).

An individual actor such as a mother who fixes breakfast every morning at 7:00 A.M. has the ability to ask if this is generally justifiable; that is, she may ask if this rule is consistent with the idea of equal opportunity. But she can also feel committed to her family. She has to take into account the conditions of who goes to work and who goes to school, and she can vary the action according to the situation, for example, on weekends. Thus, she may compromise, asking for a new breakfast time, assigning other tasks to the other members of the family, and so on.

The source of individual autonomy is the agency of the subject, that is, his or her ability to make choices and not to be completely driven by external conditions or internal instincts but also guided by given norms. The human individual can set goals and question outside demands. When Parsons says that concrete action always involves conditional and normative elements, he uses the term "normative" to refer to the realm of agency that is not causally determined but open to choice and deliberation. He is very clear about this when he speaks about setting ends:

> As so far defined, an end is a concrete anticipated future state of affairs. But it is quite clear that not this total state of affairs but only certain aspects or features of it can be attributed to normative elements, thus to the agency of the actor rather than to features of the situation in which he acts. . . . An end, then, in the analytical sense must be defined as the *difference* between the anticipated

future state of affairs and that which it could have been predicted would ensue from the initial situation *without the agency of the actor having intervened.* (Parsons, 1937/1968: 49)

When Parsons (1937/1968: 76–77) also says that action always implies "effort to conform with norms," this "effort" means the exercise of agency, because only free agents can direct action toward norms. This recognition of agency has far-reaching implications for the solution to the problem of order. Inasmuch as actors are capable of exercising free agency and conditions like external force or internal instinct to support and protect their own group do not determine their action completely in the causal sense, order between free agents could come about randomly only at given moments but not as a durable feature of their relationship, unless there were some other source of order. This is exactly the position that leads Parsons to his notion of value consensus. This, in fact, is the only possible form of order between free agents! This is what he distinguishes as normative order from the factual orders that result either from causal determination by external conditions or internal instincts or from momentary coincidence, for example, the coincidence of buyers' and sellers' interests on a market. However, their contract presupposes normative elements that need the consensus of agents. This complementarity between agency and consensus has been completely missed in the common critique of Parsons's "normative" solution to the problem of order. It is also true for a recent interpretation that parallels Parsons's normative solution to the problem of order in terms of value consensus as civil religion to Hobbes's inconsistent resort to the authority of God (Wagner, 1991). This would be nothing but an externally imposed compulsory order that is completely inconsistent with the notion of value consensus of free agents in a voluntaristic order.

Though developed in correspondence to Hobbes's search for political order, Parsons's voluntaristic solution to the problem of order is by no means limited to questions of political order. It is a solution that is relevant for any field of social action and, as such, unsurpassed by any new approaches to the problem of order, most of which ultimately imply some form of accidental or compulsory factual order. It is therefore a mistake to take leave of Parsons in this respect (Luhmann, 1982: 372; Wagner, 1991: 122). However, Parsons himself fell short of his analytical achievement, because he did not distinguish sufficiently between consensus resulting from a common life-world and agreement resulting from a discourse. He equated norms too much with the "nonrational" elements of action. Traditional norms of a life-world are nonrational; however, agreement on norms resulting from discourse is rational. Parsons tended toward the conformistic horn of the Kantian dilemma of order.

3.4 Order and Change

The interest of sociology in order is the same as the interest of natural sciences in the order of nature — discovering basic laws.

The sociological interest in order must not be confused with an ideological interest in maintaining some concrete existing order in a society; it is not at all a plea for law and order in society. The distinction between factual, normative, and voluntaristic order shows how different forms of order can exist, what features they have, and what place the autonomy of the individual has within this order.

A voluntaristic order is an order in which the individual's autonomy plays a central role in interrelating the otherwise purely accidental, compulsory, conformistic, and ideal forms of order.

Change means the change in actions themselves and in orders of action. The center of an order is the regularity with which we can expect certain actions under certain conditions. The major factor that provides for this regularity is the inclusion of individuals in a common life-world of shared rules that are taken for granted.

Insofar as these rules can be rationally questioned, they can be changed in the direction of rationally justified and general ideas.

Insofar as individuals adapt their action to changing conditions and rationally relate means under these conditions to freely chosen ends, they have the chance to deviate from what has thus far been taken for granted. In this process rules become adapted to new situations.

Insofar as individuals pursue ends disregarding the rules that have been taken for granted thus far and have enough power to enforce their action against other actors, an existing order can be changed in the direction of the ends of powerful actors, particularly charismatic leaders.

Action and Systems Theory

So far we have treated the synthesis as it was attempted by Talcott Parsons in his first book *The Structure of Social Action* (Parsons, 1937/1968). Integrating positivism and idealism, he achieved the synthetical view of voluntarism. His next major works, *The Social System* and *Toward a General Theory of Action*, appeared in 1951, the latter co-authored with Edward Shils and other colleagues. With these works Parsons moved away from a theory of action toward a theory of systems of action. We shall look more closely at whether this was a major break, meaning the replacement of action theory by systems theory, or whether the action-theoretical basis was preserved in the new frame of reference.

Social Systems, Personality Systems, and Cultural Systems

New concepts do enter the conceptual frame of reference: Action is conceived of as taking place in a situation where the actor is oriented toward cultural, social, or physical objects, and we can add organic objects. An example of a cultural object is a book that a student reads; a social object is the student group to which he or she belongs; a physical object is the seminar room in which he or she attends classes; an organic object is his or her body or the body of another person as an organism. The actor's orientation toward these objects is shaped through three different systems: the personality system, the social system, and the cultural system. This is where the systems language as distinct from the action language enters the scene. The systems have their own identity; they have boundaries that distinguish them from events outside a system and have to display mechanisms of self-maintenance in order to stay alive as systems.

Let me characterize the systems briefly, then go on to a closer analysis of each system, after that turn to the analysis of the interrelationships between the systems, and finally ask whether action theory has lost its relevance for this new systems theory (Parsons, 1951; Parsons and Shils, 1951b).

1. A *social system* is a complex of interdependent interactions that can be distinguished from situational interactions and from noninteractional elements of the situation and of actions outside this system. There are boundaries that define what is within and what is outside the system. Social norms and roles and clear rules of membership in a social system play a major part in defining those boundaries. Its major problem of self-maintenance is maintaining social order.

2. A *personality system* is a complex of interdependent need-dispositions of an individual actor that can be distinguished from situational dispositions to act and from nondispositional aspects of the situation and of action outside this system. There are boundaries that define what is within and what is outside the system. That an individual knows who he or she is and what he or she is and wants to be, that is, the idea of having an image of oneself, plays a major part in defining the boundaries of the system. Its major problem of self-maintenance is maintaining identity and self-realization.

3. A *cultural system* is a complex of interdependent symbols that can be distinguished from symbols and nonsymbolic elements of action and the situation outside this system. Ideas with their identifying function give a cultural system meaning and serve to define its boundaries. Its major problem of self-maintenance is maintaining the consistency of its symbols — its pattern consistency.

Social System

The social system (Parsons and Shils, 1951b: 190–230) is constituted by interactions. What is interaction? The meaning of interaction is illustrated as follows: an actor, whom we may call "Ego," orients his or her actions and expectations toward the actions and expectations of another actor we shall call "Alter." That is, when Ego acts in a certain way, he or she expects that Alter will react in a certain way and vice versa. And Ego shapes his or her action according to this expectation.

If I enter a small grocery, I know (expect) that the storekeeper expects me to indicate that I would like to purchase something; otherwise, I would not enter the store. Thus, I enter the store only if I am sure that I will purchase something (this is not so vital in the supermarket). The storekeeper orients his own action to my entering the store and says, "Can I help you?" He expects me to have the intention of making a purchase and acts in this direction. I expect that the storekeeper wants to serve me and does not allow self-service. Thus my answer to the question is: "Yes, I'd like six tomatoes, five navels, and four croissants." Because I expect that the storekeeper will expect me to pay, I take out my purse and wait to hear what he says: "That's $6.59." I hand over $7.00 and expect 41 cents back. He gives me the 41 cents, we both say "goodbye," and I leave the store. This is an interaction guided by the actors' mutual expectations. I do not enter the store unless I know I want to buy something, I do not serve myself, and I do not take anything away that I have not paid for. The storekeeper does not leave me alone in the store and does not make any attempt to sell me second-class merchandise, because he knows I would not come again. I direct my action not only according to my ends and available means but also according to the expectations of the storekeeper, and vice versa. The storekeeper with his expectations is a social object I am oriented to or a condition to which I have to adapt my action in the positivistic view.

Parsons and Shils (1951a: 14–16; 1951b: 105–7, 201–2) conceive of this interaction in *Toward a General Theory of Action* as an exchange of gratifications (positive sanctions) and deprivations (negative sanctions) regarding the need-dispositions of the actors. I have the need to get some fruit and bakery products, and this need is gratified if I shape my action according to the expectations of the storekeeper. The storekeeper's handing over the fruit and croissants is a gratification with regard to my needs. My purchase is a gratification for the storekeeper, because he can buy some other things with the dollars from my purchase. If he sends me out of the store when I want to serve myself, I cannot satisfy my needs, particularly if there is no other grocery nearby. My refusal to make any further purchases if I get some rotten merchandise is a deprivation for the storekeeper.

Parsons and Shils make use of two further concepts in order to describe the interaction between Ego and Alter: complementarity of actions and expectations, and double contingency of gratifications. Complementarity means that Ego's actions are oriented to Alter's expectations and vice versa. That is, the actions and expectations of each refer to the other, either in the sense of conformity of actions to expectations or in the sense of deviation of actions from expectations. The customer's request for tomatoes, navels, and croissants conforms to the storekeeper's expectation that the customer wants to buy something. If the customer looks around without asking for something, this deviates from the storekeeper's expectation. He will attempt to correct the customer's action by asking with special emphasis, "Can I help you?" If the customer does not react by indicating a wish to make a purchase, the storekeeper will ask the person to leave the store. If this reaction still does not bring results, the storekeeper may tell the person that he will call the police. Finally, the police may come and take the person out of the store. The reactions of the storekeeper in this case are negative sanctions, which imply deprivations of the customer's needs (ultimately: having to pay a fine). We can see in the reactions of the storekeeper several levels of strictness of sanctions, from a mere emphasis when asking "Can I help you?" to the person being removed from the store by the police using physical force. In the last instance, physical force is the material basis of negative sanctions.

Double contingency of gratifications means that Ego's gratifications are dependent (contingent) not only on his or her selection from alternatives for action but also on the reactions of Alter and his or her selection from alternatives for action, and vice versa. This makes predictability of each other's actions an urgent need for Ego and Alter. But what provides for this predictability? Is it merely the exchange of positive and negative sanctions that brings about social order in the sense of mutual predictability of actions? Some of Parsons's formulations point in this direction, particularly when he writes that positive and negative sanctions guide action in the direction of conformity with the actor's expectations. But this makes order ultimately dependent on the abilities of the actors to apply deceit and force. Why shouldn't a youth in the store make use of a momentary inattention on the storekeeper's part and take away what he wants? Or why shouldn't he alarm his companions in his street gang and force the storekeeper to let them do what they want? The mere threat of future vandalism could force the storekeeper not to alert the police. Here we have the situation where superior force and deceit decide on the chances for action. We have a predictable order only as long as the police are powerful enough to control every corner of the neighborhood. Otherwise there is always the possibility that a street gang will impose force on the storekeeper, or the storekeeper may indeed be successful in alerting the police, or the power of the street gang in question will be counteracted by another street gang. In this case we have a war between police and street gangs and between rival street gangs.

This is the point where Parsons and Shils (1951b: 200–202) say that a sanctioning power like the police as an agent of the state may provide for order. In this case the state is itself an agency that has monopolized physical force to a certain degree and thus is able to enforce laws made by this agency in everyday situations. The storekeeper who calls the police makes use of these laws and of the corresponding power of the police to enforce them. But what is to be done if the means of control and the force of the state are not sufficient to enforce every law in every situation? Particularly, the right of every citizen to bear arms (guns) in the United States places limits on the monopolization of physical force. What might be an effective means in securing order that is independent of the distribution and application of force would be a consensus among the interacting parties on certain norms governing their interaction. This is what Parsons refers to as the solution to the problem of order in interaction. But how does this consensus come about?

There are two ways of achieving a consensus. Either the interacting parties subsume their action under values that are universally valid or they share membership in a community. Universal values are the outcome of procedures of rational justification. These are values like personal freedom, which is reconciled with the freedom of other persons, and equality of opportunity. But these are very general measures of action and not concrete prescriptions for specific action. They do not tell the storekeeper and the customer how to coordinate their action, though they are measures of the general rights a customer and a storekeeper have, particularly rights in concluding contracts. These rights allow the customer, for example, to give back fruit that is obviously rotten and the storekeeper to refuse to change items that fulfill the normal standards of quality. But concrete actions are guided by more specific norms. And in order to act in consensus, the storekeeper and the customer must associate in a community. That means they build a feeling of familiarity and of cohesion that result from regular purchases in the same store. Both the storekeeper and the customer are a community in this case in which shared norms are anchored in a common solidarity. That this is less the case in a supermarket explains why the supermarket needs cameras to watch the customers and the small grocery store does not need them.

The smallest possible community in our example is that which exists between two actors, but normally the community comprises more than two actors, for example, the neighborhood that regularly goes to the grocery store and meets there. In a certain sense the community that reaches beyond the two actors is a stabilizing factor that always provides its support to one of the two actors who can legitimately claim that the other actor has violated a norm of the community. This is not possible in the two-person community. The community forms a moral authority that stands above the two interacting parties. But these two are themselves members of the community. That is, as members of the community, they share norms and their application to concrete situations. As individuals with personal interests and other relationships of solidarity outside the community, they experience a sanctioning power above them. That is, the consensus of the community changes into an external force when it is applied to individual and situationally changing interests.

When we take into account what I have just described as communal association, we have to correct Parsons's treatment of interaction as representing, in the first place, an exchange of gratifications and deprivations. The fact that the storekeeper and the customer communally associate with one another is a form of interaction in the same way as the exchange of goods and dollars. It finds its expression in the fact that the customer regularly goes to *this* storekeeper and not to another one, and that the storekeeper draws the attention of the customer to the lower quality of a certain piece of fruit compared with another one, even in a special service for the customer that is not profitable for the storekeeper in any way. It also finds expression in conversations beyond the mere exchange of goods and money. In these talks, both normally assure one another about the common world of the community in which they live, particularly in talks about the community. When they say, "See you tomorrow," they assure one another of the continuation of their association. It is interesting that the word *customer* derives from "custom," and that this describes behavior that is taken for granted in a community.

Another form of interaction also has to be distinguished from the exchange of gratifications and deprivations, and it is also involved in the situation of a purchase: communication. How both persons act is determined not only by the expected gratifications, deprivations, and customs they follow but also by the meaning of the words they use to communicate. If the customer says, "A pound of German potato salad," and the storekeeper gives him or her a salad, the customer may be disappointed when he or she realizes that this is not a German potato salad at all as far as he or she knows. The two assigned the words "German potato salad" a different meaning. The customer usually will not react by changing to another grocery. He or she will tell the storekeeper the next day what he or she means by German potato salad.

In terms of exchange, the economic exchange of commodities and money is embedded in a higher order *social* exchange of truthfulness and gratitude, which itself is guided by the sharing of common norms of a community. In this perspective, Parsons's and Shils's analysis of social interaction as exchange goes well beyond the framing of exchange in purely economic terms.

We can summarize that there are at least four different forms of interaction taking place at the same time between customer and storekeeper:

1. *Exchange of gratifications.* Here accidental predictability (order) is possible if the storekeeper can offer what the customer wants, and vice versa.

This is made most probable through the customer's use of money and the storekeeper's knowledge of the normal wishes of his customers. The latter is a case of communal association being applied to exchange.

2. *Mutual application of deprivations.* This is not an exchange in the pure sense, as Parsons tends to assume in his American view of conflict settlement as bargaining, but mutual threatening. Order, in this case, is the result of the controlling power of a superordinate sanctioning body, of a ruling authority with a police apparatus.

3. *Communal association.* Here order is possible when the interacting parties share the membership of a community that stands above other community memberships and above the interests of the individual.

4. *Communication.* Here order results from agreement on the meaning of the words used in communication. The application of universal norms to a situation implies a special form of communication: the rational justification of an action by explaining its consistency with universal norms, using arguments in a discourse.

Double contingency now has a more general meaning: It means that not only Ego's gratifying action but also Ego's success in applying deprivations, establishment of an association, and Ego's communication of a meaning is contingent both on Ego's selections and on those made by Alter.

I now turn to the question of the self-maintenance of a social system. The interactions taking place in a grocery store between the storekeeper and the customers form a social system. They can be distinguished from interactions and noninteractional aspects outside this system. First, there is a distinct meeting place that defines territorial boundaries (although not every social system needs territorial boundaries, it is usually the case). There is also a certain time to meet, defined by the store's hours. Who participates in the social system is defined, for everybody who enters the grocery is included in the system. In the case of the grocery store, the members of the neighborhood will act in the social system of the store. All these obvious criteria of the boundaries of the system derive from the norms governing the interdependent actions. These norms define the identity of the social system.

A special kind of norm comprises social roles that describe the behavior of an actor who takes some part in the interaction. These are norms for action commonly shared in the community. Insofar as the actors direct their expectations toward one another in terms of these norms they form role expectations that are not arbitrary and based on personal interest but normatively binding, because they are backed up by the shared norms of the community. In our example, storekeeper and customer are the two social roles that are normatively defined and are acted out by storekeepers and customers in concrete situations.

Boundary maintenance, then, means maintaining the norms of the social system, maintaining its social order. If, for example, the grocery changes over to a system of self-service it has changed its identity and its boundaries. If it was a defining norm that the grocery did not sell cigarettes but it now does, it has again changed its boundaries. Forms of action once closed out from the system are now part of the system. All this means that boundary maintenance in the system's language is based on the permanent reproduction of the different kinds of social order in exchange, mutual negative sanctioning, communal association, and communication in the language of action theory. This is a first answer to the question of whether systems theory has completely replaced action theory.

Another question is also of interest here: Does the theoretical interest in boundary maintenance close out the theoretical interest in change, as some interpreters of the Parsonian theory of social systems have complained? The answer must be: The two are complementary, and if we can answer the question of boundary maintenance, we can also answer the question of change if we reverse the argument. Change demands the introduction of new forms of action into a system, thereby attaining a new complementarity of interests, for example, when customers ask for cigarettes and self-service more and more. It demands the use of force in order to promote some new forms of action in the face of resistance, for example, when the federal courts order school busing in order to achieve racial equality of opportunity against the resistance of parents. It demands establishing new forms of communal association, for example, if the desired schools are to achieve commonly shared norms. It demands communication and rational justification, when, for example, the legitimacy of racially separated schools is questioned from the point of view of equal opportunity.

Let me now describe briefly the other two systems, the personality system and the cultural system.

Personality System

The personality system is based on the need dispositions of the individual actors (Parsons and Shils, 1951b: 110–58). Personality distinguishes each actor from the other actors, and it distinguishes those actions that are assigned to the individual's personality and to his or her responsibility from actions that come about accidentally or through compliance to external force, even to the role expectations in an interaction. This means there are two aspects of personality: one aspect in which a person's uniqueness compared to other people is distinguished and another aspect in which an identity is formed that remains stable. In his or her uniqueness and general identity, the individual finds self-realization and self-expression. Self-maintenance here means maintaining one's uniqueness, identity, and self-realization. Need dispositions are the basis of the uniqueness and identity of an actor. A need disposition is an actor's inclination to strive for certain *general* ends and to act under certain conditions in a typical way. Let us assume that achievement is a need disposition of an individual and never giving up after suffering any setback (defeat) is an inclination to act. We can expect from this individual that he or she will go on trying, regardless of whether he or she has lost in a tennis match, in a discussion on morality, or in social work against drug abuse.

Our customer also has a unique personality. He or she is inclined to prefer some food and to avoid other food, to come to the grocery every Friday in order to get everything for the whole week, to smoke a certain brand of cigarettes, to read a certain newspaper, and to ask the storekeeper for things in a certain way. The person plays the role of customer in a unique way and puts his or her personality into this role.

Boundary maintenance for the personality means that the actor is able to direct all the external demands for action toward the fulfillment of his or her personal needs and identity as well as toward the ongoing distinction from others, thus maintaining his or her uniqueness. Change means that the individual gives way to external influences and lets him- or herself be motivated by cheaper offers from the supermarket, by submission to an external authority, by new communal associations (changes in friendships, according to the saying: "Tell me with whom you go, and I will tell you who you are"), and by new communication and processes of rational justification. A person who is more committed to general principles and less committed to concrete behavioral prescriptions is able to change his or her behavior without changing his or her identity.

Cultural System

A cultural system is constituted by symbols (Parsons and Shils, 1951b: 159–89). Language, the Bible, works of literature, works of science, works of art, architecture, newspapers, styles of life, movies, theaters, pubs, restaurants, groceries, supermarkets, sports games, parks, streets, and houses are all aspects of culture. The freeway system, Hollywood, Venice, UCLA, the *Los Angeles Times*, are parts of the cultural system of Los Angeles. The campus site with its awe-inspiring buildings, the *Daily Bruin*, campus events, the restaurants, the library, the way in which courses are conducted are all parts of the cultural system of UCLA. The language spoken in the grocery, the style of its advertisements, the style of presentation of the merchandise, the storekeeper's and the customer's dress are all parts of the cultural system of the grocery. These are things that serve as symbols, and symbols have meanings that have to be determined by interpretation. The dress of the storekeeper and the customers, for example, may symbolize a middle-class style of life, not poor and not extravagant; the advertisement symbolizes the same moderate attitude; the same is true of the presentation of the merchandise. And the people speak a moderate language, neither poor nor extremely articulate. What we see is a certain consistency in the pattern of the cultural system. If the same grocery changed its style of advertising to a more aggressive type, it would not fit in with the existing cultural pattern. The same would be true if the storekeeper suddenly dressed in an extravagant style or spoke like young teenagers or intellectuals.

A cultural system always transcends the situation of interaction and the social system. The social system of the grocery shares its cultural style with every other middle-class grocery. And in this system, a language is applied that is spoken throughout the world. A cultural system is like a text that has its meaning and must be distinguished from the interpretation of the text (symbols) in a concrete social system and concrete situation of interaction. The words used in communication in the grocery are part of a language, which is just a system of symbols, either written on paper or articulated orally. The communication in which the actors *use* the language and interpret the meaning of spoken words is a form of social interaction; in distinction to cultural systems as such, communication forms a social-cultural system. Another example would be the sociology texts in a sociology course; they are part of the cultural system of sociology—they are a system of symbols. The interpretation of the text in a class is communication and thus a form of social interaction.

A cultural system maintains its boundaries when it maintains its identity, which is expressed in a certain consistency of a cultural pattern. The grocery, for example, has a moderate middle-class cultural system. The introduction of extravagant advertising would introduce into the system symbols that were formerly excluded, and thus its identity and boundaries would break down. A change of the cultural system takes place through introducing new symbols and through achieving a new pattern consistency and identity, for example, if the grocery were to change into a shop for foreign delicacies with a more extravagant appearance, and both storekeeper and customers spoke a more flamboyant language.

Interrelating the Systems

The next step concerns the interrelationships between the social system, personality system, and cultural system. We can describe these with three central terms:

1. The interrelationship between the cultural system and the social system gives rise to what we call the *institutionalization* of a cultural pattern in the social system.
2. The interrelationship between the cultural system and the personality system gives rise to what we call the *internalization* of a cultural pattern in the personality.

3. The interrelationship between the social system and the personality system gives rise to what we call the *socialization* of the personality with regard to the norms and roles of the social system.

None of these three interrelationships should be misconceived as a one-way relationship in which the cultural system dominates the personality and the social systems or the social system dominates the personality system. They are all two-way relationships. And they have to be clearly distinguished, which Parsons did not always accomplish. He partly combined and confused institutionalization and internalization, saying that institutionalization is at least partly based on internalization. And he partly confused internalization and socialization, not clearly pointing out the difference between the learning of the meaning of cultural symbols and the attaching of the individual to binding social norms.

Institutionalization

Institutionalization means on the one hand that the stock of available cultural symbols comes to be applied to social interaction in a social system; on the other hand, it means that the norms of the social system can be transcended by fully exploiting the cultural meaning of the social norms. In this way culture always becomes something more restrictive and particular than is theoretically allowed by the cultural symbols when it is applied in a social system. In the social system, processes of communal association and consensus formation bind the actors to some particular meaning of a cultural symbol, processes of interpretation link the social norms to the cultural symbols, processes of power application enforce norms against resistance, and processes of exchange open them for the interests of the actors.

For example, the English language contains more words than can be permitted in communications in the grocery store. People who deviate from this social norm are closed out of the social system. The term "potato salad" has a wider meaning than it has when applied in a particular grocery. The word "freedom" has a wider meaning than it has when applied in the grocery; the narrower definition does not include making political speeches in the grocery. But on the other hand, as far as the interacting parties have experiences beyond the confines of the particular social system of the grocery, they can question whether it is correct to assign such a narrow meaning to the English language and to specific words of this language. The more fully they want to exploit this meaning, the more the cultural system is a force for change for the social system in a general direction: in the direction of exhausting the full range of meaning of cultural systems. When the schools in the United States changed in the 1960s and 1970s from racial segregation to racial integration within not much more than a decade, this was, beside other factors such as pressure politics, an effect of fully exploiting the meaning of equality as a value of the cultural system of society and also as that value applies to the social system of schools.

In summary, institutionalization means on the one hand particularization of the cultural system, that is, the narrowing of the meaning of cultural symbols through processes of consensus formation in the social system. On the other hand it means universalization of social norms through change in the direction of a full exploitation of the meaning of cultural symbols in processes of rational argumentation. This is a process of interpenetration where culture becomes part of the social system as particularized social culture, and the social system becomes part of the cultural system as universalized social values and norms.

Internalization

Internalization means on the one hand that the individual personality finds some special interpretation of cultural symbols in the application to its need dispositions and ends. On the other hand, it means raising the individual above the pure pursuit of egoistic needs and ends and the acquisition of the ability to reflect on one's needs, ends, and actions. All reflection is an application of culture to the personality of the individual. In the process of cultural symbols being applied to individual needs and ends, those symbols become specified. The individual makes a selection out of a wide range of possible interpretations of cultural symbols. The individual has his or her personal version of the English language, prefers some words to other words, and also prefers a specific meaning of words and values like "freedom," "equality," and "moderate behavior" to other meanings. Freedom may mean for one person that he or she may drive wherever he or she wants, or see a movie with whatever content without censorship, or go to the beach every day, or make a speech on whatever subject he or she wants. In our grocery example, the individual can apply for him- or herself the middle-class cultural style and also use unusual words and meanings.

The more an individual learns the full range of the meaning of cultural symbols and is able to reflect on the appropriateness of his or her selections, the more he or she tends to justify any action by subsuming it under cultural symbols. A person's need dispositions become generalized. The competitive, young basketball player, for example, becomes a personality with an overall achievement motive that can be applied to every action, not only to basketball. This process of fully exploiting the meaning of the cultural system enables the individual also to achieve distance from the social norms of the social system. He or she can criticize any particularization of cultural symbols from the point of view of the more general meaning of the cultural system. The grocery customer can ask if it makes sense to exclude certain styles of dress from the grocery and introduce a new style. The junior student who criticizes the quarter system of UCLA in a letter to the editor of the *Daily Bruin* does not put forward his or her criticism from the point of view of personal interest but from the point of view of the values of the educational system, arguing that the quarter system does not allow a sufficiently thorough and deep acquisition of cultural knowledge.

Internalization means, on the one hand, specification of cultural symbols to personal needs and ends and, on the other hand, generalization of needs and ends in the light of cultural symbols. This is a process of interpenetration where culture becomes part of the personality in a personalized form, and personality becomes part of culture in the form of personal styles of life.

Socialization

Socialization means, on the one hand, that the individual personality accepts social norms and rules as binding for his or her action and, on the other hand, that the norms and roles become specified according to the personal needs and ends the individual actor pursues. The binding of the individual to the norms and roles always requires the inclusion of the individual in the social system. He or she must become a member who feels attached to the community. The community is a body that is above the individual and can apply positive and negative sanctions in order to produce a conformity of the individual to norms. But if the individual is to feel a commitment to the norms, he or she must identify with some agents of the community, like mother and father, and increasingly with the community as such. Then the individual has a sense of belonging to the community and of being a bearer of the norms of the community.

For example, every new customer who moves to the neighborhood increasingly becomes a member of the grocery community with the extension and intensification of associational contacts. As a result, it is not fear of negative sanctions or striving for positive sanctions that guides action but the feeling of sharing norms with others. However, the mere approval or disapproval of the community including the actor him- or herself is a latent basis of the sanctioning power of the community.

But the individual does not minutely carry out prescribed rules when playing his or her roles. The person interprets them with regard to his or her personal needs and ends and selects some aspects appropriate for him or her. The new customer may indeed introduce a style of purchasing, dressing, and speaking and emphasize aspects that have never been previously expressed in the grocery system. The student who acts in a class to question everything the professor says plays his or her role in a way that deviates from the average but not from the role of student.

To summarize, socialization means, on the one hand, a binding of the individual to social norms and roles; on the other hand, it means the application of norms and roles in accord with the needs and ends of the individual personality. This is a process of interpenetration in which the social norms become part of the personality of an individual, namely, as his or her conscience (or superego, as Freud called it) and where the individual's personality becomes part of the social system, as the actual acting out of norms and roles through individuals always defines the concrete meaning of those norms and roles.

Defensive Reactions and Deviance

In the process of socialization, social role expectations and individual need dispositions are brought into accord with one another. The failure of that process will provoke defensive reactions on the part of the individual's personality and deviant motivation with regard to role performance. Parsons and Shils (1951b: 133–37) take the following defense mechanisms from Sigmund Freud:

- *Rationalization.* Role conformity that frustrates a specific need disposition is justified by referring to the fulfillment of other need dispositions by the same behavior.
- *Isolation.* Role conformity is isolated from need dispositions that might be frustrated by that behavior.
- *Displacement.* Need dispositions that are frustrated by the demand for specific role performances are satisfied in other contexts.
- *Fixation.* The individual anxiously adheres to behaviors that safeguard him or her against possible frustrations.
- *Repression.* Need dispositions that are in conflict with social role expectations are extinguished from consciousness.
- *Reaction formation.* Dangerous need dispositions that may create frustrations are replaced by less dangerous need dispositions.
- *Projection.* Repression of dangerous need dispositions is supported by attributing them to other people who serve as scapegoats.

With regard to role performance, a failure to establish sufficient accordance between social role expectations and need disposition brings about deviant motivation (Parsons, 1951: 249–325). If this deviant motivation is suppressed by external control, compulsive role conformity results. In the active form it is expressed in *compulsive performance orientation*; in the passive form it is expressed by *compulsive acquiescence in status expectations*. If social control does not succeed in the suppression of deviant motivation, deviant behavior comes about. The active form is expressed by *rebelliousness*; its passive form is expressed by *withdrawal*.

Failure to establish accordance between social role expectations and individual need dispositions results from a lack of *support* by the socializing agents for the socializee and an unbalanced relationship between *permissiveness* and *refusal to reciprocate* with regard to the socializee's need dispositions on the part of the socializing agents (Parsons, 1951: 300).

As with his view of social interaction in this phase of developing his theory, Parsons sees the interaction between the socializing agents and the socializee primarily as an exchange of gratifications and deprivations on the basis of greater or lesser support given by the socializing agents to the socializee and, correspondingly, a greater or lesser identification of the socializee with the socializing agents. However, Parsons (1951: 283–97) opens up ways to a more complex view when he addresses the problem of legitimation. Inasmuch as social control involves legitimation, the definition of behavior as deviant or conforming depends on its justification by the common values of the collectivity. The more the deviant receives support for his or her definition by some subgroup of the society, the more he or she may withstand the punishing activities of the agents of control. Deviance, then, is part of political conflict between opposing social groups. The deviant act might be the first step toward a redefinition of social role expectations in this case. On the other hand, the less support there is for the deviant, the more his or her punishment is part of a ritual act in which the collectivity renews commitment to its norms.

Three Problems of Order

If we look back to the problem of order in social systems we can now distinguish three types of problems (Parsons, 1951: 24–45):

1. The internal problem of order: How order is established in interaction itself and in the interrelationship between different social systems.
2. The motivational problem of order: How the social system can attract the motivation of individual personalities, that is, their need dispositions and ends, to the acting out of social norms and roles.
3. The cultural problem of order: How the social system can legitimate its norms and roles by demonstrating their consistency with the wider cultural symbols (values).

The Pattern Variables

In *The Social System* and the co-authored *Toward a General Theory of Action*, both published in 1951, Parsons partly collaborated with Edward Shils to introduce a further conceptual innovation: the so-called pattern variables (Parsons, 1951: 58–67; 1967: 192–219; Parsons and Shils, 1951b: 76–91). There are five pairs of juxtaposed pattern variables. They describe alternatives for action between which an actor has to choose in every situation.

Though Parsons is not clear here, choice in this context can mean only that, in principle, an actor as a human being has the freedom to choose between these formats of action. But he or she also has *only* that choice. Freedom here means that the patterns that guide an action are not inborn instinctual behaviors but culturally chosen *norms* for action. That is, they are voluntarily selected guides for action. But the actor cannot escape the choice. Because human beings are free, they are at the same time forced to decide how to act. They are condemned to freedom, as French philosopher Jean-Paul Sartre put it in the famous core of his philosophy of existentialism (Sartre, 1943). And Parsons thinks that the pattern variables define basic choices for action that are conceived of as covering the whole range of possible human choices in situations of action. But actors do not choose on an either/or basis: their action varies along a continuum between the two extremes defined by the pairs of pattern variables. In addition, because every action is shaped by the three systems — cultural, social, and personality systems — the pattern variables determine action through these three systems. They appear as cultural values, as social norms and role expectations, and as personal need dispositions.

The five pairs of pattern variables are the following:

Self-orientation_____Collectivity orientation
Diffuseness_____Specificity
Affectivity_____Affective neutrality
Particularism_____Universalism
Ascription (Quality)_____Achievement (Performance)

As cultural values, the pattern variables are symbolically present normative patterns for action with a relatively wide scope of different interpretations and applications; as social norms and role expectations, they are more concretely formulated and binding for the actors acting in a social system; as personal need dispositions, they are specified to typical patterns an individual tends to follow in typical situations of action. Let me briefly explain the meaning of each pair.

Self-orientation means that the actor makes his or her needs and goals the criteria for deciding what action to take in a given situation. The student enrolling in a class follows his or her goal of achieving a certain standard of education in a certain subject. In Western societies, it is a cultural idea that the individual's needs and goals alone should decide which kind of education the person gets. As a social norm and role expectation, the student has to make decisions within the social system of the university on which class to take in which term. As a personal disposition, the individual student acting self-orientedly does not like the idea of anybody, for example, his or her family, making the decision for him or her. In Asian cultures, the family still has much more influence on the decisions of the individual, including higher education, a difference from Western culture that is still alive to a certain degree in the Asian communities within American society. Self-orientation, in general, means that there is a more or less wide scope for action within which individuals can follow only their own needs and goals. The market is the paradigmatic field in which individuals act self-orientedly.

Collectivity-orientation means that rather than the individual's needs and goals determining action in a situation this is done according to the collective norms and decisions of a collectivity to which the individual belongs as a member. For example, an American high school student can decide on his or her own what education to pursue or in what class to enroll, but not whether to receive education or not. Compulsory education means that the collectivity has decided this for each individual. It is a cultural idea, a social norm, and the individual has to act this out applying more or less personal dispositions.

Here is another example for comparison: A young man leaves his mother and father who live in the country and who need his support in agricultural work; he does this in order to make his living in town. He acts self-orientedly. If the same young man sacrifices his life to support the family, he acts with a collectivity orientation. In a modern society (town), self-oriented action has much more legitimacy than in traditional societies (village), where more collectivity orientation prevails.

Diffuseness means that the actor can address everything in a situation of action—that nothing is closed out and no clear criteria for the selection of actions exist. An educational institution with no differentiation of classes according to years of enrollment and no fixed program for classes and no grading of achievements implies a diffuse orientation of action.

Specificity means distinct orientation of action. An educational institution that has a program with a narrowly defined subject like mathematics and a clear differentiation of classes according to years of enrollment and grades according to achievement embodies such a specific orientation of action. If the student can interact with the teacher as he or she would with a friend and vice versa, the specific roles of teacher and student get confused with the role of friend. Thus, the orientation of action is diffuse compared to the specific teacher-student interaction, where everything is closed out that does not belong to the process of teaching and learning. Cultural values, social norms and role expectations, and personal dispositions can prefer either the diffuse or the specific orientation of action.

Affectivity means that an actor involves his or her emotions in actions. Whether or not I like another person will guide my decision on whether I want to be closely connected with him or her or want to keep more distance. And I can show my feelings toward other people quite directly without hesitation or any attempt at hiding them. I can show enjoyment, fun, excitement, anger, love, and hate. The family and relations of friendship are places where this can be done quite normally. The sports arena is another place for showing feelings. In southern European countries, public demonstration of feelings is much more normal than in northern and central European countries. The United States is in between.

Affective neutrality means that emotions are closed out from action. How an official in a bureaucracy treats my tax return has nothing at all to do with his or her feelings. In a bureaucratic organization, feelings of people toward one another have no legitimate place in actions. The same is true when a teacher grades the exams of students. Cultural values, social norms, and personal dispositions define the scope for affective and affectively neutral behavior.

Particularism means that an actor follows his or her attachment to a particular person or group and the norms of a particular group that are only part of the world of actors. It is always a commitment to someone or some group at the cost of a commitment to another person or group and at the cost of the commitment to a more comprehensive group. If a young girl tells her mother that she has been dropped from a school position by a school committee of her friends, her mother naturally will give her support. She will complain of the wrong those bad kids have done to her child. She will not look into whether her daughter was to blame for this situation. She will not ask questions in this direction. What counts for her in this situation is her attachment to her daughter and not the question of what was right or wrong from a standpoint that reaches beyond their particular commitment to one another. This is particularism.

The opposite orientation is *universalism*. In our example, the school board, which may have to deal with the committee's action, cannot take a position on the basis of a commitment to one child or the other. It has to ask who was right and who was wrong, in a more general sense, by applying legal and also moral rules that are valid for the whole school community and also beyond that community. But the girl may initiate a lawsuit at a district court. In this case, the committee decision has to be judged according to still more universal laws and moral rules. In this process, more and more universalism is the basis for action, that is, an orientation of action on the basis of a commitment to a universal community and the universal norms transcending every particular group and their norms — finally, the nation and the constitution, and beyond that, humankind and the rights of humanity. Again, cultural values, social norms and role expectations, and personal dispositions define the scope of application of these orientations of action.

Ascription (quality) means that an actor bases his or her action toward another actor on a quality that the other actor has had from birth and his or her belonging to some group or class. Acting toward somebody according to his or her age, color, ethnic origin, and/or class origin is acting on the basis of ascription. Admission to schools, colleges, universities, and jobs on this basis is ascription.

Achievement (performance) means that an actor behaves toward another actor according to the achievement the other actor has attained and according to his or her performance, that is, how well he or she does something. Admission to colleges, schools, and jobs on the basis of grades is action according to achievement and performance. Cultural values, social norms, and role expectations define the scope of application of these orientations.

Parsons's analysis of the interrelationship between doctor and patient as a professional-client relationship was the first application of the pattern variable scheme. He pointed out that in order to provide for a return of the patient to the normal fulfillment of his or her social roles, on the one hand, and to provide for the fulfillment of the patient's needs, on the other hand, there must be an interlinkage of juxtaposed pattern variables. The patient wants to gain trust. He or she approaches the doctor from self-interest, must establish a diffuse relationship, and include affectivity in liking the doctor. The patient wants to be treated particularly and on the basis of an ascribed status. The doctor has to treat the patient according to the expectations of the wider collectivity, specifically, neutrally, universalistically, and according to his or her performance. Both extremes have to be interlinked in the doctor-patient relationship. The doctor first has to accommodate to the needs of the patient, but then must lead the patient more and more to the other side of the pattern variables in order to reintegrate him or her into normal social roles in society.

The pattern variable scheme is a formal reformulation of a distinction that was drawn by the German sociologist Ferdinand Tönnies (1887/1963) between *Gemeinschaft* (community) and *Gesellschaft* (society) as special types of social association. A community is a village or a family; a society is a city or a nation-state as a whole. In Parsons's terms a community is based on the application of one side of the pairs of pattern variables, the side that encloses action more: collectivity orientation, diffuseness, affectivity, particularism, and ascription. A society is based on the opposite: self-orientation, specificity, neutrality, universalism, and achievement.

The Four-Functions Paradigm

The next step in the development of Parsons's theory of action and systems was the introduction of the famous Four-Functions Paradigm, also known as the A-G-I-L scheme, in a book entitled *Working Papers in the Theory of Action*, which appeared in 1953 and was co-authored with Robert F. Bales and Edward A. Shils. The starting point was Bales's research on small groups, particularly discussion groups and task groups. Parsons, Bales, and Shils generalized from Bales's empirical observations and made a first empirical distinction of four system problems to find that discussion groups and task groups go through four basic phases in accomplishing a task, thereby fulfilling four functions:

A: Adaptation
G: Goal attainment
 I: Integration
L: Latent pattern maintenance

A *phase* is a period of time in which the action of a group is specifically preoccupied with fulfilling one of the four functions. A *function* is a problem a group has to solve in order to survive as a social system in its environment. Four different kinds of environments correspond to the four types of problem. Survival means that a system maintains its boundaries: what interactions are part of the system and what interactions are not part of the system are clearly defined. Let me describe the four phases and functions briefly.

A. *Adaptation.* A social system like a task group has to adapt itself to its material environment. It must gather resources in order to survive. For example, let us assume a student group wants to prepare for an exam. In this case, the material environment is defined by the conditions set for passing the exam: the reading matter that has to be interpreted. In order to fulfill the function of adaptation to this external condition, the students must gather the appropriate books and copies, gather information, and organize a division of labor.

G. *Goal attainment.* A social system like a task group has to attain group goals under the condition that there are a lot of members in the group who have quite different individual goals. Thus the group needs procedures in order to make collective decisions, for example, one student may emerge as a leader and decide for the others how often they meet, in what sequences the books are read, and what interpretation of a text should be selected. Or they may decide according to majority rule or even by unanimous agreement. In any case, decisions have to be made in order to transcend the conflict of individual goals in favor of collective goal attainment.

I. *Integration.* A social system like a task group has to provide for social cohesion and solidarity, that is, integration against a background in which the participating actors all have relationships of solidarity outside the group. They are also members of other groups, such as families, groups of friends, and sporting, artistic, or study groups. Thus, the task group has to form its own solidarity and cohesion to attract members to itself. It also has to guard against internal divisions into particularized subgroups. It has to include outsiders and marginal members in the cooperation; in case of conflicts evolving from decisions in which some members are defeated by others, the group has to make sure that everybody can still feel that they are members of the group, so that the defeated members are also committed to the group decision.

L. *Latent pattern maintenance.* A social system like a task group has to find and maintain its identifying ideas with regard to the many different concrete decisions made in the group and the specific meanings every incoming member gives his or her relationship to the group. An exam preparation group must have an idea of the subject it is studying in order for its members to understand each other. This idea cannot be changed from week to week; otherwise, the group would lose its identity and break apart.

The next step in the development of Parsons' theory was to interrelate the four-function paradigm with the pattern variables, also described in *Working Papers in the Theory of Action.* In order to achieve this interlinkage, Parsons, Bales, and Shils dropped the pair comprising self-orientation and collectivity orientation. The other four pairs were divided into two pairs defining the cognitive orientation toward an object and two pairs defining the attitude toward an object.

Cognitive orientations to objects are:

Particularism_____Universalism
Ascription_____Achievement

Attitudes to objects are:

Affectivity_____Neutrality
Diffuseness_____Specificity

One side of the cognitive orientation pairs and one side of the attitude pairs is related to the four functions in the following way:

Adaptation: Universalism and achievement as cognitive orientations. Specificity and neutrality as attitudes.
Goal attainment: Particularism and achievement as orientations. Specificity and affectivity as attitudes.
Integration: Particularism and ascription as orientations. Diffuseness and affectivity as attitudes.
Latent pattern maintenance: Universalism and ascription as orientations. Diffuseness and neutrality as attitudes.

We can get a sense of the meaning of this interrelation between the four functions and the remaining four pairs of pattern variables if we describe it more empirically. In this way we can say that the fulfillment of each specific function needs a primary application of one side of one of the four pairs and secondary applications of a specific side of the other pairs. In order to explain this, I apply to the A-G-I-L schema the differentiation of means, ends, norms, and ideas I made earlier with regard to the frame of reference of voluntaristic action theory.

> *Adaptation* requires the mobilization of means; the use of means may vary between achievement and ascription, with achievement as the best precondition.
> *Goal attainment* requires an end to be set; the formulation of that end may vary from specificity to diffuseness, with specificity as the best precondition.
> *Integration* requires action to be guided by norms; the relationship to the norms may vary from affectual attachment to neutrality, with affectivity as the best precondition.
> *Latent pattern maintenance* requires the orientation of action by ideas; these may vary from universalistic to particularistic ideas with universalism of ideas as the best precondition.

In a first step, we can correlate the following functions and primary pattern variables:

Adaptation is grounded on the adequate finding of *means* to attain goals, and this must be primarily based on achievement, not on ascription. That is, in our exam preparation group the students use only those means that are best and assign tasks to those students who are best or have so far performed and achieved best at this task. They never work on the basis of what means have traditionally been applied to this task or on the basis of age, color, ethnic origin, or other such criteria.

Secondarily, the means have to be specifically distinguished in order to examine their appropriateness for achieving an end. The relationship to means and the division of labor has to be neutral; affectivity would interfere with finding the best means. The appropriateness of the means has to be proved within a universal frame of reference; they have to be tested everywhere in every situation.

Goal attainment primarily demands the clear definition of *specific ends*. A diffuse definition of ends gives no clear direction to action. If the student group decides to prepare for a sociology exam and also to have fun, the goal would be a rather diffuse one compared to the goal of preparing for an exam in contemporary sociological theory.

Secondarily, achieving a specific end requires the application of the best means, which must be found out according to achievement and performance. To ensure that actions are firmly targeted on the chosen end, the members of the student group must be attached to that end affectively. They must have an emotional involvement in achieving in sociology. In order to bring their frame of reference, the ideas that guide their actions, into focus upon the goal of the exam, this frame of reference needs a certain particularism, that is, a commitment to this class and its theme of contemporary sociological theory at the cost of a commitment to sociology or education outside the class.

Integration primarily needs the commitment of the members of the student group to the *norms* of the group based on their feeling of belonging to the group. This needs an affectual attachment to the group and its norms. The individual is emotionally a member and bearer of the group norms and does not judge them neutrally; he or she reacts with anger when norms are violated.

Secondarily, group members must close their minds and look only to the group that is orienting their action according to particularism. It is not on the basis of achievement and performance regarding the best and most profitable forms of action that the members obey the norms and act in solidarity. They act on the basis of ascription; that is, they take for granted what has traditionally been a group norm and act in solidarity toward every member of the group regardless of their achievement. The norms are diffusely defined, so that they do not provoke conflicts between goals.

Latent pattern maintenance requires that the student group has an identifying general idea, a frame of reference, which provides for continuity and identity. This idea is universal in character. It is so universal that every concrete action of the group can be subsumed under that idea. "Learning contemporary sociological theory" is a more universal idea for the group than "Learning the economic paradigm of sociology," which would be more particularistic. The idea must be acceptable for every individual member in the group.

Secondarily, the idea or frame of reference must be the firm core of the group and cannot be changed from situation to situation according to new experiences. Thus, it must be ascribed as a quality of the group and cannot be tested according to achievement and performance. Otherwise, the group would damage its identity every day. Because of its wide scope, the universal idea has a certain diffuseness; it does not define actions specifically. A wide range of different actions can be subsumed under the general frame of reference of the idea. The universality of the idea makes it increasingly empty, so that it cannot attract deep emotions, that is, affectivity. It needs neutrality. Whenever an idea is related with affectivity, it is a particularized version of this idea anchored in group solidarity.

In conclusion, the outlined assignments of pattern variables to the specific functions hold true only for the fulfillment of a specific function and are contrary to the fulfillment of another function. A concrete social system, like a study group, has to combine them all.

The Cybernetic Hierarchy of Conditions and Controls

A further step in the development of Parsons's theory of systems of action was the introduction of a double cybernetic hierarchy of conditions and controls in the late 1950s (Parsons, 1959; 1961a). In this view, the four functions and the related processes of interaction are ordered in a double hierarchy. In order to make this consideration easier, we can conceive of the interactions oriented to the fulfillment of a specific function as subsystems of interaction differentiated from one another through their own norms of behavior as defined by the particular combination of pattern variables. And we can give these subsystems specific names according to their functions:

A. The adaptation subsystem contains all interactions oriented toward adaptation.

G. The goal-attainment subsystem contains all interactions oriented toward goal attainment.

I. The integration subsystem contains all interaction oriented toward integration.

L. The latent-pattern-maintenance subsystem contains all interactions oriented toward latent pattern maintenance.

These subsystems are first viewed as being ordered in a hierarchy of conditioning with the ranking $A \rightarrow G \rightarrow I \rightarrow L$, with the energy and dynamism for action highest in A and lowest in L. Secondly, they are viewed as being ordered in a hierarchy of controls with the ranking $L \rightarrow I \rightarrow G \rightarrow A$, where information and the guidance of action are highest in L and lowest in A. This means in our example:

A. The process of mobilizing means always shows new situations for the group, which leads to changes in their actions, new techniques of reading, new reading matter, and so on.

G. This may lead to a revision of at least some subsidiary goals for the group in the subsystem of goal attainment, for example, changing the schedule for reading, abandoning reading a certain text, or perhaps even giving up the goal altogether.

I. The process of decision making involves conflict between subgroups. This endangers the cohesion and solidarity of the total group. Thus, new processes of ensuring mutual cohesion and solidarity must take place, for example, in informal gatherings.

L. The new cohesion and solidarity of the group is also a redefinition of its norms, but these norms may step outside the frame of reference given by the general idea of the group. Thus, a new and broader identifying idea must be established. In this process a dynamic change has taken place from A to G to I to L.

In the other direction:

L. In the subsystem of latent pattern maintenance the definition of an identifying idea sets the limits for the group norms formulated for concrete group action.

I. These limits define the scope for group action.

G. The group norms determine the forms and procedures of decision making (e.g., majority rule).

A. The goals delineated in decision making set the objectives toward which means and the gathering of means have to be directed and thus set their limits on the adaptation subsystem. In this direction there is a descending control and setting of limits for action from **L** to **I** to **G** to **A**.

A New Grounding of the Four-Functions Scheme

After introducing the A-G-I-L scheme on the basis of empirical generalization from the observation of task and discussion groups and after relating it to the pattern variables, Parsons provided an additional formal deduction of the four functions from the cross-classification of two fundamental variables of systems of action. He defined action in a system such that it may be directed either internally to the system or externally outside the system, and it may be instrumental for some other goal or pursued for its own sake; Parsons's term for the latter characteristic is "consummatory." Thus we get four combinations out of the cross-classification of these variables guiding action in a system, and these four combinations are linked to the four functions of the A-G-I-L scheme (Parsons, 1967: 192–219). (See figure 1.1.)

Adaptation of a system to its environment is based on an external orientation of action toward the environment and on an instrumental orientation; that is, means are mobilized for some other ends.

Goal attainment of a system is based on an external orientation toward some end beyond the present state of the system, and it is consummatory in character, because it seeks a goal for itself and not for any other reason.

Integration of a system is based on an internal orientation of action toward the system itself and its parts; it is consummatory in character, because it occurs for its own sake.

Latent pattern maintenance of a system is based on an internal orientation of action toward the system itself, and it is instrumental in character, because it provides instrumentally the legitimatory ideas applied to concrete action.

Figure 1.1   Pattern Variables and Functions of Action Subsystems

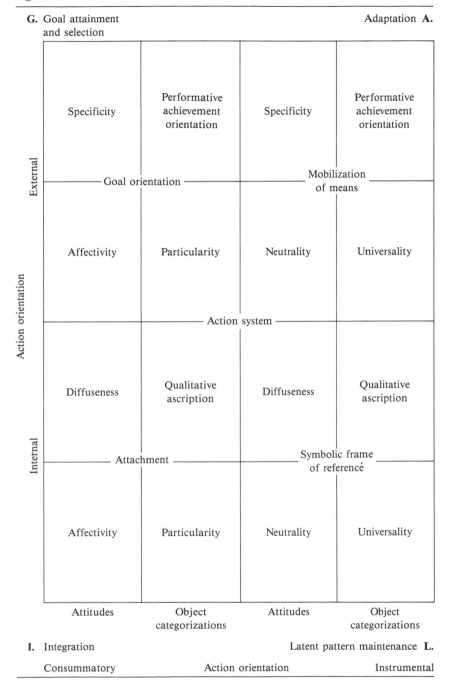

I do not find this deduction of the A-G-I-L scheme very convincing. In particular, the functions of integration and latent pattern maintenance do not fit in very well. The application of the variables "instrumental" and "consummatory," which are positivistic in character, to the functions of latent pattern maintenance and integration do not provide adequate definitions. Therefore, I propose another introduction to the A-G-I-L scheme (Münch, 1987a, 1987b). (See figure 1.2.)

I start with two basic features of action: It is always oriented to symbols and it implements the meaning of the symbols through interpretation. Thus, we have two interrelated variables defining the frame of reference of action: symbols and actions, which interpret and carry out the meaning of the symbols. The symbolic world can vary in complexity, which means that the number of symbols entering the symbolic horizon for action and the number of contradictions between symbols can vary from a small number to a large number. The alternatives for interpretation and implementing a symbol in action can also vary from a small number to a large number, resulting in lower or higher "contingency," that is, predictability of action. Both parts can vary independently of one another. Thus, we can construct a system of coordinates for action out of the two axes of varying symbolic complexity and contingency of action. This system of coordinates has four extreme points that define the boundaries of a "space" within which action takes place or, more briefly, of the action space. And these four extreme points of the action space correspond to the four functions of the A-G-I-L scheme. At the same time we get the four functions applied to the aspects of theories and to the variants of positivism and idealism. I refer again to means, ends, norms, and ideas as basic aspects of action.

A. As a rule, there are no restrictions on the symbolic representation of means for action. We can imagine whatever we want as a means for action in achieving an end. Furthermore, there can be a great number of contradictions between the means. What I do with a specific means, that is, what ends I pursue with this means, is also not restricted and completely open to my decision. Thus, we have high symbolic complexity and high contingency of action. This is a field of the action space in which action has the highest degree of variability and adaptivity to changing situations. Means fulfill the function of opening the scope for action and of adaptation with regard to changing situations. Market exchange is the form of interaction out of which means evolve. For example, I can imagine different means of getting from my house to work: bus, bike, automobile, or walking. And I can also use these means for completely different things than simply getting to work.

G. Ends for action are selections out of a great many alternative goals that are symbolically present to actors. They have to make their decision.

Figure 1.2   Pattern Variables and Functions of Action Subsystems

G. Goal attainment   Adaptation **A.**

	Modalities of objects		Adaptive exigencies represented by "symbolic" meanings of objects	
Performative	Particularistic	Universalistic	Part.[a] ← Spec.[b] ↓	Perf.[c] ← Neut.[d] ↓
	Objects of cathexis	Objects of utility	Expressive symbolization	Cognitive symbolization
Qualitative			Qal.[e] ← Aff.[f] ↓	Univ.[g] ← Diff.[h] ↓
	Objects of identification	Objects of 'generalized respect'	Moral-evaluative categorization	Existential interpretation
			Consummatory	Instrumental

(Left edge labels: **External**, **External**, **Qualitative**; right edge labels: **External**, **Internal**)

Action orientation

	Integrative standards for orientation		Orientations to objects	
External	Perf.[c] ↑ Aff.[f] →	Univ.[g] ↑ Spec.[b] →	Affectivity	Neutrality
	Goal-attainment	Adaptation	Consummatory needs	Interest in instrumental utilization
Internal	Diff.[h] ↑ Part.[a] →	Qual.[e] ↑ Neut.[d] →		
	Integration	Pattern-maintenance	Needs for affiliation	Needs for commitment
	Consummatory	Instrumental		

(Left edge labels: **Internal**, **External**, **Internal**; right edge labels: **Specificity**, **Diffuseness**)

I. Integration   Latent pattern maintenance **L.**

Consummatory   Instrumental

Action orientation

a. Particularity	d. Neutrality	g. Universality
b. Specificity	e. Qualitative ascription	h. Diffuseness
c. Performative achievement orientation	f. Affectivity	

After the decision has been reached, the specificity of the goal prescribes that it must be interpreted and carried out in a determinate way so that no alternatives are open. High symbolic complexity is accompanied by low contingency of action. This is the field of the action space where action has the highest degree of directedness toward a specific end regardless of changing situations. Ends fulfill the function of specifying the scope for action and of providing for goal attainment. Procedures of decision making are forms of interaction out of which ends emerge. For example, a student group may imagine a lot of different possible outcomes for the schedule of its meetings. After the decision to meet every Friday from 6:00 P.M. to 8:00, their action is precisely determined with regard to the time of meeting, though everybody knows that theoretically there could be other times.

I. Norms for action are taken for granted. There are no alternatives to self-evident binding norms in a community, otherwise they would have the status of ends. And within a community the norms have a definite meaning, prescribing action precisely. Low symbolic complexity is accompanied by low contingency of action. Norms fulfill the function of closing the scope for action and of providing for integration. Communal association is the form of interaction out of which binding norms emerge. For example, it is self-evident for the members of a student group to help each other. Thus, when a student asks another member of the group for some information on sociological theory, the norm of helping is applied without entering into competition with another norm, and it prescribes in its application to the situation precisely what has to be done.

L. General ideas and symbolic frames of reference give a general orientation to action. They reduce symbolic complexity through abstraction and generalization. Thus they do not have many competing alternatives. At the same time, their abstractness leaves open a wide range of interpretations and actions. Low symbolic complexity is accompanied by high contingency of action. General ideas and symbolic frames of reference perform the function of generalizing the scope for action, and they provide for latent pattern maintenance. Communication and discourse are the forms of interaction out of which general ideas emerge. For example, the idea of truth has no alternative for students discussing a sociological text, but there are many different meanings of truth and many different ways of approaching truth.

A summarizing example follows: The *idea* of truth is a general orientation for the action of academics. It has no alternatives. But it can be interpreted and approached in many different ways. *Norms* of methodology in approaching truth are prescribed within certain schools of thought. Within any particular school they have no alternatives to compete with, and they prescribe precisely the procedures for carrying out the rules. The *goals* and objectives of research toward which a research group directs its investigations need decisions that are binding. They are always selections out of a great many goals. But once selected, they determine exactly the direction investigations should take and how the goals should be carried out. The hypotheses tested in the course of the project are *means* applied in order to approach the truth and the goal of the project. There are no restrictions in formulating such hypotheses, and the same hypotheses can be used for very different ends. Truth is the idea resulting from discourse on the meaning of science, norms come from the commitment to a scientific community, ends result from scientific procedures of decision making, and hypotheses are offered on a scientific market.

The Social System and the Generalized Media of Interchange

The next step in the development of Parsons's theory of systems of action was the more detailed analysis of the social system and its application beyond the microsociological level of studying task and discussion groups to the macrosociological level of studying society. The major step in this direction was a study called *Economy and Society* prepared in collaboration with Neil J. Smelser (Parsons and Smelser, 1956). The four subsystems for the fulfillment of the four functions received specific names: The economic system fulfills the function of adaptation and of opening the scope for action; the political system fulfills the function of goal attainment and of specifying the scope for action; the (societal) community system fulfills the function of integration and of closing the scope for action; and the fiduciary system — or, as I prefer to call it, the social-cultural system — fulfills the function of latent pattern maintenance or of generalizing the scope for action. The internal structure and internal processes of these subsystems and the interrelationships between the subsystems are now at the center of studying the social system. In further steps, Parsons introduces so-called generalized media of interchange (interaction, communication) for the analysis of the subsystems and of their interrelationships: money for the economic system, political power for the political system, influence for the (societal) community system, and value commitments for the fiduciary (or socio-cultural) system. In Parsons's view, money and power change the situation of action through positive inducement or negative sanction; influence and value commitments change the intentions of actors through positive persuasion or negative and critical activation of commitments. Let me explain these new concepts step-by-step (figure 1.3).

The Subsystems of the Social System

We first examine the structures, processes, and media of interchange of each subsystem of the social system.

Figure 1.3   The Social System

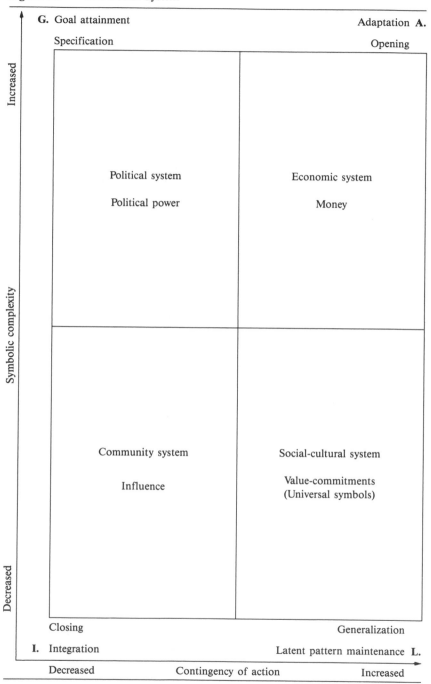

A: *The Economic System*

The function of the economic system is to provide for the adaptation (A) of the total social system to its changing environment through the mobilization of means (resources). The economic system is based on interactions in which the actors select their actions according to the principle of optimizing a set of ends, that is, of acting in the most profitable way, achieving the highest benefits when costs are subtracted. The interaction between individuals is an exchange of goods and services (gratifications, rewards). The adequate means are incentives to motivate another actor to give something away that can be useful for me. If I have a textbook entitled *Introduction to Sociology* and do not need it any longer, but I want a higher level book called *Sociological Theory*, I can look for someone who wants my introductory textbook and can give me his or her book on sociological theory. In this case, we both use the means of offering something the other wants as an incentive. But it is not easy to find someone who has exactly what I want and wants exactly what I have.

Exchange is much freer if we use a generalized medium for exchange, that is, money. In this case, I can sell my introductory textbook to somebody, get the money, and buy the textbook from some other person. In this case, the market exchange is completely open. I can imagine whatever I want and articulate that on the market, and I can do whatever I want with what I have purchased. I am also not in any way restricted in what I have to sell in exchange for my purchase. High symbolic complexity meets high contingency of action.

Like any medium of interaction, money has some specific qualities (Parsons and Smelser, 1956; Parsons, 1967; 1969).

1. Money is symbolic in character. It has no intrinsic value. A $100 bill symbolizes all the goods and services that can be purchased with it.
2. Money is a generalized medium. It can be used independently of the specific conditions and persons involved in a situation of exchange. It can be used regardless of time, place, and the persons involved in an exchange.
3. The use of money and its acquisition is regulated by a specific system of norms—the normative code for the medium. The norms regulating property, contract, labor, and currency are the guiding framework for the use and acquisition of money. Only insofar as such norms exist is money the only legitimate means of acquiring property. The use of force is forbidden. And only under this condition is money the legitimate means of paying for goods, services, and labor.
4. Money circulates between actors. I give my $20 to the bookseller for a book on sociological theory. He or she gives the $20 to the sportswear seller for a sweatshirt. But money also circulates beyond the boundaries

of the economic system, particularly when actors spend money according to social-cultural styles of consumption, distribute it among groups and individuals according to their legitimate needs, or spend it in pursuing collective goals.

5. Money undergoes processes of inflation and deflation. If I can buy a smaller amount of goods and services for $100 at time t_2 than at time t_1, it has lost some of its value; this is inflation. If I can buy a greater amount of goods and services for $100 at time t_2 than at time t_1, money has gained value; this is deflation. Both inflation and deflation are signs of crisis in the economy. The more inflation progresses, the more the poorer people fall below the poverty line. The more deflation progresses, the less money will be available altogether. Many people do not have money at all, so they cannot buy anything even if it is cheap.

6. Money can undergo a process of value creation, that is, the money available for consumer spending is accompanied by a corresponding increase in production. There are more goods and services than before. Thus, money and goods and services have increased for all producers and consumers acting on the market, not for one part at the cost of another part. In this sense value creation is not bound to what are called zero-sum conditions, in which an increase in one part of a game is necessarily accompanied by an equivalent loss in the other part, as for example in a sports match.

7. There is a value principle measuring money: utility. That is, money fulfills its function inasmuch as one can buy goods and services with it. The solvency of economic units, which may be a whole society (say, Mexico), is a standard of coordination for economic action. Solvency means being in a position to repay debts, which depends on the economic unit's (the society's) production of goods and services.

Every social system, not just society, has an economic subsystem. The economy as a subsystem of society comprises all acts of production, exchange, and consumer spending. Within a smaller social system, like a university or a college, any action in which education is offered in exchange for enrollment is an economic subsystem of this social system. Students calculate economically in which college and which class to enroll; they pay and expect an increase in their education that should improve their career chances. Particularly if there is a market in which colleges — and within the colleges, courses — compete for enrollment, economic calculations enter into the action. Another example is a student group preparing for an exam. In this group, several students "offer" solutions for parts of the exam. They compete with regard to the attention they attract from other students and with regard to their approval. In smaller economic systems like this one, some substitute for money may be involved, like attracting attention from other people and receiving the approval of other people. In this case, approval is exchanged for education, for ideas, or for solutions in preparing for exams. The utility of approval is expressed in the education, ideas, and solutions for exams it can "buy." Units often work with approval credits, that is, they work on some generalized approval. A university college that appoints a professor in order to teach a class in sociology gives some of the approval it has received from the public and the students to this professor, who has to demonstrate his or her and the university's solvency in offering education in sociology.

G: *The Political System*

The function of the political system is to provide for goal attainment (G) of the total social system under the conditions of conflicting goals through collective decision making. The political system is based on interactions in which actors pursue specific goals, according to the principle of maximizing and realizing these goals, and come into conflict with one another. In this case, an actor has to apply force in order to overcome the possible resistance of other actors pursuing their own goals. If I want to make use of a pasture and other actors want to do the same, I can construct a fence around the pasture and defend it with weapons. In this case, my decision to use this pasture (my goal) is enforced against the possible resistance of other people. Force is a means that enables an actor to enforce the realization of a goal (or decisions to pursue such a goal) under the condition that anyone else can imagine and might like to pursue goals conflicting with the actor's own; the decisions and goals can be carried out only against resistance evolving from the presence of conflicting goals. High symbolic complexity of possible ends occurs in the interaction; nevertheless, action is directed toward one alternative that is described by the goal of that actor who can apply superior force. That means low contingency of action.

In another example, a student group preparing for an exam has different members with very different and conflicting goals regarding the procedure of preparation. Nevertheless, they need to reach a decision that will be binding for all, that is, collectively binding. One student may have much more knowledge than any other member of the group. If he or she threatens the other members with withdrawal if they do not follow his or her goal, the other members will comply out of fear that the threat will be carried out. Because the more knowledgeable student has no competitors, he or she can apply that superior knowledge as a sanction insofar as withholding his or her knowledge is a deprivation for the other members. A precondition is that there is indeed no alternative source of knowledge for them. If there are several advanced students, they may struggle for leadership over the other students. But in this case we have more of a market situation in which the competing students have to make offers in order to get followers.

Deprivations and negative sanctions are always concrete means of overcoming resistance. Their effectiveness depends on the situation, particularly on how much an individual's or a group's need satisfaction relies upon the means another individual has in his or her possession. For example, the knowledge-seeking students have to rely on the knowledge-possessing student. Thus, the applicability of deprivations and negative sanctions is restricted to particular situations and cannot be generalized beyond these situations. More general in its effectiveness is physical force, because it enables an individual to prevent the gratification of whatever needs he or she wants to prevent on the part of another individual.

But the application of physical force is always in danger of being counteracted by physical force from other actors. Thus, force is not really a general means for making decisions collectively binding, that is, binding for everyone in a social system.

A more general medium for making decisions collectively binding is legitimate political power. In this case the actors in a social system establish, by rational justification and/or common tradition, certain positions and/or decision-making bodies that have the right to set and carry out goals that are binding for the whole collectivity. Farmers may, for example, live in a community that has a community assembly empowered to decide on the entitlement to use pastures. The student group may form a committee that has the right to decide on the collectively binding goals. The assemblies, committees, government bodies, and governmental officials are the only actors who have the right to make collectively binding decisions and the right to apply physical force in order to enforce the decisions. The rules of decision making may vary from unanimous agreement through majority rule to one-person decisions. Political power in this sense is a generalized medium of interaction, appropriate for political decision-making processes under the condition of high symbolic complexity of imaginable goals and the selection of one single end for action. It has the following qualities (Parsons, 1969: 352–404).

1. Political power is symbolic in character. It symbolizes all specific decisions that can be made collectively binding and all corresponding goals that can be pursued and enforced as collectively binding. The political power of the student committee symbolizes all specific decisions on how to prepare for exams.
2. Political power is a generalized medium. It can be used in any situation against anybody, without the danger of opposing force being exerted. It can be used regardless of time, place, and the persons involved.
3. The acquisition and use of power is regulated by specific norms anchored in the consensus of a community and rationally justified. In this way political power is embedded in an order of authority, which comprises

all norms describing the rights of bodies or people occupying corresponding positions to decide on goals binding for the collectivity. A constitution is such an order of authority.

4. Political power can circulate between actors, particularly in democratic political systems. Every voter hands over with his or her vote a small amount of power to a representative, to a representative body, or to a party, which hands its accumulated power over to a government. The government, in turn, hands it over to certain governmental agencies devoted to carrying out certain specific political programs. Political power also circulates to other social subsystems, particularly when it is used to give directions for economic action via economic policy, or to change associational relations through positive laws, or to make decisions on education and other cultural institutions.

5. Political power undergoes processes of inflation and deflation. If I can enforce a smaller amount of decisions with the same amount of power at time t_2 than at time t_1, political power has lost some of its value; this is inflation. A government that has the same right to decide as any former government but can enforce only a small part of the decisions made by former governments faces power inflation. If the political scene is full of new incoming power holders who crosscut each other, inflation can be expected. When, however, more decisions can be enforced with the same amount of power at time t_2 compared to time t_1, deflation occurs. Both inflation and deflation are signs of crisis. In inflation only the strong power holders have a chance to enforce decisions. In deflation there is only a small number of power holders at all, and a low level of decisions that benefit the whole system; there is a low production of decisions.

6. Political power can undergo a process of value creation. Political parties can act as political banks that attract power from voters, and they can lend this accumulated power as a credit to governments and specific political programs. If political decisions increase and become more far-reaching in this way, more power and more decisions are in circulation than before. And every small power holder (voter) can benefit from this process. In this case the conditions of a zero-sum game are overcome. The increase of power for a proportion of the actors does not necessarily involve the loss of the same amount of power for another proportion of the actors.

7. There is a value principle for measuring political power. It finds its expression in the effectiveness of political power in enforcing collectively binding decisions. The compliance of actors with collectively binding decisions based on political power serves as a standard of coordination for political action. A power holder can expect in this case that his or her decisions will be accepted as binding. This is a way of

assuring political solvency in the case of political credits; it means that the increasing production of binding decisions corresponds to received credits of power.

I: *The Community System*

The function of the (societal) community system is to provide for integration (I) of the total social system through communal association. The (societal) community system is based on interactions that have the character of communal association and proceed according to the principle of conformity to the shared norms of a life-world. The norms the actors follow are self-evident and have no competing alternatives. The actors' symbolic horizon has a low complexity. At the same time, the norms describe precisely how to act in a certain situation. This is low contingency of action. In communal interaction the actors act on the basis of belonging to a community and of sharing norms of behavior; every act assures them of their belonging to one another and to the same community. Their action takes a lot of rules for granted. They act just because one has to act in a certain way in a certain situation. If worker A tells his colleague B that he will support the strike on the next day and asks him if he will also, and his colleague answers, "Sure, I will," both act jointly on the basis of a shared belonging to the workers' community. They act in solidarity with one another. B associates with A and the other workers and vice versa because they feel that they belong together and should act together.

The shared feeling of belonging to a community, however, is a concrete means of motivating another actor to associate in a situation and conform to common norms that is restricted in its effectiveness to relatively small communities in which all members know each other. Imagine action within a family: When a mother asks her daughter to help her clean the bathroom, do the dishes, and so on, she may do no more than simply ask her daughter. She may not have to offer an incentive (money) or threaten her with deprivations (having to stay in the house this afternoon) or convince her with arguments ("It is for the sake of equality that you should do it today because your brother did it last time"). She just says the words, and her daughter conforms. The more she has to emphasize her words, the smaller is the value of their belonging to the same family. However, the mother will have no chance of getting anyone outside the family to help out with cleaning unless she pays them. The common feeling of belonging is a means of motivating concrete associational acts and conformity to shared norms, which is restricted in its effectiveness to small communities and counteracted by membership in other communities.

The development of rights of citizenship is, on the level of society as a whole, an invention that allows a much wider range of motivating associational acts and conformity to common norms. As a citizen of the United

States, I am entitled to expect conformity to the shared norms of citizenship from every other such citizen. I have the right to expect admission to
schools, colleges, universities, and jobs without consideration of my racial,
ethnic, religious, or class origin and only on the basis of achievement. Parsons
calls this right to solicit acts of association and conformity to citizenship
norms "influence."

Influence is a generalized medium, and compared to the concrete feeling of belonging it is much more far-reaching. Some people can acquire
more influence than other people. The basis for such an accumulation of
influence is provided by merits in serving the community. Members who
have performed and who continue to perform services for the community
as a whole gain appreciation and influence. Thus, people who have voluntarily served the community in responsible positions, such as mayor, deputy,
priest, committee member, club president, member of the school board,
chairman of a department, dean of the college, and so on have in this way
acquired appreciation and influence. These are also members of the community who express in their conduct of life the community norms in an
exemplary way. Conformity to community norms is the most basic precondition for acquiring influence in the community. Donations to the community, to the library, to the art museum, to schools and colleges and
universities, and to welfare programs are the obligatory way for rich people
to establish a good reputation, and thus influence, in the community. A community member who has accumulated influence can use it to motivate other
members to join certain associational activities—to contribute donations
to some new kindergarten or to join a campaign to establish a new school
or to preserve a recreational area. Influence has some general qualities in
common with the other media of interaction (Parsons, 1969: 405–38).

1. Influence is symbolic in character. It symbolizes all acts of joining in
   with any action of association and of conforming to community norms.
   The influence of a mayor, for example, is expressed in the response to
   appeals to support his or her proposal to do something about preserv-
   ing a recreational area and in other acts of this kind.
2. Influence is a generalized medium. Particularly because it is anchored
   in rights of citizenship, it transcends every particular group membership and is independent of time, place, or the persons involved in the
   interaction.
3. The acquisition and use of influence is regulated by specific norms, those
   which define membership and rights of membership in a community
   and the community norms, and it is confined to soliciting acts of association, joining community action, and conformity to community norms.
   I can accumulate influence only through membership, conformity to
   community norms, services, and donations to the community. I can use

influence only in order to solicit association, support for community actions, and conformity to community norms.

4. Influence can circulate between actors. If a reputed member of a community recommends supporting a group that wants to establish a new program of primary-school education, he or she hands part of his or her influence over to this group, for example, in a letter of recommendation. The person cannot at the same time support a group that opposes this program. He or she cannot recommend supporting everything, otherwise the member would lose his or her reputation as a serious person and thus lose all his or her influence. This means that handing over influence implies giving away some part of one's influence. Influence can circulate beyond the boundaries of the (societal) community system, for example, when it is used to get certain groups' or individuals' interests included in the process of political decision making (political lobbying), or to support certain economic enterprises (advertising with respected people), or to give values a concrete meaning (respected people talking about the meaning of freedom and equality).

5. Influence undergoes processes of inflation and deflation. If, as a citizen, I can motivate fewer people to associate, join some action, and act in conformity to community norms at time t_2 than at time t_1 with the same amount of influence exerted, inflation has occurred. A high rate of incoming new members in a community is a very common cause of influence inflation. If I had to circulate only one letter in my neighborhood in order to get people together in a joint action for the preservation of a recreational area at time t_1 and I have to write five letters at time t_2, inflation has occurred. Deflation means that I get more joint, associational, and conforming acts at time t_2 than at time t_1 with the same amount of influence exerted, for example, with one letter compared to five letters. But both, inflation and deflation, are signs of crisis. In a period of inflation only highly reputed persons and groups can motivate joint, associational, and conforming actions. In a period of deflation most people have no reputation and thus no influence. Only a small number of people do everything for the whole community, which means that there is also a low production rate of joint, associational, and conforming acts.

6. Influence can undergo a process of value creation. Respected persons, clubs, committees, and voluntary associations can act as influence banks. They gather the associative will of a great many individuals and give this collected influence as a credit to certain programs for the community: a new library, a new recreational area, a new school, and so on. In this way credit allows a more far-reaching production of associational and joint actions than an immediate give-and-take exchange of influence

and joint action. The amount of influence available increases, and the production of joint, associational, and conforming acts increases also. In this way zero-sum conditions are overcome, because the increase of influence and corresponding joint, associational, and conforming actions is for the whole community. It does not mean that one part of the community's influence grows at the cost of an influence decrease for the remainder.

7. The value principle for measuring influence is solidarity. That means influence has value only insofar as it produces acts of solidarity (association, joining in, conforming). The standard of coordinating communal action is social consensus; when I act on the basis of influence credits, there must be a real chance that I can establish consensus on some joint, associational, conforming action. Otherwise, there would be a lack of communal solvency.

L. *The Social-Cultural System*

The function of the fiduciary (or as I prefer to call it, the social-cultural) system is to provide for latent pattern maintenance (L) of the total social system through communication and an orientation to general ideas. The fiduciary (or social-cultural) system is based on communicative interaction. The actors subsume their action under general ideas, that is, under words with a general *meaning*. They can subsume a lot of different interpretations and actions under a small number of very general ideas. Low symbolic complexity is accompanied by high contingency of action. The action strives toward consistency with ideas. The actors communicate symbols (gestures, words) to one another. Their mutual reaction is determined by the meaning of the symbols. Thus, when a mother tells her children that their father is tired, they know what she means: "Please be quiet, do not ask him too much." When she reminds Andy that his brother Bill is also there, Andy knows she means: "Let Bill play with the toys, too." Within the shared communicative context the words and phrases used have a clear meaning for the communicating actors.

But one has to know this context in order to get the intended meaning of the words. The same words heard outside this context can also mean: "Father works very hard for his money" and "Bill visits Andy." The words used are indexical in character; they refer to a certain context that must be known in order to understand what they mean. Indexical symbols are context-bound means of communication, that is, means of transmitting a message in a way that the person being addressed will understand the message. The same is true with indexical norms as a specific group of indexical symbols. Mother's messages to the children are also prescriptions: "Be quiet" and "Let Bill play." They are also context bound. In another context the children do not have to be quiet, and Bill is not allowed to play with the toys, for example, in the toy shop.

The more individuals are able to assign symbols (words) a general and more abstract meaning, the more they can communicate beyond the boundaries of particular contexts. Cultural universals, words with a general meaning, and values with a general meaning can be considered as generalized media for communication. The more a language develops such universal words, the more it becomes a context-free and generalized medium for communication. Terms like "education" are more general than terms like "knowing how to ride a horse"; values like "freedom," "equality," and "reason" are more general in character than norms like "Let Bill play with your toys" or "Don't go out in the rain without an umbrella." Universal symbols of a language and universal values common to many people (which, as Parsons does, we can call "value commitments" to bring out the binding of the individual to values) are generalized media for communication that allow one to communicate beyond the boundaries of any particular cultural context. As generalized media, they have some qualities in common with other media (Parsons, 1969: 439–72).

1. Universal symbols and value commitments are symbolic in character; they symbolize all the acts of understanding the meaning of my communications and all the acts of consenting to my value communications that I can solicit in using these universals. The term "education" symbolizes all acts of understanding on the part of my partners in communication when I use this word. The value "equality" symbolizes all the acts of consenting to this premise when I refer some proposal for reforming or for conserving certain institutions to this value. This does not necessarily imply consenting to my proposal. I would obtain that consent only if I could sustain my reference to the value by good arguments.

2. Universal symbols and value commitments are generalized media. They can be used in any particular context, at any time and place, and in communication with any person.

3. The use of universal symbols and value commitments is regulated by a specific system of norms, the grammar of a language, and norms of communication and discourse. In this way using rewards, force, or influence in communication and discourse is ruled out. Everybody who is able to talk has the same right to communicate, discuss, propose, and question messages; only the consensus achieved in a free discussion between equals counts as a criterion for the universality of symbols and values.

4. Universal symbols and value commitments circulate between actors. When I tell the dean of the college at UCLA that the semester system corresponds to a greater extent to the value of providing education than the quarter system does, I have applied the universal of "education"

in a certain message to a special situation and cannot, if I wish to remain consistent, do that in a different way at a later stage. I have given away a certain application of the universal "education." The situation is analogous to not being able to use the same $20 bill to buy a pair of sneakers that I have already used to buy a sociological theory book. I have transmitted my application of the universal "education" to another actor who takes this up in order to start his or her own continuing communication. Referring to my application of the universal "education" enables him or her to hand over the communication to any third person. Handing over applications of universals establishes chains of communication without contextual restrictions. Somebody at Harvard can just as easily take up the communication and continue its course.

Universal symbols and value commitments also circulate beyond the boundaries of the social-cultural system, for example, when they are introduced into particular communities in order to ask for the universal legitimation of its norms and institutions, when they are applied to procedures of decision making in order to ask for the universal legitimacy of the procedures, or when they are applied to economic action in order to provide for its rational reflection and to define cultural patterns of work, production, and consumption.

5. Universal symbols and value commitments undergo processes of inflation and deflation. When I can solicit a smaller amount of communicative understanding and/or of consent by mentioning a universal symbol and/or value at time t_2 than at time t_1, the universal has lost some of its value; this is inflation. For example, in a time of heated discussions, the use of certain phrases like "emancipation," "law and order," and "freedom" can be overdone, so that everybody uses the phrases but nobody understands their meaning in a communicative act. Alternatively, when a lot of new participants enter a discussion, it becomes more difficult to create understanding with a few words. The opposite, deflation, occurs when I can obtain more understanding with the same universals at time t_2 than at time t_1. Here, the participants in communication are so small in number that it is easy to communicate, but I do not reach many people. Both inflation and deflation are signs of crisis. In inflation, there is much talk but no understanding. In deflation, there is much understanding but little talk.

6. Universal symbols and value commitments can undergo processes of value creation. Educational institutions like universities, widely read newspapers, and television programs can attract the communication of universals stemming from a lot of individuals. They gather these communications, give them a general definition, and hand this definition over to some other contexts of communication that are in need of general definitions for their problems and general justifications for actions.

Thus, universities can support research in certain directions, and newspapers and television programs can give their definitions and justifications to certain points of public discussion like arms control, air pollution, economic growth, and so on. They give credit to some lines of argumentation in this discussion, thus supporting them in communication and enabling them to provoke a wider understanding and/or consent than in cases where only face-to-face communications can take place.

The increased use of universals by virtue of these credits results in an increase in communicative understanding and consent. Thus, the increase is for the whole system of communication and does not favor one part at the cost of another part, as is the case in zero-sum games. For example, newspapers like the *New York Times* gather a lot of communications from correspondents, politicians, experts, and others and convert these into a final communication on a certain problem like arms control, thereby supporting a certain line of argumentation with fresh arguments. This is a credit to groups who put forward this line of argumentation. Insofar as this increases overall understanding and/or consent, an increase in the total production of understanding and/or consent has occurred.

7. The value principle for measuring the worth of universal symbols and value commitments is the integrity of a latent cultural pattern. This means that the language and the symbols used must have a certain enduring meaning in order truly to produce understanding and/or consent. The standard for coordinating communication is the consistency of a cultural pattern. When I use universal symbols and values in communication and take them as credit with a view to understanding, I must be able to mobilize understanding and consent. Otherwise, I do not communicate seriously. The precondition for such understanding and/or consent is consistency in the applied universal symbols and values. Otherwise, everybody would get confused, and nobody would understand and/or consent to a communication.

Interrelating the Social Subsystems

Let us now look at the interrelationships between the subsystems of the social system. These are fundamental for making available the specific functional contributions of individual subsystems for the social system in its entirety. For example, only when the ideas emerging out of social-cultural communication are transmitted to the areas of the community, political, and economic systems can they provide for the latent pattern maintenance of the total social system. For this to take place, an approach must first be made toward unifying ideas defining the identity of the total system in social-cultural terms; then these ideas must be applied in order to define the identifying and basic ideas of communal association, political action, and economic action. In a social system that has differentiated subsystems providing for the fulfillment of its basic functions, the subsystems have to mutually interchange their functional contributions. This interchange of functional contributions between subsystems can be called interpenetration.

Between the four basic social subsystems six interchanges and interpenetrations occur. Interpenetration is that type of interrelationship between social subsystems that allows the highest degree of fulfillment of the individual functions without the subsystem breaking apart, thus maintaining the integration of the subsystems in relation to one another. Interpenetration is a balanced interrelationship between subsystems; one does not dominate the others. It has to be distinguished from one-sided interrelationships where certain systems dominate others. Interpenetration is also an interrelationship in which the total system displays a continuously effective dynamism, because the subsystems are always in tension with one another and change each other in their marginal zones. It must therefore also be distinguished from a structure in which subsystems merely coexist in separation, whether this is a complete separation or a reconciliation within a wider frame of reference where the subsystems do not mutually influence each other.

Let us now look at the six interchanges between the social-cultural, community, political, and economic subsystems of the social system. In its most elaborate form Parsons conceives of the interchange between the subsystems of the social system as an interchange of factors and products governed by the media of interchange associated with each subsystem involved. Factors are formed by the source system according to its own criteria and transmitted to the addressee system by the former's medium of interchange, where they are processed to form products. These are produced according to the criteria of the source system but called up by the addressee system using its own medium of interchange and consumed according to its own criteria. In the following sections I will give a general explanation and a concrete exemplification of what is going on in these interchanges and conclude with a brief representation of the interchanges in terms of factors, products and media of interchange (figure 1.4).

L-I: *Social-Cultural System and Community System*

The interpenetration of the social-cultural system and community system is the area of the institutionalization of value patterns.

The social-cultural system provides legitimation of norms and loyalty demands for the (societal) community system. This means that norms guiding behavior within the (societal) community and loyalty demands involving commitment to the community gain social-cultural legitimacy only if

Figure 1.4 The Input-Output Paradigm of the Social System

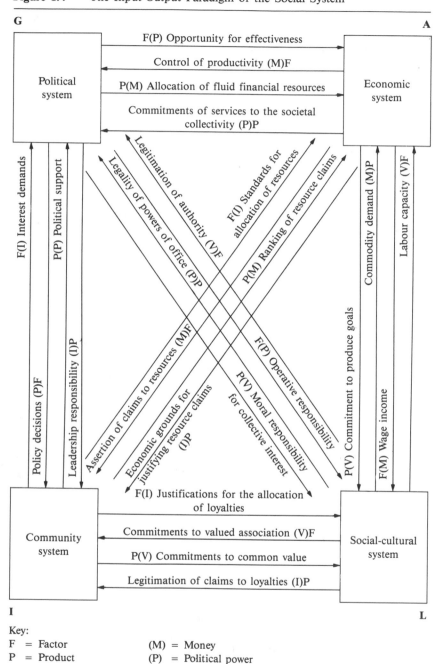

Key:
F = Factor (M) = Money
P = Product (P) = Political power
(I) = Influence (V) = Value commitment

they are consistent with more general values that have emerged out of communication and discursive argumentation. The general values can be used as critical measures of the institutionalized norms in a community.

A sociology department, for example, is a community that has norms guiding the teaching of sociology: a certain number of courses with a certain subject matter and a binding definition of certain areas of sociological knowledge and of sociology texts every student has to read. In addition, there are more general values such as extending and deepening the education of students with the best available knowledge, advancing knowledge, and seeking truth. To the extent that advances in knowledge are achieved in sociological discourse, pressure is created to apply such advances in teaching, since the values demand that students' knowledge be deepened. Thus, in the light of new sociological knowledge, the courses and readings that had traditionally been obligatory may lose their legitimacy, so that new courses and new texts have to be introduced. A department's demands of loyalty from the departmental community also lose their legitimacy when they imply teaching courses and assigning readings that are out of touch with the progress of sociological knowledge. Professors who are engaged in research and in teaching fulfill an important function in transmitting new knowledge to the educational process. The social-cultural system of the department is the ongoing sociological discourse; the community system is based on the norms for teaching (and also for research) and on the loyalty demanded from its members. The transmission of values and ideas from sociological discourse to the norms of teaching involves measuring the legitimacy of norms and loyalty demands against universal symbols, values, and ideas and confronting norms and loyalty demands with arguments that force them to justify themselves in terms of their consistency with such universal values and ideas. In this zone of interpenetration an existing consensus on norms is questioned in order to achieve a new consensus in which there is more consistency between institutionalized norms and general values and ideas.

In another example, the school system of the United States in the 1950s was racially segregated. This was the institutionalized norm, based on consensus and influence (reputation) of the dominating white majority. The social-cultural discussion, meanwhile, was placing more and more emphasis on the value of equal opportunity as a basic cultural value. The two sides were no longer in consistency with one another. The legitimacy of the norms of the educational system was called into question until they were changed, and the institutionalization of desegregation as a norm of the educational system brought about a new consistency and a broader consensus in the societal community. An important means of transmission between the social-cultural discussion and the societal norms institutionalized in the societal community is public discussion.

In the opposite direction of the interchange between the social-cultural and the community systems, the community system penetrates the social-cultural system by producing commitments to values based on influence (reputation). Values like "equal opportunity," "freedom," and "rewards based on achievement" become binding in character only if there is a consensus in the community on those values and if membership of the community at the same time attaches the individual to the consensually borne values. Thus, the commitment to values is not an outcome of their rational justification but a product of communal association involving influence (reputation) as a generalized medium of interaction. This implies that the binding commitment to values is always a commitment to a certain interpretation and particularization of the values out of a wider range of possible interpretations.

But the horizon of thinking in the community is narrowed to a certain interpretation that has no competing alternative within the community. What "extending and deepening education with the best available knowledge" means is defined by the common view on knowledge in the departmental community. In a very strict empirical department strongly devoted to empirical quantitative sociology (like Wisconsin and Michigan), a new interpretation of the classics and new theoretical debates will not be included within the meaning of that value of "extending and deepening education with the best available knowledge"; the members of the department, because they belong to this community, are committed to a certain interpretation of the educational value that has no alternative within the community. New members (and students) become committed to this interpretation through the influence (reputation) of the older members, particularly of the most reputed ones. The basis of this influence is the mutual sense of belonging to the departmental community.

We turn now to the second example: What the value "equal opportunity" concretely means in social interaction and in which way individuals are committed to this value are questions of communal association and influence in the societal community. In the 1950s, for example, desegregation in education and affirmative action were not included in the dominant interpretation of "equal opportunity" in the United States' societal community. But insofar as respected public leaders (e.g., Martin Luther King, John F. Kennedy, Lyndon B. Johnson) and reputable associations, organizations, parties, churches, and denominational groups put their influence (reputation) into the campaign for desegregation and later affirmative action, the latter became more and more part of the common and binding interpretation of "equal opportunity." The majority moved from segregation toward desegregation. In this way criticism of segregation for being inconsistent with "equal opportunity" is based on the application of universals to concrete situations and on argument. The commitment of people to this interpretation, however, has its basis in the influence of reputable members of the societal community. The result is a growing inclusion of minorities in the societal community; they become citizens with equal rights and can in this way partake of each citizen's influence on others, though this process has by no means completely achieved its goal.

In terms of factors, products, and media of interchange the described interchange has to be conceived as follows: The social-cultural system sends *commitments to valued associations* as a factor carried by value commitments and *legitimations of claims to loyalties* as a product carried by influence to the community system. The latter sends *justifications for the allocation of loyalties* as a factor carried by influence and *commitments to common values* as a product carried by value commitments to the social-cultural system.

L-G: *Social-Cultural System and Political System*
The interpenetration of the social-cultural and political systems is the area of specification of values and justification of decisions.

The social-cultural system provides legitimation for political authority. This means that the norms guiding the procedures of political decision making have to be justified in terms of universal values and ideas in rational discourse in order to gain cultural legitimacy. The values emerging out of social-cultural discussion serve as critical measures for political institutions and, in a secondary way, even for the positive laws enacted in political decision making. A department of sociology, for example, has its procedures of decision making; it has an executive committee that decides on new appointments, on appointments of visiting professors and scholars, on the initiation of new teaching programs, on availability of word processing, and so on. It also has its cultural communication and discourse between colleagues on sociology, research, and teaching. A central value in the cultural system of the department applying to procedures of decision making is the fellowship between colleagues, which means that every colleague in the department has the same right to raise questions and suggest certain decisions and that no decision should be made that is to the considerable disadvantage of some and cannot be justified by professional standards.

Thus, insofar as the procedure of decision making does not provide for opportunities of each member of the department to speak, it can be criticized from the point of view of basic values of the cultural system that are transmitted in this way via social-cultural communication and discourse to the political system. Social-cultural discourse is applied to procedures of decision making. Discourse directed toward this object forms a zone of interpenetration between pure social-cultural discourse and political decision making. Not only the procedures of decision making but also the decisions themselves can be measured against basic values; they have cultural legitimacy only when their consistency with the basic values can be proved. This is not a direct derivation of decisions from values, because different decisions might all be consistent with the values. But it is, nevertheless, possible to state what would be inconsistent with the values. Different decisions can be made, for example, on the eligibility of department members for merit increases, but each of them has to carefully review the qualifications of the members; otherwise a decision has no cultural legitimacy and can be debated and questioned.

In another example, a state government (political system) may decide on the construction of a new airport in a certain area. After the decision, people in that area may protest that they had no chance to put their claims into the decision-making process, because there was no hearing of interested parties affected by the decision. They can file a lawsuit, and the political decision could be turned down by a court decision stating that the failure to include a public hearing in the decision-making process is inconsistent with basic principles of the Constitution. In this case, the court decision is a linking mechanism between social-cultural discussion referring to the values of democratic participation and political decision-making procedures.

But it is not only in the formal sense that a political decision can be refuted by a court decision; this can also be done in the substantial sense. A law or governmental act can be turned down by court decisions, and finally by a decision of the Supreme Court, if it contradicts principles of the constitution of a state or of the federal system. For example, school board decisions in southern states refusing the admission of black students to all-white schools were refuted by federal court decisions in the 1960s. The mixture of social-cultural discourse and political decision making in court decisions can be seen in the fact that court decisions need an extensive justification through the application of constitutional principles to specific cases.

On the other hand, it is the majority position among the judges that decides a case, and the decision of the majority is mandatory for everybody and can be enforced through legitimate political power. For example, federal police enforced the school attendance of black students in a white college against the wishes of Governor George Wallace of Alabama as he stood in front of the main entrance in 1968. But the minority vote in a court decision is also publicized so that it remains in public discussion and may become the majority vote in a later court decision. In many civil rights cases, the minority vote of earlier decades became the majority opinion in the 1960s.

In the opposite direction, political decisions are always selections out of the horizon of cultural values and out of their scope of interpretation as they are discussed in social-cultural discourse. This means that every political decision also has aspects that involve cultural meaning. In this way political decision making determines which parts of the cultural system become concrete reality in everyday actions. The decision making of the sociology department's executive committee, for example, specifies which parts of sociological knowledge become included in the teaching program of a certain quarter. The research committee decides on the priority of a certain research area and directs funds and appointments to this research area. There are also other fields of research that may get less funds and appointments or may not get any attention. Thus, the decision making in the department selects from sociological culture what then becomes concrete teaching and research in the department, and this concrete teaching and research, for its part, defines what is the dominating sociological culture in the department. In this way political decision making based on the mobilization of power permeates and shapes sociological culture. It is important to have votes in a committee, that is to say "power," in order to shape the selected departmental culture.

In another example, every governmental act is a decision that has cultural meaning and selects certain aspects from the wider range of culture to give it a certain expression. When the federal government of the United States increases or cuts social welfare programs, this determines what equality in the United States is in fact, not only in theory; when federal laws define criteria for police action, they also determine the concrete meaning of cultural values such as "freedom" and "equal treatment before the law." When the city government of Los Angeles decides to extend the freeway system and the international airport, it concretizes what freedom in Los Angeles means: to get anywhere one wants to go in the most convenient way. These are decisions based on the mobilization of votes that express political power.

In terms of factors, products, and media of interchange, the social-cultural system sends *legitimations of authority* as a factor carried by value commitments and *legality of powers of offices* as a product carried by political power to the political system. The latter sends *operative responsibility* as a factor carried by political power and *moral responsibility for collective interest* as a product carried by value commitments to the social-cultural system.

L-A: *Social-Cultural System and Economic System*
The interpenetration of the social-cultural and the economic systems is the area of the cultural definition of economic production and consumption and of the economic calculation of cultural thought.

The social-cultural system provides for the legitimation and cultural shaping of economic action. This means that cultural values emerging from social-cultural communication and discourse set a frame of reference within which economic action takes place. Economic action can vary to a great extent, but it has cultural legitimacy only if it does not violate the culturally legitimated boundaries. Our sociology department has an economic subsystem. Externally, it competes with other departments with regard to student enrollments, research funds, appointing reputable professors, the appearance of its publications, or which theories are best proved. Furthermore, it engages in an exchange of ideas and makes contracts to cooperate in research projects with other departments and with industry. Internally, the members of the department also compete for these scarce resources, engage in exchange, and conclude contracts.

The social-cultural shaping of this economic action means that the advancement of knowledge and its transmission to society via education and publication is a basic value that defines the boundaries of economically based actions. This means that the department is not culturally legitimated to raise funds for programs that have nothing to do with the advancement of knowledge, and it is not allowed to fake data in order to gain a reputation for what ostensibly are excellent research results. Furthermore, the department is obliged to abide by the terms of any contracts it concludes. Also, insofar as it gives approval and funds for research it cannot do this on the basis of affiliations but only on the basis of achievement in research and teaching. The same is true of the individual members of the department. Research and teaching are forms of labor and to a certain degree economically calculated by both the employee and the employer. However, the form of this work is shaped by cultural values. In addition, research and teaching result in advanced knowledge and education, which are economic products, but products shaped by cultural values. These cultural values define the criteria of adequate knowledge and education.

In another example, in economic production and exchange, individuals calculate economically the profits of production and exchange. But they do it within a cultural frame of reference defined in social-cultural communication and discourse. Every economic actor has a certain education providing for some basic values and for knowledge he or she applies in economic action. The orientation toward achievement in a career, toward abiding by rules of contract, and toward placing a high value on equal opportunity is based on cultural education and discussion. Standards for the production of goods and services, the application of scientific knowledge in economic production, and styles of consumption are based on social-cultural communication and discourse and define the boundaries for economic action. An engineer who wants to introduce a new technology transmits cultural knowledge to the economic system. A consumer who dresses in a moderate middle-class style also transmits cultural values to the economic system.

In the opposite direction, the mobilization of economic resources for cultural values permeates the social-cultural system. This means that cultural values cannot be transformed into everyday concrete action without economic resources being mobilized: money, libraries, theaters, campuses, art galleries, and so on. In this way, economic calculation exerts an influence on the ups and downs of cultural values, making culture dependent on market conditions and transforming culture into fashion. Cultural values, ideas, and programs that can attract resources have much more chance of getting into the market and of achieving a public presence. Research areas in the sociology department that serve economic interests attract a lot of money, and the department can extend programs and research staff, hence gaining more cultural presence through sheer quantity than less subsidized areas. In this way, economic calculations in the department exert an influence on what kind of knowledge becomes culturally salient during a certain period.

Let's return to our broader example. The income from labor is a basic resource for living a certain style of life. The increased income of the whole mass of people in the United States over the past hundred years has contributed to the salience of what we call mass culture: movies, television, automobiles, leisure activities, uniform styles of dress and housing, and uniform styles of food—hamburgers, hot dogs, and sandwiches. The investment in high technology has consequences for culture in transforming styles of writing and communication to suit computer language. Education, the arts, movies, and television shows attract investment based on economic criteria in different ways, and this investment contributes to the production of the culture of the United States. But it isn't only investment in culture in its everyday sense that contributes to the production of culture. All economic investment and production results in products that have not only a utility value but also a cultural meaning, symbolizing a style of life: Coca-Cola, McDonald's, skyscrapers, freeways, and cars have a cultural meaning, and the variation of this meaning is influenced by economic calculations and investments. As symbols with cultural meaning, they cross the boundary between the economic and the social-cultural system and become part of the social-cultural system. This means that the economically produced cultural symbols come to be included in the social-cultural definition of meaning on the basis of communication and discourse.

In terms of factors, products, and media of interchange, the social-cultural system sends *labor capacity* as a factor carried by value commitments and *commodity demands* as a product carried by money to the economic system. The latter sends *wage income* as a factor carried by money and *commitments to production of goods* as a product carried by value commitments to the social-cultural system.

I-G: *Community System and Political System*

The interpenetration of the community and political systems is the area where social control and political responsibility are constituted.

The (societal) community system provides for normative and judicial control of political decision making. This means that the political actors involved in the decision-making process have to be attached to the norms guiding the procedure of decision making, and this is possible only when they are included in a (societal) community, feel that they belong to this community, and are committed to its common norms. The common law in England and the United States and the emergence of citizenship have been major steps in modern Western societies toward establishing such a societal community. For the citizen, political decisions are binding not only because political power can enforce them but also because the procedural norms of decision making are borne by every citizen because of his or her membership in the societal community. Reputation acquired in communal association also gives the individual actor his or her right to put personal interests into the process of decision making. The influence of reputable people and social groups gives interests and themes a "community license" to be heard and carefully regarded in the political decision-making process. Political actors have to rely on reputation in the societal community in order to gain support (votes, power) for political decisions.

In the sociology department, decisions are binding for all members insofar as the rules of decision making are borne by the departmental community and each member feels attached and committed to this community. Each member who wants to take part in the process of decision making has the influence, by virtue of his or her membership, to be heard and paid due regard for his or her opinion and interests, and each member who wants some specific decision (e.g., an appointment of a visiting professor) needs the support of other members, which he or she can gain by using his or her influence on (reputation with) other members of the department. The executive committee may decide on the appointment of a new professor. Its decision will be accepted by all other members as binding regardless of the nature of the decision provided the committee has abided by the commonly shared norms of decision making. Whoever wants to contribute his or her opinion to this decision has, as a member of the community, a basic influence, which implies an entitlement to be seriously heard; someone who wants to gain support for a certain decision has to put his or her reputation into this process. The more highly respected members can put in more influence (reputation) and have a better chance of obtaining a decision in accordance with their own opinions.

Here is another example. A new air pollution act of the state government of California will be accepted as binding by every citizen and group of citizens insofar as those individual citizens and groups feel committed to the rules of decision making. Every citizen and group has some degree of reputation that allows their opinions to be heard. Those who want to have the air pollution act enacted in a certain form have to gain political support from other citizens and groups by using influence (reputation). But the more respected people and groups can put more influence into this process than the less reputable.

In the opposite direction, political leadership and the organization of communal associations through positive law based on political decisions are outcomes of political decision making and penetrate the (societal) community system. In this process associational relationships acquire the character of formal legality based on positive laws.

In the sociology department, the chairperson and the executive committee are both positions with rights to decide and the power to enforce certain decisions. In their decisions to extend some areas of research and teaching and to cut funds for other areas, the chairperson and the executive committee lead the whole department, that is, the whole community, in a certain direction of research and teaching. They take responsibility for this decision for the whole departmental community, not only for parts of it. An active leader of a department can provide for a lot of movement in new directions, thus also changing the character of the departmental community, particularly the traditional horizon of teaching and research in the community. The formal decisions change the substance and character of the norms of the community. They become based on formal decisions, not on tradition; the rights of individual members and the distribution of resources among them become formally defined and are no longer just traditions as they used to be.

For example, the presidency of the United States is a position with a considerable amount of power to make decisions, though in many cases the president also needs the consent of Congress. But a president can lead the whole nation in a certain direction, as exemplified by President Reagan's changes in the nation in the 1980s toward a stronger emphasis on political strength in international relationships, on competition in society, and on cutting expenses in social welfare, also emphasizing people's self-responsibility while deemphasizing the responsibility of society for their well-being. He changed the character of the societal community, of its basic norms of association. Political decisions and new laws emerging from these decisions replace institutionalized norms. The process in the 1960s and 1970s had moved in a quite different direction. Political laws then changed the segregation among people and led to more equality in association.

In terms of factors, products, and media of interchange, the community system sends *interest demands* as a factor carried by influence and *political support* as a product carried by political power to the political system. The latter sends *policy decisions* as a factor carried by political power and *leadership responsibility* as a product carried by influence to the community system.

I-A: *Community System and Economic System*

The interpenetration of the community and economic systems is the area where resources are allocated to the community and the community exerts control over economic activity.

The (societal) community system provides for the normative regulation of the economic system. Insofar as economic actors are committed to a community and to common norms, their interactions come to be regulated by these norms. A market community is a specific linkage between the (societal) community system and the economic system. The sociology department's economic actions, its external and internal competition, exchanges, and contracts, become ordered and predictable for the actors insofar as the members involved in competition, exchange, and contracts feel committed to the departmental community. Norms of competition that prohibit faking data and norms of contract that prohibit breach of contracts are applications of community norms to economic behavior. A natural community norm, for example, is not to harm a fellow member of one's own community. Another aspect of regulation is the ranking of interested demands for resources (funds) from the community. The norms of the community may, for example, prescribe that every member should get the same amount of resources or that every member should get resources according to his or her achievement that contributes to the overall reputation of the department. In any event, one needs reputation in the community in order to obtain resources.

In another example, if economic actors do not feel associated in the same community and perceive one another as strangers, they do not feel committed to common norms regulating their competition, exchanges, and contracts. It is only when such a market community is established that normative regulation of economic behavior comes about. The same is true with ranking demands for resources. If societal groups do not conceive of themselves as members of the same societal community, they cannot influence each other and will not reach a shared ranking of interested demands for resources and of the distribution of rewards. Poor people may feel closed out of all distribution processes; achievement as a basis for the distribution of resources (rewards) may be considered as a device for the successful to keep on being successful and for the unsuccessful to remain that way too. Affirmative action, for example, is a normative regulation interfering with the pure logic of competition, providing the basis of equal opportunity.

In the opposite direction, the economic system provides the resources necessary for life in the community and for communal association to occur at all. The distribution of resources via economic competition also determines who can most closely associate with whom. Also, the market's penetration of the community changes community life, which acquires aspects of individual choice and calculation. Whom individuals associate with becomes a question of individual utility calculation. Communal relationships are no longer traditionally prescribed but a matter of free individual choice. In the sociology department, any economic mobilization of resources has its influence on the community. Research can be done on a larger scale, including new appointments and a lot of research assistants; teaching can be done on a larger scale. This changes the patterns of association. Particularly the market of research brings together researchers on the basis of individual choice and breaks long-existing traditional commitments.

Each donation people make to their community is a form of mobilization of economic resources for the community system. The mobilization of economic resources is the basis for community life, which needs some means of association: common meeting places, the town hall, the church, and means of communication and transportation. The large-scale development of such resources changes the character of communal association. Individuals can choose the place where they live and can communicate and associate over long distances. This demands new forms of association and of "belongingness." The inputs from the economic system into the community system call for the development of new forms of association: the freely and temporarily chosen association that is not exclusive in character but compatible with a lot of other associations according to different interests. Voluntary and pluralistic association becomes the prevailing form.

In terms of factors, products, and media of interchange, the community system sends *standards for allocation of resources* as a factor carried by influence and *rankings of claims to resources* as a product carried by money to the economic system. The latter sends *assertions of claims to resources* as a factor carried by money and *economic grounds for justifying claims to resources* as a product carried by influence to the community system.

G-A: *Political System and Economic System*

The interpenetration of the political and economic systems is the area where resources are mobilized for collective goals and economic activity is directed.

The economic system provides the resources that can be applied to carrying out collective goals that are based on political decision making. For example, the funds, personnel, research data, and theoretical knowledge accumulated in economic competition, exchange, and contracts in the sociology department are transmitted to its political system when the research committee decides on how these resources ought to be used for research projects in the department. In another example, the tax paid by individuals and corporations is a transmission of economic resources to the political system, within which political decisions determine what collective goals will be carried out with the available resources. When the government of a city decides to build new colleges, it applies part of its tax resources to a specific collective goal.

In the opposite direction, political decision making provides for steering the economy in directions determined by collective goals. For example, when the research committee of the sociology department decides on the extension of a certain research area, it gives the internal and external competition for funds and personnel a certain collectively decided direction. For another example, when the federal government decides on a budget, this is always combined with spending money for certain products leading to increased activity in corresponding industries (e.g., military equipment). Tax exemptions for investment in new technologies, overall tax policy, budgetary policy, or perhaps even industrial planning by the state (like the French system) all provide directions for economic action and form an input from the political to the economic system.

In terms of factors, products, and media of interchange, the political system sends *opportunities for effectiveness* as a factor carried by political power and *allocation of fluid financial resources* as a product carried by money to the economic system. The latter sends *control of productivity* as a factor carried by money and *commitments of services to the collectivity* as a product carried by political power to the political system.

The System of Action

Thus far we have considered the internal processes and structures of interaction and the differentiation and interrelation of subsystems of interaction. Yet interaction also takes place in an environment that contains noninteractional elements (see Parsons, 1951, 1959, 1961a, 1961b, 1978; Parsons and Shils, 1951a; Parsons and Platt, 1973; Lidz and Lidz, 1976). According to the scheme of symbolic complexity and contingency of action already introduced, interaction covers the field of structuredness where low symbolic complexity is combined with low contingency of action. If we step beyond the field of interaction in the total action space, we have to deal with the interrelationships with the environment in three directions. The symbolic structure of culture constitutes an environment with reduced symbolic complexity and increased contingency of action; the behavioral processes of learning form an environment with both high symbolic complexity and high contingency of action; the dispositions of the human personality form an environment with high symbolic complexity and reduced contingency of action. Conceived in this perspective, the order of interaction is a question of not only its internal constitution but also its external interrelationship with culture, personalities, and behavioral systems. In a more general view we are interested here not only in the order of interaction but also in the order of action in a more comprehensive sense.

The Subsystems of the Action System

Let us first characterize the internal qualities of the subsystems of action and then analyze their interrelationships. In order to complete our analysis of norms as constitutive elements of order, we concentrate again on the normative aspect of action (figure 1.5).

Figure 1.5   The System of Action

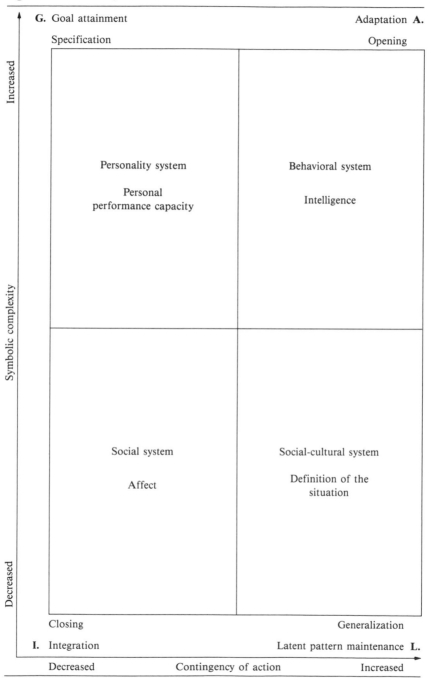

L: *The Cultural System*

Cultural systems are systems of symbolic constructions that are made up of cognitive, expressive, normative, and meaning systems. If we consider only cultural norms, we have to take into account that they are abstractions from any social context and have an objective meaning that is independent of social and individual interpretation. For example, the work of Max Weber belongs to the culture of sociology. This work has an objective structure that goes beyond Weber's personal knowledge of his work and beyond every interpretation. That is, it contains a potentially infinite number of possible interpretations. But as long as cultural systems are measured according to criteria of validity (truth, identity, consistency, coherence), there is an internal logic of development. Thus, interpretations of Weber's work are not arbitrary in character; they undergo a process of selection according to their tenability if confronted with the reality about which they make propositions. It is not Weber's own view of his work that is the criterion of selection but the reality to which an interpretation relates. Weber's view is in itself only one possible interpretation that has to be assessed according to the criterion of truth.

We may not only postulate a developmental logic of cognitive systems approaching truth in the process of selection of propositions by permanent criticism in Karl R. Popper's (1963, 1972) sense but also assume the possibility of a developmental logic of expressive, normative, and meaning systems that is also based on selection by criticism, thus closing out errors step-by-step. In this way expressive systems are measured according to the criterion of identity they provide for a multiplicity of individual expressive feelings; normative systems are measured according to the criterion of consistency they provide for a multiplicity of particular norms of social systems; and meaning systems are measured according to the criterion of coherent meaning they provide for a multiplicity of human actions in the world. Insofar as symbolic constructions are permanently confronted with criticism that applies these measures we may expect a logic of development of cultural systems to "approach" validity in the mathematical sense, that is, approaching more and more validity but without ever attaining it completely.

Thus, cultural systems always have the potential to transcend every concrete institutionalized societal culture in particular social systems. Cultural systems are applied to action by definitions of the situation. For example, the concept of social action is constitutive for Weber's work. We may use this concept as a device for defining a concrete event in the world as social action. This definition of the situation allows us to apply the whole framework of Weber's sociology to analyze the event at hand.

The developmental logic of cultural systems leads to the attainment of ever more generalized symbolic constructions. In this process culture can be subsumed under a few abstract premises such as the idea of truth for the culture of science: Symbolic complexity is reduced by generalization. But these abstract principles leave a wide range open for possible interpretations and applications to action: Contingency of action is very highly developed.

I: *The Social System*

In social interaction, we refer to social interpretations of cultural symbols. The internal logic here is how individuals come to mutually predictable interpretations of symbols, how they attain socially binding and common constructions of symbols. For example, Weber's work is interpreted by sociologists who constitute a social system because they are engaged in social interaction. This system of interaction of sociologists is composed of discourse, decision-making processes, markets, and communal association, which all contribute to the process of institutionalizing interpretations of Weber's work as socially binding. There may be some basic elements that are shared by all sociologists. All sociologists may share the conviction that every student of sociology should learn Weber's basic categories at the beginning of his or her studies. However, there are variations from one department to another in the way this is done, that is, the way the department community designs a concrete course on Weber's basic categories. But the way in which this course is run in a specific semester is the result of departmental decision-making processes.

At the same time, discourse on Weber's categories continues in the wider social system of sociology including the sociology course under consideration. There is also competition between sociologists in general and between participants of the course in particular with regard to new, influential, and more tenable interpretations of Weber. In this way there is always something socially binding in the treatment of Weber by students of sociology. They cannot avoid being examined on his basic categories. This socially binding Weber is much more restricted in character than the cultural Weber. But at the same time, in a complex and contingent social system there are always processes at work that interfere with this restriction, linking the socially binding Weber to the more universal cultural potential—opening his work to new interpretations but also specifying him in concrete questions and answers in processes of decision making.

Socially binding interpretations of culture are applied to concrete situations by affect based on the attachment to and identification with others. Alter accepts interpretations of Ego on the basis of his or her attachment to or identification with Ego. Socially binding interpretations of cultural systems close the horizon of possible interpretations and in this sense reduce symbolic complexity. At the same time they are much more concrete in content than cultural systems as such, thus prescribing action, that is, ways of applying interpretations of cultural systems to concrete situations in a much more determined way; at the same time they reduce contingency of action. Weber's work, as a cultural system, allows a great deal of interpretation. This is symbolic complexity for the social system; it is reduced by attaining a socially binding interpretation, which does not leave open very different ways of application; that is, it reduces contingency of action.

G: *The Personality System*

Our next step is to examine the personal Weber. Every sociologist interprets Weber's work in a specific way according to personal knowledge and disposition. Though each sociologist has learned Weber's work in the social interaction of sociology courses, his or her interpretation of Weber is never identical with that of the teacher and of the other participants. They may have found a consensus on specific aspects of Weber's work at the end of the course and before the examination. But the individual has acquired not only the social Weber of his or her study group but also the cultural Weber. One can read *Economy and Society* only on the basis of one's general capacities of understanding language. One can read Weber from one's personal experience and can continue reading Weber and include all of one's new experience after the course. One applies one's Weber interpretation to concrete situations (e.g., in discussions) on the basis of one's performance capacity, that is, the ability to select out of a multiplicity of interpretations and a multiplicity of aspects in Weber's work a specific interpretation and aspect relevant to the solution of the intellectual problem discussed in a concrete situation. Facing high symbolic complexity of possible interpretations and aspects an individual is nevertheless capable of selecting one alternative as binding for action, that is, for his or her contribution to the discussion.

A: *The Behavioral System*

Next, we come to the learning processes of the behavioral system. A student's acquisition of Weber's work is also a behavioral learning process. The individual invests his or her intelligence in studying Weber's work. The higher the levels the student achieves in this process, the more he or she will be able to intelligently discuss, interpret, and apply Weber's work, leading to completely new interpretations and applications. In this way, intelligent interpreters of Weber supply us with innovations that may change our view of Weber's work. Intelligence is the medium that allows the student to apply Weber's work to explain reality on the one hand and to confront it with the multiplicity of events in reality on the other. In order to do that, the person has to formulate an increasing number of empirically testable hypotheses derived from Weber's work. He or she raises symbolic complexity but can also confront the hypotheses in a great number of different tests with the manifold reality: contingency of his or her action is also very high.

Interrelating the Action Subsystems

Let us now examine the interrelationships between the subsystems of action characterized above. In the most advanced terms Parsons conceives of the interpenetration of subsystems of action as an interchange of factors and products that is carried out by generalized media of action (figure 1.6).

- Definitions of the situation are oriented toward the *constitutive grounds of meaning* of the human condition. The appropriate standard of value is the *value rationality* of action, grounded in moral authority. To reflect a more strictly cultural understanding of that medium, we should replace the term "value rationality" with "meaningfulness of action in a cultural framework."
- Affect is oriented toward the *institutionalization of meaning* relevant to society. The value standard is the *unity of meaning* (harmonization) of identities based on social imperatives. Affect is the general medium of the social system, which encompasses value commitments, influence, power, and money as special forms.
- Personal performance capacity is oriented toward the *internalization of relevant meaning* for the personality. *Means-end rationality* (*Zweck-rationalität*) serves as the standard of value based on practicality, that is, the possibility of being able to carry out actions.
- Intelligence is oriented toward *grounds for cognitive validity and significance*. The value standard is the *cognitive rationality* of action, grounded in cognitive standards.

L-I: *Cultural System and Social System*

In the interrelationship between the cultural system and social interaction, the institutionalization of the cultural symbolism in social systems takes place. This relationship involves tension between the developmental logic of attaining cultural, socially independent validity and the socially binding interpretation of culture. In the process of institutionalization, culture becomes linked to social interaction, and, by virtue of its own developmental logic, it exerts pressure on social institutions to change in the direction of cultural validity. The linking mechanism here is the intellectual *criticism* of social institutions in the light of cultural values, which always steps beyond any concrete *societal* culture. In the other direction, processes of *consensus formation* define certain interpretations of cultural values in social institutions as socially binding, thus reducing the total cultural potential to a concrete societal culture. Most theories of institutionalization do not disentangle precisely enough these two counteracting processes of institutionalization. They particularly neglect the fundamental process of criticism and the dynamic potential of the cultural developmental logic.

Figure 1.6 The Input-Output Paradigm of the Action System

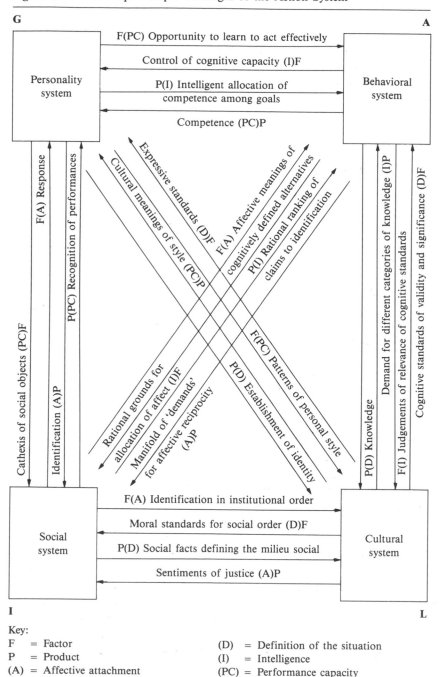

Key:

F   = Factor   (D) = Definition of the situation
P   = Product   (I) = Intelligence
(A) = Affective attachment   (PC) = Performance capacity

In terms of interchange of factors and products carried out by generalized media, the cultural system sends *moral standards for social order* as a factor carried by definitions of the situation and *sentiments of justice* as products carried by affect to the social system. The latter sends *identification in institutional order* as a factor carried by affect and *social facts that define the social milieu* as a product carried by definitions of the situation to the cultural system.

L-G: *Cultural System and Personality System*

The interrelationship between the cultural system and the personality of the individual is the context of internalization of culture in the personality system. Here, too, culture exerts a pressure of rationalization on the individual personality. The more an individual is exposed to the developmental logic of culture, for example, via longer phases of education up to university education, the more that individual feels compelled to justify his or her actions in the light of cultural knowledge, expressions, norms, and meaning constructions. This involves the *application* of culture to individual action. In the other direction, there is a process of *selecting* culture for the uses of the individual personality. That is, each personality has its own problems, and the individual judges the total potential of culture with regard to its *relevance* for the solution of personal problems. Insofar as the individual transmits his or her selections to culture, for example, if a person writes a book selecting Weber's study of capitalism and relating it in his or her interpretation to the question of the work ethic in our times, the personal selection out of the cultural system contributes new elements to the cultural stock. In this process culture is the outcome of innumerable creative individual acts.

The compulsory influence of cultural rationality on the individual personality should not conceal the fact that, on the one hand, the individual personality creates new culture in his or her selection of cultural elements in order to solve personal problems and that, on the other hand, cultural generalization of the individual horizon also frees the individual from his or her commitments to the particularistic societal culture. Certainly a person has acquired culture in processes of interaction. But the person's ability to interpret language enables him or her to discover in the transmitted societal culture the whole underlying potential of the cultural system as an independent system of objective meaning—the deep structure of culture. Only a theory that can clearly distinguish culture in its objective quality from societal culture will also grasp this aspect of internalization, which does not mean conformity to societal norms but acquisition of the cultural potential that transcends every societal culture. Parsons always conceived of internalization as a relationship between cultural and personality systems, not social and personality systems, thus opening this concept to the cultural dynamic.

It is an irony that his theory was constantly misrepresented as involving the accommodation of the individual to the pressures of the social system by sociologists who favored theories that do indeed fail to clearly draw a distinction between culture in its objective quality and societal culture in its binding character. In this respect, Parsons transcends Durkheim, Freud, and Mead, who were inclined to reduce culture to societal culture, and also Piaget and Kohlberg, who emphasized the cognitive developmental aspect of pure culture in the individual without, in any systematic way, bringing it into interrelationship with the social dimension of interpreting culture.

In terms of the interchange of factors and products carried out by generalized media, the cultural system sends *expressive standards* as a factor carried by definitions of the situation and *cultural meanings of style* as a product carried by performance capacity to the personality system. The latter sends *patterns of personal style* as a factor carried by performance capacity and the *establishment of identity* as a product carried by definitions of the situation to the cultural system.

L-A: *Cultural System and Behavioral System*
The interrelationship of the cultural system and behavioral processes of learning confronts culture with the multiplicity of events in reality, on the one hand, and gives situationally varying experience a frame of reference on the other hand. The individual uses all his or her situationally changing experience and all his or her perception of reality as a test case for cultural constructions of reality. This is the process of *testing* culture, which opens culture for innovations. In the other direction, the use of the cultural framework is a process of *ordering* experience.

In terms of the interchange of factors and products carried out by generalized media, the cultural system sends *cognitive standards of validity and significance* as a factor carried by definitions of the situation and *demands for different categories of knowledge* as a product carried by intelligence to the behavioral system. The latter sends *judgments of relevance of cognitive standards* as a factor carried by intelligence and *knowledge* as a product carried by definitions of the situation to the cultural system.

I-G: *Social System and Personality System*
The interrelationship between social interaction and the individual personality is the context of motivating the individual to participate in social interaction. The expectations of interacting parties shape the dispositions of the individual insofar as he or she identifies with social objects and learns to live out his or her need dispositions in socially acknowledged ways. This is the process of social *molding* of personal dispositions and the place for Freud's superego. But insofar as the individual has the chance to shape his or her action in social roles according to need dispositions, there are counter-

acting measures against a one-way domination of the social system over the personality. In this process the individual plays social roles according to his or her *role interpretation* and thus contributes to the social definition of roles.

In terms of the interchange of factors and products carried out by generalized media, the personality system sends *cathexis of social objects* as a factor carried by performance capacity and *identification* as a product carried by affect to the social system. The latter sends *response* as a factor carried by affect and *recognition of performances* as a product carried by performance capacity to the personality system.

A-G: *Behavioral System and Personality System*

The interrelationship between behavioral learning processes and the individual personality constitutes the mobilization of behavioral resources. An individual gives his or her learning a specific *direction* according to personal aims, dispositions, and problems. The person does not learn arbitrarily but according to a plan aiming in a specific direction. In the other direction, the individual is open for innovations from the learning process and *redefines* his or her aims, dispositions, and problems in the light of growing experience.

In terms of the interchange of factors and products carried out by generalized media, the personality system sends *opportunities to learn to act effectively* as a factor carried by performance capacity and the *intelligent allocation of competence among goals* as a product carried by intelligence to the behavioral system. The latter sends *control of cognitive capacity* as a factor carried by intelligence and *competence* as a product carried by performance capacity to the personality system.

I-A: *Social System and Behavioral System*

The interrelationship of social interaction and behavioral learning processes is the context for the social organization of learning. Insofar as a social system is open for the learning of its individual members, these learning processes *change* permanently the definition of social knowledge and social roles. The student of Weber who gains new insights may or may not immediately transform this progress in learning into social knowledge and into the shaping of his or her role as a sociology teacher or student. In the other direction, the binding character of *standards* of learning is constituted in social interaction. Without such standards learning would be blind and could not be accumulated or transmitted to other individuals.

In terms of the interchange of factors and products carried out by generalized media, the social system sends *affective meaning of cognitively defined alternatives* as a factor carried by affect and *rational rankings of claims to identification* as a product carried by intelligence to the behavioral system. The latter sends *rational grounds for the allocation of affect* as a factor carried by intelligence and the *manifold of "demands" for affective reciprocity* as a product carried by affect to the social system.

Conclusion

The order of interaction is a question not only of the internal composition of interaction but also of the external interrelationship of interaction within the whole system of action. These interrelationships may also range from accommodation via mutual isolation, reconciliation, conflict, and interpenetration to domination. The interpenetration of subsystems creates a complex and contingent order. In this case, we may consider a specific subsystem in its structures and processes within its environment. This subsystem is then the microsystem; the whole system in which it is embedded within its environment is the macrosystem. What is micro and what is macro are questions of perspective. If we look at the social system within the action system, it is a micro system. If we see market exchange within the social system, the former is micro, and the latter is macro.

The Human Condition

In the later years of his life, Talcott Parsons was deeply concerned with the most basic anthropological question of the human condition. The collection of essays in his final book, *Action Theory and the Human Condition*, published in 1978, one year before his death, gives viable expression to these studies. By turning his attention to this area, Parsons now incorporated his notion of the action system in the more basic system of the human condition (Parsons, 1978: 323–433). This new system is composed of the telic, action, organic, and physico-chemical systems. Each of these four subsystems performs one of the four functions according to Parsons's overall functional scheme on the level of the human condition. Their processes and interchanges are also coordinated by generalized media (figure 1.7).

The Subsystems of the Human Condition

First, we will examine the subsystems of the human condition system, their structures, processes, and media.

L: The Telic System

The telic system performs the function of latent pattern maintenance by way of defining the most basic (transcendental) conditions of meaning in human life. Low complexity of meaning constructions is accompanied by high contingency of events that can be covered by these constructions. The generalized medium of the telic system is *transcendental ordering*, which

Figure 1.7   The Human Condition

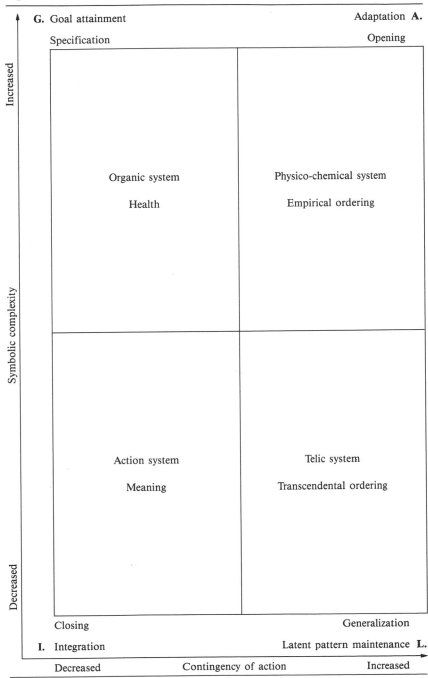

G. Goal attainment

Specification

Adaptation **A.**

Opening

Increased

Symbolic complexity

Decreased

Organic system

Health

Physico-chemical system

Empirical ordering

Action system

Meaning

Telic system

Transcendental ordering

Closing

I. Integration

Generalization

Latent pattern maintenance **L.**

Decreased   Contingency of action   Increased

is related to the orientation category of *transcendentality*. The latter is a general frame of reference for meaningful human existence. From the human perspective, this frame of reference is the most general basis for physico-chemical order, organic order, and order in action. The relevant evaluation standard from the human viewpoint comprises *transcendental argumentation* (or logic) in the sense of Kant's three critiques of reason.

The fact that the human being can live only as long as there is meaning for him or her in life is the most basic transcendental condition of human existence. Here is the source of the universal human quest for meaning that gives rise to religion of whatever kind as a universal phenomenon. When in present times we seek after the meaning of a civilization that destroys its own environmental resources, we pose the question of meaning in an immediately relevant form. This is why the quest for meaning will survive concrete religion and why it is completely wrong to expect the irrelevance of this condition of human life after the breakdown of the historic religions. It is also impossible to replace answers to questions of meaning by answers to questions of secular morality, as Jürgen Habermas (1981: 375–85) has put it in his criticism of Parsons's idea of the telic system.

I: *The Action System*

The action system performs the function of integration by way of ordering events in meaningful systems. In human thought only a small part of what could be possible under the meaning conditions of human life becomes realized. For example, every religious meaning construction is a selection from a wider range of possible constructions. These religious meaning constructions also determine what can be meaningful action in a more definite way than the conditions of meaningful human existence in general. In religious communities, the range of possible meaningful action becomes even more closely defined. Low complexity of meaning constructions is accompanied by low contingency of action. The generalized medium that allows us to coordinate human action is *meaning* that is ordered by the rules of language. Meaning is related to the orientation category of *generativity*, the frame of reference for the articulation of meaningful symbolizations of a language. It allows the creation within its system of an infinite variety of linguistic symbolization, all from the same basic linguistic elements. The relevant evaluation standard is the *understanding* (*Verstehen*) of expressions of meaning.

G: *The Organic System*

The organic system, of which the human organism is a part, is a goal-directed system; its relation to its environment is controlled by cybernetic feedback processes. It performs the function of goal attainment and is the site of organic evolution via processes of reproduction, mutation, and natural selection. High complexity of possible events is accompanied by low contingency of real events via processes of goal direction and natural selection. The medium that operates here is *health*, which is a generalized expression for very different characteristics of specific parts of the organism. Health is related to the orientation category of *teleonomy*, which represents a general frame of reference for the functioning of the organism. The evaluation standard is *diagnosis*.

A: *The Physico-Chemical System*

The physico-chemical system is the site of physico-chemical structures and processes and performs the function of adaptation within the whole system of the human condition. It provides the resources for the other subsystems. High complexity of possible events is accompanied here by high contingency of real events. The system's medium is *empirical ordering* as expressed in the laws of physics and chemistry. These laws cover a multitude of physico-chemical processes, so that these processes can be used and transmitted via technology to other systems. The medium that allows this transmission is *empirical ordering* by natural laws. Empirical ordering is related to the orientation category of *causality* as the general frame of reference. The relevant evaluation standard is the *adequacy of causal explanations*.

Interrelating the Human Condition Subsystems

Parsons goes on to construct a model of the interpenetration of these subsystems of the human condition from the point of view of the human actor in terms of an interchange of factors and products carried out by the generalized media of the human condition. (See figure 1.8.)

L-A: *Telic System and Physico-Chemical System*

From the interpenetration of transcendental conditions and physicochemical processes, we obtain the *constitution of natural order*, according to Kant's *Critique of Pure Reason* (Kant, 1781/1964a, for translation, see 1952a). The telic system sends *categories of the understanding* (e.g., causality, interdependence, substance) *and forms of intuition* (space, time) as a factor carried by transcendental ordering and *generalization of knowledge* as a product carried by empirical ordering to the physico-chemical system. The latter sends *sense data* as a factor carried by empirical ordering and *orderliness of nature* as a product carried by transcendental ordering to the former.

L-I: *Telic System and Action System*

From the interpenetration of transcendental conditions and action, the *constitution of the order of action* results according to Kant's *Critique of*

Figure 1.8   The Input-Output Paradigm of the Human Condition System

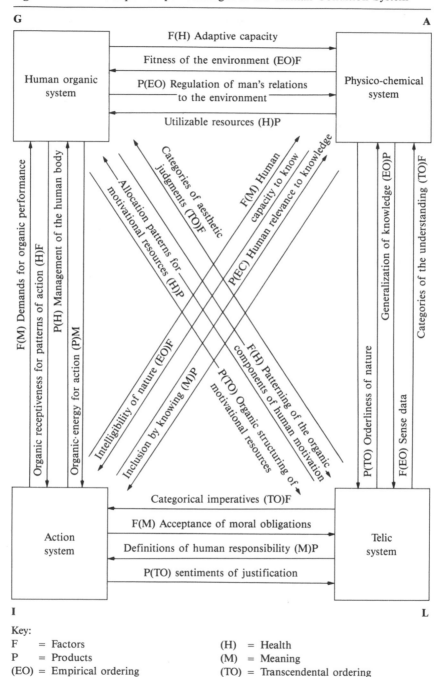

Key:
F   = Factors   (H) = Health
P   = Products   (M) = Meaning
(EO) = Empirical ordering   (TO) = Transcendental ordering

Practical Reason (Kant, 1788/1964b; for translation, see 1952b). The telic system sends *categorical imperatives* as a factor carried by transcendental ordering and *definitions of human responsibility* as a product carried by meaning to the action system. The latter sends *acceptance of moral obligations* as a factor carried by meaning and *sentiments of justification* as a product carried by transcendental ordering to the former.

L-G: *Telic System and Organic System*

From the interpenetration of transcendental conditions and organic goal orientation, the *purposiveness of organic life* is formed, according to Kant's *Critique of Judgement* (Kant, 1790/1964c; for translation, see 1952c). The telic system sends *categories of aesthetic judgments* as a factor carried by transcendental ordering and *allocation patterns for motivational resources* as a product carried by health to the organic system. The latter sends *patternings of the organic components of human motivation* as a factor carried by health and *organic structuring of motivational resources* as a product carried by transcendental ordering to the former.

G-A: *Organic System and Physico-Chemical System*

From the interpenetration of organic goal direction and physico-chemical processes we obtain the *mobilization of physico-chemical resources for organic life.* The organic system sends *adaptive capacity* as a factor carried by health and *regulations of man's relations to the environment* as a product carried by empirical ordering to the physico-chemical system. The latter sends the *fitness of the environment* as a factor carried by empirical ordering and *utilizable resources* as a product carried by health to the former.

G-I: *Organic System and Action System*

From the interpenetration of organic goal direction and action, the *motivation of action* emerges. The organic system sends *organic receptiveness for patterns of action* as a factor carried by health and *organic energy for action* as a product carried by meaning to the action system. The latter sends *demands for organic performance* as a factor carried by meaning and *management of the human body* as a product carried by health to the former.

I-A: *Action System and Physico-Chemical System*

From the interpenetration of action and physico-chemical processes, the *meaning and cultivation of nature* is formed. The action system sends *human capacity to know* as a factor carried by meaning and *human relevance to knowledge* as a product carried by empirical ordering to the physico-chemical system. The latter sends the *intelligibility of nature* as a factor carried by empirical ordering and *inclusion by knowledge* as a product carried by meaning to the former.

Personality Development and Socialization

The theory of the development of the human personality outlined by Parsons
was shaped by his interpretation of Durkheim's and Freud's work and, in
the 1950s, by his collaboration with James Olds, who introduced a behavioristic perspective. Later on, this behavioristic approach was complemented by
Piaget's cognitive psychology as introduced by Victor and Charles Lidz
(Parsons, 1951, 1964, 1978; Parsons and Bales, 1955; Parsons and Platt, 1973;
Lidz and Lidz, 1976).

In the perspective of Parsons's theory, the human personality emerges
as an autonomous system from the interpenetration of the organic needs,
drives, desires, and instincts of the individual with the factual, social, and
cultural environment. This gives rise to a personality that is composed of
four subsystems: Id, Ego, Superego, and Ego identity (Ego ideal). The interaction between socializee and socializing agents shapes the character and
development of all these aspects of the personality, not only the emergence
of the superego as it was conceptualized by Freud (1923/1972).

Personality development in the outlined four dimensions has different
meanings:

> *Adaptive upgrading:* The Id learns to situationally adjust to ever more
> complex, contingent, and rapidly changing situations by using its
> intelligence.
> *Differentiation:* The Ego acquires the ability to manage the attainment
> of different goals.
> *Inclusion:* The Superego becomes capable of coordinating an ever greater
> number of solidarities and loyalties.
> *Value generalization:* The Ego identity reaches higher levels of value
> generalization and has the ability to subsume a greater number of
> specific ideas and actions under very general ideas and values.

Socialization and personality development is an ongoing process of interaction between a socializee and socializing agents that involves object relations, object cathexis, identification, and internalization as basic elements.
This process can be roughly differentiated into three basic stages: (1) mother-
child interaction in childhood; (2) extended interaction with mother, father,
brother, sister, peers, and teachers in the transition from childhood to youth;
and (3) further extended interaction with peers and adults in the transition
from adolescence to adulthood.

Mother-Child Interaction

The interaction between the infant and his or her mother is central to
the first stage of personality development. The child learns, via reward and

punishment, the first patterns of behavior and control over impulses, for example, schedule of nutrition, cleanliness, walking, and talking. These are the first steps of the adaptive upbringing of the Id.

The mother is the first object the child relates to. She becomes an object of cathexis the more she satisfies the baby's needs for nutrition, pleasure, acceptance, and erotic stimulation. The child becomes oriented toward the attainment of goals; the Ego develops and differentiates.

The closer the relationship, the more the child will identify with his or her mother. Both form a unit of social attachment; identification of the child with mother grows. Identification with its mother is the basis of the child's conformity to mother's norms. In this way the Superego begins to emerge in a preliminary form; inclusion takes place.

The closer the attachment, the more the child will love his or her mother. Love is a generalization of mutual attachment. It becomes the first mediating link for generalization. The child acquires a more generalized self-awareness and self-confidence, sees him- or herself in terms of not only good or bad acts but also of being a good (or bad) boy or girl. His or her identity is based less on specific rewards and punishments and more on a general love attachment—to be someone who is loved and loves, is accepted and accepts, is a good boy or girl or a bad one. Ego identity develops. Values of higher generality become internalized by the child. These are the first steps of value generalization.

Extended Interaction: Mother, Father, Brother, Sister, Peers, and Teachers

The more the interaction of a child extends beyond the mother-child unit, the more the child will establish new object relations, object cathexes, identifications, and internalizations. The father gains importance in interaction, and he turns out to be an obstacle for the continuation of the love attachment with the mother. This gives rise to the Oedipal crisis, particularly with a male child. A girl's object relations also become more complex. The child has to give up the erotic attachment to his or her mother. This is a first loss of cathected objects, a first separation. The closed character of the mother-child social system no longer continues to exist. New cathexes and identifications of a more complex nature are open for the child.

Identification with father introduces an authority relationship and imposes conformity to norms that come from wider society and are represented by the father. The attachment to the father, in erotic terms, has a neutral character. This generalized attachment is the mediating link for internalizing more general values: achievement, universalism, neutrality, and specificity. In cases of a single mother or where the mother and father both work, this transition from a close emotional and particularistic community to a more neutral, specific, achievement-oriented, and universalistic society has to be initiated also by the single mother or by both partners in order to open up ways toward the wider society.

A still more complex nature and higher level of identification and attachment emerges from relating to brothers, sisters, the family as a whole group, peers, teachers, and school. In this process, higher levels of adaptive upgrading, differentiation, inclusion, and value generalization of the personality are reached.

From Adolescence to Post-Adolescence and Adulthood

College is the site of a new stage of socialization where still higher levels of personality development are attained. The student experiences a new loss of objects. He or she leaves family and friends to go to college.

New object relations, object cathexes, identifications, and internalizations become established. The student first identifies with and becomes attached to his or her student peers on the basis of solidarity and equality. This gives support. But next to this, identification with his or her teachers on the basis of an authority relationship moves the student toward higher levels of rationality. Reward and punishment via grades shape learning according to new patterns of thought and behavior, now based on the expertise of teachers and the value of cognitive rationality. This gives further impetus to adaptive upgrading.

As more complex object relations and object cathexes are established in the wider academic community, the Ego becomes more differentiated and oriented to a more complex set of goals. This process is sustained by the academic community when it constitutes a relatively complex total society. Identification with the academic community strengthens the student's commitment to the norms of cognitive rationality and provides for inclusion in a wider, even international society. Inclusion in extended academic discourse is the basis for internalizing the value of cognitive rationality: value generalization.

The outcome is a personality that attains higher levels of intelligent behavior (Id), competent decision making (Ego), coordinating multiple solidarity relationships and loyalties (Superego), and value generalization (Ego identity).

Socio-Cultural Evolution

From the mid-sixties on, Parsons turned his interest to questions of sociocultural evolution, particularly to questions of the evolution of the system of modern societies and their fate (Parsons, 1966, 1967: 490–520, 1971, 1977a: part 3). Interpreters of Parsons's work have evaluated this evolutionary turn as a repudiation of his initial statement in *The Structure of Social Action* of 1937: "Spencer is dead" (Parsons, 1937/1968: 3). This, however, is inadequate. When Parsons consigned Spencer to the grave in 1937, he was taking issue with Spencer's utilitarianism and simple naturalistic Darwinism (Spencer, 1972; Darwin, 1977), particularly in the light of Durkheim's criticism of Spencer and of the contributions of Marshall, Pareto, and especially Weber to understanding the role of institutions and ideas in social life and history. Parsons had not forgotten the lessons he learned from these authors when he turned to questions of socio-cultural evolution in the mid 1960s. Particularly, Weber's universal history of the world religions and their impact on historical development is very much present in Parsons's theory of socio-cultural evolution.

A Multidimensional Approach to Socio-Cultural Evolution

Parsons's theory is neither utilitarian nor Darwinistic in a simple sense. He pays particular attention to the intrinsic features of the various dimensions of socio-cultural evolution and gives special emphasis to the interrelationship between wider cultural systems (e.g., religions) and particular societies. He tries to reveal which types of institutional developments provided certain types of societies with higher capacities to deal with different types of problems on an ever larger scale: problems of adaptation to natural exigencies via mobilization of scarce resources, of attaining a complex set of specific goals via differentiation of parts performing specific functions within an organized whole, of integrating an ever more complex set of groups and individuals into one societal community, and of founding an ever wider range of institutions, decisions, and actions upon a consistent system of ideas. Evolution with regard to these four problems, which are defined according to Parsons's four-function paradigm, means developing higher capacities to solve those problems (Parsons, 1966: chapter 2; 1971: chapter 2). Whether and under what conditions a society does indeed produce such capacities is a very different question, which was neither raised nor answered by Parsons. He was much more interested in outlining the specific advances that were made by primitive societies compared to nonhuman organizations of life, that is, to animal proto-societies, of archaic societies compared to primitive societies, of intermediate societies compared to archaic ones, and of modern societies compared to intermediate ones, along the lines of the four problem areas.

Evolution is thus multidimensional in character. Differentiation—which was Spencer's master scheme—is only one dimension in the process of evolution. According to Parsons, it has to be complemented by adaptive upgrading, that is to say, cumulative learning leading to the establishment of ever more intelligent technologies and ever more comprehensive, complex, and deeper scientific knowledge. Thus, the study of socio-cultural evolution is also a study of the evolution of scientific knowledge on the basis of rational criticism in discourse. This is where we would have to include the evolutionary philosophy of science as formulated by Karl R. Popper (1972).

A further dimension of socio-cultural evolution is the widening scope of inclusion of different groups and individuals in an ever more complex but nevertheless integrated societal community. In this view socio-cultural evolution is the evolution of structures of solidarity from the most simple forms of tribal societies to the most complex forms of modern multi-group societies. Here, Parsons expands on Durkheim's (1893/1973a) study of the transformation of solidarity structures from mechanical to organic solidarity in the process of socio-cultural evolution. Finally, reaching higher stages of socio-cultural evolution also involves what Parsons calls value generalization. This means that systems of cultural ideas are increasingly abstracted from their concrete contexts of formulation at a particular historical time and place and are thus better able to serve as measures for the legitimation *and* criticism of any particular norm, institution, decision, or action in any society. This is obviously where Parsons extends Weber's (1920-1921a/1972a, 1920-1921b/1972b) universal history of world religions. It is also where he meets with Habermas (1981).

Thus Spencer is only one and a very limited source of Parsons's theory of socio-cultural evolution, which becomes as qualified in its contribution as was intended by Parsons's critique of Spencer, which he formulated in 1937. Luhmann's theory of functional differentiation corresponds much more to Spencer's original idea than does Parsons's more multidimensional theory of socio-cultural evolution. In a sense, Parsons's theory attempts to attain a synthesis of Anglo-Saxon utilitarian Darwinism with French structuralism and German idealism.

In dealing with socio-cultural evolution, Parsons looks first at the core of the societies under study: their structure of solidarity that characterizes what he calls the societal community. Here he is interested in how much a certain type of society has succeeded or not succeeded in developing structures of solidarity that allow for an integration of an ever more complex set of groups and individuals in one society. This is the problem of *inclusion*. Then he looks at the differentiation of other institutions from the societal community along the lines of the remaining three functional problems: religion, polity, and economy in their relation to the societal community and their capacity for *value generalization, differentiation*, and *adaptive upgrading*. The differentiation of these institutional complexes from the societal community, however, does not mean their complete separation but, rather, the farther evolution progresses, their interrelation in a balanced interchange of factors and products that necessitates the establishment of intermediate systems in their zones of interpenetration performing the function of integrating the differentiated systems. The main steps of socio-cultural evolution are briefly summarized below.

Primitive Societies

Primitive societies like the Australian Aborigines (Parsons, 1966: chapter 3) have evolved beyond animal proto-societies because of the establishment of (1) language, magical religion, and a constitutive symbolism that defines a common identity; (2) rituals and structures of solidarity based on kinship and specific rules of intermarriage; (3) a more advanced differentiation of labor according to sex and age; and (4) a more advanced use of tools in order to adapt to the natural environment. All these complexes, though, are very closely bound together within the community of the tribe. Higher forms of primitive societies like the African kingdoms move toward more abstraction in their belief system, a more complex societal community composed of different clans, and a more complex differentiation of labor and more advanced technology.

Archaic Societies

Archaic societies, like ancient Egypt and the Mesopotamian empire, evolved beyond primitive societies in the following respects (Parsons, 1966: chapter 4): (1) The invention of written language and the abstraction of religious belief to a system of thought that differentiates the divine order from the terrestrial order and subsumes the latter under the reign of the former, allowing a much wider range of institutions and activities to be embraced in cultural terms. The Egyptian idea of *Maat* is such an archaic religion. (2) In terms of solidarity these empires integrated a much more complex set of groups in one societal community, based on the establishment of commonalities in belief, organized labor, and political rule. (3) Labor was differentiated in a much more complex way. However, solidarity was divided between the ordinary people and those who participated in the administration of political authority in an official position. (4) Technology advanced to the level of specialized knowledge of a more complex and abstract nature. The Egyptian empire succeeded in establishing an enormous bureaucratic organization of divided labor. The archaic societies display the beginnings of the differentiation of the institutional complexes of religion, labor, and polity from the societal community while retaining strong ties to the societal community under the leadership of political authority. The establishment of kingdoms, or in Egypt the establishment of pharaonic rule, was the major integrating factor for these differentiated institutional complexes.

Intermediate Historic Empires

Intermediate historic empires, like China, India, the Islamic empires, and the Roman empire, evolved beyond archaic societies because of the advances they achieved in the following respects (Parsons, 1966: chapter 5):

1. They extended the techniques and use of written language, which became the basis of an unprecedented abstraction of human thought and knowledge. Religion, philosophy, and mathematics flourished to form widely expanding and widely diffusing systems of thought.

In China, Confucius gathered together the thought of an educated elite of literary officials who ran the administration of the state to build up a system of ideas that lasted for centuries. The main thrust of this thought was the conception of a balanced order of the world—the Tao—and a balanced order of society—the Li—to which one had to accommodate in order to maintain that balance. Whereas Confucianism interpreted this integration as conformity to the existing social order, the marginal Taoism founded by Laotse conceived of it as a mystical union with the Tao.

In India, the intellectual caste of Brahmins created a highly abstracted idea of the world as an eternal circle of life with the doctrine of retribution and reincarnation. Every action in this life would be retributed after reincarnation in the next life in a higher or lower caste. For ordinary people, the path to salvation here was conformity, while for the privileged it was retreat from responsibility for one's actions in this world by adopting an indifferent attitude to fulfilling externally imposed obligations, or concentration on the essence of being by way of ascetic meditation techniques.

Buddhism developed a conception of an eternal order of Nirvana, which an individual could enter by total retreat from the thirst for life.

Islamic thought, as established by the Prophet Mohammad, took up the idea of one ruling God from ancient Judaism and from Christianity. Yet its thought remained legalistic and never succeeded in forming an abstract system of ideas capable of ordering the whole range of complex life. As the complexity of life continued to grow, then, Islamic thought inevitably became repressive. Because of its close links with military conquest, it also tended to serve as a legitimating ideology for authoritarian regimes.

The achievement of the Roman empire was not so much its religious thought (this, like its Greek counterpart, conceived of the gods in very human terms) as its idea of a natural order that was binding both for deities and for human beings, which again was derived from Greek thought.

2. In terms of solidarity, these intermediate empires established a widespread societal community comprising a whole set of tribes, clans, castes, and strata that associated within it. However, membership of this single community was still differentiated into higher or lower order membership depending on one's place within the hierarchy of groups. The Islamic empires never overcame the split between ethnic groups, which very often took the form of one or several groups being oppressed by a ruling group. The Roman empire advanced well beyond the others in that it developed a general idea of citizenship that integrated every full citizen within one societal community. However, the Roman empire did not succeed in integrating its many

territorial areas on the basis of this idea, which originated in the much smaller Greek city-states. The Romans' most lasting achievement was the establishment of Roman law, which performed the function of integrating in an unprecedented way both a people and a territory that grew increasingly complex in terms of economic trade and political decision making.

3. In terms of goal attainment, these empires registered an advance by establishing a complex division of labor that was organized mostly in terms of political administration and also in terms of market organizations.

4. Technology and empirical knowledge were advanced by pioneering inventions on an experimental basis.

The institutional complexes of religion, polity, and economy advanced in their differentiation from the societal community to form autonomous systems, with their own carrier castes and estates. Their integration relied mostly on the congruence of functional differentiation with the hierarchy of castes and estates.

Seedbed Societies

Two rather small societies did not develop to become large empires or to exist independently very long in their own right but nevertheless served as crucial cultural innovators with lasting effects on the socio-cultural evolution of Western civilization: Israel and Greece (Parsons, 1966: ch. 6).

Israel is the source of Judeo-Christian culture and contributed three basic elements to that culture: first, the conception of a transcendent legislator God; second, the conception of a moral order commanded by Him, which transcended any existing mundane order; and third, the conception of a holy community that had to execute His mandate by serving as His instrument in transforming this evil world into a better one.

The Greek city-states formed the source of a high abstraction of philosophical thought, particularly of dialogical argumentation that became the model of Western reasoning. The concept of citizenship of the Greek *polis* served as a model for a form of societal integration that was independent of primordial group memberships and developed only within Western civilization, first in the Roman empire, then in the medieval city, and then in the Western nation-states after their democratic revolutions.

The System of Modern Societies

Turning to the evolution of the system of modern societies, Parsons emphasizes that they form an interdependent system with a common Western culture (Parsons, 1971: chapter 3).

Ancient Cultural Roots

The roots of Western culture have to be located in the cultural innovations of ancient Israel and Greece and in institutional innovations of the Roman empire, particularly in Roman law. The primary bearer of these cultural innovations after the breakdown of those civilizations was early Christianity. Christ complemented the image of the universally commanding God by the image of the universally loving God. The missionary work of Paul separated membership in the Christian community from ethnic and political affiliations. This separation paved the way for the propagation of Christianity as a cultural system independently of any concrete political society. The teaching of Origen and Augustine and the elevation of Christianity to the status of a state religion after a long period of persecution led to a reconciliation of its teaching with the mundane order and played down its original order-transforming power. The same is true of its establishment as a major power in the medieval system of the feudal division of power. Scholastic teaching conceived of the world as a well-integrated hierarchical order in which everybody has his or her proper place, whether rich or poor, saint or sinner.

The Renaissance

A first breakthrough to modernity came with the Renaissance, when the potential for abstraction and dialogical reasoning that was encapsulated in ancient Greek thought was rediscovered and brought into interpenetration with empirical experimentation. It represented the birth of modern science, which connects rational thought and logical reasoning with empirical experimentation and technological invention. This entailed a great deal of collaboration between scholars, artists, artisans, and engineers, which was unprecedented and broke through the established feudal order of estates. Its social basis was the evolution of citizenship in the medieval cities.

The Reformation

The Reformation reestablished the order-transforming power of Christian religion. First, Luther made proper faithful conduct in a person's calling to God a matter for everybody everywhere in social life and thus transmitted the monk's asceticism to every sphere of social life. However, Luther's Protestantism remained bound to the traditional order and power of the reigning political authority. According to his teaching of the two kingdoms, one had to submit to God in religious matters and to the secular political authority in matters of this world. His teaching also entailed mystical elements in his conception of the individual as a vessel that has to be filled by the contemplative feeling of unity with God. Not work but the right inner feeling is the way of salvation.

The true order-transforming power of Christian teaching was revealed by Calvin and his theory of predestination and by the Puritan sects in

England and the Netherlands alongside other Protestant currents like Pietism, Methodism, Baptism, and the ideas of the Quakers, which Max Weber called ascetic currents of Protestantism. Calvin reintroduced the commanding God of the Old Testament and the conception of the human being as His instrument in executing His mandate to transform the sinful world into a better one to His glory. His teaching of predestination did not lead to fatalism but left the individual with the agonizing question of whether he or she was one of the Elect and part of the community of saints. According to Calvin, nobody could know. However, his followers moved to the position that one cannot influence God's decision, but one can see in one's conduct of life whether one is part of the Elect or not. According to Calvin's idea of the human being as God's instrument in building the world to His glory and according to the status of most Puritans as bourgeois people who were used to placing work at the center of their lives, the consequence of this situation was extreme pressure to establish proof of one's elected status by untiring work in one's profession and by actively building a society to the glory of God. The most extreme example of this instrumental activism was John Winthrop's founding of Massachusetts in New England as a "city on a hill" to which the whole world would look as an example of God's rule and which had to do all in its power not to fail in the eyes of God. The idea of a covenant with God resembled that of the ancient covenant of the people of Israel with Yahweh.

The consequence of this religious revolution was the breakthrough of the fundamental tension between God's moral commands and the sinful world that introduced a permanent pressure to change in the direction of a closer correspondence between the worldly orders and God's prescribed moral order. In connection with economic activity this pressure to change set free an approach to work that Max Weber called the spirit of capitalism: restless professional work without consuming all the fruits of this work but with the permanent reinvestment of those fruits into further economic enterprises. In connection with political activity, this pressure set free the idea of government as an agency of change in the realization of a better world. In connection with social activity, this pressure set free the idea of a society that had to be organized according to God's moral laws. This was the cultural innovation that finally led to the breakdown of the authority of tradition.

Enlightenment, Citizenship, State, and Capitalism

The Enlightenment did not change this breakthrough but radicalized it in secular terms. The world now had to be actively changed according to the universally valid ideas of rationality, freedom, and equality. The development of mass media and universal education brought an unprecedented amount and rapidity of cultural development and an unprecedented impact of a central culture on every sphere of society.

In the present time, the development of electronic media and of universal higher education have pushed us into a new stage of cultural production and its impact on society. There has never been a society in human history that was so deeply penetrated by culture as the present-day system of modern societies. This cultural revolution in the Western world was the cultural basis for further innovations in all institutional spheres that nevertheless also had to involve other internal innovations (Parsons, 1971: chapters 5, 6): The industrial revolution established rational capitalism as a distinctive system that reached unprecedented sophistication in mobilizing resources to transform them into goods and services on ever higher levels of societal wealth. The democratic revolution institutionalized a conception of citizenship that was able to integrate an unprecedented multitude of classes, strata, and groups into one societal community. The more this transformation proceeds the more people and groups are entitled to equal rights to take part in society's economic wealth via property rights, its political decision making via political rights, its social welfare via social rights, and its culture via rights to education. The latter process leads to what Parsons calls the educational revolution. Another major transformation that complements these revolutions is the establishment of the modern state as an agency of permanent change.

Thus, we have four major transformations along all four problem areas of Parsons's functional scheme that distinguish the system of modern Western societies from any other type of society:

1. A system of ideas that claims universal validity and exerts a permanent pressure on society to change toward a closer correspondence to it.
2. A system of citizenship that includes a multitude of groups in one societal community.
3. A differentiated government that is conceived as an agent of permanent change.
4. A system of rational capitalism that has developed an unprecedented capacity to innovate in its technological adaptation to ever higher demands.

The Network of Interlocking Systems

A characteristic of these differentiated systems of modern societies is that they are not as unidimensionally organized as those of the intermediate historic empires but have incorporated elements of all other systems. In addition, they are integrated not by the congruence of status and functional differentiation but by the establishment of intermediate systems that serve as mediating links between the differentiated systems.

Institutional achievements of modernity like the establishment of legal systems, constitutional courts, and party systems have to be viewed as intermediate linkages between political government and the societal community, the socio-cultural systems of intellectual discourse, and the economic systems of freely articulating interests. These systems are not functionally specialized; they are systems of negotiation between the exigencies of political decision making, social solidarity, cultural legitimation, and satisfaction of interests. There is no one-dimensional code that could govern the functioning of such systems. Instead, there is a multidimensional interplay of various exigencies. It is within such mediating systems that most decisions and actions are worked out.

In this way, modern societies establish an ever more complex network of interlocking systems. Thus, the establishment of new systems in modern societies is not only a consequence of functional differentiation but also, and to a much greater extent, a consequence of the institutionalization of mediating links between functionally specialized systems — and, indeed, between mediating systems that are already established. At present, we are witnessing an enormous trend toward the creation of such mediating links within the economy, the polity, the societal community, and the socio-cultural systems, for example, the establishment of quality circles in business firms or of new forms of interdisciplinary scientific research creating new mediating disciplines.

The same trend, though, also covers the interrelationships between the basic societal systems. Today, most decisions and actions are worked out not within a closed autonomous system but in intermediate systems of negotiation between the contradictory exigencies of functionally specialized systems. The theory of socio-cultural evolution put forward by Talcott Parsons has the potential to open our eyes to these developments. It therefore stands in the forefront of current and future societal development. Compared to this level of theorizing, theories of systemic differentiation are reflections of earlier stages of socio-cultural evolution and not state-of-the-art instruments for understanding societal developments. In a certain sense they are relics of "Old European thought," as Niklas Luhmann (1982, 1984) likes to label such outdated theories — however, without realizing that his own theory of systemic differentiation fits precisely into this category.

According to Parsons's analysis, the system of modern societies displaying the outlined features of a network of differentiated *and* interpenetrating systems with very specific contributions to solving the four functional problems on ever higher levels of capacity first emerged in northwestern Europe, with Britain taking the lead (Parsons, 1971: chapters 4, 5). Here we have an evolution of the concept of citizenship on the national level and the differentiation and interlocking of religion, societal community, government, and industrial capitalism. The other European societies follow this pattern, but with less success in various dimensions. In the twentieth century, the lead was taken by the United States (Parsons, 1971: chapter 6; see

Lipset, 1963). Parsons claims that the United States managed to establish a new differentiation and interlocking of religion, societal community, polity, and economy with the establishment of its Constitution in 1789, which separated church and state and introduced a new potential for a common citizenship encompassing a multitude of groups, for a new conception of voluntary association among people in a complex network, for mass participation in citizens' rights, a new conception of human agency in mastering the wilderness of the world, and a new conception of individualistic economic activity to form a capitalism of mass production.

Beyond these developments we can say that the establishment of interlocking systems of negotiation between differentiated systems is a peculiar feature of American society that is much more developed there than in the Continental European societies in particular, for these still correspond more to the model of differentiated societies. The system of checks and balances, the system of voluntary associations, the importance of the courts and of the so-called regulatory commissions in the political system all have had their effect on the idea of negotiating between contradictory demands and interests stemming from different functional systems and social positions in society. This is where we can see characteristics of American society that will feature in future developments in all Western societies.

The lead in evolution in the system of modern societies by the United States has become a fact in the twentieth century—however, a much debated fact in European eyes, which are critical, whether from the standpoint of a backwardly oriented traditionalism and authoritarianism or from the critical intellectual point of view of radical ideas of rationality, freedom, and equality. The first type of criticism is certainly outdated, whereas the second type is a necessary part of that dynamic tension that has pushed the modern societies forward since their origination in the European cultural revolutions. The most advanced society also calls for the most advanced intellectual criticism. Talcott Parsons himself saw the home of intellectual criticism still located in European societies.

The development of the modern societies has also been accompanied by countermovements that lead backward to earlier stages of socio-cultural evolution (Parsons, 1971: chapter 7). Parsons calls them fundamentalistic movements. Should these ideas become reality, modern societies would be thrown back to lower levels of complexity, mostly to simple traditional or authoritatively organized societies. One such society in modern times has been the Soviet system of socialism, which dissolved completely after the revolutions of 1989 because of its regressive character in evolutionary terms.

A great problem is transmission of the Western type of socio-cultural evolution to modernity to non-Western societies. The introduction of Western technology often destroys the traditional basis of those societies without building up the institutional and cultural structures that make up what we call a modern Western society. Thus these societies are torn between the authoritarian regimes of the right and the left. Parsons's analysis of the many preconditions that need to be fulfilled to create a modern society is information enough to warn us that the way to modernity is impossible for non-Western societies unless they undergo changes that last for generations to come.

Nevertheless, Parsons is one of those who believe in the project of modernity and who do not see an alternative way to the future that could compete with it. Contemporary announcements of the end of modernity, of the advent of postmodernity, and of the New Age that synthesizes modern achievements with the Asian idea of a balanced world order would have evoked in him nothing but a belief in modernity's strength to absorb such movements within its own path to the future. In this light, such movements are the stuff from which modernity receives its never-ending power of renewal. This interpretation of Parsons's overall commitment to the project of modernity has to be conceived independently of his concrete judgments about the progressive or regressive ("fundamentalist") nature of particular social movements like the student movement of the 1960s. He believed in the rightness of Franklin D. Roosevelt's politics of the New Deal in the 1930s and of the civil rights movement in the 1960s and 1970s. He was an American liberal with a strong belief in modernity's and especially America's power of permanent renewal.

Social Stratification

In the early phase of structural functionalism, the work of Kingsley Davis (1949) and Wilbert E. Moore (1946) attracted much interest. Their coauthored article "Some Principles of Stratification" was widely read and criticized (Davis and Moore, 1945). In this article, the authors argue that each society will develop an unequal distribution of rewards, such as money, power, or prestige, because it has to attract people into positions designed to satisfy its basic survival needs. These positions are of unequal attractiveness to people. They are also of unequal importance to the society's survival needs. The source of the unequal attribution of importance to different positions is the prevailing value system, which determines the importance of survival needs and of positions for serving those needs. Talented and qualified people who could fill those positions are in short supply to varying degrees. Thus, doing the job associated with a certain position, like road worker, civil servant, sales manager, nurse, doctor, or teacher, is more highly rewarded the less attractive the job is and/or the greater the importance attributed to that position according to society's prevailing value system and the smaller the supply of talented and qualified people for the position.

This theory has been criticized for a number of reasons (Tumin, 1953; Huaco, 1966). It has been argued that the stratification system might display more dysfunctional than functional effects for society's survival because it entails disruptive conflict between the less well rewarded and the better rewarded classes, because the upper classes might use their definitional power in order to define the importance of positions to their advantage, which again might increase disruptive class conflict, or because the existing class system itself determines the chances of people to qualify for positions, which also might generate conflict. The importance assigned to positions and the supply of people for the positions are results of the class structure itself rather than working as independent causes of that class structure. The latter argument represents an alternative provided by conflict theory to explain the class structure of a society. In this perspective the dominant class consolidates and perpetuates the class structure of society by its power to determine which positions are needed for society and which are more important or less important, and by its power to open or close the paths toward those positions.

It is not difficult to find truth on both sides of the debate. The differentiation of society into classes gives unequal access to public discourse about the need and importance of positions, and it gives unequal access to the qualifications needed for filling the positions. This class differentiation of society is always a source of conflict. Thus far, conflict theory is right. On the other hand, the more public discourse expands, penetrates society, and involves spokespeople of various classes, groups, and strata, the less the definition of need and importance and the opening of ways to qualify for positions are uniform replications of the existing class structure and the more they need a broader legitimation by a broader consensus spanning different classes, groups, and strata. Otherwise, society would dissolve into permanent class struggle. This is the element of truth contributed by the functionalist perspective. It was Gerhard Lenski (1966) who tried to work out such an integrated theory of stratification.

It is remarkable that Parsons's (1940/1954a, 1954b, 1977b) own attempts at explaining social stratification remain marginal to the outlined debate on the functionalist theory of stratification, though they would have helped to avoid the failures of Davis and Moore. Parsons concentrates his approach on the sources of a *legitimate* system of social stratification. There might be various factual reasons for the distribution of positions and corresponding rewards in society, like access to money, power, or influence; however, insofar as a system of stratification is a legitimate one, it depends on the grading of positions according to the value system on which society has reached a consensus. The value system implies a grading scale according to which positions and the services of their incumbents to society are *evaluated*. It is only the prestige attributed to positions and their incumbents that results from the application of the value system, not the acquisition of money, power, or other privileges. The latter might come from other sources.

Because Parsons distinguishes clearly between the grading scale anchored in the value system and the factual distribution of ranks in terms of money, power, or influence, his approach allows us to recognize that there is a potential tension between the value system and the factual distribution of ranks in terms of money, power, or influence. The latter can be called into question in the light of the value system. In modern societies the value system further entails the tension between the right to equal opportunity on the one hand and unequal rewards according to individual achievement on the other. Thus, the more public discourse is open and addresses such tensions, legitimacy will be attributed only to the system of stratification inasmuch as it does not entail inequalities that result from any sources other than unequal achievement under conditions of equal opportunity. In this process, the value system works as a dynamic force of social change rather than as a source for the stability of the existing stratification system. Legitimacy also will be absent the more there is a split in the value system itself and a lack of consensus and the more public discourse leads to dissension on the basic values that are to be used in evaluating positions in society. Particularly Parsons's (1977b) final treatment of social stratification opens up ways toward such a view, though we have to state more explicitly what is only implicit in his approach. Thus, factual stratification has various sources in the access people have to money, power, and influence, yet its legitimacy depends on the mobilization of value commitments with regard to values on which consensus needs to be established in public discourse.

Summary

Action Theory

1.   Positivism

1.1   Conceptual frame of reference
       (1) Ends
       (2) Means
       (3) Conditions
       (4) Principles
       (4.1) Principle of rational choice of means relating to ends under
             certain conditions
       (4.1.1) Principle of optimizing several ends
       (4.1.2) Principle of maximizing one single end
       (4.2) Principle of natural selection
       (5) Action
       Residual categories: Ideas, norms, customs. The principles of optimizing and maximizing are themselves fixed, that is, based on norms.

1.2   Propositions

1.2.1 Whenever different actions are at an actor's disposal, the actor chooses the alternative from which he or she expects the optimum of realization of ends.

1.2.2 Whenever different actions are at an actor's disposal, the actor chooses the alternative from which he or she expects the maximum realization of one end (goal).

1.3   Theoretical solution of the problem of order

1.3.1 A predictable order of actions results when the calculations of how to optimize ends (or maximize one single end) by all actors involved in a situation converge to form a certain pattern of behavior.
       Technological advice: Always provide for the free mutual adaptation of actions; never make preliminary restrictions.

1.3.2 A predictable order of actions results when the external conditions are structured in such a way that the behavior of all actors involved is oriented in a specific direction.
       Technological advice: Impose a superordinate authority with a determined end and centralized power on the actors.

1.4   Predictions

1.4.1 If an action no longer results in an optimum realization of ends, it will be given up.
       Falsifying instances: Every action that is maintained irrespective of its economic outcome, for example, maintaining the custom of always going to the same grocery even if the nearby supermarket is cheaper. The action is not calculated economically.

1.4.2 If an action no longer results in the maximum realization of an end, it will be given up.
       Falsifying instances: Every action that is maintained irrespective of its contribution to the maximization of an end. For example, if we select a specific program in order to prepare for an exam and retain a part of it for discussion even though we know it is no longer required for the exam.

2.   **Idealism**

2.1   Conceptual frame of reference
       (1) Ideas
       (2) Norms
       (3) Conditions
       (4) Principles
       (4.1) Principle of subsuming an action in the presence of certain conditions under a generally valid idea.

(4.2) Principle of deriving an action in the presence of certain conditions from norms that are taken for granted.

(5) Action
Residual categories: Ends, means, economic calculation of optimum of ends, maximizing an end.

2.2 Propositions

2.2.1 Whenever different actions are at an actor's disposal, the actor chooses the action that can be subsumed under generally valid ideas.

2.2.2 Whenever different actions are at an actor's disposal, the actor chooses the action that can be derived from norms that are taken for granted.

2.3 Theoretical solution of the problem of order.

2.3.1 A predictable order results when all actors involved in a situation agree on generally valid ideas.
Technological advice: Let actors transcend their personal interests and see what is valid from the point of view of reason, that is, let them engage in a rational discourse with arguments.

2.3.2 A predictable order results when all actors involved in a situation share common rules that are taken for granted.
Technological advice: Actors must form a community with close intimate relationships, a stable membership, mutual solidarity, and a stable tradition in which their action becomes a matter of habit.

2.4 Predictions

2.4.1 If an action is not consistent with a generally valid idea, it is not chosen.
Falsifying instances: Every action chosen that is not consistent with generally valid ideas. For example, a student who uses illegal means in writing his or her paper in order to have advantages compared to other students violates the idea of equality of opportunity.

2.4.2 If an action does not conform with the norms of a community, the members of the community do not perform this action.
Falsifying instances: Every action that is chosen by community members though it does not conform with the community's norms. For example, a student who tells an outsider stories of his or her group even though it is a group norm not to tell anybody anything of what is going on within the group.

3.   Voluntarism

3.1 Conceptual frame of reference
(1) Ends
(2) Means

(3) Conditions
(4) Norms
(5) Ideas
(6) Action

Residual categories: The theory claims to be inclusive and, therefore, not to need any such categories.

3.2   Propositions

3.2.1   The more the actors calculate the optimum outcome of their action and the more they act under the conditions of exchange and competition, the more frequently they change their action (variability of action).

3.2.2   The more actors calculate the maximum outcome of an action for one single end and the more they act under the condition of dominance and conflict, the more their action maintains a specific direction (directedness of action).

3.2.3   The more an actor subsumes his or her action under general ideas, the more his or her action maintains a general identity and continuity irrespective of situational change (identity of action).

3.2.4   The more an actor derives his or her action from norms that are taken for granted, the more his or her action maintains a regularity by following a certain predictable pattern irrespective of changing situations (regularity of action).

3.3   Theoretical solution of the problem of order.

As far as its predictability is concerned and the regularity of behavioral patterns, order in action is a result of establishing norms that are taken for granted in a community; yet, given the need to maintain a lasting identity despite situational change, it equally has to be related to general ideas through discourse. Likewise, the need to be variable in the face of changing conditions and means makes it a result of economic calculation, and the need for it to direct actions toward a specific end means that it has to be enforced by a superordinate authority with sanctioning power.

Technological advice: Depending on the features an order is supposed to display, different measures have to be applied: the formation of a tradition among a closed group, discursive argumentation of enlightened actors, economic calculation, or the imposition of power and authority.

3.4   Predictions

3.4.1   If an actor calculates the optimum outcome of an action and the action does not contribute anything to that optimum, it is changed. *Falsifying instance:* A large amount of economic calculation but a low rate of change in action.

3.4.2   If an actor calculates the maximum outcome of an action, the action that is directed so as to contribute to the maximum attainment of an end singled out by the actor is maintained.
Falsifying instance: A large amount of maximization but a low directedness of action.

3.4.3   If an actor subsumes his or her action under general ideas, the actor maintains an identity in his or her action even if it does change.
Falsifying instance: Much orientation to general ideas but a low identity of action.

3.4.4   If an actor derives his or her action from norms taken for granted, he or she maintains a regular pattern of behavior.
Falsifying instance: Much commitment to norms but low regularity in patterns of behavior.

Systems Theory

4.   Social Systems

4.1   Functions

4.1.1   The more social action is guided by communication, discourse, and value commitments, the more it will maintain a general pattern.

4.1.2   The more social action is guided by communal association, solidarity, consensus, and influence, the more it will conform to definite norms.

4.1.3   The more social action is guided by authority and power, the more it will move in a specific direction, even if a great many alternative ways of acting are imaginable.

4.1.4   The more social action is guided by market exchange and money, the more it will vary with the change of situations (available means and given conditions) and the more it will enhance its adaptive capacities.

4.2   Interpenetration

4.2.1   The more value commitments penetrate the societal community, the polity, and the economy, the more social norms, the exercise of authority, and market behavior will change in the direction of generalization, that is, more broadly justified patterns.

4.2.2   The more influence penetrates public discourse, the polity, and the economy, the more propositions, the exercise of authority, and market behavior will conform to definite norms.

4.2.3   The more political power penetrates public discourse, the societal community, and the economy, the more propositions, social norms, and market behavior will be forced in the directions that are backed up by political power, even in the face of resistance.

4.2.4   The more money penetrates public discourse, the societal commu-
        nity, and the polity, the more propositions, social norms, and the
        exercise of authority will be upgraded in their level of production
        and will be adapted to changing conditions and goals.

4.3   Production

4.3.1   The more value commitments are backed up by influence, political
        power, and money, the greater will be their capacity to transmit
        messages.

4.3.2   The more influence is backed up by value commitments, political
        power, and money, the greater will be its capacity to mobilize support.

4.3.3   The more political power is backed up by value commitments,
        influence, and money, the greater will be its capacity to enforce col-
        lective decisions.

4.3.4   The more money is backed up by value commitments, influence, and
        political power, the greater will be its capacity to allocate resources,
        goods, and services to articulated needs.

4.4   Mediation

4.4.1   The more communication is mediated by value commitments, the
        greater will be the extent and scope of mutual understanding.

4.4.2   The more communal association is mediated by influence, the greater
        will be the extent and scope of support received.

4.4.3   The more the exercise of authority is mediated by political power,
        the greater will be the extent and scope of enforced collective
        decisions.

4.4.4   The more market exchange is mediated by money, the greater will
        be the extent and scope of transactions of resources, goods, and
        services.

4.5   Dynamics and Growth

4.5.1   The more the demand for understanding, support, collective deci-
        sions, resources, and goods and services outstrips their supply as it
        grows between time t_0 and t_1, the greater will be the increase in the
        number of units of the corresponding media that need to be spent
        on them, that is, the higher will be the rate of inflation.

4.5.2   The more the supply of understanding, support, collective decisions,
        resources, and goods and services outstrips the demand for them
        as it grows between time t_0 and t_1, the greater will be the decrease
        in the number of units of the corresponding media that need to be
        spent on them, that is, the higher will be the rate of deflation.

4.5.3   The more and the more rapidly the supply of media of interaction
        grows without a corresponding increase in the supply of products,
        the greater will be the rate of inflation.

4.5.4   The more the supply of media of interaction falls behind the growth in the supply of products, the greater will be the rate of deflation.

4.5.5   The more the supply of media of interaction and production grow together, the more understanding, conformity, collective decisions, and goods and services will grow in the whole system and overcome zero-sum conditions.

5.   Action Systems

5.1   Functions

5.1.1   The more action is guided by symbols and definitions of the situation, the more it will maintain a general pattern.

5.1.2   The more action is guided by social interaction and affect, the more it will be ordered in a predictable way.

5.1.3   The more action is guided by personal dispositions and performance capacity, the more it will move in a specific direction, even if a great many alternative ways of acting are imaginable.

5.1.4   The more action is guided by behavioral learning and intelligence, the more it will vary with the change of situations and the more it will enhance its adaptive capacities.

5.2   Interpenetration

5.2.1   The more definitions of the situation penetrate social interaction, personal dispositions, and behavioral learning, the more they will change in the direction of generalization, that is, more broadly justified patterns.

5.2.2   The more affect penetrates cultural symbolization, personal dispositions, and behavioral learning, the more they will be ordered in a definite way.

5.2.3   The more personal performance capacity penetrates cultural symbolization, social interaction, and behavioral learning, the more they will be directed toward specific goals.

5.2.4   The more intelligence penetrates cultural symbolization, social interaction, and personal disposition, the more they will vary according to the change of situations and the greater will be their adaptive capacity.

5.3   Production

5.3.1   The more definitions of the situation are backed up by affect, performance capacity, and intelligence, the greater will be their capacity to convey messages.

5.3.2   The more affect is backed up by definitions of the situation, performance capacity, and intelligence, the greater will be its capacity to coordinate social interaction.

5.3.3   The more performance capacity is backed up by definitions of the situation, affect, and intelligence, the greater will be its capacity to make and carry out decisions.

5.3.4   The more intelligence is backed up by definitions of the situation, affect, and performance capacity, the greater will be its capacity to adapt to varying situations.

5.4   Mediation

5.4.1   The more symbolization is mediated by definitions of the situation, the greater will be the number and scope of comprehensible messages.

5.4.2   The more social interaction is mediated by affect, the greater will be the number and scope of coordinated social interaction.

5.4.3   The more personal decision making is mediated by performance capacity, the greater will be the number and scope of decisions that can be made and carried out.

5.4.4   The more behavioral learning is mediated by intelligence, the greater will be the amount and scope of successful adaptation to varying situations.

5.5   Dynamics and Growth

5.5.1   The more the demand for meaning, coordination of interaction, personal decisions, and behavioral adaptation outstrips their supply as it grows between time t_0 and t_1, the greater will be the increase in the number of units of the corresponding media that need to be spent on them, that is, the higher will be the rate of inflation.

5.5.2   The more the supply of comprehensible messages, coordination of interaction, personal decisions, and behavioral adaptation outstrips the demand for them as it grows between time t_0 and t_1, the greater will be the decrease in the number of units of the corresponding media that need to be spent on them, that is, the higher will be the rate of deflation.

5.5.3   The more and the more rapidly the supply of media of action grows without a corresponding increase in the supply of products, the greater will be the rate of inflation.

5.5.4   The more the supply of media of action lags behind the growth in the supply of products, the greater will be the rate of deflation.

5.5.5   The more the supply of media of action and production grow together, the more comprehensible messages, coordination of interaction, personal decisions, and behavioral adaptation will grow in the whole system and overcome zero-sum conditions.

6.   The Human Condition

6.1   Functions

6.1.1   The more events are guided by transcendental conditions, the more they will maintain a general pattern.

6.1.2   The more events are guided by action, the more they will be coordinated.

6.1.3   The more events are guided by organic conditions, the more they will display a goal-directed character.

6.1.4   The more events are guided by physico-chemical processes, the more they will vary with the change of conditions.

6.2   Interpenetration

6.2.1   The more transcendental ordering penetrates action, the organism, and physico-chemical processes, the more they will maintain a general pattern.

6.2.2   The more meaning penetrates transcendental conditions, the organism, and physico-chemical processes, the more they will be coordinated.

6.2.3   The more health penetrates transcendental conditions, action, and physico-chemical processes, the more they will be goal directed.

6.2.4   The more empirical ordering penetrates transcendental conditions, action, and the organism, the more they will adapt to changing situations.

6.3   Production

6.3.1   The more transcendental ordering is backed up by meaning, health, and empirical ordering, the greater will be its capacity to maintain a latent pattern.

6.3.2   The more meaning is backed up by transcendental ordering, health, and empirical ordering, the greater will be its coordinative capacity.

6.3.3   The more health is backed up by transcendental ordering, meaning, and empirical ordering, the greater will be its goal-directing capacity.

6.3.4   The more empirical ordering is backed up by transcendental ordering, meaning, and health, the greater will be its adaptive capacity.

6.4   Mediation

6.4.1   The more transcendental conditions are mediated by transcendental ordering, the greater will be the number and scope of events that can be conceived in a consistent system.

6.4.2   The more action is mediated by meaning, the greater will be the number and scope of actions that can be coordinated.

6.4.3   The more organisms are mediated by health, the greater will be the number and scope of organic processes that can work in a goal-directed way.

6.4.4   The more physico-chemical processes are mediated by empirical ordering, the greater will be the number and scope of such processes that can be adapted to each other.

6.5   Dynamics and Growth

6.5.1   The more the demand for latent pattern maintenance, coordination of action, organic goal direction, and physico-chemical adaptation outstrips the supply as it grows between time t_0 and t_1, the greater will be the increase in the number of units of the corresponding media that need to be spent on them, that is, the higher will be the rate of inflation.

6.5.2   The more the supply of latent pattern maintenance, coordination of action, organic goal direction, and physico-chemical adaptation outstrips the demand as it grows between time t_0 and t_1, the greater will be the decrease in the number of units of the corresponding media that need to be spent on them, that is, the higher will be the rate of deflation.

6.5.3   The more and more rapidly the supply of media of the human condition grows without a corresponding increase in the supply of products, the greater will be the rate of inflation.

6.5.4   The more the supply of media of the human condition lags behind the growth in the supply of products, the greater will be the rate of deflation.

6.5.5   The more the supply of media of the human condition and production grow together, the more latent pattern maintenance, coordination of action, organic goal direction, and physico-chemical adaptation will grow in the whole system and overcome zero-sum conditions.

7.   Personality Development and Socialization

7.1   Functions

7.1.1   The more the human organism interacts with varying conditions, the more intelligence will be mobilized and the more the human personality will acquire the competence to cope with varying situations in attaining goals.

7.1.2   The more the human organism identifies with social objects, the more affect will guide action and the more the human personality will acquire self-control and a moral conscience that subjects the personal attainment of goals to discipline and definite rules.

7.1.3   The more the human organism is confronted with cultural symbolization, the more definitions of the situation will guide action and the more the human personality will acquire a general identity that maintains a general pattern in any concrete adaptive, goal-oriented, or rule-guided action.

7.1.4   The more the human organism has a chance to stand against its factual, social, and cultural environment, the more performance capacity will be mobilized and the more the human personality will acquire a strong Ego.

7.2   Growth

7.2.1   The greater the number and scope of situations with which the human personality is confronted, the greater will be the growth in its competence to mobilize knowledge for attaining goals.

7.2.2   The greater the number and scope of people and social circles with whom the human personality identifies, the greater will be the growth in its capacity to coordinate a wide range of loyalties.

7.2.3   The greater the number and scope of symbolizations with which the human personality is confronted, the greater the number and scope of action that the personality will be able to render consistent within its identity, and the greater will be its capacity to reflect.

7.2.4   The greater the number and scope of opportunities to resist that are available to the human personality, the greater will be its capacity to maintain a unique identity, to differentiate from others, and to resist constraints and temptations.

8.   Socio-Cultural Evolution

8.1   Functions

8.1.1   The more resources a society can mobilize, the greater will be its capacity to adapt to varying situations.

8.1.2   The more a society achieves functional differentiation while maintaining the coordination of divided labor, the greater will be its capacity to attain an ever greater number and scope of different goals.

8.1.3   The more a society manages to include a multitude of groups in one societal community under the notion of a common citizenship, the greater will be its capacity to coordinate an ever greater number and range of social interactions.

8.1.4   The more a society manages to generalize its value system, the greater will be its capacity to maintain a basic identity in an ever greater number and range of transformations.

8.2   Growth

8.2.1   The more a value system has been differentiated from a concrete society and interpenetrates with it, the greater will be the rate of value generalization and of transformation of the society in the direction of ever more generalized and demanding values.

8.2.2   The less a value system has been differentiated from a concrete society, the more the two will mutually support each other in maintaining a traditional cultural and social order.

8.2.3   The more a value system has been differentiated from a concrete society yet does not interpenetrate with it, the more the value system will end in abstract mysticism and the more the society will be left to its own traditional and/or dynamic powers of communities, power holders, and interests.

8.2.4   The more a society succeeds in establishing intermediate systems for mediating between conflicting functional demands by interpenetration, the greater will be its capacity to increase adaptation, goal attainment, integration, and latent pattern maintenance at the same time.

9.   Social Stratification

9.1   The stronger the correspondence of the system of social stratification of a society to its value system and the stronger the consensus on that value system, the stronger will be the stratification system's legitimacy.

9.2   The weaker the correspondence of the system of social stratification of a society to its value system and the stronger the consensus on that value system, the weaker will be the stratification system's legitimacy and the stronger will be the cultural pressure on the system to change.

9.3   The less there is consensus on the value system in society, the less the system of social stratification will be accepted as legitimate and the more it will exclusively result from access to money, power, or influence, thus constituting a factually existing but illegitimate system.

Critical Assessment

It was Talcott Parsons who made the most thoroughgoing attempt to attain a synthesis in sociological theory, though he did not succeed in all respects. His greatest achievement is the provision of a formal frame of reference that can be used for integrating the conflicting paradigms in one system. However, his attempt at synthesis was biased from the beginning toward a search for the factors that explain order in social life, and that search was conducted with a very Durkheimian approach to the question of order. His position was fundamentally shaped by his sharing of Durkheim's critique of utilitarianism, which is right in its core but tends to do away with the contribution of utilitarian thought to understanding social action.

Parsons's first solution of the problem of order in *The Structure of Social Action* (Parsons, 1937/1968) has been widely misunderstood by critics who point out forms of predictable interaction that do not result from commonly shared norms. This, however, is not a falsification of Parsons's statement, the intention of which is to bring out the point that any other form of coordinating social action, like external force or a convergence of interests, does not yield the same bindingness and thus uniformity and stability of social action as do commonly shared norms. Parsons himself admitted that there are "factual" compulsory and accidental forms of order resulting from external force and converging interests. Also, what he calls a "normative" order as distinct from a factual one is based on the consent of freely choosing, reasonable actors and is thus a type of order that is attainable only on the level of the human being's capability to attain freedom and reason. This is one aspect of calling his position "voluntarism."

However, Parsons did not maintain the distinction between general values and concrete norms, between reason and conformity, consistently at that time and tended to understand the normative solution of the problem of order in terms of conformity to norms, thus closing out the opposite to this position, namely, agreement on the basis of reasoning and discourse. He did not fully work through the Kantian problem of order and fell into the traps of conformism instead of clearly maintaining the tension between idealism and conformism, though he was well aware of these opposites in the distinction between objectivism and historicism in the idealist tradition of thought (Parsons, 1937/1968: 473–88). This is why he was inclined to merge Weber's notion of the impact of ideas on social life with Durkheim's notion of collective representations. A full understanding of the problem of order in social action, though, must maintain the tension between accidental, compulsory, conformistic, and idealistic forms of order in a general theory of voluntaristic order, which means including market exchange, conflict, and discourse in the production of order much more than Parsons really did.

The next step in the development of Parsons's sociology formulated in *The Social System* (Parsons, 1951) and *Toward a General Theory of Action* (Parsons and Shils, 1951a) did not completely do away with his conformistic bias. Parsons approached human action in the interpenetration of the social, personality, and cultural systems predominantly with the question of how the order of action is produced out of this interchange. He extended the question by distinguishing the social, motivational, and cultural problem of order. In his preoccupation with order he did not clearly distinguish between institutionalization, internalization, and socialization, intermixing them in one complex with socialization in the lead position (Wrong, 1961). On the other hand, elements of a behavioristic view of human action entered the scene. He conceived of interaction as an exchange of gratifications and deprivations, thus playing down the dimensions of association and communication. His theory of personality development was later influenced by Durkheim, Freud, and the behaviorism of his collaborator James Olds. It formulated the preconditions for the emergence of a rather conformistic type of personality. However, further development of his theory on the level of the general action system introduced elements of Mead and Piaget via collaboration with Victor and Charles Lidz, so that he approached a much more complete theory of personality development in the interpenetration of the systems of personality, behavioral learning, social interaction, and cultural symbolization, thus pointing out the ways to the conformistic, reflective, rebellious, and variable aspects of the personality. However, a full understanding of these dimensions of personality development requires further inclusion of the contributions of Piaget, Kohlberg, Simmel, and Mead into the frame of reference of Parsonian action theory.

The same is true of Parsons's theory on the level of the social system, which is formulated from the perspective of order production and gives special emphasis to the corresponding mechanisms in the interchange between the subsystems of the social system. However, with the formulation of the four-function scheme, Parsons did overcome his original merging of values and norms, reason and conformity. He was now able to clearly distinguish between these two dimensions, between cultural and social system on the general action level and fiduciary and community system on the social system level. Particularly in his theory of socio-cultural evolution, he recognized the order-transforming power of general cultural ideas and values that transcend any concrete social system, and of intellectual reasoning that transcends the belief system of any particular community.

Parsons's four-function paradigm allows adequate attention to be paid to all dimensions of social life and social development, to solidarity, and to discourse, power, and market exchange as well. However, a full realization of the potential of this theory needs much more inclusion of the contributions of the different paradigms that have specialized in investigating one of these dimensions. The conceptualization of the socio-cultural system needs to be renewed by discourse theory and symbolic interactionism, that of the community system by structuralism, phenomenology and ethnomethodology, that of the political system by conflict theory and structuration theory, and that of the economic system by rational choice theory and Marxism. If this is done, Parsonian theory can provide the overall frame of reference for working on an ever more finely interwoven network of sociological theory as a common undertaking of all sociologists, whatever their home base may be. With regard to the often raised question of whether Parsons's turn to systems theory did break away from the basic insights of his earlier action theory, we should have learned from this chapter: Parsons's systems theory does not change any of his earlier insights. It is an extension but no refutation of action theory.

Critical assessments of Parsons's work have been produced time and again. Of the many works available, I particularly mention Black (1961), Loubser, Baum, Effrat, and Lidz (1976), Bourricaud (1977, for translation, see 1981), and Alexander (1982–1983, volume 4). An earlier assessment was also made by this author (Münch, 1987a). Robert Holton and Bryan Turner

(1989a) have advanced our understanding of Parsons's view on the economy in society.

Further Developments

A number of scholars have worked directly with Parsons or indirectly alongside his approach to stretch the theory beyond its original boundaries. For example, Neil J. Smelser (1959, 1962) has introduced many more elements of economic theory and conflict theory into his work on the British industrial revolution and on collective behavior. Robert N. Bellah (Bellah, 1957, 1970, 1975; Bellah, Madsen, Sullivan, Swidler, and Tipton, 1985) has extended the theory farther into the realm of communication, morality, and meaning construction in his work on religion and morality in Japan and the United States. Shmuel N. Eisenstadt (1963, 1966, 1973) has extended the approach in his historical-developmental and comparative studies largely by explaining the specific path to modernity in different cultures and societies. Edward Shils (1972, 1975) has advanced our understanding of social order and of the role of intellectuals. Bernard Barber (1952/1968, 1957, 1963, 1978, 1983) has advanced the sociology of science, professions, and inequality. Edward Tiryakian (1962, 1975, 1977, 1978, 1983) has enriched the Parsonian approach by drawing on phenomenology and by rereading the classics. Rainer Baum (1976a, 1976b, 1981) has done so with theoretical work on the generalized media of interchange and with historical work on the Holocaust as has Roland Robertson (1980, 1990) with his work on globalization. Harry Johnson (1973, 1976) has explored the working of communication and media. Leon Mayhew (1971) has developed the analysis of institutions and activities in society, and Dean Gerstein (1981) the analysis of drug addiction. Victor and Charles Lidz (1976) have incorporated elements of Piaget's cognitive psychology. Mark Gould (1976, 1987) has formulated a Marxist revision of Parsonianism. The collection of essays published by Jan J. Loubser, Rainer C. Baum, Andrew Effrat, and Victor M. Lidz (1976) in honor of Parsons gives evidence of scholarly work of the highest quality carried out within the Parsonian framework.

Jeffrey C. Alexander (1982–1983, 1985, 1987a, 1987b) has provided a detailed account of this potential for variety within Parsonian theory and has also given a balanced assessment of Parsons's strengths and weaknesses. He argues forcefully for a multidimensional renewal of Parsonian theory. His work is a good proof of the revitalization of Parsonian action theory and analytical functionalism in the 1980s, which he has called "neofunctionalism." He has contributed very much to renewing Parsonian theory. Within the framework of neofunctionalism, younger scholars like Paul Colomy (1985, 1990a, 1990b), Frank Lechner (1984, 1985, 1989), and David Sciulli (1984, 1986, 1988, 1989) are advancing sociological theory in a fresh new way (Sciulli and Gerstein, 1985).

In Germany, Parsons's work has regained recognition since the 1970s (see Alexander, 1984). Scholars like Enno Schwanenberg (1970, 1971) and Stefan Jensen (1980) have contributed illuminating interpretations of Parsons's sociological theory. Bernhard Giesen (1980, 1991) and Michael Schmid (1982) have elaborated an important evolutionary approach of sociological theory that relates to and goes beyond Parsons. Bernhard Miebach (1984), Karl-Heinz Saurwein (1988), and Harald Wenzel (1991) have extended our understanding of Parsons's work with new and innovative reconstructions. And I have worked on revitalizing Parsonian theory by way of rereading the classics and incorporating the achievements of competing contemporary theories and by applying the framework to comparative historical studies on the development of modernity (Münch, 1982, 1984, 1986, 1987b, 1991; for translation, see 1987a, 1988).

Later on we will examine Niklas Luhmann's (1984) systems theory. Here we must recognize that Luhmann started his great undertaking from the work of Parsons. We will also deal with Jürgen Habermas's (1981) renewal of critical theory by way of combining the theory of communicative action with systems theory. In doing so Habermas draws on Parsons. The revitalization of Weberian sociology initiated by Wolfgang Schluchter (1979, 1988) is indebted to the work of Parsons. In the United States, the influence of Parsonian theory declined after the late 1960s. However, with the revitalization that has taken place since the beginning of the 1980s, it is again very much alive.

In this context I mention the work of Amitai Etzioni (1961, 1968, 1988). Though not a Parsonian in the strict sense, he has nevertheless tried to develop a comprehensive social theory similar to Parsons's approach that interrelates knowledge, power, consensus, and the mobilization of resources in order to understand and explain the complex nature of society, though with much more emphasis on the dynamics of societal development. He emphasizes the interaction of those factors in the production of what he calls the active society, that is, a society that actively develops itself.

I also mention the work of Walter Buckley (1967) at this point. He tried to explore the potential of general systems theory for advancing sociology. He is not a Parsonian, but his work does relate to the systems element in Parsons's work. With his strict systems approach, he misses the core of Parsons's voluntaristic action theory.

Two

EMPIRICAL FUNCTIONALISM:
ROBERT K. MERTON

IN THE late 1940s and the early 1950s, the Department of Sociology at Columbia University in New York rose to attain an outstanding position in American sociology. In the 1950s, it was the only equally ranking competitor of Parsons's Harvard Department of Social Relations. Since that time American sociology has become much more polycentric in character. However, Columbia is still one of the leading departments. The rise of Columbia's sociology to its prominent position in the late 1940s and early 1950s was particularly due to the work of two scholars: Robert K. Merton and Paul F. Lazarsfeld. Merton (1949/1968d, 1968e) created an empirical version of functionalism that aimed to develop theories of the middle range, such as theories of deviance, in contrast to the analytical functionalism of Parsons and his preoccupation with grand theory. Lazarsfeld developed the quantitative methodology that was appropriate to this kind of middle range empirical functionalism (Lazarsfeld and Rosenberg, 1955). The main object domain of the studies conducted in this context was the institutional structure of society. Social structure, organizations, occupations, professions, and science became the areas most widely studied by Columbia empirical functionalists and other outstanding Columbia sociologists. This is why we start here with an analysis of the specific character of institutions, institutional structures, or simply structures.

The Institutional Structure of Social Life

Every society is at least to a minimal degree founded on institutionalized patterns of recurrent behavior, that is, patterns of behavior that do not change quickly according to a change of situations and that cannot be easily

119

changed by individual actors engaged in action regulated by these institutionalized patterns. Without such institutionalized patterns of behavior, action would be unpredictable, and the coordination of the actions of individuals would have to be achieved anew from chaos all the time.

Certainly life in society always involves unexpected actions, misunderstandings, miscoordination, and conflict. However, there is also at least some confirmation of expectations by the behavior of others, mutual understanding, coordination, and consensus. That means there are recurrent, persistent patterns of behavior upon which people can rely when they are about to plan their actions. We call such recurrent patterns of behavior "institutions" or "institutional structures," or simply "structures." Behavior that is institutionalized in a society and combines with other behavior to form an institution is obligatory for the members of society acting in a situation to which the established institution applies. Behavior regulated by an institution is prescribed by a set of norms that make up the normative structure of an institution. Thus, there are two aspects of institutions: a set of norms that are binding for the members of a society and a pattern of recurrent, persistent behavior that corresponds to these norms. There are certainly always a number of deviations from the norms. However, these do not call into question the existence of an institution as long as these deviations provoke sanctions by the members of society and as long as the deviant cannot mobilize enough power and legitimation of his or her action to get societywide support. The more the deviant succeeds in this respect, the more likely it is that the institution will undergo structural change.

Wherever and whenever people act, they at least partly reproduce such institutionalized patterns of behavior. People who go to a certain place to worship, who marry and raise children, who take part in a cocktail party, who go to school and to college, who vote in an election, who buy food in the supermarket, who conclude a contract of employment, who carry out a job, or who stop their car at a red traffic light thereby follow a pattern of conduct that does not come about accidentally in a situation of action but is the same for many people in many instances and many situations over a considerable time. It is behavior that is certainly motivated by individuals' desires but not freely chosen and created in the situation. It is behavior embodied in the society's stock of knowledge and prescriptions of which every member makes use in carrying out certain actions and in satisfying individual desires. This behavior is available to the individual as a member of that society; other behavior is not available to the person and at the very least it would provoke negative sanctions by the other members of society.

Many of our actions carry out such institutionalized patterns of behavior. And it is these institutionalized patterns of behavior that make up the identity of a society. If we want to get to know a society we have to look at what is typically recurrent behavior of its members and not at what comes about accidentally from situation to situation. If we want to get to know an individual person we will try to uncover the recurrent features of his or her behavior. It is no different with societies. In learning to know the specific character of a society, we have to uncover the recurrent behavior patterns in the interactions between its members.

Early Functionalism

This institutional dimension of societal life is the object domain of an approach to studying society that became the dominant paradigm of sociology in the 1940s and 1950s: structural functionalism. The groundwork for this paradigm was laid down by Durkheim (1895/1973b) and then by the leading anthropologists who studied the working of primitive societies: Radcliffe-Brown (1922, 1935, 1952) and Malinowski (1922/1961, 1926, 1948). Durkheim established the social fact as the object domain of sociology. As he put it, the social fact is external to the individual, exerts a constraint on him or her to act in certain ways, is universal in character, that is, universally binding for each member of a society, and has to be studied like a thing, that is, an object *sui generis*, which can be separated from the individual dispositions of actors. Social facts are institutionalized patterns of behavior in the above-described sense. According to Durkheim they are there before an individual carries out his or her action in a certain situation, and they will still be there after this action is finished.

An actual case of marriage, for example, is but one instance of a procedure carried out many times before and after this actual case occurs. And all marriages are carried out in a similar way. Thus, what the actual case contributes to the procedure is mostly the actual motivation of the actors, but this is framed according to the preceding and proceeding pattern of marriage. What is of interest for the sociologist is not why the two people marry but how they do it and why it is done in a typical recurrent way in that society.

Radcliffe-Brown and Malinowski studied the recurrent practices they observed in tribal societies, practices like the exchange of goods and presents, rites of initiation, commemoration of the dead, funerals, magic, punishment, and assembling. These are the institutionalized patterns of interaction that make up the specific character of the societies they studied. The anthropologists were not interested in ephemeral activities but in the typical phenomena of those societies. Therefore, they concentrated on the institutional structure. What gave rise to structural functionalism as a paradigm of analysis was the way in which they approached an explanation of the *persistence* of these phenomena. They aimed at discovering the functions that the carrying out of specific practices fulfilled for the working and persistence of the society under study. Especially the maintenance of integration and solidarity of society became the prominent reference point for such functional analyses. An institutional practice was explained by its contribution to the integration and solidarity of society. However, other reference points were also introduced, particularly by Malinowski: biological needs of the members of society, like the need for nutrition, psychic needs of the members of society, like the need for support, and socio-cultural needs of society, like integration and solidarity.

The origin of this organismic theorizing lay in analogizing society to biological organisms, an approach put forward by leading social thinkers in the nineteenth century. Auguste Comte, Albert Schäffle, Herbert Spencer, and René Worms contributed to this emerging organismic social thought in the second half of the nineteenth century. It was, on the one hand, favored by the success of biology as a model of scientific thought and, on the other hand, influenced by a desire to point out ways of finding an ordered society.

Durkheim explicitly addressed the question of a functional explanation of institutional practices in his *Rules of Sociological Method* (Durkheim, 1895/1973b), but he did not advocate functionalism as a paradigm. He clearly stated that it was not enough to point out the function of a social phenomenon in order to explain its existence; the cause that brought it about would also have to be discovered. According to his commitment to explaining social phenomena by social phenomena and not by other phenomena like biological and psychic ones, he also required that cause and function have to be social in character. Thus, the functional part of this explanation of a social phenomenon has to be related to social and not individual needs, as the causal part has to be related to social and not individual causes.

Take, for example, the Australian aborigines who were studied secondarily by Durkheim (1912/1968). They gather on a regular basis in order to carry out certain religious rites. This is apparently an institution. How can we explain this institution? There is, on the one hand, the cause: The people do not come together casually but in a regular way. It is not a coincidence of independent individual wishes to meet that brings about the meeting but an obligation they feel commonly as members of that collective to continue with a common tradition. This is the social cause that conditions the members of that society to participate in the meeting. This social cause of members' participation has to be distinguished from the social cause that contributes to their feeling of an obligation to continue with the established tradition. This feeling emerges from their mutual solidarity. Now, the very effect of the common celebration of religious rites is that they confirm the solidarity of people engaged in these rites. We can say that the institution of regularly carrying out religious rites has the social function of confirming the solidarity of society inasmuch as all relevant members participate in these rites independently of whether these people know about this effect or not. This is the functional part of the explanation.

It refers to the function of the institutionalized practice for the maintenance of solidarity in that society.

As we can see in this explanation, there is a circular effect in the practice of religious rites. People feel obligated to meet in order to commonly practice a religious rite, because they are mutually committed to each other in solidarity. This causes them to follow the call of the meeting's organizers and causes the organizers to call the society's members together. On the other hand, the very gathering and common practice of the rite strengthens their solidarity as an (unintended) effect, which is the social function of that meeting and the cause of their feeling of obligation to participate in future meetings.

Durkheim himself does not relate causal and functional analysis in this circular way. However, the example is drawn from Durkheim's study of religion of the Australian aborigines and can be used as an exemplification of his commitment to point out the *social* causes and *social* functions of a *social* phenomenon (Durkheim, 1895/1973b: 89–97). Their mutual stabilization in a circular flow is a special case of relating cause and function to each other; we can do it by interpreting Durkheim's analysis of religious rites in the way outlined above. The social function of a social phenomenon is the effect it has on the society, for example, on the maintenance of its solidarity. In a sense it is just the effect resulting from a specific cause.

What is special about functionalism created by anthropologists after Durkheim is its claim to explain a social phenomenon simply by the functions it fulfills, without engaging in an analysis of its causes, not even in the way outlined above, where cause and function are mutually interrelated in a circular flow. The persistence of society becomes the very cause for the existence of a social phenomenon fulfilling a positive function for the maintenance of society. For Malinowski (1926), every social phenomenon fulfills an indispensable function for the whole of society. It satisfies biological needs for food, shelter, and reproduction, psychological needs for support, or needs related to maintaining culture and social organization, like institutions of exchange, decision making, social control, and education. The society organizes action in order to fulfill biological needs that give rise to additional psychological needs, which again give rise to sociocultural needs for the organization of action on a higher level.

Though Radcliffe-Brown (1935) opposed Malinowski's emphatic functionalism and called his own approach structuralism, he nevertheless often couched his analyses in functionalist terms, that is, he gave functional explanations of social practices. He denied that every social phenomenon exists because it fulfills a necessary function; he emphasized that assuming the unity of society is only a hypothesis on which a functional explanation of a social phenomenon as contributing to the persistence of society proceeds and not a postulate that every society displays such unity. He also argued that we cannot assume universal needs of any society; we can assume only particular conditions of existence of particular societies. Nevertheless, his explanations of the institutions he discovered in primitive societies were very often functional in character. For example, he explained the existence of lineage systems by their contribution to the maintenance of solidarity and the avoidance of conflict. They determine the distribution of property rights among families without which conflict would arise each time an actual property owner died. The lineage system exists because it helps to avoid conflicts on property rights and thereby helps to maintain solidarity. This is a functional explanation of lineage systems simply by referring to the function they fulfill for maintaining solidarity in society. The logic of such a functional explanation reads as follows:

A. Whenever a society exists, it will display a minimal solidarity.
B. Whenever there is a lineage system, it will contribute to maintaining solidarity.
C. Society *a* exists.

D. Society *a* has a lineage system.

The derivation of sentence D from sentences A, B, and C is not correct. The reason is that there may be other social practices that secure the maintenance of minimal solidarity; thus, the very existence of a society does not allow us to conclude that there is necessarily a lineage system. The fact that such a system exists, however, is not enough proof to preclude the maintenance of solidarity by institutions other than the lineage system. In fact, the lineage system may be badly designed, so that it actually gives rise to conflict. If society displays solidarity, this must come from sources other than the lineage system. Thus, there may be a lineage system that causes conflict in a society that nevertheless has some solidarity. Therefore, the existence of a society is not a sufficient reason for explaining the existence of a lineage system.

In some cases, a lineage system may be well enough designed to preclude conflicts so that it supports solidarity, which again is a source of its acceptance and its application in concrete cases. This would be an instance of a circular relationship of cause and effect similar to that pointed out with Durkheim's analysis of religious rites. Thus we could transform Radcliffe-Brown's functional explanation into a circular causal one. However, normally such a procedure would not be a sufficient explanation for the existence of a lineage system. A complete analysis would have to point out the way in which it became established and institutionalized and the way in which it is stabilized. It may have been established by a dominating group, legitimized by certain basic ideas of the society, and stabilized by social control and procedures of legitimation. These are elements that continuously contribute to the reproduction of the lineage system and that go much beyond the mere existence of society. It is these special processes that have to be included in a sufficient explanation of institutions but do not enter an explanation purely couched in functional terms of relating a structure to a necessary function for the maintenance of society.

Postulates of Functionalism

Robert K. Merton (1949/1968a) formulated a paradigm of functional analysis that starts with basic criticism of three postulates of prevailing types of functionalism, postulates that are particularly rooted in Malinowski's version of functionalism. The postulates are functional unity, universal functionalism, and functional indispensability.

Functional Unity

Functional unity means that a society is an integrated whole and that the members of that society live in harmony and solidarity with each other. In this case, it is assumed that an institutionalized social practice and belief is explained by its existence, because it fulfills a positive function for the maintenance of society as a whole. Radcliffe-Brown formulated this principle as a hypothesis to the effect that, in explaining functionally the existence of a social phenomenon, we have to presuppose the unity of a society. Otherwise, the effects of that social phenomenon would be contradictory, being positive for some parts of society and negative for other parts or even the whole society.

Malinowski argues against Radcliffe-Brown that the sociological school has overemphasized the solidarity of primitive society and has disregarded the individual in order to show that a functional explanation has to point to the functions of a social practice or belief for the whole culture and the individual. Thus he explains the primitive belief in the supernatural not only by the positive function it fulfills for the integration, technical and economic efficiency of culture as a whole but also by its positive function for the biological and mental welfare of the individual member. As Merton puts it, he does not really abandon the postulate of functional unity but only adds the further postulate that a social phenomenon has to be additionally explained by its function for the individual members of society.

Merton is certainly right when he calls into question the assumption that societies display the property of functional unity. For example, if only a particular group of society participates in a particular religious rite and others have their own rites, these rites help to maintain the group's solidarity but work contrary to the maintenance of solidarity between groups in that society. As he notes, the assumption of functional unity may be fairly adequate for primitive societies but not for more advanced societies composed of different groups with different religions, life-styles, and interests. However, he seems to miss the specific message of the postulate of functional unity. When Radcliffe-Brown argues that a social practice or belief has to be functionally explained by its contribution to the maintenance of total social life under the hypothesis that society is an integrated whole, he just wants to preclude the feasibility of a functional explanation if the condition of unity is not fulfilled. Whenever there is no such unity, the existence of a social practice or belief has to be explained by reasons other than its function for the maintenance of society, because it has no such uniform function. For example, it has to be explained by the domination of a specific group in society that makes use of a particular practice because it corresponds to its beliefs, even though it raises conflicts with other groups in society.

Malinowski's addition of the requirement to also show the positive function of a social practice or belief for each individual member of society is an even further sharpening of the requirements for an adequate functional explanation. It is based on the assumption that without such effects for the individual members a practice or belief can also have disruptive effects and can provoke opposition that works against the persistence of the social practice or belief. Radcliffe-Brown assumes that a functional explanation is inadequate if society is not an integrated whole; Malinowski also assumes this inadequacy if it cannot be shown that a social phenomenon has positive functions for each individual member of society. What Radcliffe-Brown and Malinowski formulate are not postulates that every society displays functional unity and that a social phenomenon has positive functions for the total society and even for each individual member but strong requirements for functional explanations derived from the formal character of physiological explanations of the working of organisms. Only if these requirements are fulfilled can we assume that there are no forces in society that work against the maintenance of a social practice or belief, for example, opposing groups or individuals. Only in this case can a social phenomenon be part of an integrated whole, and only then can it be explained in its existence (it would be better to say: persistence) because it fulfills a positive function for the maintenance of that whole.

As Merton admits, primitive societies come much closer to this model of an integrated social system than more advanced societies do; therefore, the anthropologists are not completely wrong in working on this assumption when they advance functional explanations of social practices and beliefs. However, what is left if we abandon the postulate of functional unity as Merton proposes? We would do nothing but weaken the requirements for functional explanations! Functional explanations become completely arbitrary if we do not require the conditions of an integrated whole. If these conditions are not fulfilled, it would be better to seek explanations of social phenomena other than functional ones. What Merton proposes becomes much more inadequate than the functional explanations of the anthropologists: a functional explanation of a social phenomenon, though the society under consideration does not fulfill the requirements for the adequacy of such explanations. This is not progress; it is regression. We ought rather to give up the functional type of explanation when we study nonintegrated societies.

Universal Functionalism

The second postulate criticized by Merton is the postulate of universal functionalism, which states that every social phenomenon fulfills a positive function. This was particularly postulated by Malinowski. Merton is again right when he denies that every social phenomenon plays such a role in society. There are many social phenomena that contribute nothing to the continuation of society or even endanger its continuation. However, this is again not the point Malinowski wishes to make. What he says has to be interpreted in conditional terms. If society is a working whole, like an organism, it is composed of parts that all make specific contributions to the working of society. If society is not such a working whole, the functional approach to explaining its features is not feasible. Thus, the postulate of universal functionalism has to be read as an additional requirement for functional explanations and not as a statement of fact. Only if we can assume that a social system is a working whole can we look for functional explanations of its parts; otherwise, we have to look for other types of explanations. Merton misses this point, which runs in the same direction as his own argument. Instead, he introduces the requirement of a net balance of positive and negative functions of a social phenomenon for society or for a social group powerful enough to enforce the phenomenon. Here again he seeks to maintain the strategy of functional explanation under conditions that are not adequate for such a strategy. If society is not a working whole composed of parts contributing to its working, we have to be very cautious with functional explanations of social phenomena.

Functional Indispensability

The third postulate criticized by Merton is the postulate of functional indispensability, which means that a social phenomenon is indispensable in fulfilling a function for society and its individual members, as formulated by Malinowski. Merton is again right when he argues that there are often alternatives to a particular social phenomenon that can fulfill the same function. Thus, the practice of belief is not indispensable. But he again misses the point. What Malinowski states has to be interpreted not as a statement of fact but as a requirement for functional explanations. Only if we can preclude the possibility that there are alternatives available within a society for fulfilling a specific function, and only if we can assume that this specific function is a prerequisite for the maintenance of society, can we explain functionally the existence of a social phenomenon. Otherwise, we have to turn to other, namely, causal or interpretive, explanations. Merton, however, maintains the functional approach even under this condition and wants to look for structural constraints, which narrow the range of possible alternatives, rather than for nonfunctional explanations.

Generally, we can say that Merton criticizes the postulates of functional unity, universality, and indispensability as statements of fact and does not recognize their nature as requirements for adequate functional explanations. As he himself admits, anthropologists studying closed communities were much more able to work on these assumptions than sociologists studying more advanced societies, which do not fulfill these requirements. However, because he does not interpret the postulates as requirements for adequate functional explanations, he commits the much more dangerous error of advancing functional explanations as a strategy for studying modern societies. Let us see how he tries to accomplish this task.

A Paradigm for Functional Analysis

We can set out Merton's paradigm for functional analysis in the following twelve statements (Merton, 1949/1968a: 104–8):

1. The items to which functions are imputed have to be standardized social phenomena, like "social roles, institutional patterns, social processes, cultural patterns, culturally patterned emotions, social norms, group organization, social structure, devices for social control, etc." (Merton, 1949/1968a: 104). Thus, functional analysis concentrates on the institutionalized recurrent patterns of interaction and not on the ephemeral aspects of social life.
2. The subjective dispositions of actors performing a social practice have to be outlined and have to be distinguished from the objective consequences of that practice.
3. The objective consequences of an item have to be demonstrated insofar as they have positive, negative, or neutral effects on a given system. Positive effects are functions, negative effects are dysfunctions, and neutral effects are nonfunctional. The balance of functions and dysfunctions has to be assessed. Functions can be manifest, that is, intended and recognized by participants in the system, or latent, that is, neither intended nor recognized.

4. The units for which an item has consequences and therefore fulfills functions and/or dysfunctions have to be distinguished: "individuals in diverse statuses, subgroups, the larger social system, and culture systems" (Merton, 1949/1968a: 106).
5. The functional requirements for maintaining a system have to be specified.
6. The mechanisms through which functions are fulfilled have to be specified. These are more general types of institutional forms of which particular items under consideration are specific instances, for example, authority as a mechanism for reaching collectively binding decisions and the concrete patriarchal system in a society as a special instance of authority.
7. The functional alternatives for fulfilling a particular function have to be demonstrated.
8. The structural context in which an item operates has to be described and analyzed with regard to its narrowing effects on the range of possible alternatives for fulfilling a particular function.
9. In order to analyze structural change as much as social statics, attention has to be paid to when dysfunctions are kept under control within a particular structural context and when they accumulate into stress and strain so that they exert pressures for structural change leading to a reduction of stress and strain.
10. Functional explanations have to be validated in comparative analysis.
11. Functional analysis has to be kept neutral in ideological terms without preoccupation with the conservative stabilization or radical change of a social system.
12. When describing a social practice that is explained functionally, the following aspects have to be included:
   a. location of the participants in the social structure,
   b. alternative modes of behavior excluded by the pattern,
   c. emotive and cognitive meaning of the pattern for the participants,
   d. a distinction between motivation and objective behavior, and
   e. behavioral regularities that are part of the pattern but not recognized by the participants.

Application, Examination, and Critical Assessment

In practicing functional analysis, Merton uncovered latent functions of a phenomenon in order to explain it. He gave some examples of such an analysis (Merton, 1949/1968a: 109–36).

Informal Groups and Conspicuous Consumption

Merton argued that the Hawthorne Western Electric Studies came to fruitful explanations when the latent functions of standardized practices of workers and informal organization were discovered (Roethlisberger and Dickson, 1939; Mayo, 1945). As Veblen (1928) demonstrated in his study on the leisure class, the continuous pattern of consuming highly esteemed products by the leisure class can be explained by referring to the function this pattern fulfills for confirming the reputed status of people who want to be considered as members of this class. This is called conspicuous consumption. However, can we explain the informal group organization and its corresponding pattern of productivity by its latent function for the working of the organization and/or the solidarity of the group and/or the identity of individual workers? It is unavoidable that workers cooperating daily will form a group on their own that defines its own standards of productivity the more they are autonomous in this regard, whether or not this has positive functions for the company, the group, or the individuals. In many cases this phenomenon creates strain for all: the company, the group, and the individuals. Nevertheless, it exists, which demonstrates that its existence cannot be explained by referring to positive functions. The same is true for conspicuous consumption. The very existence of this pattern creates a lot of stress for the individuals who feel pressure to participate, because they would otherwise endanger their status. Thus, the explanation is not a positive function for attaining status but the pressure that leading figures exert on those who want to be associated with them.

Social Structure and Anomie

His most widely read article, "Social Structure and Anomie" (Merton, 1949/1968b, 1949/1968c), is considered by Merton as an example of functional analysis. It is also an example of a theory of the middle range that he opposed to grand theory like Parsons's (1937/1968, 1951) action theory aiming at covering the whole human world (Merton, 1949/1968a). Middle-range theory goes beyond practical empirical generalizations but does not aim to cover the whole of society. It tries to explain a specific feature of society in a systematic way. The feature that is of interest here is the existence of conforming and deviating behavior with regard to the norms institutionalized in society. The argument of the middle-range theory constructed for explaining this feature of society runs as follows.

A society's culture, on the one hand, sets goals of desirable states of affairs for its members. On the other hand, it defines the legitimate means for attaining these goals. If both parts of that culture are equally binding for the members of society, there is a state of equilibrium. If one part is more binding than the other, disequilibrium exists. Such disequilibrium calls for behavior that will restore the equilibrium. It exerts pressure on the individual members of society to adapt their behavior to this situation. According to Merton, there are five types of adaptation to society's cultural structure. The first two are:

1. The more there is a state of equilibrium and goals and means are equally binding, the more individuals will react by conforming to the goals and the institutionally prescribed means.
2. The more goals dominate and the means for attaining them are weakly institutionalized and the less individuals have access to legitimate means, the more individuals will react by applying illegitimate means, which is innovation.

The second hypothesis applies particularly to American society, which is committed to achievement and wealth much more than to the legitimate means for achievement and does not give everybody the same access to these legitimate means. Thus, it exerts pressure to adjust to this disequilibrium by applying illegitimate means; this pressure is most strongly felt by the disadvantaged lower classes. Referring to Durkheim, Merton calls this disequilibrium a state of anomie.

The remaining three hypotheses can be formulated as follows:

3. The more means are strongly institutionalized but goals are less salient, the more individuals will conform to the means without considering their effectiveness in attaining the goals, which is ritualism.
4. The less goals and means are institutionalized, the less individuals will be attracted by society's goals and means and the more individuals will retreat from society, which is retreatism.
5. The less goals and means are institutionalized and attract individuals and the more individuals are committed to personal goals and means, the more individuals will react with rebellion against society.

Though Merton does not formulate these hypotheses explicitly but simply provides a typology of forms of adaptation to societal culture, we can set out the hypotheses on the basis of his various arguments in the text. The question then is, What is functional about this analysis? The hypotheses can be formulated in causal terms as shown above. There is nothing functional about them. What is functional is the background argumentation. Merton seems to assume that a certain state of the cultural structure of society, namely, the equilibrium or disequilibrium of goals and institutionalized means, and its relationship to the social structure of opportunities to apply legitimate means necessitate particular forms of behavior, that is, forms of adaptation, so that individuals can live within such a society. The individual's need for balance seems to be the final reference point of this functional analysis. The need for balance means that the individual tries to adjust his or her behavior to internalized goals and/or means. That is, Merton seems to assume that individuals' internalization of goals and means parallels their weak or strong institutionalization in society. Confronted with the opportunity structure of society, they are forced to choose a particular type of behavior in order to act consistently with their internalized goals and/or means. In the case of conformity, they have enough opportunities to conform to internalized and institutionalized goals and means. In the case of innovation, they do not have enough opportunities and therefore are forced to apply illegitimate means in order to attain the goals that are much more strongly institutionalized and internalized than the means.

We can add to Merton's constraints the access to illegitimate means as a condition for choosing them, as Cloward has argued. According to Cloward (1959) an individual will not become deviant if he or she has no access to illegitimate means. This access to illegitimate means can be explained on the basis of Edwin Sutherland's (1939: 1–9) theory of differential learning based on differential contacts:

6. The more an individual is confronted with positive definitions of deviant behavior and the more chances he or she has to learn its techniques, the more likely it is that the individual will engage in deviant behavior.

In the case of ritualism, people's overcommitment to institutionalized and internalized means precludes any look at the effectiveness of the means for attaining the goals. In the case of retreatism, the institutionalization and internalization of goals and means is so weak that people are not at all attracted to society and tend toward retreat. They cannot act according to something to which they are not committed. In the case of rebellion, there is a conflict between institutionalized and internalized goals and means. The individual committed to goals and means that are contradicted by society's institutionalized goals and means cannot do anything other than revolt against society.

The general line of Merton's argument in "Social Structure and Anomie" points out how certain social structural constraints have a narrowing effect on the functional alternatives generally available for an individual to achieve balance between his or her action and his or her internalized goals and/or means. The reference point is the balance between an individual's internalized goals and/or means and his or her action. The items explained functionally are forms of adaptation. Which one will be selected is explained by the structural constraints that exert a narrowing effect on the range of alternatives.

Is this an adequate functional explanation? We can say that, as stated in the outlined form, it is more adequate than the examples given with the Hawthorne Western Electric studies and with conspicuous consumption. The reason is that there is a reference point and an attempt to narrow the range of functional alternatives by referring to structural constraints. However, it takes a lot of clarification and precision to bring about this structure of argumentation from Merton's rather vague formulations. And the exposition of the hypotheses in causal terms demonstrates that the functional explanation can be replaced by a causal one.

The Role-Set

A further example of Merton's functional approach is the theory of the role-set (Merton, 1957). Merton distinguishes status and role as basic elements of social structure. A status — like father, mother, son, teacher, lawyer, salesman, customer — is a position in a social system involving designated rights and obligations expressed in the patterned expectations of others. The role is the behavior of the status occupant that is oriented to these patterned expectations. Each status is related to a whole series of reference groups, each of which has its own expectations. Thus, there is an array of roles associated with a status, each one related to a specific reference group. This is what Merton calls a role-set. The teacher plays a different role with regard to the different reference groups in his or her role-set. He or she is confronted with the expectations of pupils, of parents, of colleagues, of the school board, and of the principal and behaves in a different way with regard to each one of them.

The role-set always involves a certain number of conflicting expectations. The different positions of reference groups in society give rise to different values and interests and thus to different and conflicting role expectations. Too much of this conflict endangers the functioning and progress of society. In order to cope with this functional requirement, society needs mechanisms for avoiding, limiting, and resolving conflicts in the role-set. Every society that keeps on working and functioning has institutionalized such mechanisms. Merton discovered six different mechanisms for resolving conflict in the role-set that are part of the social structure and not simply individual strategies, as he emphasizes:

- The importance of a status for the individual is relative. For the teacher, his or her occupational status may be of central importance, whereas for other individuals in the role-set, their status and corresponding relationship to the teacher may be only of peripheral importance. This difference in the importance given to various statuses limits chances of intense conflict.
- Differences of power in the role-set work as means of limiting conflict. The more powerful reference groups can enforce their expectations more effectively; a coalition of weaker reference groups increases their power and thus the effectivity of their expectations; and a balance of power gives the teacher more chances to play off the reference groups against each other.
- Not all role activities of a status occupant are observable to all members of the role-set to the same degree. This contributes to avoiding conflict.

- Inasmuch as the reference groups become aware of the conflicting character of their expectations, they will be more occupied with settling this conflict. The status occupant is thus relieved of resolving the conflict in role expectations for him- or herself.
- The occupants of the same status, like teachers, who are confronted with similarly conflicting role expectations can give each other support and thus make it easier for each one to deal with the conflict.
- In a limited number of cases, the individual who is confronted with too much conflict in a role-set may abridge the relationship. Inasmuch as this opportunity is given to individuals, there is a tendency toward abridging role-sets with too much conflict and maintaining those with a workable degree of conflict. Nevertheless, a certain amount of residual conflict will always remain.

Merton's theory of the role-set can be summarized as follows:

1. Society is composed of interrelated statuses and roles.
2. The status is a certain position in society; the role is behavior of status occupants oriented to the role expectations of reference groups related to that status.
3. The interrelationship of a status with different reference groups makes up a role-set.
4. The different positions of reference groups in society give rise to diverging and conflicting values, interests, and role expectations.
5. The more society keeps on functioning, the more it develops mechanisms for avoiding, limiting, and resolving conflicts in role-sets like relative importance of various statuses, differences of power between those in the role-set, insulation of role activities from observability by members of the role-set, observability of conflicting demands by members of the role-set, mutual support among status occupants, and abridging the role-set.

The Political Machine

A more explicit functional explanation is put forward by Merton for a widespread phenomenon in American democracy: the political machine (Merton, 1949/1968a: 126–36). This is an informal association of people led by a boss who infiltrates the political system so much that this association becomes the true acting body in local political decision making. Affiliation with this organization becomes the most important precondition for political success. Where the political machine has been established, nothing can be done without its support, let alone in the face of its resistance. The machine is particularly a phenomenon of big cities.

How does Merton explain this phenomenon in functional terms? He first describes the phenomenon as an institutionalized practice. It is the item that has to be explained. Then he points to a structural feature of American democracy that gives rise to a need for informal leadership: the splitting of power by the system of checks and balances as it was designed by the Founding Fathers who wrote the U.S. Constitution. This is a functional prerequisite of the political system: leadership in order to provide for making collectively binding decisions even if there is conflict. The political machine fulfills this prerequisite. It provides leadership that can break through the splitting of power in the system of checks and balances.

However, this is not the only need that is served by the political machine. It also serves the needs of very different groups. First, it provides help and support for the weak and poor independently of bureaucratic restrictions — thus in a much more flexible way than the official bureaucracy. Second, it helps legitimate business by way of regulations, new chances for making profits, privileges, and reduction of competition without establishing permanent governmental control. Third, it does the same for the illegitimate businesses of smuggling, drugs, and prostitution. Fourth, it provides chances for upward mobility within the machine itself for all those who do not feel strong enough to achieve without such support.

This is Merton's functional explanation of the political machine. It is based on the following general proposition:

> The more the functions of a social practice or belief for the maintenance of a social system outweigh its dysfunctions for it and the more its functions for serving the interests of social groups outweigh its dysfunctions and the greater the number and power of these groups, whether such functions or dysfunctions be manifest or latent, the more this social practice or belief will persist once it has been established.

The persistence of the political machine is explained by this general proposition. It has to be noted that the explanation applies only to the *persistence* of the political machine *once it has been established*. Its establishment has to be left to historical circumstances. All we could say in this regard is that the conditions responsible for the persistence of the political machine contribute to making it easy for political actors to get it established. However, the fact that we were able to couch Merton's argument in causal terms demonstrates that we can carry out his analysis without committing ourselves to truly functional explanations.

What is left then is the substantial character of the argument. Here we can see that Merton's structural functionalism is concerned with explaining institutional structures as persisting aspects of social life. The change of these institutional structures is explained by accumulated dysfunctions, strain, stress, and anomie that run contrary to maintaining an ordered social life. Thus, change is provoked by disorder and moves society toward establishing a new order of institutional structures.

What is the substantial nature of Merton's explanation of the political machine? In the foreground is its usefulness for several groups. If we go back to Merton's general exposition of the paradigm, we see also that the groups served by the machine must be more powerful than those it does not serve. There is also a more general need of the total social system served by the political machine: the need for collectively binding decisions that presupposes leadership. As Merton points out, there must be a *convergence of interests* of powerful social groups and of the whole community in order to have an institutional structure sufficiently supported, which secures its persistence. It is this *convergence of interests* that bears the whole weight of his explanation. If there were no convergence of interests he would have to explain the institution by the interest of the most powerful group served by that institution. In taking this line he replaces the anthropologist's reference point of primitive solidarity by the convergence of interests backed by power. This is a transformation of functionalism that seems to be necessitated by the features of modern societies, which are much more heterogeneous in character than primitive societies. Generally seen, Merton is right to make that transformation, but he misses the minimal contribution of solidarity and related aspects of association to the stabilization of institutional structures even in modern societies, and he misses completely the contribution of processes of legitimation and de-legitimation to the stabilization and destruction of institutional structures.

An institution becomes more binding in character even in modern societies as different groups are drawn together in common practices in this institution that contributes to building a common life-world. In this case the institution becomes part of the life-world of different groups and thus builds a bridge between these groups that is more than just a causal convergence of interests. The merging of the institution with the life-world of the groups makes its persistence more independent from serving concrete interests. It then can persist without serving any interests.

Moreover, without sufficient legitimation by the prevailing cultural values in processes of communication and discourse, an institutional structure is always in danger of being attacked by opposing groups. Its continuation presupposes legitimation by prevailing cultural ideas. On the other hand, a contradiction between cultural ideas and institutional structures exerts pressures for change in the direction of bringing the structures closer to the ideas.

There have been successful attempts at destroying political machines by introducing local government without party affiliation. Political machines were destroyed in some cities when institutional reform was enacted that was based on de-legitimation of the political machine in the light of the

U.S. Constitution. Without a systematic place for legitimation processes within our theoretical framework we could not explain these destructions of political machines.

Unfortunately, there is no place for such processes of legitimation and de-legitimation in Merton's paradigm of structural functionalism. It is preoccupied with the convergence of interests of groups with enough power to enforce their interests. This is certainly an important dimension in explaining an institutional structure; however, it is not enough for a complete explanation. We also have to study the course of power conflicts in their own logic, the association of groups and people in an institution including how it merges with the life-world of these groups, and the processes of legitimation and de-legitimation. In order to accomplish this task we have to consult theories of power and conflict, of the normative structuring of the life-world, of communication, discourse, and legitimation.

Consulting theories of economic transactions can improve the arguments on converging interests. For example, we have to know that an institution is a collective good and is not spontaneously provided the larger a society grows, even in cases of converging interests. Its establishment and continuation need additional support, for example, the action of political entrepreneurs who take the lead in creating and running institutions. In the light of this argument, Merton underemphasizes the role of the boss in the political machine. Without an active boss there would be no political machine; it is in danger or even breaks down when the boss retreats and no new boss is in sight. We have to be aware of the outlined deficiencies in Merton's structural functionalism without denying its merits. These merits lie in drawing our attention to what constitutes a society and makes it unique and different from other societies, its forerunners, and its followers—the institutionalized patterns of social life rather than the ephemeral aspects of that life. However, the convergence of interests is but one answer to the question raised by structural functionalism. This question needs a much more complete answer, and we cannot arrive at this answer without the aid of the many other paradigmatic contributions to sociological theory (see Sztompka, 1974, 1986).

THREE

STUDIES IN DELINQUENT SUBCULTURES: ALBERT J. COHEN AND JAMES F. SHORT, JR., WALTER B. MILLER, MILTON J. YINGER, GRESHAM M. SYKES, AND DAVID MATZA

A SOCIETY may be guided by a dominating culture. However, this dominating culture does not penetrate every corner of society. To varying degrees, there will be room for subcultures that have their own values and norms. Classes, status groups, age groups, professional groups, regional groups, and religious groups do not reproduce the dominating social culture but build up subcultures of their own. Behavior that deviates from the dominating values and norms is very often nothing but an outcome of conformity to the values and norms of a subculture. Such a subculture exists because of incomplete inclusion of the corresponding groups in the dominating societal culture. Its members may simply perpetuate the traditionally handed-down behavior patterns of the subculture or they may receive from conformity to the subcultural norms those rewards that they do not receive from the wider society because they are insufficiently successful in conforming to its norms. In the first case, the subculture is reproduced from generation to generation just because it is a milieu of its own. In the second case, it becomes established and is reproduced because it satisfies the needs of its members for rewards withheld by the wider society. Both paths toward the establishment and reproduction of subcultural behavior patterns are possible and may even mutually support each other.

Studies in delinquent subcultures of this kind have to be seen as steps away from the structural-functional approach and toward what became established as phenomenological sociology. The influence of pragmatist studies in neighborhoods, communities, and other social milieux is also visible in these studies when regular behavior patterns are viewed as an adaptation to external social conditions. However, the explanation of deviant behavior by its conformity to the values and norms of a subculture is clearly a step toward a phenomenology of the immediate normative life-world in which the behavior of human individuals is embedded. This is why we can interpret such studies as movements starting from a critical assessment of structural functionalism that continue with elements of pragmatist sociology and approach a phenomenological type of sociology.

Subcultures of Delinquency:
Albert K. Cohen and James F. Short, Jr.

Albert K. Cohen and James F. Short, Jr. (1958) conceive of delinquent gangs as subcultures that emerge from structural strains in society. Delinquent gangs make up a subcultural milieu that provides solutions to problems of status and self-respect for youngsters inasmuch as the normal solutions of achieving in society are out of their reach. In functional terms, the gang is a phenomenon of the youngsters' adaptation to the structural conflict between valued achievement and the inability to achieve by legitimate means. In pragmatist terms it is a means of adapting to the demands set by the environment in practical conduct. However, Cohen and Short go beyond this functional and pragmatist explanation of delinquent gangs in describing their subcultural milieu and explaining the behavior of their members in terms of conformity to the norms of that subculture. In doing so, they move a step toward the phenomenological explanation of behavior by understanding it as an instance of a regular pattern of behavior embedded in a normative life-world.

Much delinquent behavior is embedded in such a subculture, composed of beliefs and values that are built up in communication between people who are in a similar position in the social structure and live closely together. The delinquent subculture opens up ways of achieving a reputable status within its boundaries as an alternative to inaccessible paths to status achievement that predominate in the wider society. The subculture's paths to status achievement become normal conforming behavior for the youngsters. This also contributes to neutralizing the apparent deviation of their behavior from the dominating law. A youngster is confirmed in the rightness of his or her behavior, which seems to be deviant in terms of the dominating culture.

Cohen and Short distinguish six types of juvenile delinquent subcultures:

1. The parent male subculture. It is nonutilitarian, malicious, negativistic, and versatile. It is oriented to short-run hedonism and group autonomy.
2. The conflict oriented subculture. Composed of large gangs, it is well organized and determined by toughness. The prevailing behaviors are drinking, sex, vandalism, gambling, and stealing.
3. The drug addict subculture. Drug addiction and criminal behavior go hand in hand. The subculture can be organized in two ways: (a) as a

group on the periphery of violent gangs or (b) as an independent group in its own right.

4. Semi-professional theft. Three elements are involved: (a) using strong-arm methods of obtaining money, (b) "fencing" stolen articles, and (c) stealing things for one's own needs.
5. The middle-class delinquent subculture. This group deliberately courts danger and cultivates sophisticated, irresponsible playboy manners and tries to play adult roles in devotion to sex, liquor, and automobiles.
6. The female delinquent subculture. This group comprises mostly women who have trouble in establishing durable relationships with men. They are often objects of exploitation by men and thus become involved in drug addiction and prostitution.

Lower Class Culture and Delinquency: Walter B. Miller

In his study "Lower Class Culture as a Generating Milieu of Gang Delinquency," Walter B. Miller (1958) argues:

> In the case of "gang" delinquency, the cultural system which exerts the most direct influence on behavior is that of the lower class community itself — a long-established, distinctively patterned tradition with an integrity of its own — rather than a so-called "delinquent subculture" which has arisen through conflict with the middle-class culture and is oriented to the deliberate violation of middle-class norms. (Miller, 1958: 5–6)

With this premise Miller points out that we have to understand the particular norms of the lower class and its youth in order to explain patterns of gang delinquency. The latter is a normal outcome of these norms. It is behavior that conforms to lower-class norms — and it has to be explained in terms of this conformity rather than in terms of deviation from middle-class norms. Conformity to his subcultural norms automatically brings the lower-class boy into deviation from middle-class norms. In taking this position, Miller steps farther away from functionalist or pragmatist explanations than Cohen and Short and closer toward a phenomenological approach to studying delinquency.

In approaching his explanatory program, Miller tries to uncover the latent cultural milieu that underlies the behavior of lower-class delinquent gangs. He describes this milieu with concepts that denote so-called *focal concerns* of the lower class and its youth. Focal concerns describe what is important for the members of a subculture, how they see the world, and how they are disposed to act. Miller distinguishes six focal concerns of a lower-class subculture:

1. Trouble. Getting into trouble is partly avoided, partly confers prestige, and sometimes is a covert means of being cared for. It is concerned with law-abiding and law-violating behavior.
2. Toughness. This is oriented to physical prowess, strength, endurance, athletic skill, and masculinity. It devalues softness and female character.
3. Smartness. This is the ability to outsmart, outwit, outfox, dupe, "con," and "take" others and to avoid being outwitted, duped, or "taken" oneself.
4. Excitement. This involves the venture into a world of risks involving alcohol, sex, and fighting. Ventures into excitement often cause trouble, which gives rise to periodic attempts to withstand the excitements of the risky world followed again by periodic involvements in that world.
5. Fate. The course of events and of one's life is interpreted in terms of luck and misfortune.
6. Autonomy. There is an overt rejection of subordination but a covert acceptance of subordination in order to avoid trouble resulting from one's involvement in risky behavior.

These are the focal concerns prevailing in the American lower class. The delinquent gang is embedded in this subculture and contributes to reproducing its focal concerns. Thus it is normal for the lower-class male youngster to join one of the many gangs; it is not a deviation from the focal concerns prevailing in his milieu.

Additional features of lower-class subculture contribute to the youngster's motivation to join a gang. A gang is part of the peer group to which the youngster is committed. The peer group is particularly important for the lower-class youngster because of the weakness of the family. Households are very often female-based. Families are broken. The peer group makes up for some of the deficiencies of the family. It is a much more stable and solid primary group, which gives the youngster (a) a sense of belonging, and (b) status. Its activities demand a high level of in-group solidarity. This binds the youngster all the more to the peer group and to the gang.

Though the gangs are well aware of the law-violating character of their behavior, they carry it out as part of the normal subcultural concerns. The gang fight, for example, frequently involves violations of the law but is nevertheless an outcome of conforming to the concerns for trouble, toughness, smartness, excitement, fate, and autonomy.

Miller summarizes his approach to explaining gang delinquency as conformity to a subculture as follows:

1. Following cultural practices that comprise elements of the total life pattern of lower-class culture automatically violates certain legal norms.

2. In instances where alternate avenues to similar objectives are available, the non-law-abiding avenue frequently provides a relatively greater and more immediate return for a relatively smaller investment of energy.
3. The "demanded" response to certain situations recurrently engendered within lower-class culture involves the commission of illegal acts.
4. The dominant component of the motivation of "delinquent" behavior engaged in by members of lower-class groups involves a positive effort to achieve status, conditions, or qualities valued within the actor's most significant cultural milieu. (Miller, 1958: 18)

Subculture and Contraculture: Milton J. Yinger

Milton J. Yinger (1960) has extended the study of subcultures by introducing what he calls a contraculture in an article on "Contraculture and Subculture." According to Yinger there is an enormous variability of culture within some societies; they entail various subcultures.

Yinger sets out to clarify the term "subculture," which has been used to denote: (a) panhuman phenomena, (b) ethnic, regional, or class enclaves in a society, and (c) countervalues to a dominating culture. He proposes to use the term "subculture" to denote any cultural deviation of a social milieu from a dominating culture and to use the term "contraculture" when the deviating values and norms are in explicit conflict with the dominating culture. In analyzing adolescence, Yinger points first to the fact that this is a social role one has to play in society as an adolescent. In this aspect adolescence is part of a wider social system and still not a separate subculture. However, it becomes such a subculture when adolescents build up their own system of values, interests, games, speech patterns, and aesthetic tastes. Fashion movements can also be part of a particular adolescent subculture. When, however, adolescents are in conflict with the adult world and devote themselves to countervalues, they establish a contraculture.

Delinquent gangs have to be analyzed as contracultures when they arise from frustrations in achieving within conventional society. The lower class and artists very often constitute features of a contraculture.

Techniques of Neutralization:
Gresham M. Sykes and David Matza

Gresham M. Sykes and David Matza (1957) added a further aspect to the studies in delinquent subcultures in an article on "Techniques of Neutralization: A Theory of Delinquency." Their emphasis is on the legitimation of delinquent behavior. According to Sykes and Matza, juvenile delinquency cannot be explained simply as righteous adherence to a countervailing subculture, because most juvenile delinquents do experience guilt and shame. Juvenile delinquents live in the contradiction of approving of the law but deviating from that same law. This is a conflict they have to resolve so that the fact of delinquency can be reconciled with the acceptance of the law: techniques of neutralization. Sykes and Matza distinguish five such techniques:

1. The denial of responsibility means accusing someone else of being responsible for the delinquent act, even the victim.
2. The denial of injury plays down the injuries done to the victim.
3. The denial of the victim defines the delinquent act as rightful retaliation or punishment.
4. The condemnation of the condemners blames the people who condemn the delinquent act as motivated by some malicious intentions.
5. The appeal to higher loyalties places the loyalty to one's friends above the loyalty to other people and to the law.

Critical Assessment

Studies of delinquent subcultures have turned our attention to the embeddedness of behavior in a normative life-world that immediately surrounds the individual and may deviate from the dominating culture or may even be in conflict with that culture. This is called a subculture or a contraculture. Deviant behavior then has to be explained as patterned according to the norms of the subcultural or contracultural milieu. This is a step toward the phenomenological analysis of the life-world underlying any social behavior. Whenever behavior displays a regular pattern within a community, it has to be explained in terms of its embeddedness in such a normative life-world. This is the dimension of social behavior best explained by phenomenological studies. However, such studies need extensions in order to cover social behavior completely. They also have to take into account the reward calculations of actors in order to explain the *variations* in delinquent behavior. This is the instrumental-adaptive aspect of deviant behavior as pointed out by Cohen and Short. The *violence* of deviant behavior needs explanation in terms of the conflict between a contraculture and the dominating culture as emphasized by Yinger. The *continuity* of delinquent behavior needs explanation by the availability of neutralization techniques, as demonstrated by Sykes and Matza. In combining all these aspects we move closer toward a comprehensive explanation of social behavior.

FOUR

THE STRUCTURE OF EVERYDAY LIFE: THE PHENOMENOLOGICAL SOCIOLOGY OF PETER L. BERGER AND THOMAS LUCKMANN

SOCIOLOGISTS IN the United States and in Germany have developed an approach to the social world that gives special emphasis to the processes in which the reality of the social world and its normative structures are constructed by human actors. Their search is less for structures in their formal, objective, and constraining character and more for the construction of meaning in social reality. Studying the procedures by which social actors construct the reality in which they live is the subject matter of this approach. It is called phenomenological sociology, or sometimes social constructionist sociology, because it sees the world as it appears to the human being as made up of phenomena constructed by the human actors themselves. Discovering the basic processes that guide this reality construction is the task of phenomenological sociology.

Structural functionalism and phenomenology share the orientation toward studying the normatively structured aspect of the social world and are thus both different from positivistic approaches, which see the social world primarily in terms of interests, exchange, and money or goals, conflict, and power. The ordering of the social world and how it comes about is their preoccupation. Thus, they try to understand the normative and regular patterns of social life. However, they do it in different ways. Whereas the structural functionalist reveals the functions behind the normative structures that exert their constraint on the human individual, the phenomenologist discovers the essential meaning common to certain patterns of life and the processes by which people create this meaning.

Intellectual Roots: The Phenomenologies of Edmund Husserl and Alfred Schutz

German philosopher Edmund Husserl (1859–1938) laid the philosophical foundations of phenomenology. He carried on the tradition of nineteenth-century German idealism in the most idealist manner (Husserl, 1900–1901/ 1928, 1950; for translation, see 1960, 1970).

In Husserl's philosophical view the construction of reality is the work of the consciousness of the human being. A person relates to reality in what Husserl terms the "natural attitude," which takes things perceived in the environment as factually given and ordered objects. However, the ordered appearance of these objects to the human being is a construction of his or her consciousness, which is basically intentional in its relationship to the world. The consciousness of the individual approaches the world with intentions and thereby constructs reality as it appears to him or her. If I approach the behavior of someone else with the intention of watching that person's attacks on me, I will see the preparation or carrying out of an attack in any of his or her behavior. The task of phenomenology is to reconstruct the generally occurring processes in which the human being's consciousness constructs reality as it appears. In this way the human being "apprehends" reality, that is, he or she takes that reality into possession.

The construction of reality proceeds according to the method of phenomenological reduction. The individual orders perceived reality according to the pure form, the invariant properties of his or her consciousness and thus reduces the perceived world to that which appears essential to the person according to the given properties of his or her consciousness. The phenomenologist reconstructs this process and carries out a phenomenological reduction of the individual's reality construction to the essence of the invariant properties of his or her consciousness, eventually reaching the transcendental ego, which is the locus of the unity of consciousness and the origin of the ordering work of reality construction. Every aspect of the empirical world that is not a part of the properties of pure consciousness is "bracketed" and set aside as something that is not relevant for the study of the reality constructing processes of pure consciousness.

Because Husserl locates the ordering of knowledge in the formal properties of pure consciousness — in the transcendental ego — he has a problem explaining how different egos can construct a common world view. In his later work Husserl (1950, for translation, see 1970; written 1929/1932) introduced the concept of the life-world in order to deal with this problem. The life-world is the ordered world out there as it appears to the human individual in his or her natural attitude. Because people live in a community, they share a common horizon that is their life-world. However, Husserl conceived of the life-world very much from the standpoint of the individual consciousness. Inasmuch as I see the other person as someone like myself, I assume that he or she has the same view of the world. Thus there is still a reduction of a collective phenomenon, the life-world, to the working of the individual consciousness.

The German philosopher Alfred Schutz (1899–1959) introduced Husserl's phenomenological approach into sociology. He emigrated to the United States in the early 1930s and from then on taught at the New School of Social Research in New York. He also practised law as a counselor until 1956, when he finally concentrated exclusively on his scholarly work. Schutz was much more concerned with the *social* construction of reality than with its construction by the human being's consciousness (Schutz, 1932, 1962, 1964, 1966; for translation, see 1967).

According to Schutz, an individual lives in an *Umwelt*, a *Mitwelt*, a *Vorwelt*, and a *Folgewelt*. The *Umwelt* is constituted by relationships to people who are the immediate companions of the individual. These are we-relationships. The *Mitwelt* is constituted by relationships to more remote types of actors and structures to which the individual relates via typifications. These are they-relationships. The *Vorwelt* is constituted by the individual's relationships to his or her predecessors and is realized in his or her interpretations of the past. The *Folgewelt* is constituted by the individual's relationships to events in the future in his or her action carried out with the intention of bringing about effects in the future.

Of the four worlds, the *Mitwelt* is the one that is most structured according to prevailing typifications by which the individual's view of the world and his or her corresponding action is guided. This is the paramount subject matter of a sociology that tries to discover how human actors construct their reality in a common social process. The *Vorwelt* is open to sociological analysis, because the sociologist can reconstruct what happened in a definite way in the past. The *Folgewelt* is less accessible to sociological analysis, because of the indeterminacy of future events. The *Umwelt* is characterized by the idiosyncracies of persons and thus no object domain for generalizable sociological knowledge.

Schutz elaborates the idea that human action involves *meaning* and *motives* that have to be kept separate. He distinguishes between *objective* and *subjective meaning, because motives* and *in-order-to motives.* The meaning of an action is determined by the interpretation given to that action. The objective meaning of an action is determined by the interpretation intersubjectively given to that action that corresponds to intersubjectively shared typifications. The subjective meaning is the actor's own interpretation. Motives are reasons for action. A because motive is a reason for an action determined by a past history of events. An in-order-to motive is a reason for an action that stems from the purpose of realizing a certain end in the future. Thus, an attack made by one person against another may have the objective meaning of an unjustified attack insofar as nobody can see grounds for it in the light of commonly shared patterns of interpreting attacks. It may have the subjective meaning of a justified attack for the actor, because he or she sees the object of his or her attack as a danger. The because motive may be a history of bad and dangerous encounters with the other actor. The in-order-to motive may be the goal of preventing the assumed opponent from starting his or her own attack.

The major conceptual device elaborated by Schutz is the concept of the life-world, which became the master concept of phenomenological sociology. The life-world is made up of all those typifications that people share and use in their common practice. This is the locus of their reality construction. The life-world is an intersubjectively shared world, a stock of knowledge composed of typifications, skills, useful knowledge, and recipes for viewing and interpreting the world and for acting in that world. It is the security base for our lives. From here we explore the world according to systems of relevance. We mobilize the social stock of knowledge in our action according to its relevance for the situation. Inasmuch as human action explores the world concretely beyond the realm of the known and onward into the complexities of its unknown features, the recipes of the social stock of knowledge are eventually challenged. Instead of being in accordance with the unproblematic, taken-for-granted world, the human being faces problems. The world becomes problematic and necessitates the reconstruction of the social stock of knowledge. However, the starting point for this reconstruction is always the existing life-world stock of knowledge, which exerts its structuring effect on any new construction of social knowledge. The human individual can never escape the life-world in which he or she lives.

For phenomenological sociology, the paramount methodological postulate is that the sociologist has to reconstruct the actors' social construction of reality. The sociologist must make sure that his or her reconstruction can be confirmed by the constructions of the actors themselves. Therefore, qualitative studies of the life-world of actors with mountains of interview data characterize the work of the phenomenological sociologist. According to Schutz, the sociologist's constructions have to be *relevant* to the life-world of the actors under study; they have to be *adequate* with regard to their own reality constructions; they have to be *consistent* in themselves; they have to be *compatible* with corroborated existing knowledge or disconfirm and replace that knowledge; and they have to be *subjectively meaningful* to the actors who are the subjects under study.

Schutz was well aware of the shortcomings of Husserl's monadic phenomenology, which tried to explain the ordered nature of the world as it appears to the individual in terms of the formal properties of a single individual's consciousness. Elaborating on Husserl's concept of the life-world, he went on to demonstrate the intersubjective nature of that life-world.

Nevertheless, for Schutz, the structures of the life-world were something given, a precondition that determined how the individual experienced the world, namely, in an ordered way. What he did not address sufficiently was the question of how this intersubjectivity is constituted in processes of association and communication. Instead, it is treated as something that imposes itself on the individual as an external constraint (see Habermas, 1981: 194–205). This is also apparent in Schutz and Luckmann's coauthored work on *The Structure of the Life World* (1973).

The work of Schutz has been brought to the attention of a wider sociological public by the collaboration between a representative of the German academic world, Thomas Luckmann, and a representative of the American academic world, Peter L. Berger. The publication of their work, *The Social Construction of Reality* (1966/1971), initiated a growing recognition of sociological phenomenology as a distinctive approach to understanding and explaining the social world. This is why we center our examination of this paradigm around the work of Berger and Luckmann. Thereby, we will see that Berger and Luckmann slightly move away from Schutz's concentration on reconstructing the social world as an objective phenomenon that is best exemplified and structured by the typifications of a common culture toward their interest in the life-world as an everyday world that immediately surrounds the individual and is constructed with day-by-day interactions. They emphasize much more the subjective aspect in the construction of the life-world. For them, objective structures and subjective construction of structures meet in the life-world, whereas for Schutz, the life-world is more a part of the objective structure that imposes its constraint on the individual in his or her subjectively motivated action. In Schutz's view, there is a realm of private knowledge, but this knowledge nevertheless has its sources in the social stock of knowledge. Biography is always shaped by the existing culture of the life-world. There is a realm of freedom where the individual can act as a free agent. But this is no more than a place where he or she makes choices among different plans and projects offered by the social stock of knowledge.

In distinction to this objectivist conceptualization of the life-world as a structure that predetermines the space of action, Berger and Luckmann tend to conceive of it as an area of life where existing structures and their subjective constructing meet. In their view, the life-world is much more an everyday matter that is defined in interaction day by day. It is an overlapping area of *Umwelt* and *Mitwelt*, if we take Schutz's terms in order to characterize Berger and Luckmann's position, whereas for Schutz the life-world is closer to the *Mitwelt*. In a sense Berger and Luckmann have introduced an element of American symbolic interactionism into phenomenological sociology and thus turned it away from Schutz's German-based search for objective meaning structures toward a more American view of everyday meaning constructions in everyday situations. The German sociology of the life-world (*Lebenswelt*) has become the American sociology of everyday (negotiated) life. Nevertheless, Berger and Luckmann have preserved elements of the more objectivist approach, even by way of borrowing from Durkheim, so that their phenomenological sociology keeps enough distance from symbolic interactionism to be recognized as a distinct paradigm of sociological analysis. Let us now look at their approach in detail.

Berger and Luckmann's approach to phenomenological sociology is not as concerned with the goal-attaining and profit-maximizing strategies of social actors as are conflict and economic theories. Their primary concern is how social actors see and come to see and interpret social reality. The order of this reality is viewed not as resulting primarily from strategic action but as an order that emerges from interpreting the world in common social practices. The order of social life is not a question of accommodating conflicting goals and profit-maximizing behavior; it is a question of arriving at a commonly shared view and interpretation of social reality and of understanding one another. How social actors construct such a commonly shared view and interpretation of social reality in common practices is primarily of interest for the phenomenological way of asking the question: How is social order possible? And this is indeed an approach that places that question at the center of its interest. Compared to the Parsonian statement that social order cannot solely emerge from power struggle or economic transaction and needs to be rooted in the commonly shared values and norms of a solidary community, phenomenology tries to go deeper into a description and analysis of this world of commonly shared values and norms. This world is seen as an overall interconnected social reality, as social actors see and experience it and deal with it.

Everyday Life Reality

Social actors see, experience, and deal with different social realities. However, there is one paramount social reality that provides the basis for all these different realities. This is the reality of everyday life (Berger and Luckmann, 1966/1971: 33–42). Any analysis of the order of social reality has to investigate its roots in the reality of everyday life and in the common, everyday practices of people. The reality of everyday life is ever present; it constantly imposes itself on the individual, who cannot escape its rule. Because of its ever-present nature, taking on the view of everyday life becomes the natural, self-evident, and unquestioned attitude of the individual. This *ever-present, inescapable nature* is the first feature of the reality of everyday life. It is quite natural for us to get up in the morning like everyone else, to go to school or to work, to use a toothbrush in order to clean our teeth, to have breakfast, lunch, and dinner at certain times, to have guests visiting in the evening rather than in the morning, to have the car washed on Saturday, to go out on Friday or Saturday, to like clean air and clean water, to wait to be seated in a restaurant by the waiter or waitress, to keep a certain minimum distance from other people in public places, to come on time to an appointment, to keep quiet in a sacred building, to not interrupt a speaker before the floor is open for discussion, to pay in dollars and not in bananas at the supermarket. These facts of everyday life seem to us quite natural, because we do not know of realities that would be contrary in character. We experience these facts from day to day; our whole day is minutely determined by these facts. They are constraining and natural facts at the same time — constraining because we cannot escape them without losing our orientation in life and natural because we cannot imagine a different reality.

In the terms established by Emile Durkheim (1895/1973b), everyday life is an integrated set of social facts that have an objective character, exist like things, are external to the individual, are unchangeable and impose their pressure on the individual, and are universally binding in character. They are binding for all of us.

Berger and Luckmann say that the individual's consciousness is in a wide-awake state of tension in everyday life because of its imperative character. However, this assumption seems to be rather questionable, because the tension of consciousness normally increases as one experiences unexpected new events and remains low with the normal process of everyday life where everything happens the same way as usual.

The second feature of the reality of everyday life is its *ordered character*. In Berger and Luckmann's terms, people "apprehend" it as an ordered reality, which means that people see, interpret, and acquire it as such a reality in the course of their normal lives. Events do not occur casually in everyday life; they occur in a specific order that regulates life from morning to night. There is a recurring temporal order to what I do and whom I meet from morning to night: family, colleagues at work, the cashier at the supermarket, my tennis partner. I have a specific weekly program at school or at work that tells me what I have to do at what time. When I talk to someone, the grammar and vocabulary of the language we use predetermine an ordered way of doing this. Everyday life is filled with programs that give my life a specific order, programs that I did not establish by myself but were in existence long before I started to follow them in my life. This order did not arise out of my own voluntary decision nor does its continuation depend on it. It will continue to exist even after the end of my life. It is this independence of the individual's subjective decision that makes the reality of everyday life completely predictable. We can expect a lot of things and order our personal life according to these things, because we know they will happen independently of the will of the people involved in these events as social actors. Everyday life is, in this sense, an objectified reality, a reality that exists independently of subjective will and that places its own stamp on that will.

The organization of everyday life for me is *centered around the here and now* of my bodily existence and presence. I am most familiar with what surrounds me immediately: my family, my neighborhood, my workplace, my friends at the sports club, my city, my country. What is immediately accessible to me is the closest circle of my everyday life; this constitutes my center around which are assembled realities of growing remoteness. The farther these realities are from the center of my everyday life, the less I am interested in them and the less I know of them. I am completely familiar with my home, fairly familiar with my neighborhood and my workplace, somewhat less familiar with my city, less familiar still with my country, and distinctly unfamiliar with foreign countries. These are different zones of everyday life differing in their closeness to me. I can approach the remote zones only by starting from my center and by relating them to that center.

The reality of everyday life is an *intersubjective, commonly shared world.* I share this world with all those people with whom I associate regularly. Because of our close association we experience the same events, act in the same situations, and have many chances mutually to confirm and disaffirm what we see, what we know, think, and want. Because we share life in this way, we are able to come to a common view and understanding of it. The commonsense view of the world is rooted in this sharing of life. With my family and with my friends and my community I share a common view and understanding of the world, because we live together and mutually support each other in arriving at such a view and understanding. It is much more difficult to reach a concretely determined intersubjective view and understanding of the world when people are more remote from each other. Here the intersubjective world resides much more in abstract typifications.

In everyday life we *take reality for granted.* The natural attitude assigns the experienced reality of everyday life a self-evident character. Nothing is questioned. Everything appears to be quite natural and common. Because we live in the reality of everyday life like fish in water, we cannot imagine alternative realities. The regularities of everyday life are something we need just like each breath we take. The natural attitude of everyday life does not leave room for doubt about whether something is real or unreal, right or wrong. Things are taken to be unproblematic, because the routines of everyday life provide solutions for everything that can happen within its confines.

However, this does not mean that I am unable to experience new facts and would never be confronted with new problems. There are always such new events that interrupt normal proceedings. This endangers the security I have within the confines of the reality I take for granted, and it calls for strategies to cope with that problem. Suddenly, there are problematic elements in my life. The student confronted with a new question he or she has never dealt with, the mechanic confronted with a machine he or she has never seen, the mother who suddenly sees her child resisting her advice—these people see the unproblematic proceeding of everyday life interrupted and see themselves confronted with something problematic. How can they cope with this situation? From the point of view of the natural attitude of everyday life, they can cope with this problem only by establishing links between the unproblematic core of everyday life and these problematic events. After the first disturbance, the student, the mechanic, and the mother see similarities between things they know and their new experience. They solve their problem like they have solved other problems. The student does so by recalling a similar question; the mechanic recalls working on a similar machine; the mother recalls noticing similar behavior in her child. In this way they incorporate the new events into the existing body of everyday life. The problematic is assimilated into the unproblematic. In a sense this is phenomenological reduction: reducing the problematic to the unproblematic, the unknown to the known, the unfamiliar to the familiar, incorporating every new experience and event into the body of the commonly shared and self-evident reality of everyday life by establishing links of similarity and common meaning.

Certainly our world does not consist only of the reality of everyday life. Moreover, what is everyday life for some people may be a remote reality for me unless I have a close relationship to these people. There are also many realities that are shared by only a certain number of specialists, for example, the realities of the different sciences. In Berger's and Luckmann's terms these are *finite provinces of meaning*, because their existence is limited to a small set of specialists; whereas the reality of everyday life does not have such narrow limits. It is the basis all people in a society share, and it embraces all those finite provinces of meaning within its confines. Whenever we endeavor to get to know something of such a specialist's world we do so by way of an excursion that starts from the reality of everyday life and returns again to this reality after a while. Such specialists' worlds can become a regular part of social reality only if they can be linked to the language of everyday life. If the sociologist were unable to explain the meaning of basic terms by using everyday language, sociology would never gain new adherents and be established as part of societal knowledge. I may describe "playing a social role" as performing actions in a certain position, for example, as a student, teacher, guest, or host, according to the expectations people direct in a society at people who are in such a position. In doing so I make use of everyday words in order to explain the meaning of the sociological term "social role," which is a part of the finite province of sociological language. Teaching sociology to undergraduates constantly involves such back-and-forth references between the reality of sociology and the reality of everyday life.

Everyday life is *structured spatially and temporally*. This world has a spatial and temporal order. There are specific places for doing specific things at home, in public places, and at work. At home, each member of the family may have a room where he or she has a private sphere or only some members may have such a sphere. There are also rooms for cooking, eating, sitting around, working, and bathing. Any reorganization of this order according to which rooms are used is a reorganization of the socially ordered world. The same holds true for the temporal order. Day, week, month, and year imply a specific temporal order in which different things are done. The temporal order of breakfast, lunch, and dinner cannot be reversed at will from day to day. We cannot turn the volume up on our stereo as loudly as we want in the middle of the night.

Social Interaction

The way in which I come to share the world of everyday life with others is social interaction (Berger and Luckmann, 1966/1971: 43–48). The closest form of social interaction is face-to-face interaction. The roots of social interaction as such are formed at the beginning of our lives in the interaction between mother and child. In face-to-face interaction, the other presents him- or herself in full reality. As interaction grows ever closer and continues, I get to know more and more of the other person's subjectivity. We can establish an intersubjectively shared world that entails much of our personal subjectivity.

On the other hand, the more superficial the contact between two actors becomes, the more they see each other only in specific aspects that are relevant for the situation—only as certain types of people, not as concrete persons. We make use of *typificatory schemes* in order to minimally identify the other person. For example, when I encounter a man at the gas station, I may first see him as a typical American who is able to enter conversation spontaneously and to exchange cards. From the card I learn that he is sales manager at a company that produces furniture. I assume he is a typical salesman and evaluates people according to their budget for consumption. After some time I realize he is very entertaining but also respectful with regard to my person, has a liberal political opinion (which I may regard as untypical for a salesman), cares a great deal for his children, prefers a simple lodge to a luxury hotel, and so on. As we talk to each other for a longer time, my first typification becomes more and more modified and is replaced by a picture of a concrete person. However, I have less chance to engage in such conversation the more interaction remains guided by typificatory schemes, which become the more anonymous the farther removed the partner of interaction is.

The image I have of people I have never actually met is an anonymous one. There is a progressive anonymity in our typificatory schemes the more remote the people are with whom we interact or about whom we have some opinions without having had the chance of meeting them. Typificatory schemes make remote worlds accessible to us. Without such typifications we could not act beyond the limited sphere of our closest relationships. The more social life expands beyond these close circles, the more it becomes ordered according to typificatory schemes with progressive anonymity.

Language

A further device that leads social life beyond face-to-face interaction is *language* (Berger and Luckmann, 1966/1971: 49–61). Language originates in everyday life and in concrete situations of social interaction; however, in distinction to the very special bodily expressions of feelings in specific situations, language transcends human subjectivity. The expression of sadness in my eyes when I say goodbye to a close friend can be understood in this situation only by the two of us. It cannot be transmitted to another situation at another place and to other people. Yet the phrase in my letter to my friend, "I was very sad when you were leaving last Sunday," is something that can be read again in different situations and places and at very different times by many different people. It is knowing the meaning of sadness in a situation of separation that allows us to recall that situation as many times as we want. The language phrase "I was very sad when you were leaving last Sunday" is an objectified expression or an objectification of the very singular light in my eyes and of my inner feeling at that time. The phrase can be used universally and understood by everybody who has learned that language.

My feelings in the situation cannot be transmitted beyond that situation. Language is an objective system of signs; inner feelings remain subjective in character. Because of its objective character, language has a generalizing and leveling effect on the expression of feelings. It is a general typification of feelings that can be very different on the subjective level. My feeling of sadness could have been very different from the feelings of my friend at the time he or she was leaving me. Language as an objectified social fact equalizes the expression of feelings and constrains us to express feelings in words other people may understand but which are inadequate for expressing our true feelings. However, the other side of this coin is the enormous expansion in the experiences, feelings, wishes, opinions, and attitudes that can be conveyed by the use of language with universal character. Language is an objectified system of signs or symbols that can be detached from their origin; the meaning can therefore be understood independently of the situation of origin.

Language is organized in the same way as social reality is organized in general. It originates in everyday life in which we speak everyday language.

This is the root of every more specialized language. Any specialized language can be understood in a society only when its special terms can be explained in everyday language. Language is the receptacle containing our social stock of knowledge. Only the knowledge that is set into language, particularly written language, can be transmitted from generation to generation. Language is ordered in degrees of familiarity; we are very familiar with our everyday language and knowledge, but we are less familiar with languages and knowledge the farther they are away from us. Accordingly, language and knowledge are differentiated in terms of relevance for me. What immediately surrounds me has greater relevance than things at a remote distance.

Society as Objective and Subjective Reality

Thus far we have seen how the reality of everyday life appears as an imperative, ordered, intersubjective, self-evident, and unproblematic world, ordered spatially and temporally and objectified in typificatory schemes and language. Human conduct is constantly ordered by these features of everyday life, which does not leave to the individual any decision on how to act. It is a pre-established program that everybody carries out in everyday action without imagining any alternatives. This view is opposite to the view of economic and conflict theory, which presupposes that the individual is always in the situation of making choices between alternative goals and means according to the principles of maximization or optimization of ends. There is no such choice in much of our daily conduct, because this conduct only carries out a pre-established program. Whenever such choices are made, they occur on the basis of the everyday order about which we do not decide. This everyday order exists before any individual begins to make choices. This pre-established character of everyday life cannot be fully explained in terms of economic and conflict theories. The phenomenological approach has much more to say about this feature of everyday life.

What we have learned from Berger and Luckmann so far is what this order of everyday life looks like. We have a description of it; and this description tells us that there are features of everyday life that cannot be traced back to economic transactions or power struggles. We now want to know the processes that contribute to producing and maintaining this order of everyday life. According to Berger and Luckmann, these are institutionalization, legitimation, and socialization. The processes of institutionalization and legitimation produce society as an objective reality; the process of socialization establishes society as a subjective reality within the individual personality. It is important to know that institutionalization, legitimation, and socialization do not play a fundamental part in conflict and economic theorizing; if anything at all, they can have only a derived status. In the phenomenological perspective, they are at the center of sociological analysis.

Institutionalization

Berger and Luckmann (1966/1971: 65–109) approach the question of institutionalization with a consideration of the remarkably low level of determinacy of human conduct by the instinctual steering of behavior. Compared to animal behavior, that of the human being is determined and regulated by instincts to only a very minimal degree. Whereas animal behavior is mainly—though not exclusively—regulated and held in balance by instincts, human behavior would be very chaotic if it were regulated only by the existing instincts. Human life would be full of frustrations, because there would be no connection between human conduct and the satisfaction of needs. Nevertheless, human conduct is not so chaotic as one would expect it to be from the point of view of its instinctual regulation.

The first origin of this regulation of human behavior is the much more highly developed ability of the human being to learn compared to other animals. We can call this the extraordinary plasticity of the human individual. His or her behavior can be shaped in many different ways according to different kinds of learning within different environments. The human being can live in very different environments and develops different behavioral schedules within those environments. On the other hand, human conduct is normally more regulated than would be expected from the point of view of individual learning. As Durkheim put it, the individual is a bundle of drives leading in many different directions. Just learning how to satisfy these drives does not establish an order within the individual that tells him or her how these drives relate to each other and how to satisfy them. According to Durkheim, there is nothing within the individual that would allow the establishment of such an order from within. In this respect, the individual is dependent on an order that surrounds him or her and guides his or her conduct. This is what social order gives to the individual. Being born into an existing social order frees the individual from many decisions on how to act and from disorientation with regard to the question of how to act in a specific situation. This Durkheimian answer to the question of why the human individual needs social order is also the answer given by Berger and Luckmann.

The question then is, How does social order originate? According to Berger and Luckmann, it is produced by human action. Whereas a human being is a social product and needs social order, and society is an objective reality that imposes its pressure on the individual, the objective reality of society has nevertheless been produced in human action. What interests us here is how social order comes to be produced in human action. This is the point at which we have to turn to the processes of institutionalization and legitimation.

Institutionalization is a process by which casually and freely chosen forms of human conduct acquire a binding character for the individual in a certain social context, milieu, group, or society. What may formerly have been a matter of choice is no longer open to voluntary decision; it is obligatory for everyone. For example, some friends meet at a bar on Friday night on several occasions. These are casual gatherings of people who get on well together. However, over time, the group may establish restrictions: newcomers are no longer accepted; people who do not come regularly hear from their fellows that they are unreliable and have to fear being closed out of the group; and latecomers are reminded of the regular time of meeting. In this way it becomes binding to be a member of the group in order to have access to the meetings, and it becomes obligatory to come on time and regularly to those meetings. This is the process that turns a casual gathering into an institution. An institution consists of rules that regulate a specific type of behavior among certain people who build up a milieu, group, organization, or society. The members of the above-mentioned group are obliged by the established institution to limit the people who meet regularly on that day to those already in the group, not to talk to outsiders, and to come on time and regularly. Their associational behavior is guided by that institution.

What is the basis of the obligatory character of the institution? Berger and Luckmann are not very clear about this, but we can add that there must first be a growing feeling of mutual belonging coming from spending evenings together. This feeling of mutual belonging establishes the commitment of the individual to the group that implies solidarity to the group and its members in cases of needed support and loyalty to its opinions and directives. Inasmuch as the feeling of mutual belonging, commitment, solidarity, and loyalty have been established, the group's rulings acquire an obligatory character for its members, who feel obliged to carry out its rules. This does not mean that there are no cases of deviance. However, it does mean that the group reacts uniformly toward deviant behavior by applying sanctions: reminding the deviant of the rules, reducing his or her status in the group, looking upon him or her as an unreliable person, denying him or her certain privileges, and excluding him or her from group action and finally from the group itself. These are the qualities of a group that make its rules a firm institution and not just a set of casual expectations of behavior.

Berger and Luckmann point out three major aspects that are involved in the process of institutionalization—habitualization, sedimentation, and tradition—together with social roles representing the institutional order.

Habitualization is the process in which causal behavioral conduct takes on a regular form and can be expected in similar future situations. Our example of turning the casual gathering of people into a regular meeting of friends is a case of habitualization. After some casual gatherings, it becomes a habit of the group members to come to the same place on Friday night. Casual behavior is now turned into predictable behavior. Habitualization frees people from the insecurity that accompanies any new encounter and behavior. The individual can rely on what he or she knows and is led to maintain established lines of conduct. Conversely, it is easier for the partners-in-interaction of the individual to be able to predict his or her behavior when that individual follows habitualized lines of conduct. Therefore, both parties to the interaction are inclined to support a movement of conduct toward habitualization.

Habitualization is effective only for those people who themselves take part in the process. It cannot be transferred to other people. Thus, an institution would always be terminated when those people who had been engaged in establishing it left the scene. However, we know that many institutions have lifetimes well beyond those of their founders. The process that allows this expansion of an institution's existence can be called *sedimentation*, which turns habitualized behavior into a tradition. Sedimentation occurs when an institution becomes articulated in language, either in oral or written form. If the friends who meet regularly on Friday night not only gather on the basis of habit but also talk about it, telling each other to meet regularly on Friday night and saying nobody should be late, the institution becomes more apparent to them. Let us assume they form a club whose objective is to play pool on Friday night at a certain place. They may also go on to write a constitution for the pool club. This constitution specifies the conditions under which one can be a member, determines membership fees, and regulates the behavior of the members. As soon as these rules have been written down, they can be transmitted to any new member in the same way.

As time goes on, there may be a complete turnover in the membership, but the pool games on Friday night at a specific place can continue to exist, with the same behaviors taking place. In this way the institution of playing pool at a certain place on Friday night becomes independent of its creators and of any persons. It is simply a *tradition*, which is regularly occurring behavior rooted in the remote past. We can say under these conditions that people have always played pool at that place on Friday night as long as we can remember, and they will do so in the future. When we ask why people do this, the answer is: Because that is what they have always done. Tradition is the firm basis of an institution, because it limits questions about the reasons for doing things in a certain way. The answer that it has always been that way cuts off any further enquiry. Certainly, a tradition has to be kept alive by regularly doing what the tradition is. It is only because people regularly meet at that place on Friday night that the tradition is firmly established in people's consciousness. Both past and present merge in this way, and it is this merging of past and present that makes a tradition so stable.

Lack of a past to which we can refer our present actions and lack of actualization in present action hinder the firm institutionalization of forms of human conduct.

A further major element of institutions is their *representation in social roles*. When the pool club has formally established membership, has established rules of membership, and hands out membership cards, the social role of being a member of the pool club has been created. Beyond the role of ordinary member the club can add the roles of president, council member, and novice. These roles then represent the institutional order of the club's pool playing. The definition of social roles establishes responsibilities for the maintenance of an institutional order. It is not just regularly observable behavior that occurs here; now we have individuals who take over roles and, in this way, responsibility for at least part of the institutional order. Being a member, council member, or president of the pool club implies an obligation to care for the club and its institutional order. On the other hand, the definition of these roles makes the corresponding behavioral conduct independent of concrete persons. People may go; roles remain the same. Social roles are objectified behavioral conduct required of everybody who takes on these roles.

An institutional order can be more or less *integrated or segmented*. The institutional order of modern societies is much more segmented and loosely integrated than that of primitive societies. The segments of the institutional order of modern societies represent subuniverses of meaning, constituted by specific roles and languages. The roles and languages of science, the market, bureaucracy, family, and religion are very different from each other. For these to be integrated, their specific languages and knowledge need to be retranslated into the commonsense language and knowledge of everyday life.

Institutional orders undergo processes of *reification*. This means that people conceive of the institutional order as something that is naturally given, has always been so, and will always be so in the future. The institutional order appears to be a natural fact, unchangeable by human will. People forget its creation and continuation by human action or may even see the institutional order as a reflection of a higher divine order. Reification is a process that stabilizes institutions and curtails individual freedom to create, re-create, and change institutions.

Legitimation

Thus far we have explained the process of institutionalization that establishes social order. The maintenance of this order depends largely on the process of legitimation to which we now turn our attention (Berger and Luckmann, 1966/1971: 110–46). Legitimation answers the question, Why is social life controlled by specific rules making up institutional orders? Why should members of the pool club come regularly to their meetings? Why doesn't the club allow each person to decide when and how often to come? This may be a question asked by a member who feels too much pressure regarding his or her participation in the meetings. Answering this question in such a way that the asking member consents to the rule and feels obliged to conform is giving a legitimation of that practical imperative. Any institution is set up by a number of such practical imperatives. Giving these practical imperatives the status of legitimacy is the task of processes of legitimation. Such a process of legitimation assigns a normative dignity to the practical imperatives and cognitive validity to the objectified meanings of the institutional order. In this way a practical rule is transformed into an obligatory norm; practical knowledge is transformed into universally valid knowledge. Deviation from the obligatory norms and the valid knowledge is no longer just the wrong way of doing and knowing something but a violation of a sacred order.

Legitimation always traces the validity of a particular practical imperative or of practical knowledge back to more general norms and knowledge that are held as valid. The rule of regular participation in meetings in the pool club may be legitimated by saying that the members coming to the meeting would not find enough partners to play with and would therefore be wasting their time if only a small number of the members came. As a result, the club would break apart. This legitimation refers to the norms of not letting down one's fellow members and of keeping solidarity as well as to one's interest in not losing the chance of having pool partners. A person who feels committed to the club and to the norm of not letting fellow members down or who has an interest in maintaining the group will then accept the legitimacy of the practical imperative of regularly taking part in the meetings if he or she is convinced of the correct derivation of the practical imperative from the more general norms and interests. The person must be convinced that not regularly participating in the meetings would really violate the norms of solidarity and trustworthiness or really break the club apart. With regard to the norms, he or she must see that those more general norms entail the practical imperative as a special instance in their meaning; with regard to the interest in maintaining the club, he or she must believe in the empirical statement that irregular participation breaks the group apart. This is the structure of any legitimation of practical imperatives and knowledge: deriving practical imperatives from more general norms by way of subsuming particular norms as special instances under the meaning of more general norms, or by way of relating them to more general interests with the help of empirical statements. In the case of practical knowledge, this knowledge is subsumed under more general knowledge as a special instance.

The legitimation of an institutional order can reach different levels of generality: immediate legitimation, rudimentary theoretical propositions, theories, and symbolic universes. In our pool club, the legitimation of regular participation by referring to solidarity, trustworthiness, and interest in maintaining the group would be an *immediate* one. A *rudimentary theoretical proposition* would involve postulates about the proper conduct of people in a voluntary association, thereby legitimating solidarity and trustworthiness themselves with statements such as: "No group can exist without the solidarity, loyalty, and trustworthiness of its members. Thus, in order to maintain group life we have to expect those qualities from our members." This is a rudimentary theoretical legitimation of solidarity, loyalty, and trustworthiness in group life.

The next level of legitimation has the maintenance of voluntary groups as its object domain. Here we need more *generalized theories* of the proper organization of human life, such as: "The human being needs a type of organization that reconciles human freedom and the human need for social order. Voluntary associations are the best type of organization of human conduct that meets the two requirements of freedom and order, because the individual has a choice between alternative associations, but within the association he or she is committed to its institutional order."

Finally, we reach the level of even more general *symbolic universes*, which address the values of human life themselves. Here the reconciliation of freedom and order in human conduct has to be legitimated, for example, in statements like: "It is the very nature of human existence to be free and nevertheless to live in community with one's fellows. The two can coexist only in social organizations that reconcile freedom and order."

Climbing up the different levels of legitimation, we began by tracing back regular participation in group meetings to solidarity and trustworthiness and continued by tracing back these norms to the maintenance of group life in a rudimentary theory of voluntary associations. Then we traced voluntary association back to the reconciliation of freedom and order in a theory concerning the proper organization of human life. Finally, the reconciliation of freedom and order was traced back to the ideas of the nature of human existence, thereby reaching the level of a global symbolic universe. In this process we reached ever more general statements that made their predecessors on the lower levels their object of legitimation. The generalization starts with a specific group, goes on to voluntary association in general, continues with the more general question of social organization of human life, and reaches the most general level of the nature of human life as such.

On the level of the nature of human life, we become involved in the most general debates, which involve the symbolic universes of mythology, theology, philosophy, and science. The more this level is involved in processes of legitimation, the more these processes become dominated by specialists of legitimation: *intellectuals*. The mystagogue, the theologian, the philosopher, and the scientist are the corresponding intellectual types that interpret and apply the ideas of symbolic universes to concrete questions. The intellectuals can take on more or less powerful positions in society. In general, because the continuity of an institutional order depends on recurrently linking back its rules to the most general ideas of a prevailing symbolic universe, intellectuals as specialists for that task have an influential position in society. How powerful they are depends on the degree to which they make up a closed group that has monopolized the interpretation of the world in a society and on the degree to which this group has direct access to political power and leadership. In ancient China the *literati* civil servants were a very powerful and influential group of intellectuals because they presided over both the means of interpreting the world via the teachings of Confucianism and the means of political rule via bureaucratic positions. In ancient India, the Brahmins were very influential but less powerful than the Chinese *literati*; they had monopolized the interpretation of the world via the teachings of Hinduism, but the means of political rule had been monopolized by a special military caste, the Kshatriyas.

In our modern society intellectuals are still influential but not very powerful, and they are always confronted with competing ideas. They preside over the means of interpreting the world, but they do not form a homogeneous group interpreting one single symbolic universe. They are split into many different types and groups of intellectuals interpreting competing subuniverses of meaning: theologians of different religions, philosophers or scientists of different schools or in different disciplines, journalists of different political leanings, and experts in different professions. As an additional constraining factor, they do not occupy strategic political and administrative positions. Modern societies have a pluralized symbolic universe and a pluralized group of intellectuals.

This does not mean, however, that processes of legitimation have become unimportant. The contrary is true. The number of people who are concerned with intellectual matters and who participate in processes of legitimation has constantly grown. Therefore, questions of the legitimacy of institutional order are much more frequently raised. What is different now from more homogeneous ancient societies is that there is much more competition in this process and hence much more change. What seems to be legitimated today will appear illegitimate tomorrow, because the critique of institutions becomes ever more sophisticated.

In ancient societies there was mostly a dominating interpretation of a single symbolic universe that had to struggle only with heresies. Most "heretics" lived in a state of suppression and were able to challenge the

dominant ideology and intellectual group only in extraordinary revolutionary situations where the regime could be overturned. In modern society there
is no such stable relationship between dominant ideology and heresy; rather,
there is a permanent competition between more or less influential ideologies and intellectual groups. The legitimation of an institutional order thus
depends on two interrelating factors: the ability of intellectuals to provide
consistent and powerful interpretations of the world that can beat their rivals
and the ability of intellectuals to get access to positions of influence and
power in the mass media, bureaucracies, political parties, and governments.
The maintenance or change of institutional orders is therefore an outcome
of the interplay of legitimation and power struggle.

Socialization

Thus far we have been concerned with society as an objective reality,
and we have been looking at the institutionalization and legitimation of social
order as processes by which this objective reality is produced and reproduced.
However, there is also a subjective side to this process: society as a subjective reality. This implies the questions, How is society represented in the subjective consciousness of human individuals? and, How is society shaped by
the subjective consciousness of these individuals? These questions are at
the very core of an analysis of the process of socialization.

Berger and Luckmann (1966/1971: 149–204) distinguish primary and
secondary socialization. Primary socialization takes place in early childhood,
normally within the family, while secondary socialization continues this
process in different settings at school, at work, or with friends.

A first characteristic of *primary socialization* is that there is only one
family, one social milieu, and one reality of everyday life in which a child
undergoes that process. The child has no choice of parents, family, milieu,
and reality. The child incorporates this reality only through constant contact with his or her parents and family. No access to reality is independent
of their mediating function. Therefore, the relationship to parents and family
is most important for the process of socialization. The primary precondition for incorporating social reality is the identification of the child with
what are termed "significant others": mother, father, brother, sister, aunt,
and uncle. What the child learns of social reality — knowledge of facts and
norms — is immediately linked with his or her picture of and affection for
those significant others. Only inasmuch as the significant other awakens the
child's positive affection and trust will the child identify positively with the
surrounding social reality and incorporate knowledge and standards of conduct with a positive feeling.

There is not only an identification with significant others but also a
growing self-identification in the process of socialization. The child learns

to identify him- or herself in terms of what these significant others call the child and say about him or her. Positive self-identification cannot emerge from this process if there is no positive identification transmitted from the agents of socialization to the child.

In the process of socialization, the relationship to significant others is expanded more and more to encompass the relationship with the so-called generalized other. It is increasingly a case not just of a mother getting angry if her child does not come home in time for dinner. Others also get angry. The child learns that everybody thinks like this. Thus the consciousness of "Mom does not want me to come late to dinner" turns to the generalized consciousness of "Others get upset if I am late." This state of consciousness is backed up not only by Mom, but also by everyone, that is, by a generalized other. In this process the subjective consciousness of the individual takes on more and more general views and merges with the objective reality of society.

This process continues in *secondary socialization*, although it involves a greater choice of significant others and also more confrontation with different views of the world. Secondary socialization implies relationships to significant others that cannot be as deeply affectual as those of primary socialization. There is much more formality and anonymity in this process. Therefore, it does not implant its realities in the individual as deeply as the process of primary socialization does. Change in these realities and how they are incorporated into the individual's identity takes place much more easily than any change in the primarily acquired subjective consciousness and identity. This is all the more true the more the individual is confronted with competing world-views, as is the case in the ongoing process of secondary socialization in modern societies.

Nevertheless, the maintenance and change of subjective realities, consciousness, and identity always involves not only the change of conceptual schemes but also the change of significant others. There is always a social basis to changes in subjective consciousness. On the other hand, no subjective consciousness will be maintained without its constant revitalization in the association with like-minded significant others. A personal religious ethic will be maintained as a lively ethic only if it is constantly revitalized in the association with the religious community. A change of personal religious ethic will take place only if it is backed up by association with a new religious community. On the level of ideas, the individual needs a plausible reinterpretation of his or her biography in order to establish a new consistent identity. Every change of identity is a process of resocialization of the individual, which implies the reorganization of his or her consciousness and social contacts. Maintenance and change of identity both take place in constant conversation with others and go hand in hand. Attempts to maintain a certain self-concept often necessitate the modification of inconsistent attitudes.

The Problem of Understanding Meaning:
Phenomenology and Hermeneutics

Phenomenological sociology tries to understand the meaning of the world in which human actors live rather than to explain events in that world causally. Therefore, the methodological problems involved in understanding (*Verstehen*) the meaning of the world of human actors have always been of major interest to phenomenology. This is an interest that is shared with the humanities (*Geisteswissenschaften*) and their method of hermeneutics, which has been used for interpreting texts since Dilthey (1883/1968, 1924/1964) raised the question (see chapter 9, volume 1).

The phenomenology of Edmund Husserl (1900–1901/1928, 1950) played a major part in further developments. For Husserl the master device for attaining objective knowledge in cultural studies was the method of phenomenological reduction. Phenomena under study have to be stripped of everything that is irrelevant to the question raised by way of "bracketing" and setting aside those irrelevant aspects. In this way one comes to the essence of a phenomenon. Ordering the pure properties of consciousness located in the transcendental ego produces objective knowledge in the sense that it is ordered in character. Inasmuch as knowledge can be traced back to the formal properties of pure consciousness it is objective for the human being. Husserl failed with his approach in that he was not able to account for the objectivity of knowledge in terms of its intersubjectivity. There was no way from the single consciousness to knowledge that is objective in the sense that it is held to be valid intersubjectively. When he introduced the concept of the life-world in order to cope with this problem in his later work (Husserl, 1950; for translation, see 1970), he did so from the standpoint of the individual consciousness. Intersubjectivity is created inasmuch as I live with other people in a common life-world in which I assume that the other persons are like myself and have the same view of the world as I do.

Generations who followed Husserl had to struggle with this problem. Martin Heidegger (1927/1949) tried to surpass Husserl's phenomenology with his existential philosophy, which was concerned with the question of how the human being's understanding of his or her existence (*Seinsverständnis*) constituted human existence. Alfred Schutz (1932, 1962, 1964, 1966) moved Husserl's philosophical phenomenology centering around the human consciousness toward a sociological phenomenology that aims at revealing the modes of socially constructing intersubjectively shared knowledge. In doing so he took up the concept of the life-world introduced by Husserl in his later work. For Husserl and Schutz the life-world is the ordered world as it is experienced by the individual in his or her natural attitude of taking that world for granted. For Husserl the objectivity of the individual's knowledge of that world has to be proven by reducing it to the formal properties of the human consciousness. For Schutz the objectivity of the individual's knowledge of that world has to be proven by arriving at a common, intersubjective interpretation between the observer and the observed actors who make up the world under study. This is the position also taken by Berger and Luckmann. Further widely read contributions to this problem have been provided by Schütze (1975) and Schütze, Meinefeld, Springer, and Weymann (1973).

In its approach to revealing the preconditions of intersubjectivity in processes of understanding the world of actors, phenomenology merges with hermeneutics as the method of interpreting texts. Phenomenology starts with the meaning construction of the human consciousness and goes on to search for the conditions under which intersubjective meaning between the consciousness of two or more human individuals can be constituted. Hermeneutics starts out from the meaning that is located in a text and goes on to search for the conditions under which the human individual can arrive at a true understanding of the text's meaning. For phenomenology, meaning is first a subjective and then an intersubjective phenomenon. For hermeneutics, meaning is first an objective phenomenon residing in a text and only secondarily also a subjective and intersubjective one inasmuch as the human individual understands the meaning of a text and shares this understanding with other individuals.

Any hermeneutic interpretation of a text has to deal with the problem of the so-called hermeneutic circle. This means that we always have to start with a preconceived idea of the meaning of the text and then understand every single part in the light of our preconceived idea of the whole. However, every single part that we read also contributes to our understanding of the whole. The circle is unavoidable but does not necessarily militate against any chance of revising our idea of the whole by our understanding of single parts. Some parts of a text may be easy to understand from the point of view of our preconceived idea; other parts may not. The latter can give us reason to revise our understanding of the whole. In this process, hermeneutic work is a permanent back and forth process between the preconceived ideas of the whole and single parts. The parts are the test cases of our preconceived idea, similar to the way in which single facts are test cases for general scientific theories.

The classical source of hermeneutics is the work of Wilhelm Dilthey (1883/1927, 1924), introduced in volume 1, chapter 9. A major advance in the methods of hermeneutics has been made by Hans Georg Gadamer (1960, for translation, see 1975), who took the work of Heidegger (1927/1949) as his starting point. According to Gadamer, we come to a valid understanding of texts inasmuch as we are able to establish a virtual conversation (*Gespräch*) with the author of a text. In doing so we start from a certain pre-understanding (*Vorverständnis*) and aim at a mutual understanding with the author of the text. This procedure is completed by embedding our conversation with the author of the text in his or her conversation with his or her contemporaries and our conversation with our contemporaries. The more the conversation proceeds, the more the horizon of the text's author with his or her contemporaries, on the one hand, and the horizon of the text's interpreter and his or her contemporaries on the other will merge with one another. The interpreter and the author alike will ultimately live within a common life-world. This is the point of valid understanding. In this process the interpreter assumes a perfect character of the text as long as he or she can correct mistakes from the point of view of perfect understanding of the text.

The development of hermeneutics after Gadamer's work has shifted toward a closer analysis of the reception process from the point of view of the reader of a text. Jauss (1982, 1989) has elaborated a new "reception aesthestics" that concentrates on the horizon of expectations with which a reader approaches a text.

Beyond the work of German hermeneutics, important contributions to the interpretation of cultures have been made by Claude Lévi-Strauss (1962, for translation, see 1966), Roland Barthes (1967, for translation, see 1983), Mary Douglas (1966, 1973), Paul Ricoeur (1971), Clifford Geertz (1973), and Marshall Sahlins (1976).

This is the major methodological thrust of contemporary *phenomenological* and *hermeneutic* approaches in the social sciences. They aim at understanding the meaning of the cultural world and see social action, social structure, and society primarily as embodiments of meaning that either is constituted intersubjectively or derives from a given text (see Winch, 1958; Grathoff, 1973; Apel, 1979; Bleicher, 1980; Sica, 1986; Brown, 1987, 1989). Phenomenology and hermeneutics are mostly concerned with understanding given life-worlds and texts in their structure. This is why they have been dealt with here under the heading of the structure of social action. However, inasmuch as they are extended to studies of the rationalization of culture and of cultural dynamics, as is the case with Weber's cultural studies, Habermas's discourse theory, or Luhmann's systems theory, on the one hand, or symbolic interactionism and the dramaturgical theory of communication, on the other hand, they reach right into the symbolics of social action.

Summary

1. The more social action is rooted in the routines of everyday life, the more it will proceed according to a stable and regular order.
2. The more everyday life's reality is an imperative, ordered, intersubjective reality that is taken for granted, the more it has ordering effects on social action.

3. The more social reality is objectified in typificatory schemes, social roles, and language, the more social order will continue to exist independently of its creators.

4. The more the human individual, who is instinctively unordered and open to the world, is required to display order in his or her personality and behavioral conduct, the more the individual needs guidance by social order.

5. The more an institutional order is backed up by the commitment of members to a social group or society, their solidarity, and loyalty, the more obliged the members will feel to carry out its rules and the more uniformly they will react to deviations by applying sanctions reestablishing the validity of the institutional order.

6. The more social order is backed up by institutionalization involving habitualization, sedimentation and tradition, and social roles as representatives, the more stable and predictable it will be.

7. The more a social order becomes reified, the more it will continue against the will of people.

8. The more human action becomes objectified in social roles and language, the more it produces society as an objective reality.

9. The more objectified social reality imposes itself on the individual, the more it will make mankind a social product.

10. The more an institutional order corresponds to more basic and generally held ideas, the more it is viewed as legitimate.

11. The more an institutional order can be traced back from immediate legitimation to rudimentary theoretical propositions, theories, and symbolic universes, the more it will continue to exist independently of particular changes in interests and norms.

12. The more an institutional order is backed up by mythology, theology, philosophy, or science, the more it will be considered as legitimate.

13. The more an institutional order is considered as legitimate, the longer it will continue to exist.

14. The more homogeneous an intellectual group is as interpreter of the world, the more homogeneous the symbolic universe is, and the more it has monopolized the interpretation of the world, the deeper and more effective will be its influence on the legitimation of social order.

15. The more an intellectual group has access to positions of political power, the more effectively it will turn its world-view into institutional orders.

16. The more effective primary socialization is, the more the objective reality of society will be represented in the subjective reality of the individual.

17. The more positively a socializee identifies with significant others, the more he or she will incorporate the social reality mediated by those others in his or her subjective consciousness and identity and the more the socializee will see him- or herself as others do.

18. The more the relationship to others becomes extended, the more the view of others will be generalized.
19. The more an individual relates to generalized others, the more his or her subjective reality merges with the objective reality of society.
20. The more an individual associates with significant others, the more he or she will maintain those views that are consistent with theirs and change other views in order to make them more consistent with theirs.

Critical Assessment

In an evaluation of Berger and Luckmann's sociological phenomenology, the first point to note is that it gives us important, indeed vital, access to the cultural world that surrounds social life and provides the stable basis that is essential for regularly ordered and predictable social action to take place. None of the positivistic paradigms of conflict and economic theory can replace this phenomenological contribution to sociological knowledge in its own terms. However, sociological phenomenology itself has its shortcomings and cannot serve as an all-embracing approach to the social world. Its main contribution to sociological knowledge is its analysis of the roots of social order in everyday life and its production and reproduction in processes of institutionalization, legitimation, and socialization. These are the processes that produce and reproduce the stable and predictable elements of social life. In the view of sociological phenomenology, we approach a sociological object by studying the everyday rules guiding social life, the commitment of members to a social group, their solidarity and loyalty making the rules binding for the members, and the processes of institutionalization, legitimation, and socialization.

The object domain of sociological phenomenology is systems of meaning. The relationship between different elements of these systems and between these systems and social behavior is not one of cause and effect but one of reason and logical consequences. Pointing out such relationships in an analysis of the rules guiding everyday life and of the processes of institutionalization, legitimation, and socialization is not a simple matter of drawing up formalized propositions of cause and effect. Rather, a close analysis of meaning relations is what is required. We cannot take it as a shortcoming of sociological phenomenology that it cannot be reduced to a parsimonious set of propositions like conflict and economic theory. This difference is an inevitable part of the difference between hermeneutic and positivistic approaches to sociological theory. In terms of hermeneutic phenomenology, we *understand* an action or a rule in its meaning by tracing it back to the meaning of everyday life's cultural systems and more global symbolic universes. In terms of positivistic economic and conflict theory we *explain* an action by tracing it back to a cause according to a proposition on the empirical relationship between cause and effect (Hayes, 1985).

However, social life *in toto* is not as stable and predictable as it would appear in the view of sociological phenomenology. It throws much less light on the processes that undermine and destroy this stability. Economic calculations and transactions that contribute to permanent changes of behavior lie outside the conceptual apparatus of sociological phenomenology. The same is true of the power struggle and domination that leads to the enforcement of goals even against existing traditions and for argumentation and discourse that not only legitimate existing institutions but also criticize and delegitimate them and give rise to a permanent change of institutional orders in the direction of ever more broadly conceived values like freedom, equality, rationality, and mastery of the world. The revitalization of order in everyday action always involves processes of economic calculation and transaction, domination, and discursive reasoning. In our example of the pool club, the members will not continue to participate if they do not expect a further maximization of their utility from that behavior; the club can be turned toward much more far-reaching goals by an effective leadership that uses power in order to secure the compliance of the members. In this way the club could be changed into a criminal organization dealing in drugs. The club could also be changed by an enlightened membership debating on the proper rules of conduct leading to more freedom of individual decision with regard to participation or to more equality between members in enjoying the privileges of the club and taking part in its decisions.

Even the production and reproduction of the cultural world from the point of view of an approach that concentrates on this part of social life cannot be explained in all its features in terms of sociological phenomenology. It does not give enough access to the contingencies and variable elements of everyday life practices themselves. This is what we can learn from Goffman's analysis of the strategic aspects of everyday interaction and from Garfinkel's ethnomethodological studies of everyday practices (to which we will turn in the next chapter). The approach also fails to point out sufficiently how cultural change is initiated in procedures of conversation and discourse involving criticism of institutional orders and a change toward more rationality. This is the object domain of symbolic interactionism and discourse theory with which we will be concerned later on in this book.

Yet another area where there is a lack of clarity is in how Berger and Luckmann deal with the question, Where do the roots of an intersubjectively upheld order of everyday life lie? Berger and Luckmann do not sufficiently address association, community, solidarity, consensus, and uniform sanctioning of deviations in addition to communication between members of a community as the most forceful roots of an intersubjectively upheld order of everyday life. Their analysis tends instead to disintegrate into a conceptualization of the structures of everyday life, like external objects, on the one hand, and the perception, recognition, and internalization of these structures by single individuals. What is not revealed sufficiently is the constitution of intersubjectivity in the cooperation and communication between people who form a community.

Finally, however much hermeneutics and phenomenology have contributed to our knowledge of the preconditions of establishing intersubjectivity of meaning between the interpreter and author of a text, between subject and object, and between observer and observed, they still have not been able to raise and answer the question of how to prove validity claims between them. Whether or not the interpreter of a text is in agreement with the text's author about its meaning is one thing, but whether the two are in agreement about the text's validity claims is quite a different matter. The first aim will be reached by establishing a common life-world; the second, however, requires the claims to be tested in the criticism of a discourse. In order to deal with this problem we have to go beyond phenomenology and hermeneutics to consult Habermas's (1981: 152–200) theory of testing validity claims in discursive procedures.

Related Work

Phenomenological sociology has been successful in inspiring qualitative studies of life-worlds over the past thirty years. Among those who explicitly promoted this progress in the United States are George Psathas (1973, 1979) and Harold Garfinkel (1967). Both have built upon the approach to construct what is called ethnomethodology (to which we will turn in the next chapter). There is some overlap between phenomenology, ethnomethodology, and symbolic interactionism in the United States because they share the American way of life. This is why these approaches are sometimes grouped together under the heading of the interpretive paradigm that is juxtaposed to the normativist paradigm in its objectivist and structuralist sense. This is the common thrust of an influential collection of essays representing the "interpretive paradigm" published by Jack Douglas (1970).

Another center of phenomenological sociology is Germany, where Joachim Matthes (1969, 1983, 1985), Richard Grathoff (1973, 1983, 1989), Fritz Schütze (1973, 1975), and Hans Georg Soeffner (1989, 1992) have provided particularly influential contributions to this development. Ulrich Övermann (1979, 1985) has developed an approach of objective hermeneutics out of phenomenological sociology. Objective hermeneutics aims at reconstructing the objective meaning expressed in any particular instance of a biography or a social act. The collaboration of Thomas Luckmann and Peter L. Berger in writing their influential work, which we examined in this chapter, is good evidence of a particular German-American coproduction in developing phenomenological sociology. The Germans are more engaged in the philosophical foundations of phenomenological sociology and in the objective structures of the life-world; the Americans are more interested in the empirical realization of that enterprise and in the permanent production and reproduction of the life-world in everyday situations. This division of labor results from their training in different academic and societal life-worlds, though there is enough scope for overlap between them.

FIVE

THE SOCIAL WORLD AS AN ACCOMPLISHMENT OF SOCIAL PRACTICE: HAROLD GARFINKEL'S STUDIES IN ETHNOMETHODOLOGY

GROWING OUT of phenomenology, a new approach in studying the organization of the social world in the practices of social actors was developed by Harold Garfinkel. Garfinkel's various contributions to this project were assembled in *Studies in Ethnomethodology* in 1967. They investigate the methods according to which members of a society make accounts of the social world that surrounds them and, in doing so, actually make that world. Because each society and each social situation is unique in character, making accounts of these unique worlds is like making accounts of specific ethnic societies. It is like the practice of ethnography. Studies in ethnomethodology, then, examine the methods members of a society apply in doing that ethnographic work; this is the origin of the expression "studies in ethnomethodology." The title of Garfinkel's book expresses the fact that he himself carries out studies on the ethnomethodology employed by the members of a society. Ethnomethodology is not what Garfinkel does but what the members of a society do, and Garfinkel brings this to light. Therefore, it is more precise to call Garfinkel's work "studies in ethnomethodology" and the work of members of a society "ethnomethodology." Nevertheless, in a less precise usage, the term "ethnomethodology" has been used to characterize Garfinkel's sociological approach itself. Here I shall mostly use the terms "studies in ethnomethodology" or "ethnomethodological approach" to characterize the work of Garfinkel and his followers.

Objective Reality as an Outcome of Accounting Processes

Garfinkel starts his project with a critique of conventional sociology. According to this critique, conventional sociology sees social reality as an objective reality in the sense of Durkheim's (1895/1973b) concept of a social fact. In this view, a social fact has to be treated like a thing that is external to the human individual, exerts a constraint on the individual, and is universal in character. It is an objective reality like physical reality. Conventional sociology tries to gain access to this objective reality by applying methods of gathering data, methods such as interviews, surveys, participant observation, and gathering documents on social phenomena. All these methods have in common the fact that they have to rely on accounts given by people, whether these are the accounts of lay people or those of professional sociologists or of both.

A study of rates of criminality that gathers data from the statistics of police departments does not simply "discover" an objective reality of crime rates that is there independently of the practice of gathering data. What appears as objective reality is instead the result of the very process of gathering data. What the professional sociologist or anybody else gets to know are the accounts of criminality rates made by the police and his or her account of the police's accounts. The professional sociologist who gathers data by participant observation produces something qualitatively quite the same as the police's accounts of criminality. Both the police as sociological lay people and the professional sociologist share a central naivity. They assign an objective reality to their accounts that is independent of the accounting process itself. Whatever sophisticated method the professional sociologist applies, he or she cannot overcome the central participation of the accounting process in the construction of reality. It is not that the scientist comes closer to objective reality than lay people; it is just that he or she arrives at a different reality because of the different methods used and because of the different understanding of rationality that stands behind the different methods. What appears as objective reality depends on the methods people use in accounting for reality. Police officers' accounts of criminality depend on the categories they use in coding crime cases, on their interpretation of these categories, on their perception of cases in the light of their understanding of the categories, and on their practical methods of relating cases to categories.

Many contingencies exist in various police departments in gathering the data. Whether an incident is reported as a crime case depends on the interpretation a police officer and people affected give to the case and on their inclination to report a case. Thus, some types of criminality are much more frequently identified as criminal and are more easily reported than others. Physical violations of property rights through theft are more likely to be identified and reported as criminal than violations of property rights through deceit. There is a great reluctance to identify and report sexual delinquency and molestation, abuse, and ill-treatment of women and children, particularly when these acts occur within families. What appear in crime statistics are not acts as such but acts defined as criminal in the process of accounting. Members of society, that is, people witnessing and affected by certain acts and police officers gathering data on those acts, identify and report some acts as criminal and ignore others. They make the social reality of criminality in that society as much as the people who actually perform the acts.

The objective reality as it appears to the members of that society is a product of two sources: people who perform certain acts and people who make accounts of these acts. Hence, the objective reality of criminality as it appears to us is also made by both criminals and people who identify and report crimes. This is the commonsense reality in our society. There is no other commonsense reality, and there is no objective reality outside this commonsense reality. An act that is neither identified nor reported as delinquent in a society just is not delinquent in that society. Delinquency is not a physical thing but an act that has to be assigned the meaning of delinquency by the members of a society. It is an act that exists through a certain meaning, and this meaning is an outcome of an encounter between a physical act and its definition by the performer, by affected people, and by observers who are members of the same society. It is an accomplishment of social practices.

Yet, all this does not imply that there is always consensus on the assignment of meaning to an act and on its identification and reporting. There may be enormous differences between the people who perform an act, those affected by it, those who observe it, and finally those who observe the observers of the act. The latter might be professional sociologists who analyze the crime statistics of police departments. Let us take the case of a Californian who was seized by the police while strolling in a middle-class white neighborhood at night. He was accused of vagrancy. He himself defined his act as a stroll, which is not at all delinquent. People in the neighborhood who witnessed his stroll at night may have felt threatened by him, because usually nobody goes for a stroll in an American middle-class neighborhood at night. In another country this is much more usual, and therefore nobody would be irritated by someone "strolling." The people affected by his behavior in the American middle-class neighborhood identified the act as threatening vagrancy. The police did the same and reported the act as vagrancy.

The professional sociologist who observes the police officer's reporting act may come to the conclusion that the officer identified and reported the act as vagrancy because the man did not look like the normal, white, middle-class man on a stroll. If he had looked like that, he would not have been accused of vagrancy. The professional sociologist sees the accounting process of the police influenced by prejudices about appropriate white, middle-class appearance and behavior and may try to influence the process of accounting when drawing up his or her account by inserting a bias toward more tolerance regarding appearance and behavior. Whether the sociologist succeeds in doing so depends on his or her influence on the white middle-class neighborhood and on the police. Any success in this direction leads to a change in the method of formulating accounts of certain types of behavior and thus to a change in social reality as it appears to us. In many cases, however, the normal process of accounting works according to the views prevailing in the community and in the group of agents of that community who perform the task of identifying and reporting, that is, giving an account of acts as delinquent or not delinquent. In general, the cases can range from the situation where actors, affected people, police, and professional observers (like sociologists, lawyers, and judges) define an act in the same way to the situation where they all give different accounts. In the latter case, no uniform social reality exists; instead, there is a struggle between many different social and subjective realities. What is then binding reality has to be found out in the accounting process of a court decision. Who succeeds in court determines what becomes dominating reality.

The phenomenon that social reality is an accomplishment of accounting processes does not originate solely in the decision between an actor who acts and a public that gives an account of the actor's action. We never get an action simply presented as a physical thing. The actor has to define his or her action. Thus, what we see is a linkage between a physical act and the account of the actor. When a husband presents flowers with the words "I love you" to his wife, the act of handing over the flowers is accounted by him as an expression of love. This is how his act occurs in the world and makes up social reality. We do not receive a physical act from the actor; rather, we receive an accounted act. Even without words he or she conveys a meaning, that is, an account, of his or her action. But of course, this is not the whole story. Whether the presentation of flowers makes up a couple's social reality also depends on the wife's interpretation and on the support both get from the social environment for their interpretation. If a woman answers that her husband's purpose in bringing her flowers is just to distract her attention from his affection for another woman, and if she succeeds in getting more support for her definition, it is her account that constitutes their social reality, independently of whether the husband is attracted to someone else or not.

We can sum up by citing Garfinkel (1967: vii):

> The objective reality of social facts [is] an ongoing accomplishment of the concerted activities of daily life . . .

This view of social reality can be analyzed with reference to five points. First, there is no objective reality transcending the here and now of the very process of accounting in a particular social situation. There are no universal elements of social reality but only particular elements with limited validity. Every expression in language is indexical in character. Second, objective reality as it appears to us is reflected in the practice of accounting. Third, actions in their social context have to be analyzed as practical accomplishments with regard to making up social reality. Every social setting has its own rationale in accomplishing the task of making up social reality. There is, accordingly, no difference in principle between the lay person's and the professional sociologist's access to reality. Fourth, the ethnomethodological approach does not add another particular account of social reality to the existing lay and professional sociological accounts but provides us with the only generalizable knowledge about the universal phenomenon of making social reality with methods of accounting this reality. Fifth, social actors are not "judgmental dopes" whose actions follow the prescriptions of preexisting common values and norms; in fact, they themselves make those values and norms in the very process of making accounts of social reality.

Indexicality

Every account of social reality relies on the use of indexical expressions (Garfinkel, 1967: 4–7). These are expressions with a particularistic meaning; that is, they refer to a particular context that is the only one allowing them to be understood: "here," "there," "yesterday," "I," "he," and "she" are commonly known indexical expressions. I cannot understand what they mean or to whom they refer if I do not participate in the situation in which they are used by an actor. But, as Garfinkel puts it, every term of language bears indexical elements. These are elements that belong to the specific situation in which they are actually used. They can therefore be correctly understood only by participants in that situation. For the police officer who arrested the person in the case we referred to earlier, the term "vagrancy" may have meant walking around wearing dirty clothes and without a recognizable destination. For the professional sociologist in the situation of analyzing the case from his or her point of view, "vagrancy" may mean "living day and night without a job and without income completely on the street and from the street." Both the police officer and the professional sociologist make use of the term "vagrancy" but in different ways and interpretations. "Vagrancy" has a different meaning in their different situations. To understand the term one has to participate in the context, because only the context reveals its meaning.

Because the social world is made up of such indexical accounts it consists in particulars that cannot be universalized and thus cannot be simply "applied" in other contexts in the way of deriving the particular instance from the universal term, norm, or value. They have to be re-created in every new context. Therefore, the process of accounting is always a new creation of social reality, because "yesterday" is a different context from "today." As Don H. Zimmerman and Melvin Pollner (1970) have put it: Social reality is an occasioned corpus:

1. It has no regular and stable elements.
2. Action is a "corpusing" and "decorpusing" activity and not the uniform application of general rules.
3. The elements of that corpus are unique and not generalizable.
4. The production of an occasioned corpus is based on practices of assembling and reassembling.
5. Insofar as members of a society take the social world for granted, they take the occasioned corpus as background, but it is a background that is itself in the process of being remade.
6. Observing members' practices in assembling and reassembling the corpus makes the familiar world look strange. What has been taken as objective reality turns out to be a mere social construction. Thus, we can say that ethnomethodological studies reduce the familiar social reality to unfamiliar practices of making that reality, whereas traditional phenomenology reduces unfamiliar phenomena to the familiar phenomena of everyday life.
7. It is the societal members' practices that create the occasioned corpus. This is the only general phenomenon in a world composed of ever-changing particulars. In the example of a police department's work dealing with vagrancy, the message of Zimmerman and Pollner is that the police officers do not simply and uniformly "apply" the general term "vagrancy" according to general rules of dealing with cases; rather, they create the terms and norms that guide their action in the very process of that action. What "vagrancy" is and what appropriate treatment of suspects is are matters produced in the situation of interviewing a suspect. It is the actual practice of this police officer, here and now, in interviewing the suspect, that defines the meaning of "vagrancy" and "appropriate treatment of suspects" in that situation. The officer's action puts one element into the corpus of the police department's social reality; the action of fellow officers puts another element into that corpus. Their action tomorrow in another situation may erase the elements of today and add a different version of "vagrancy" to the corpus. By acting in this way, police officers constantly assemble and reassemble the corpus that makes up their social reality. It is an occasioned corpus, because its elements are derived by occasional acts that can be replaced by other occasional acts. However, it is always their practice that makes social reality anew. This, at least, occurs universally.

Garfinkel is certainly right when he points to the indexicality of any term of language. However, he also exaggerates. Because there are terms that are widely used in different contexts and because people communicate beyond narrow contexts, the meaning of terms becomes universalized step-by-step. Garfinkel denies the fact that there are universal contexts of communication in the modern world that distinguish their terms, statements, norms, and values from those of narrow and particularistic contexts of communication. They impose their view of reality on the reality views of the narrower contexts. For example, in the 1950s and 1960s, when the Supreme Court of the United States decided against discrimination in civil rights cases, it formulated not just one particular view of civil rights to add to those of the school boards of Southern states but one that was held to be more universally valid, because it was based on a more universal discourse than those of the Southern school boards and states. This more universal view was then imposed on those school boards, which had to carry them out according to the Court's ruling. The schoolboards could not do anything other than carry out the Supreme Court's decision. This is a relationship between a universal norm and a special instance of its application. Certainly, the school boards made many attempts to interpret the norm so that they were able to live with it, but there was no total escape from the universal meaning of the norm; escape was only minimal. But this room left for the particular reinterpretation and re-creation of the norm of precluded discrimination does not imply that there is no relationship between a universal norm and a particular instance.

Another example pointing in the same direction would be the worldwide discourse on human rights. The outcome of this worldwide discourse is a growing universalization of the meaning of human rights, so that it is becoming increasingly difficult for dictatorships and totalitarian regimes to uphold their practices of dealing with people opposed to them according to one particular interpretation of the meaning of human rights quite different from other particular interpretations. The situation is changing more and more in that direction: they cannot provide accepted legitimation of their practices before the universal public engaged in a universal discourse on human rights. They may continue with their practices, but they cannot define them as legitimate practices. Here, too, the universal meaning of certain values imposes itself on particular practices based on universal contexts of communication and discourse. Garfinkel is so preoccupied with his analysis of the indexicality of accounts that he loses touch with reality and reifies his analytical perspective of indexicality to claim that the nature of social reality is nothing but indexical. This is a fallacy of misplaced concreteness. He takes an analytical element of reality for its totality.

Reflexivity

We can derive from the above analysis that social practice has a specific reflexivity (Garfinkel, 1967: 7–9). It occasions a certain social reality and is therefore reflected in that social reality as it appears in documented accounts. These documented accounts are, on the other hand, starting points for further social practice; thus, they are reflected in social practice, however, in the unique way in which social practice reinterprets and reassembles accounts of social reality. Social practice is reflected in accounts of social reality; accounts of social reality are reflected in social practice.

Practical Accomplishments

It is true that every social context has its own rationale and that the accomplishments of actors in giving accounts of social reality have to be analyzed with regard to the contingencies of their social context (Garfinkel, 1967: 9–10). However, this does not mean that there are no elements in social practices that reach beyond a particular context but that some contexts are wider than others and even embrace them within their confines, so that the corresponding rationality of these contexts is also wider and more valid. We can explain Garfinkel's position with the comparison of lay people and professional sociologists in making accounts of social reality. Lay people and professional sociologists both get access to social reality through accounts of that reality. It is not that professional sociologists arrive at a more objective reality than lay people; their realities are not more or less objective, but just different; their methods are not more or less rational, but proceed according to different rationalities. It is, for example, quite rational for the police to identify an act as vagrancy and not as a stroll according to a person's appearance in order to have at least some method of differentiating the two and being able to make decisions that are supported in the community within which they do their work. It is, however, also quite rational for the professional sociologist to identify the behavior of the police as prejudiced and to leave the question open as to whether the behavior was vagrancy or a stroll. In doing so, the sociologist accomplishes the task of preventing the police from making unjust accusations.

The police officer and the professional sociologist belong to different social settings within which each is oriented toward different goals and therefore proceeds according to different rationalities. It is an instrumentalist view of rationality that stands in the background of Garfinkel's statement that lay people and professional sociologists differ not in the degree to which they get access to objective reality but only in the type of rationality that guides their methods of accounting. The police officer's methods are rational as an effective means of arriving at clear-cut decisions that are supported in his or her community. The professional sociologist's methods are rational as an effective means of preventing prejudiced and unjust court decisions. However, the professional sociologist's context of communication may also be wider than that of the police officer and even embrace that context. In this case, the sociologist has not only a different particular rationality compared to the police officer but also one that is wider and more universal and therefore more valid than the officer's rationality.

Accounting

What makes ethnomethodological sociology different from other accomplishments is that it studies — in a transcendental or metatheoretical way — the generalizable methods by which members of a society or a social setting, in a specifically rational way, actually make social reality in their daily practices of accounting that reality (Garfinkel, 1967: 31-34). It seems that the ethnomethodological approach provides us with the only generalizable knowledge, because it overcomes the naive approach to reality and takes on a position that transcends the naive approaches by making the methods inherent in such approaches into its object domain. Whereas the naive approaches create objective reality in processes of accounting that reality, and do so from the always particular view of a particular social situation, ethnomethodological studies reveal this particularity from a universal viewpoint: *Every* account is particular. Moreover, because making social reality through processes of accounting is a universal phenomenon, it provides us with universally applicable insights. In this perspective the ethnomethodological approach is not just one particular perspective beside other particular perspectives; it is not an account of social reality like other processes of accounting. More than that, it makes this process of accounting its object domain and therefore brings to light knowledge that transcends any single accounting process as such.

In truth, however, the achievement of the ethnomethodological approach is based on a retreat to the level of epistemology, that is, of the theory of knowledge itself. In retreating to this level it proposes a sociological epistemology that competes with other epistemologies. On the other hand, it does not compete with sociological theories that try to come to accounts of social reality able to embrace more particular accounts. The ethnomethodological view even denies the possibility of such an accomplishment. But this is just a disclaimer that is not grounded in sound reasoning. Pointing out that social reality is made in processes of accounting and that these processes are bound to particular situations does not preclude the possibility of the methods designed for accounting being improved so that they can cover different particular methods of accounting. Giving up this purpose of scientific inquiry results in complete relativism. Garfinkel makes a good sociological point for such a position of relativism, yet it is not good enough.

From the sociological point of view, the improvement of sociological language and methods relies on the expansion of social situations to the extent that, for the sociologist, the whole world and the whole of history merge in one social situation, because he or she intends to bring together whatever information can be gathered. At least social situations can be more or less narrowly constricted; likewise, there are social situations that are less narrowly constricted than other situations and embrace the latter within their confines. Therefore, their accounts embrace the accounts of the narrower situations and are more universal in character. Thus, pointing out that social situations are different and constitute different realities does not preclude there also being a relationship whereby narrower situations are subsumed under wider ones, which allows the latter to transcend the former in their accounts of social reality. This is the social basis on which universally valid knowledge is approached.

That there is a social basis and that social reality is made in processes of accounting does not imply that there is no progress from more particular to more universal knowledge. Let's take the example of two physicians. The first has patients residing in a small neighborhood, while the second has patients residing in the whole community including that neighborhood. The second thus has a broader basis for accounting reality than the first, not just a different one. His or her basis includes the basis of the first one. Therefore, his or her accounts of social reality embrace the total community and transcend those of the first physician, thereby approaching more universal validity. This is why we do not have to turn to relativism from Garfinkel's insights. They are useful but not a sufficient argument for relativism. Building sociological theories in universal terms is not sufficiently proved to be doomed to failure by Garfinkel's sociological epistemology.

Actors Are Not Judgmental Dopes

We can derive an evaluation from the foregoing analysis. Garfinkel is right when he points to the phenomenon that social action is not just a uniform and unreflected implementation of preexisting norms and values (Garfinkel, 1967: 18–24). Social actors are not judgmental dopes. An action requires actors to give a value or a norm a meaning, and they accomplish that according to the situations in which they act. They allot their meanings on the basis of which interpretation is rational in which situation. Here too, however, Garfinkel takes one element of reality to represent its totality.

Actors have to interpret norms according to their situations, but situations do not just exist side-by-side. They are very often organized in a hierarchical way and in a way in which one situation embraces another and transmits its reality to the particular situations. We have given the examples of Southern school boards and dictatorial regimes faced with the rulings of universal discourse on civil and human rights. They are not judgmental dopes in the sense that they will do anything to interpret the meaning of civil and human rights according to their own interests; however, the people who engage in discourse on these rights are also not judgmental dopes in that they refuse to believe what would be a derivation from Garfinkel's relativism: that Southern school boards' and the Supreme Court's interpretations of civil rights stand side-by-side as two particular meanings of civil rights, and Amnesty International's and dictators' interpretations of human rights stand side-by-side as particular meanings of human rights. They claim that universal discourse is a procedure that makes them able to make judgments about which position is more universally valid.

Cases

Garfinkel has given numerous exemplifications of his main thesis that social reality is the accomplishment of situationally specific processes of accounting reality. One example is the practice of the Suicide Prevention Center in Los Angeles (Garfinkel, 1967: 11–18). The members of that center had to code "unexplained" deaths with a coding scheme distinguishing natural death, accident, suicide, homicide, and categories in-between. Garfinkel demonstrates that the members interpreted the meaning of the scheme according to the particular context in which they acted. They did so according to their specific rationale. This points to the indexicality of the terms. The coders were not able to fill out documents under the coding scheme without inventing ad hoc interpretations of facts. The scheme is made up not of universal categories applied to specific instances but of particular terms that become reassembled in the very process of coding.

In UCLA's Outpatient Clinic students had to fill out coding schemes in order to determine what aspects of a patient's career had led to his or her treatment in the clinic (Garfinkel, 1967: 18–24, 186–261). The students interpreted the coding schemes according to their understanding of the social world of the clinic. This shows the indexicality of its terms. The students turned to the practice of "ad-hocing" in order to work with the scheme. The particular scheme is thus reassembled in a new particular context.

In another experiment, students reported a conversation between husband and wife to another person: first repeating their words, then giving a more extensive interpretation. Asked to make the interpretation more extensive and precise, they were unable to do so. They were not able to generalize completely from the original context to the new context. This is so because of the indexicality of the expressions used in the conversation. The students added only new particular terms to the particular repetition of the words of the couple. The original conversation reads thus (Garfinkel, 1967: 38–39):

Husband: Dana succeeded in putting a penny in a parking meter today without being picked up.
Wife: Did you take him to the record store?

Husband: No, to the shoe repair shop.
Wife: What for?
Husband: I got some new shoelaces for my shoes.
Wife: Your loafers need new heels badly.

Summary

1. The more people make accounts of social reality, the more they will make use of indexical expressions and the more social reality will have a particular, not generalizable meaning linked to a specific social context.
2. The more people make accounts of social reality, the more this reality will reflect the accounts of these people.
3. The more people make accounts of social reality, the more their practical accomplishments in doing so will be guided by the practical rationale of their situational context.
4. The more people make accounts of reality, the more they reproduce that reality in their practical action.
5. The more people make accounts of social reality, the less actors are under constraint to carry out preexisting norms.
6. The more people make accounts of social reality, the more social reality changes according to the changing situations according to which accounts are made.

Critical Assessment

As the formulation of the six propositions shows, Garfinkel makes more postulates that social order has certain characteristics than he points to the specific conditions under which social order really does have a contingent basis, which he universalizes too much. We would have to formulate the qualification that whenever social contexts are structured like markets and involve competition between equals, the processes described by Garfinkel hold true. However, this is not the case in all contexts or at all times. Discourse, communal association, and domination are structures that have very different effects. In pointing out these effects we have to correct Garfinkel's view of social reality.

In a sense, Garfinkel's view of social reality reflects a specific Anglo-Saxon practice: The practice of deciding lawsuits according to common law, which differs from the Continental European practice of codified law. Common law is indeed an occasioned corpus that is assembled and reassembled in any new practical decision. Common law emerges from nothing other than particular court decisions; thus, it is an occasioned corpus of particulars. Continental European codified law is very different, however. It is a system of general norms that is applied to specific instances in court decisions.

Whereas the work of the common-law judge is evaluated according to the criterion of whether he or she has provided for a fair procedure, the work of the Continental European judge is evaluated according to the criterion of a correct application of the objective (!) meaning of the preexisting law. The Bill of Rights of the U.S. Constitution and the work of the Supreme Court have introduced an element of derivation of particular instances from general rules, whereas, in the Continental European legal system the autonomy of judicial decision has introduced elements of making the law by assembling and reassembling particular decisions. In its totality social reality entails both cases, and it is a fallacy of misplaced concreteness to take one of them for the total reality.

In a paradoxical way, Garfinkel's radical theses reflect the methods of making accounts of social reality that are commonly found in American social practice. His accounts of social reality are heavily influenced by the commonsense accounts of that reality prevailing in the particular context of American society. It seems that we need more universal contexts of communication and correspondingly more universally valid sociological approaches in order to overcome these shortcomings of the ethnomethodological approach.

Summing up, we can say that Garfinkel's studies in ethnomethodology are particularly attuned to pointing out the variable contingencies under which the social reality of everyday life is produced. Their message is that the reality of everyday life as it is characterized by traditional phenomenology as a reality that is taken for granted is a very contingent reality that emerges from the ongoing process of people making accounts of that reality. He points out its particularity and uniqueness for every particular social context; it is a reality without any chance of being generalizable. He also demonstrates that this reality does not simply impose itself on actors. These actors are not judgmental dopes who carry out prescribed ways of acting. The actors are always engaged in interpreting norms in a way that is appropriate for their situation, which gives their action a special context-bound rationality. This is why strategies of "ad-hocing" are so important in interpreting norms. These norms are defined in specific ways by ad hoc interpretations appropriate to specific situations.

Thus, Garfinkel gives us insights into the highly variable and contingent nature of elements of social life that seem to be very stable from the point of view of traditional phenomenology: their stability is just made in specific situations and is not something that transcends these situations. Garfinkel points to the production of social order in a nevertheless contingent reality as an outcome of the "concerted activities" of actors in every concrete situation.

However, Garfinkel exaggerates his argument and gets out of touch with elements of reality working against the contingent and variable basis of social order. Applying his view of social reality, we would be unable to explain why certain meanings of social reality remain stable through various situations, because they are controlled by the same community holding up those meanings. A judge acting under common law is in a particular court situation, but he or she is also a member of a community that transcends any particular situation and upholds certain interpretations of the law. Therefore, there will not be so much particular contingency in every new case.

Applying Garfinkel's perspective, we would also be unable to explain why certain meanings are able to claim more universal validity than others: because they result from more universal contexts of discourse. The Supreme Court's discourse is more universal than that of a Southern school board.

Applying Garfinkel's perspective, we would finally be unable to explain why certain meanings can be imposed on actors who have no choice than to carry them out: because these meanings are imposed by way of applying superior power.

If we keep these limitations in mind, Garfinkel's studies in ethnomethodology provide us with interesting insights into the contingent nature of producing social order in social practice.

Related Work

Garfinkel's *Studies in Ethnomethodology* (1967) have stimulated further research particularly in the areas of studying court procedures in dealing with delinquents, doing conversational analysis, and studying procedures in scientific research. He has influenced scholars conducting studies in ethnomethodology as a common undertaking, scholars like Aaron V. Cicourel (1964, 1973, 1974), Harvey Sacks (1963, 1972a, 1972b; Sacks, Schegloff, and Jefferson, 1974), Emanuel Schegloff (1968, 1980, 1987; Schegloff and Sacks, 1973; Schegloff, Jefferson, and Sacks, 1977), Melvin Pollner (1987), Don H. Zimmerman (1970), Lawrence D. Wieder (1973), Karin Knorr-Cetina (1981), and John Heritage (1984). In recent years, Garfinkel himself has particularly studied the processes of knowledge production in the natural sciences together with Michael Lynch and Eric Livingston (Garfinkel, Lynch, and Livingston, 1981).

PART TWO

The Politics of Social Action

Six

THE FUNCTIONS OF SOCIAL CONFLICT: LEWIS A. COSER

THE REEMERGENCE of the sociology of conflict in American sociology in the 1950s is considerably indebted to the work of Lewis A. Coser. His book on *The Functions of Social Conflict* became an integral part of sociology after its publication in 1956. In this book, Coser did not, like Dahrendorf, develop a radical conflict theory of society that places the struggle for power and coercion at the center of sociological analysis. The dependence of the conflict process and its outcome on the power the actors involved can mobilize is not the primary concern of Coser's analysis of social conflict. He does not formulate a theory that relies primarily on the power relationship between conflicting actors and on their ability to mobilize power resources in order to predict the course of conflict. Coser does not construct a conflict theory in this sense. His primary concern is with the integrative functions of social conflict for groups and for society as a whole.

He starts with the observation that the American sociology of the time viewed social conflict primarily as a disruptive phenomenon of society, producing strain and tension, something at deviance with the normal "healthy" state of society needing to be brought under control so that society can function normally. Coser remembers that this wasn't originally the view of the first two generations of American sociology. With their emphasis on social reform, they saw conflict as an inevitable element of the societal process and of social change. Only after sociology became more academic in character and after its empirical branch became concerned with working for business and administration was conflict interpreted as being disruptive in character and being in need of control.

In order to reestablish a much more positive view of conflict. Coser makes extensive use of Georg Simmel's classic treatment of it, originally published in German as *Der Streit* in 1908. He starts each chapter with a statement by Simmel and then gives close analysis of this statement leading to a qualified reformulation. Two types of assumptions on social conflict are considered by Coser: assumptions on the conditions that increase or decrease the intensity of conflict and assumptions on the internally and externally integrative functions of conflict for the groups engaging in it.

Intensity of Conflict

Coser's first assumption on the intensity of conflict derived from Simmel in his proposition 2, which says that a social relationship that provides opportunities to express discontent and to openly settle conflict avoids the danger of being disrupted by accumulated hostility and withdrawal resulting from the continuous suppression of opposing drives. Giving people a chance to express their discontent immediately keeps the intensity of conflict lower than suppressing such discontent until it bursts out after having been accumulated to reach a much higher level. Likewise, safety-valve institutions for acting out hostility within certain limits, which sometimes also distract from the original object of hostility, work against the accumulation of conflict and provide some release, keeping down the intensity of conflict to a relatively low level. However, permanent displacement of hostility prevents people from expressing their discontent and society from changing in a direction that would reduce this discontent. Thus, under this condition, discontent does accumulate after all and becomes all the more violent in character. Summing up these insights we can formulate the following proposition:

1. The more there are opportunities available for openly expressing discontent in a social relationship and the more there are institutions for doing so in a society (including those that allow the displacement of discontent) and the less displacement hinders social change and accumulates the original discontent, the less likely it is that conflict will break out in a highly intense, hostile, and disruptive form.

Another factor that determines the intensity of conflict is the mingling of a specific conflict on mutually exclusive aims, actions, and outcomes with a general hostility rooted in former frustrations among the conflicting parties. Coser speaks of realistic and nonrealistic conflict or elements of conflict in this case. A realistic conflict exists between two parties who cannot attain their goals at the same time and to the same degree—where one party's goal attainment occurs at the cost of the other party's goal attainment. Acting out this conflict is a means toward a specific end. There can be other means of reaching that end. For example, leaving the field to the opponent and looking for gains in another field or making gains after the opponent has been satiated would lead one toward the same goal without having the costs of acting out the conflict. Thus, realistic conflicts will be avoided or kept within narrow limits inasmuch as the actors see alternative means of reaching their ends. However, a general hostility rooted in accumulated frustration cannot be replaced by something else; it is not a means toward an end but an end in itself. It can only be diverted from one object to another object. Its intensity, however, will remain on the same level. We can formulate the following propositions:

2. The more alternatives to acting out a conflict an actor has with regard to attaining a specific goal, the less intensely that conflict will be acted out.
3. The more frustrated an actor is from former experiences, the more intense will be his or her hostility directed toward any object.

The next considerations Coser makes deal with the effects of combining realistic and nonrealistic elements of conflict. First, he points out that according to Simmel's analysis social conflict does not always involve general hostile impulses and that hostile impulses can be expressed without a basis in realistic social conflict. However, the more the two become connected, the more intense the conflict will be. Thus we can formulate:

4. The more realistic social conflict becomes connected with general hostile impulses, the more intensely that conflict will be acted out.

The question that interests Coser then is: In which type of social relationship hostility is most intense in character when it bursts out? Referring to Simmel's analysis, Coser shows that close relationships always entail converging and diverging motivations, harmony and conflict, love and hate. In a relationship in which the partners look for deep harmony, every minor discontent is also a potential source of deep conflict. Love implies hate whenever this love is confronted with disappointing experiences. Neutral relationships, on the other hand, do not involve negative feelings as much, because they do not entail very positive feelings. We can formulate this as follows:

5. Whenever one enters a close relationship, this relationship will feature positive and negative feelings at the same time.

Continuing on this line of thought, we can say that conflict becomes more intense the closer the relationship becomes:

6. The closer a relationship, the more intense the conflict.

The reasons for formulating this proposition are easy to understand. A conflict between very distant parties concentrates only on the specific object of discontent and does not involve the whole person. It is a normal phenomenon to have such conflicts. There is also more tolerance with regard to the behavior of other people in more distant relationships. Those people just do not interest us very much, so we can tolerate much more. We do not expect their opinions to conform to our own norms and show loyalty to us. However, we do expect much more conformity and loyalty of people with whom we have close relationships, so very minor deviations from our expectations give rise to deep disappointment and generate proportionately radical and intense reactions. Thus, when conflict arises in such relationships, it will be fought out with high intensity.

A completely different factor that affects the intensity of conflict is its ideologization. As long as conflict remains confined to a specific object of discontent, for example, two parties in conflict over whether or not to construct a new road, it can be kept within limits. However, connecting the specific positions in such a conflict with a basic ideology transfers the conflict on to a much deeper level of discontent—turns it away from personal opinions that can be more or less appropriate and toward impersonal ideologies. Now it is a question not of how to find an adequate solution, mostly by some compromise, but who is right and who is wrong. Because the clashing ideologies both have to claim truth for their position, there is no midway resolution of the conflict available by way of compromise. It has to be fought right through to the final consequences. An ideology claims absolute truth, and truth cannot be compromised. Thus, we can formulate Coser's proposition 12 in the following way:

7. The more a conflict on a specific matter involves ideological positions, the more intensely the conflict will be fought out.

Internal Conflict and Internal Integration

Thus far, we have discussed Coser's analysis of the conditions that affect the intensity of conflict. We now turn to his analysis of the effects of internal conflict on the integration of social groups and societies.

First, there is the phenomenon that there are always some dissociating elements in social relationships and it is by acting them out in conflict settlement that unity can be reestablished. In loosely structured groups and an open society that allow for conflict settlement in this way, the acting out of conflict is an inevitable element of consensus formation. However, in totalitarian societies, the acting out of conflict would entail questioning the dominant ideology and would therefore tend to result in disruption according to the proposition on ideological conflict. Thus, conflict settlement works as a process of consensus formation only insofar as there is an agreement on basic values and ideological conflict is kept within the limits of this basic agreement. We can formulate Coser's corresponding proposition 7 in this way:

8. The more there are opportunities for conflict settlement in loosely structured groups and open societies and the more there is basic agreement on values and ideological conflict is kept within these limits, the more conflict settlement will result in reestablished unity and consensus.

Continuing this line of thought, we can say that the normal acting out of conflict in social relationships and societies is not a sign of weakness and instability; rather, it is a sign of strength and stability. A strong and stable relationship is much less endangered by conflict than a weak or unstable one. In the latter case, conflict has to be suppressed because of the danger of moving further apart. Thus, the absence of open conflict can be a result of suppression, which is a sign of weakness in the relationship. On the other hand, a strong and stable relationship is not in danger of breaking apart when faced with conflict and can, therefore, leave more room for open conflict. We can formulate Coser's proposition 8 in the following way:

9. The stronger and the more stable a social relationship, the less its integration will be endangered by open conflict and the more room it will leave for openly acting out conflict.

External Conflict, Internal Integration, and Identity

The next set of propositions Coser discusses is concerned with the effects of external conflict on the internal identity formation and integration of the group.

First, there is the phenomenon that conflict with another group makes visible the boundaries of a group, its membership, and the values, norms, and forms of behavior the members of that group share in common. The identity of the group is affirmed and reaffirmed against the identity of other groups. Coser's corresponding proposition 1, part one, can be formulated in this way:

10. The more social groups are involved in conflicts with other groups, the more their boundaries and their identity are affirmed and reaffirmed.

Continuing on this line, we can say that the members of a group are bound together by the conflict acted out against some opposing group. The conflict gives an immediately perceptible emphasis to their common identity and to their distinction from outsiders—it actualizes their common solidarity and common feelings toward each other. To see a fellow member of our group attacked by some outsider affects our feelings of solidarity with that fellow member and causes us to give him or her support. We may have many quarrels with our sisters, friends, party rivals, and co-workers, yet in the face of an attack on them from the outside we do not hesitate to give them our support. We can formulate Coser's corresponding proposition 9 in this way:

11. The more a social group is in conflict with an out-group, the more its internal cohesion grows.

However, the spontaneous solidarity of group members is not the only possible outcome of external conflict. In many cases there may be internal controversies preceding the external conflict, and these controversies are not always set aside by the internal opponents when the external problems present themselves. In this case, the leadership of the group tends to suppress the internal controversies with the support of the group majority in order to be able to react in a uniform way toward the out-group. As a result, the group becomes intolerant with regard to even minor deviations from group opinion and group solidarity. This is increasingly true the smaller the group and the more the group is engaged in persistent struggle with the outside. Finally, established large groups can tolerate a lot more internal deviations because outside conflict does not endanger the very existence of the group. According to Coser's proposition 8, they are under less pressure to suppress internal conflict. In this context, we can formulate Coser's proposition 10 in the following way:

12. The smaller a social group, the less firmly it is established, and the more it is engaged in external struggles with the outside world, the more intolerant it will become internally and the more it will suppress internal deviation and conflict.

Thinking further along these lines, we can imagine that the conflict with an external enemy can serve as a welcome device for group leaders to strengthen internal cohesion and to suppress deviation and conflict within the group. That can be particularly expected in groups that are not firmly established from within, lack spontaneous consensus, and are weak and unstable but nevertheless have a leadership aiming to bind the group together with whatever means at hand. Rigidly organized groups also fall into this category. They cannot tolerate internal deviation and conflict and will tend to suppress them by invoking a conflict with an external enemy. It is also possible to turn the group's attention toward an internal dissenter in the face of external conflict in order to invoke the group's pressure for conformity within. We can formulate Coser's corresponding proposition 11 in this way:

13. The more rigidly a social group is structured and the weaker and more unstable its spontaneous solidarity, the more its leadership will invoke conflict with an external enemy and/or an internal dissenter in order to mobilize the group's pressure for internal group conformity.

External Conflict and External Integration

We are now left with Coser's propositions on the integrative effect of external group conflict upon the external relationship between social groups.

First, there is the second part of his proposition 1, which is concerned with the phenomenon that conflict between groups contributes to accentuating their position within and relationship to society at large. Because the conflict between the groups continuously reaffirms their boundaries, mobility from one group to the other becomes minimized; thus the existing social structure is stabilized. We can formulate Coser's proposition 1, part two, in this way:

14. The more social groups in a society continue to be in conflict, the more they will reaffirm their boundaries and the more they will minimize social mobility and thus will stabilize the existing social structure.

Conflict also has unifying effects for the relationship between the antagonists. First, the acting out of conflict brings the antagonists together and establishes at least a minimal amount of mutual association and even commonality. The antagonists begin to share a common situation that can be the beginning of a growing relationship moving beyond conflict, even into the realm of solidarity. Former enemies may get to know each other in this way and develop a mutual respect for one another. This is the associational basis for establishing rules of conduct between the conflicting partners. The more such rules actually are established, the more orderly the acting out of conflict will be and the more the two parties will be able to further establish links leading beyond violent conflict. Without this mingling of conflict settlement with human association invoking a sense of solidarity, no mutually accepted peace could arise from violent conflict.

On the other hand, conflict acted out under the guidance of common rules very often brings together people and groups who really need each other. This is the case with all competition in sports. Sporting competition brings people together to establish relationships between friends. Furthermore, conflict settlement as it is established in Common Law procedures is the origin of norms based on conflicting parties having arrived at some new agreement. And conflict with deviators from norms brings the existence of these norms to a new awareness and into the consciousness of people, thus re-creating the social bond. We can summarize Coser's corresponding proposition 13 in four hypotheses:

15. The more people or groups associate in settling conflicts, the more they also establish social bonds between one another that give rise to mutual respect and concern and to the establishment of common norms of conflict settlement.
16. The more people associate in regulated sporting competition, the more they establish relations of friendship.
17. The more a society acts out the conflict on norms, the more it will establish new norms, thereby creating new social bonds.
18. The more society acts out conflict with deviators, the more it reaffirms its norms and the existing social bonds.

A further consequence of the acting out of conflict is the interest of a conflicting party in the unity of its opponent. The reason is that a unified opponent is more predictable in behavior than a divided one. Conflict settlement with the leadership of a divided group does not always secure peace with the other part of that group. We can formulate Coser's corresponding proposition 14 in this way:

19. The more groups are interested in predicting the behavior of their opponents, the more they will be interested in their unity.

In addition, conflict establishes and maintains a balance of power insofar as acting it out informs each group about the other's strength and this leads to efforts to meet the opponent's resources of power. Without such a steady test of power the relationship may easily come into disequilibrium without being discovered by the parties of conflict until the conflict really bursts out. We can formulate Coser's corresponding proposition 15 in this way:

20. The more groups test their power mutually in conflict settlement, the more they will be able to watch their opponents' power and thus establish a balance of power.

Finally, conflict reaffirms associations and coalitions or gives rise to new ones. This is the case because conflict with an opposing group will bring a group closer to others who are similarly opposed to it. Furthermore, groups in conflict with an opponent will explicitly seek the support of other groups. This leads to associations and coalitions on the part of the opponent too, thus creating an extended web of associations and coalitions. These associations and coalitions will last longer when they are rooted in former relationships and in common characteristics. We can formulate Coser's corresponding proposition 16 in the following two hypotheses:

21. The more a group is in conflict with an opposing group, the more it will reaffirm existing associations and coalitions with other groups or will establish new ones.
22. The more associations and coalitions reach beyond the specific cause of helping each other and involve earlier relationships and common views, the longer these associations and coalitions will last.

This is the analysis of social conflict Coser presents in his *Functions of Social Conflict* in 16 propositions. He has supplemented this analysis by a collection of essays, *Continuities in the Study of Social Conflict*, published in 1967. These essays do not change the major thrust of Coser's view; they just give more commentary and an expansion and application of the view formulated in the earlier book. We therefore can confirm our formal presentation of his analysis of social conflict by reference to the propositions presented in the earlier book.

Critical Assessment

Coser's view of social conflict is not one of conflict theory that works with a concept of power at the core of its conceptual frame of reference. Instead, Coser is concerned with conditions determining the intensity of conflict that do not reside in the power mobilized by the parties in conflict; he examines the consequences of certain forms of conflict settlement beyond the outcome of conflict itself. He shows how openness in articulating dissent (which is like an open *market* for articulating opinions) reduces the intensity of conflict, whereas the involvement of general hostility, ideology, and closeness of relations intensify conflict. Markets open chances for articulating dissent and prevent the accumulation of suppressed conflict. Aggressive hostility rooted in personal frustration introduces unspecified aggressive energy from the human personality into otherwise specific social conflicts, thus heightening those conflicts. Ideology closes the mind and sets limits on the ability of conflicting parties to turn to other means and to compromise. This is a cultural element exerting its influence on conflict. A communal element influencing the intensity of conflict is the closeness of social relationships.

Looking at these influences on the intensity of conflict, one can see that they are not political in the strict sense and do not lie inside the power mobilization process of the conflicting parties. Here we have features of markets, personalities, cultures, and communities that exert specific effects on social conflict, thereby determining its intensity. In offering his theory, Coser provides a valuable extension of the conflict perspective by these elements that are primarily treated in theories concentrating on markets, personalities, culture, and community. What he does not point out explicitly in any of his propositions are the factors internal to the power game that affect the intensity of conflict. Here we would have to expect an increase in conflict intensity if the conflicting goals are noninterchangeable. With the diminishing number of alternative goals and means and with the amount of power available on both sides:

23. The less interchangeable the goals and means involved in a conflict and the greater the power that can be mobilized, the more intensely a conflict will be acted out.

Furthermore, we would have to distinguish between intensity and violence as Dahrendorf has emphasized and Coser has agreed with in his *Continuities in the Study of Social Conflict* (Coser, 1967: 3). We would expect strong intensity of conflict with all the above-mentioned factors present but little violence the more the parties of conflict are committed to common norms of conflict regulation rooted in a shared community. Thus, competition in democratic politics can be very intense but involves little violence, whereas politics in unstable underdeveloped societies involves both strong intensity and a large amount of violence. In democratic societies, the conflicting parties share the rules of the game much more than in underdeveloped societies. We can formulate this in the statement:

24. The more intensely a conflict is acted out and the less it is regulated by common norms shared by a common membership in a community, the more violence will be involved in the conflict.

Thus far we have considered Coser's propositions on the intensity of conflict. What is characteristic of them is that they introduce factors affecting social conflict that reside outside the analytical dimension of the power game in markets, personalities, cultures, and communities. Thus Coser extends the theory of social conflict toward a more comprehensive theory not concentrating solely on the elements of goals, means, and power. However, he does so without formally starting out from the internal effects of goals, means, and power on the intensity of conflict. He extends conflict theory without starting from its very core: the constellation of means, ends, and power and the power game.

The same applies to Coser's treatment of the consequences of acting out conflict. Coser is not concerned with the determination of the outcome of social conflict by the constellation of power and with the disruptive effects of acting out conflict on society but with the integrating effects on groups and intergroup relationships. This is the point at which he diverges from conflict theorists like Dahrendorf and Collins. First, he shows that conflict settlement is a precondition for finding consensus in loosely structured groups and in an open society. Conflict in this sense is a sign of strength and stability within a group or society. Then he demonstrates how external conflict affirms and reaffirms internal group boundaries, group identity, cohesion, and group pressure on conformity. He also points to the phenomenon that rigid but weakly established groups tend to use enemies as a means of increasing group conformity. Then he points out how conflict settlement establishes association between the conflicting parties, an interest in their unity, and a balance of power. Finally, he demonstrates how conflict involves the formation of associations and coalitions of mutual support. What we see here are the effects of acting out conflict on the internal and external integration of groups and societies. This does not mean that Coser denies that there are disruptive effects of conflict on groups and societies. He is well aware of these effects and explicitly notes the conditions under which conflict has the integrative effects pointed out in the propositions. We can also turn the propositions on their heads to see that conflict has rather disruptive effects the more the conditions formulated in the propositions are absent from any particular conflict. Thus we have here the elements of a theory that points to the effects of conflict reaching beyond the outcome of the conflict processes itself, namely, the attainment of goals and the distribution of benefits, right into the field of culture and social structure, consensus, and community.

In this sense, Coser again extends the strictly conflict-theoretical view because he specifies the conditions of consensus and community formation in a world that is characterized by conflict. However, he does so with an eye primarily upon achieving integration. The disruptive effects of conflict have to be seen by turning his propositions the other way around: to the *lack* of conditions for integration. In particular, the negative conditions comprise the lack of markets for openly articulating conflict, the mingling of general aggressivity with social conflict, the ideologization of conflict, rigidity of group domination making any deviation of opinion an act of disloyalty, the lack of commonly shared norms to regulate conflict, the lack of opportunities to associate with and to get to know one's opponent, the lack of opportunities to mutually test one's power or of opportunities to form associations and coalitions, and the intensification of outside conflict in order to increase internal group pressure. All these are conditions under which conflict has disruptive effects, and we can derive them from Coser's analysis of the conditions governing conflict intensity and group integration by way of acting out conflict just by reading the analysis from right to left. However, this does not mean that Coser has formulated a balanced theory of the disruptive and integrative effects of conflict; his main emphasis is on the analysis of the integrative effects.

A theory of social conflict concentrating on the disruptive effects would add further conditions leading to disruption through conflict, particularly by laying more emphasis on the constellation of goals, means, and power and on the violence involved in social conflict. With these qualifications in mind we can make good use of Coser's analysis of social conflict. Nevertheless, we have to bear in mind that this analysis is not couched in terms of a conflict theory of society placing goals, means, power, and domination at its center, but that it tends instead to borrow from theories addressing the formation of consensus and integration. In this way it ought instead to be read as a supplement to strict conflict theory. In reality it is closer to functionalism than to strict conflict theory, because its main object of investigation is the integration of social systems. With Jonathan H. Turner (1986), we may therefore call it conflict functionalism. However, his deep knowledge of the varieties of sociological theory have taken Coser beyond the limits of narrow versions of conflict theory and functionalism as well (see also Coser, 1971).

SEVEN

A THEORY OF
DOMINATION AND CONFLICT:
RALF DAHRENDORF

TOWARD THE end of the 1950s, criticism of the then dominant functionalism converged particularly on the question of conflict and change in society. The critique proclaimed functionalism's inability to provide for explanations of conflict and change. The leading figure in this critical movement against functionalism became Ralf Dahrendorf, who tried to establish a view of society concentrating on conflict and change: a theory of conflict (Dahrendorf, 1958a/1965, 1958b, 1958c, 1959, 1961, 1967; for translation, see 1973, 1979).

The Functionalist and the Conflict View of Society

Dahrendorf does not deny functionalism any worth for understanding and explaining what is going on in society. However, in his eyes, functionalism is preoccupied with one side of society, namely, the structures and processes that contribute to upholding society and to keeping it in a state of equilibrium. To this functionalist view of society he opposes another view, which emphasizes what contributes to the destruction of society. He characterizes the two opposing images of society in four pairs of contrasting postulates. The functionalist view consists of the following four postulates:

1. Every society is a relatively persisting configuration of elements.
2. Every society is a well-integrated configuration of elements.
3. Every element in a society contributes to its functioning.
4. Every society rests on the consensus of its members. (Dahrendorf, 1958c: 174)

The conflict view entails the following four postulates:

1. Every society is subjected at every moment to change: social change is
   ubiquitous.
2. Every society experiences at every moment conflict: social conflict is
   ubiquitous.
3. Every element in a society contributes to its change.
4. Every society rests on constraint of some of its members by others. (Dahrendorf, 1958c: 174)

Dahrendorf does not want to replace the functionalist view by the conflict view; rather, he wants to add the conflict view in order to have a more
complete picture of society. He says every society includes at least parts of
both models; every society is partly stable *and* partly changing, entails elements providing for stability *and* elements providing for change, is partly
integrated *and* partly disintegrated due to conflict, and is partly based on
consensus *and* partly based on constraint. Dahrendorf is surely right in
emphasizing this double force within society, and he is also right in turning
our interest to the conflict view. However, he simplifies the functionalist
model so that it is unable to account for processes of change and conflict.
A closer analysis of Parsons's theory, which is considered to be the leading
functionalist approach to society, shows much more potential in accounting for conflict and change than Dahrendorf's functionalist model would
admit.

The postulates formulated by Dahrendorf are nowhere actually stated
in this way. It would be false from the beginning to postulate that every
society is stable, well-integrated, composed of elements providing for its functioning, and based on consensus. Why should any functionalist have been
naïve enough to make such statements about society? The opposite view
concentrating solely on conflict is, however, as false as the functionalist view.
This is the other side of Dahrendorf's insight that both models are partly
true: they are also both partly false by implication. Whether society
approaches the functionalist or the conflict model cannot be answered in
a general way, for in reality every single society occupies its own position.
Because theory has to answer questions in the former general way, this is
not a question for theory. Interesting questions for theory have to be formulated along lines such as this: Which are the different conditions providing for stability on the one hand or change on the other hand, for integration
or conflict, for consensus or constraint? Which are the different qualities
characterizing social order based on constraint or social order based on
consensus?

Taking up the last question, Parsons's theory tells us that order based
on constraint is unstable because it always has to face the struggle for power,
whereas order based on consensus is more stable. Applied to conflict settlement, this assumption implies that conflict settlement based on consensus

about the rules under which it should take place is more predictable and stable in character than conflict settlement that lacks this consensual basis. Dahrendorf himself makes such an assumption in his discussion of empirical conditions of conflict settlement without making it explicit to the reader that, in that instance, he is applying a proposition of Parsons's theory of the conditions providing for social order. These are the interesting questions as far as theory building is concerned. Dahrendorf addresses these questions after having introduced his two models of society when he makes an attempt to construct a theory of conflict.

The Origination of Conflict and Structural Change

Dahrendorf tries to identify the roots of conflicts in the structure of society. He is not interested in the conflicts arising from casual encounters between people and groups in situations where they happen to have contradictory goals. His concern is with the enduring causes of enduring conflicts. This is the reason why he looks at the structure of society that is a lasting feature of society in order to identify the origins of such conflicts. Because conflict is a confrontation of opposing groups, Dahrendorf's first question is: In what way do conflicting groups originate from the structure of society? The second question he asks is: In which forms do conflicts between social groups occur? And his third question is: How does conflict between such groups give rise to change in social structures?

Dahrendorf's basic answer to his first question is that the structural causes of social conflicts have to be sought in the relationships of domination in a society or in any smaller social organization under study. According to Dahrendorf, every social organization is divided into two opposing groups: the dominators and the dominated, the rulers and the ruled. The rulers are bearers of positive authority roles; the ruled are bearers of negative authority roles. Unless these two groups are organized and act in a unified way, they simply build up quasi-groups with latent conflicting interests. The rulers should be interested in maintaining the status quo; the ruled should be interested in changing social structure in the direction of overthrowing the established authority and gaining access to authority positions. Though Dahrendorf does not formulate his statements in propositional form, we could formulate a first proposition, thereby changing Dahrendorf's existential statement on the ubiquitous existence of dominating relationships and conflicting latent interests into a conditional statement:

1. The more the structure of a social organization is characterized by a relationship of domination between rulers and ruled, the more these two will make up quasi-groups with conflicting latent interests regarding the maintenance or change of the status quo.

However, conflict will become visible in overt action only if the quasi-groups become organized enough to act in a coordinated way toward each other. We may formulate the underlying intent of what Dahrendorf has to say in the following propositional form:

2. The more quasi-groups of rulers and ruled become organized to build up interest groups, the more they will act toward each other in a coordinated way.

What is stated in this proposition is a condition for turning latent conflict into manifest conflict:

3. The more interest groups of rulers and ruled act in a coordinated way, the more they will turn their latent conflict into a manifest conflict resulting in the struggle between maintaining and changing the status quo.

This struggle between rulers and ruled gives rise to a chance of social change that involves overthrowing the established authority to a greater or lesser degree. Though Dahrendorf does not state it explicitly, we can easily conclude that it must be the success of the ruled that leads to social change:

4. The more the ruled successfully fight against the rulers, the more social change will take place.

These are the major four statements of Dahrendorf's conflict theory in a more precisely formulated propositional form. Extending his argumentation, Dahrendorf states some further conditions that allow the initial conditions of the second, third, and fourth proposition to be met: organization, severity of conflict, and structural change.

As to the conditions under which interest groups are organized, Dahrendorf differentiates between social, political, and technical conditions. In the social sense, members of a group should be able to communicate. Closeness contributes to bringing people together to communicate. The less people live closely together, the more they will need a network of mediated communication. Furthermore, the interest group has to be able to recruit active members from the latent quasi-group. In a political sense, the political right to organize is a major precondition for forming interest groups. In a technical sense, a group needs material means, founders, leaders, and an ideology in order to be able to act in a coordinated and effective way. This is what later on Tilly (1978) called resource mobilization in his theory of revolution. We can summarize these conditions in the following proposition:

5. The more interest groups can communicate, recruit members from the quasi-group, have the political right to organize, and have the material means, founders, leaders, and an ideology, the more they will be able to organize and to act in a coordinated and effective way.

When considering the severity and intensity of conflict, Dahrendorf mentions two factors that have moderating effects on how conflict is carried out: social mobility and the social regulation of conflict through rules of conflict settlement. Social mobility opens ways to move up to authority positions that make it less urgent to use the path of violent power struggle in order to gain access to authority positions. Rules of conflict settlement make the acting out of conflict a normal phenomenon of everyday life, which proceeds in predictable and nonviolent ways and gives the ruled a chance to get their share without being forced to take recourse to violent action. We can formulate this, too, as a proposition:

6. The more social mobility and rules of conflict settlement open up the chance for the ruled to get their share, the lower will be the severity, intensity, and violence of the conflict.

Coming to the question of structural change, Dahrendorf mentions two factors: the capacity of the rulers to stay in power and the capacity of the ruled to exert pressure. A corresponding proposition would read as follows:

7. The weaker the capacity of the rulers to stay in power and the stronger the capacity of the ruled to exert pressure, the more far-reaching and thoroughgoing a structural change will take place.

Critical Assessment

Thus far, we have outlined Dahrendorf's attempt at formulating a theory of conflict and structural change. Examining the explanatory power of this theory we have to make some qualifications. We can make these partly with the help of Dahrendorf himself.

Conflict and Change

As regards the origins of conflict, Dahrendorf unfortunately starts with a rather narrow view. We can imagine a lot of social conflicts that do not originate from an established structure of domination. Inasmuch as people unite with common interests and act in the direction of realizing these interests they form groups. As soon as there are at least two groups that differ with regard to their interests there is a chance that one group might realize its interests only at the cost of the other group's realization of its interests. And this holds true regardless of whether the two groups are in a relationship of superordination and subordination to one another. A local community may be divided into two groups, one group favoring the settlement of a new industrial plant, the other group opposing this settlement without being in a clear-cut relation of domination. Here, the same conditions for making the latent conflict manifest, for organizing interest groups, and for the intensity of conflict are effective. As regards the conditions for structural change, we can reformulate that the capacity of the two groups to apply power and to exert pressure decides on their success and on whether change, for example, building a new industrial plant, will take place or not.

Thus far we have to extend Dahrendorf's view of conflict in order to include conflict between groups who do not stand in a clear-cut domination relationship to each other. Correspondingly, the conflict may be about maintaining or changing the status quo, but it may also be about which part of the social structure to maintain and/or in which direction to change the other parts. The conflict between two rival revolutionary parties can be as violent as the conflict between rulers and ruled. We can reformulate Dahrendorf's first proposition as follows:

> The more the structure of a social organization gives rise to divided latent interests, the more likely it is that quasi-groups will build up around these latent interests and will come into conflict over the realization of one interest at the cost of an opposing interest.

Starting from this generalization of the first proposition, we can continue with the second proposition and generalize the third proposition:

> The more interest groups act in a coordinated way, the more they will turn their latent conflict into a manifest conflict resulting in the struggle to enforce one interest at the cost of opposing interests.

The fourth proposition has to be generalized in this way:

> The more power and pressure a group can mobilize, the more social structure will be maintained or changed in accordance with its interests.

Adding some thoughts to this generalized fourth proposition, we can now expect structures of domination to emerge from the power struggle, a question not raised by Dahrendorf. Whereas Dahrendorf only states the ubiquitous existence of structures of domination, we can formulate a proposition on the conditions giving rise to domination:

The more a group has succeeded in conflict and has changed social structure in accordance with its interests, the more it will establish its domination over the other groups in a social organization.

Having generalized Dahrendorf's conflict theory beyond the area of conflict between rulers and ruled, we can now discuss the limitations we have to make. First, we have to question Dahrendorf's assumption that relationships between rulers and ruled give rise to conflict about maintaining or changing the status quo in every case. Is it always the case that the rulers want to maintain the status quo and the ruled want to change it and overthrow and replace the established power? A closer look shows us that this is not so. Rulers frequently take a lead in changing the social structure against the interests of groups that prefer to maintain the status quo, even groups that are not part of the ruling class. An example is former Soviet leader Michael Gorbachev, who had to enforce his reform program in the 1980s against the resistance of many different groups that wanted to maintain the existing order. On the other hand, many subordinated groups do not want to change the existing order and act in support of the rulers maintaining that order.

This is apparently contrary to Dahrendorf's first proposition. A most important source for the lack of any power struggle in a relationship of domination is that domination and power may be firmly entrenched in the ideas of legitimate authority shared by both rulers and ruled. It is astonishing that Dahrendorf assigns any stable relationship of domination the quality of legitimate authority when he characterizes the structure of domination by referring to Max Weber's (1922/1972c: 122–24) conception of legitimate authority. In this view, to use Dahrendorf's words, authority is composed of the following characteristics:

1. Authority denotes a relation of supra- and subordination.
2. The supra-ordinated side prescribes to the subordinated one certain behavior in the form of a command or prohibition.
3. The supra-ordinated side has the right to make such prescriptions; authority is a legitimate relation of supra- and subordination; authority is not based on personal or situational chance effects but rather on an expectation associated with a social position.
4. The right of authority is limited to certain contents and to specific persons.
5. Failure to obey the prescriptions is sanctioned; a legal system (or a system of quasi-legal customs) guards the effectiveness of authority. (Dahrendorf, 1958c: 177)

In the light of this view, which makes the legitimacy of supra-ordination and subordination the very essence of authority and authority the very essence of domination, it has to be asked how conflict and the attempt of the ruled to overthrow the established power is supposed to arise in authority relationships. Why should the ruled want to overthrow an established authority they consider to be legitimate? It would be self-contradictory to do that. Thus, Dahrendorf contradicts himself. He has an idea of authority that does not allow for the rise of conflict with regard to maintaining or changing the status quo, whereas he states, on the other hand, that the very existence of authority is the ubiquitous source of conflict in society. How can we avoid this contradiction? We can do so by qualifying Dahrendorf's first proposition on the origin of conflict. This proposition holds true only inasmuch as an established authority is insufficiently backed up by ideas of legitimacy. Whether this is the case or not, however, depends not on who has more power but on who succeeds in justifying the right to exercise power in the established way or the right to oppose power as it is established.

The social basis for this success is not the successful settlement of conflict but successful argumentation in discourse. Both government and opposition have to relate their claims to the same underlying ideas generally accepted in society as valid. To be sure, processes of legitimation can themselves involve power struggles with regard to using the best positions to propagate ideas; however, inasmuch as any power struggle would dominate discourse, the result would be the imposition of ideas through power without the assent of the losers of the battle. Legitimacy of authority and opposition can come about only if claims are discursively justified. Only inasmuch as processes of legitimation are rooted in discourse will the results of these processes be universally accepted as valid by all parties participating in this discourse. Thus, the question of whether an established authority is considered legitimate by rulers and ruled can be answered not by a theory of conflict involving the application of power but only by a theory of discourse involving the application of arguments. In the light of these considerations, we can qualify Dahrendorf's first proposition in the following way:

> The more the structure of a social organization is characterized by relationships of domination between rulers and ruled and the less this relationship is anchored in common ideas of legitimate authority by discursive procedures, the more these two groups will build up quasi-groups with conflicting latent interests regarding the maintenance or change of the status quo.

What we have pointed out for the rise of conflict between rulers and ruled can also be applied to the question of structural change. Normally, claims for maintaining or changing the established order imply argumentation in the light of basic ideas. The more this is the case and the more these ideas are rooted in a common culture, the less the direction of change will result only from the amount of power that can be mobilized for stability or change and the more the direction of change will come from processes of legitimation. We can formulate this as follows:

> The more a claim for the maintenance or change of an order can be justified in procedures of discourse and the more these procedures dominate in a society, the more social order will be maintained and developed in the direction of those claims.

In the light of this proposition, we have to qualify Dahrendorf's proposition on the capacity of rulers and ruled regarding the maintenance or change of the social structure:

> The less a claim for maintenance or change can be justified in discursive procedures and the less procedures of discourse are established in a society, the more this relationship will hold true: The weaker the capacity of rulers to stay in power and the stronger the capacity of the ruled to exert pressure, the more far-reaching and thoroughgoing a structural change will take place.

The question of legitimation is not the only one insufficiently answered by Dahrendorf's conflict theory. A second question conflict theory cannot answer is the question of the roots of the peaceful regulation of conflict. Dahrendorf only states the thesis that social regulation of conflict has a moderating effect on the intensity of conflict; he does not enter into any discussion as to where this social regulation might come from. A more detailed analysis would have to deal with the question of how a society can escape the transposition of the power struggle to the struggle over social regulation. If social regulation itself were to come only from success in the struggle for power, it would not lend any more predictability, order, and moderation to conflict settlement than the unrestricting acting out of conflict itself. Every regulation would be in danger of being overruled by the mobilization of power. This may indeed be the case; however, any peaceful settlement of conflict would then not be possible.

To the extent that regulation does have a stable, predictable, and binding character, it must have roots in a different sphere from power struggle. It is the solidarity of a community embracing all conflicting parties, its consensus at least with regard to the rules of conflict settlement, and the unified approval/disapproval, positive, and negative sanctioning with regard to rule conformity and nonconformity that back up the social regulation of conflict. This is information we do not obtain from a theory that places power struggle at its center. We can qualify Dahrendorf's proposition on social regulation of conflict in this way:

The more social regulation of conflict is backed up by solidarity, consensus, and unified sanctioning embracing the conflicting parties, the more conflict will be acted out in predictable, peaceful, and moderate forms.

The information enabling us to qualify Dahrendorf's theory of conflict in this way has to come from a theory of solidarity and consensus formation.

A further qualification of Dahrendorf's conflict theory has to be made with regard to alternative ways toward change in social structures. Dahrendorf himself mentions social mobility as a force that reduces the intensity of conflict. Social mobility gives a social organization flexibility and makes it open to change without necessitating violent conflict. Change here takes place by way of individual utility maximization rather than collective struggle for power. A theory of economic action would tell us that the domination of markets in a society paired with individual striving for profit will open up paths for individual mobility and will contribute to dissolving group ties and therefore reduce group action and conflict. We can formulate Dahrendorf's mobility proposition more precisely:

The more markets and individual profit maximization dominate in a society, the less established are group ties and, therefore, group action and conflict.

This is a proposition that has its roots not in conflict theory but in economic theory. Specifying the explanatory direction of conflict theory to dealing with power struggle as such makes us understand the internal logic of power struggle more precisely than any unspecified mixture of conflicting theories like that created by Dahrendorf. However, consciously qualifying conflict theory by applying theories of discourse, consensus, and profit maximization considerably extends our view of the nonconflictual forces that penetrate and guide the course of conflict (for an extended view, see Hondrich, 1973).

Role Constraint

Dahrendorf's conflict theory of society is very much present in his theory of social roles as constitutive elements of society imposed on the individual by the sanctioning power of reference groups who back up these roles (Dahrendorf, 1958a/1965; for translation, see 1973). According to Dahrendorf, sociology singles out the network of social roles imposed on the individual as its distinctive object domain. Sociology sees the human individual as a member of society who carries out social roles defined by society. In doing so, sociology constructs analytically a *homo sociologicus*, a specific perspective of the human individual that is the counterpart of biology's biological man, psychology's psychological man, economy's economic man, and political science's political man, all of which are analytical perspectives in their own right.

Social roles are not created by the individual; they are imposed on him or her by society. They are social facts in the sense defined by Durkheim. They were there before an individual was born, and they will be there after the individual's death. Moreover, they exert a constraint on the individual. They are external, universal, and constraining in character. We follow laws, go to school, vote, marry, have a job, go out for dinner, care for our children, get orders from superiors, communicate with other people, hear, see, speak a language, and act, and there is always one phenomenon present in shaping all this: society. Society is present in the *roles* we play in these actions: citizen, student, voter, husband or wife, salesperson, civil servant, lawyer, customer, father or mother, subordinate, speaker, listener, and actor. These roles relate to specific positions in society, which is a network of positions with corresponding roles. A position signifies the place where an individual stands in the societal network. The social role comprises the socially given expectations as to how the occupant of a social position has to act, ought to act, or is allowed to act in various situations. Insofar as we know the positions of an individual, we know much about his or her predispositions to act and to think in certain ways. We can derive this from the corresponding roles as they are determined by society. But we do not know anything about an individual's very personal predispositions to act and think from these positions and corresponding roles. What a teacher does and thinks as a teacher is known to us by the very fact of his or her being a teacher, but not what the teacher does and thinks as a unique person outside his or her fulfillment of role expectations.

The social role comprises role behavior and role attributes (appearance). It is divided into role segments. For example, the role of the teacher is differentiated into the segments of its relation to the corresponding roles of pupils, parents, colleagues, school board, and principal.

Social roles are quasi-objective complexes of rules for behavior that exist independently of the individual. Their substance is determined or changed not by the individual but by society. The roles have an obligatory character for the individual. What, then, is the basis of the obligatory character of social roles? Dahrendorf's answer is *sanctions*—mostly negative sanctions (that is, punishments) and sometimes positive sanctions (that is, rewards) guarantee the obligatory character of social roles. There are three levels of obligation in role expectations: expectations that one *must* act in a certain way, expectations that one *should* act in a certain way, and expectations that one *may* act in a certain way. The more binding expectations are backed up by more severe sanctions. A president of an association *must* be financially trustworthy. This is backed up by negative legal sanctions. He or she *should* not participate in competing associations, and this is backed up by sympathy as a positive sanction or social exclusion as a negative one. He or she *may* volunteer in collecting money, which is backed up by approval as a positive sanction or antipathy as a negative sanction.

Who defines role expectations? The answer is "society." But who is that made up of? "Reference groups" is the more specific answer. These reference groups are in direct interaction with the bearer of a role. Students, parents, colleagues, school board, and principal are the different reference groups for the schoolteacher. Their expectations can be in contradiction. This brings about internal role conflict. However, conflict can also come about from contradiction not only between expectations within one role but also between the different roles actually played by an individual. As a teacher, a spouse, a parent, a party member, the person is again confronted with conflicting expectations: This is inter-role conflict.

What then decides which one of the conflicting expectations is more obligatory than the others? In Dahrendorf's perspective, it is the sanctioning power of the reference groups that is crucial in determining the obligatory character of their expectations. Those reference groups that are in a central position have more power and can enforce their expectations against conflicting pressures.

Inasmuch as the individual wants to save any freedom and individuality facing the constraints exerted on him or her by social roles, the individual can achieve that only to the degree that he or she is capable of escaping the sanctioning power of reference groups. Freedom and individuality can be achieved only outside the constraints of social roles, not in playing them.

We can summarize Dahrendorf's theory of social roles in the following statements:

1. Society is a network of social positions and corresponding social roles.
2. Social roles are imposed by society on the individual.
3. Social roles are societal expectations defining what one may, should, or must do in a social position, enforced by sanctions reaching from weak positive to strong negative ones.
4. Social roles are composed of role expectations directed at the occupant of a position by different reference groups.
5. An individual can be confronted with contradictory expectations according to the different expectations of reference groups related to one role or different roles.
6. The more sanctioning power a reference group has, the more it will enforce its role expectations against conflicting expectations.
7. The more the individual wants to save any freedom and individuality, the more he or she has to escape the constraints of social roles.

Dahrendorf's role theory explains why social roles can regulate the behavior of individuals even though the roles are against their individual dispositions and are conflicting in character: because the sanctioning power of reference groups overcomes resistance, and the amount of power decides the rank order of role expectations. However, social roles have more features besides the fact that they are enforced against resistance and conflicting expectations. Dahrendorf's conflict theory of social roles does not provide tools for explaining these features.

Role expectations often vary in substance from situation to situation and from individual to individual, and the latter play them independently of the power behind them. This has to be explained by reference to the intelligence mobilized by the individual and to the negotiations between the actors involved. Some role expectations have a binding quality independent of available power. This has to be explained by the commitment of the individual to a community—the solidarity, consensus, and uniform reaction of that community to deviations. Legitimacy of role expectations is not brought about by sanctions. It requires the anchoring of role expectations in ideas and values that are held as generally valid in a discussing community.

There are other aspects of the individual's freedom and individuality besides escaping the constraint of social roles: using social roles for personal self-realization, for securing one's rights, for expanding one's scope of freedom against others, and for expanding one's horizon and autonomy. All these aspects are not covered by Dahrendorf's conflict theory of social roles.

Related Work

Conflict theory concentrating on the major class divisions and conflicts in society has developed as a rebellion against structural functionalism in American sociology since the late 1950s. Particularly influential contributions have been provided by C. Wright Mills (1956) and Alvin Gouldner (1960, 1963, 1971, 1980).

PART THREE

The Economics
of Social Action

EIGHT

SOCIAL EXCHANGE THEORY:
GEORGE C. HOMANS

IN 1958 George C. Homans published an article on "Social Behavior as Exchange" in the *American Journal of Sociology*. This article initiated a movement toward reestablishing economic thinking in sociology, along with methodological individualism and even psychological reductionism, stating that the laws of behavioral economics and behavioral psychology constitute the foundation of any sociological law. According to this approach, any macrosocial phenomenon can be explained by the laws of economics and psychology. Such views of the social world had been nearly wiped out by Talcott Parsons's attack on utilitarian thought in his *Structure of Social Action* of 1937 and by the domination of functionalism in the 1950s. Three years later, in 1961, Homans's *Social Behavior, Its Elementary Forms* gave a full account of the new economic paradigm. This book became very influential in the 1960s. A revised edition came out in 1974; it was designed to make the argument more powerful in the light of criticism that arose in the wave of the book's success.

The theory outlined in the book was soon labeled "exchange theory," although in the revised edition Homans did not fully accept the label, because in his understanding the basic propositions of the theory are more general in character and do not cover exchange processes alone. Nevertheless, applied to social interaction, the theory is specified to become a theory of social exchange. Therefore, in sociological terms we can still speak of an exchange theory. Because we are dealing with sociological theories, exchange theory is what interests us here (see also Homans, 1950, 1958, 1961, 1962, 1964, 1967, 1974, 1984).

Interaction as Exchange

In the light of Homans's exchange theory, social interaction is always seen and interpreted as social exchange, as an exchange between two actors taking place in a situation that includes only these two or—with growing complexity—other actors who are considered possible parties of exchange by the two actors under consideration. What the parties do is exchange rewards. Homans conceives of a reward as something an actor finds valuable and would like to have or would like to have occur. The actor has preferences; he or she prefers to see one thing happen and not some other thing. This may be something that comes from an innate need, drive, or desire or something that has developed as a wish in the personal history of an actor. What an actor regards as a reward may be something to eat, a friendly smile from a beloved person, a piece of information, or the receipt of other people's approval, of help in doing one's work, or of support from someone when arguing against an opponent. To continue the range of possibilities, the reward may be the attainment of consensus with other people, having a chance to help other people, being seen as altruistic by them, being seen simply as a nice person, making more money, getting a new pair of Levi's, being invited to a party, and so on. There may be many things people would see as rewards, but there are always things that are rewarding for someone but not for everyone. Not everybody has the same preferences, but everybody has some preferences according to which he or she feels rewarded by events that contribute to their realization.

People normally organize their preferences in a certain rank order. However, this is not a ranking of all the preferences they have in mind. Normally, a situation in which an actor has to decide which action to perform does not involve all preferences an actor may have but only a few of them, so that he or she has only to decide which of two, three, or four outcomes of his or her action is more valuable, that is, contributes to realizing the highest of, say, three preferences. However, whenever the preferences touched by an action are very close in their rank to one another, the actor is in a severe inner conflict and does not know how to act.

Inasmuch as there are things people would like to have and to have happen, there are also things they would *not* like to have or to happen—things they want to avoid. They do not like to be blamed for having done something; they do not like to have certain people's company; they do not like to be robbed of their freedom, to lose someone's love or companionship, or to get bad grades in school. These are things that are the opposite of rewards and are known as punishments. Rewards and punishments are in a converse relationship to each other. Withholding rewards represents a punishment to the person who is striving for those rewards. Similarly, avoiding punishment is rewarding for a person. The child who sees that mother's love is withdrawn because the child has behaved contrary to the mother's expectations feels punished inasmuch as he or she wants mother's love. Gaining back mother's love or avoiding its withdrawal in the first place is rewarding for the child. Sometimes a person can be confronted with a situation in which he or she has to choose between a more or a less severe punishment. Avoiding the more severe punishment is then felt to be rewarding in Homans's terms. A person confronted with the choice "Your money or your life" will hand over the cash and feel rewarded with life itself and a new appreciation of the term "survival."

The actor in exchange theory's terms is seeking rewards and avoiding punishment. Applied to the analysis of social interaction, this means actors enter those relationships with others and stay with those relationships that provide rewards and/or avoid punishments; and they avoid or leave those relationships which are not rewarding but punishing. People look for one another in order to have someone to receive rewards and to avoid punishments, and they hide from one another in order to avoid punishment, which in itself is then a reward.

Taking the example from Homans (1961: 30–50), we can imagine a man in an office doing some paperwork. He is new in this job and still not experienced enough to get along with his work without any problems. Homans calls him Person. We can assume that Person would like to be able to solve his problems in order to do his job according to the expectations of his organization. Thus, he feels rewarded by having solved any problems. The question is, How will he solve the problems? This is a situation in which he may look for someone in his department who has more experience and would be able to help him. At this point, a co-worker enters the situation; according to Homans we call him Other (we may continue to refer to Person and Other as males for simplicity's sake only). Receiving help from Other would be Person's reward, and this would be the reason for Person to enter into social interaction with Other. But what reason might Other have to enter into social interaction with Person? In terms of exchange theory, the only reason would be Other's expectation of being rewarded by Person (and/or by some third party) in exchange for his help. Thus, people enter into social interaction when they can expect to receive rewards from the other parties in that interaction. Because this expectation is mutual, social interaction always implies the exchange of rewards. Social interaction is social exchange. Actors who have enough experience in social interaction have learned that people expect rewards when entering social interaction; they are prepared not only to expect rewards on their own part but also to expect the expectation of rewards on the part of others they begin to interact with. They are prepared to give back rewards when they are themselves rewarded.

Now, what sort of thing might Person offer to Other in return for the help he needs at work? There may be quite a number of alternatives available.

For example, he may invite Other out to dinner or arrange for Other to purchase electronic equipment at discount rates. These offers would imply the exchange of services for commodities under the barter form of economic exchange. But Person may also pay for Other's services in money. This would place their interaction in the category of market exchange, in which commodities and services are traded for money acting as a universal exchange medium. The use of money frees the exchanging parties from the need to encounter just the right person who has what they want and wants what they have. In the latter case, Person might spend a long time looking for someone able to help him who also liked what he had to offer. Taking money in return for a service performed allows one to go out and have the dinner one wants with the company of one's own choice such as a close friend rather than the person for whom one has performed the service.

However, Homans gives special emphasis to the fact that many exchanges do occur in which money is not implicated, and he seeks to cover many more fields of interaction with this wider concept of exchange than pure economic exchange expressed in terms of money. Life in the family, organizations, communities, friendships, work, sports, communication, and groups always implies exchange of rewards without involving money. Even barter exchange (whether of commodities for commodities, services for services, or commodities for services) does not account for all remaining instances of exchange. What are of special interest to Homans are exchanges that involve immaterial rewards like consonance with other people, conformity to group norms, personal integrity, approval from other people, and love between friends. Approval from other people, which we can call social approval, is a rather general reward that has some qualities similar to money, according to Homans. Being approved of by other people puts me in a position in which I am much more likely than I would be without that approval to receive support for something I would like to do. A highly approved person finds open doors — it is easy for him or her to influence other people. Thus, having received social approval a person can turn it into many different things, for, like money, it can buy many goods and services. This is the reason why a person may accept social approval for his or her services, something that may not be rewarding immediately and intrinsically but can be turned into many different rewarding things. Because of this quality of being able to buy many different immediate rewards, social approval itself becomes something people look for and may experience as rewarding. In this way social approval can become an intrinsic reward, and people can enjoy receiving it.

Turning back to Homans's example of social exchange between Person and Other, we now can see a further alternative open to Person in order to remunerate Other for his help: being grateful and giving his approval. Thus we have an exchange of Other's help for Person's approval. But we have to determine the meaning of approval more precisely than Homans did. It makes a difference whether Person keeps his approval of Other to himself or whether he publicly approves of Other as someone you can rely on whenever you need help. In the first case, the things Person's approval can buy for Other are only things from Person, for example, the occasional dinner or opportunities for good deals in electronic equipment, or Other may simply be pleased to gain approval. In the second case, Person's approval publicly announced also buys many different things from among the whole group of people sharing Person's approval of Other. This second type of social approval has more far-reaching effects.

The Propositions

Let us now turn to the laws that govern social behavior according to Homans's theory and apply the corresponding propositions to social exchange. Homans (1961: 51–82; 1974: 5–50) formulates a theory of elementary social behavior in terms of propositions that he borrows from behavioral psychology, particularly from the principles of operant learning discovered by Burhus F. Skinner (1938, 1953) in studies of animal behavior. Homans sees in these principles the basic elements of any behavior, also of human behavior. Going on from that, because social interaction, social organization, institutions, and social structures are composed of those elementary forms of behavior, we can gain the most general insights into the working of social interaction, organization, institutions, and structures by studying the basic forms of behavior and by applying the basic propositions emerging from this investigation to the more complex features of social interaction, order, organizations, institutions, and structures. Thus Homans's strategy of theory building is deductive and reductionist in character. He starts from basic and general propositions in order to apply them to explaining singular phenomena, and he claims that sociological hypotheses on social phenomena can be derived from the basic propositions of behavioral psychology when we apply them to social phenomena. Homans states five propositions:

   I. The success proposition
  II. The stimulus proposition
 III. The value proposition
 IV. The deprivation-satiation proposition
  V. The aggression-approval proposition

Let us now examine these five propositions.

The Success Proposition

The success proposition is as follows:

For all actions taken by persons, the more often a particular action is rewarded, the more likely the person is to perform that action. (Homans, 1974: 16)

This proposition comes from studying the learning processes of animals. A hungry pigeon in a cage may discover that pecking a metal key will release a grain of corn. In the beginning the bird pecks the key accidentally, but with each grain of corn it releases in this way, the probability that it will peck the key once more increases. The connection between pecking the key and being rewarded with a piece of corn becomes established in the animal's mind. On the other hand, the smaller the number of rewards resulting from pecking the key, the less likely it will be to peck the key again.

Further research has led to some specifications of the success proposition. Thus, the shorter the time interval between the behavior (e.g., pecking) and reward (corn), the more the connection becomes implanted in the animal and the more likely it is that the behavior will be performed in the future. Behavior that is rewarded at irregular intervals is not established as behavior likely to occur as fast as behavior that is regularly rewarded, but it also takes longer to extinguish that behavior by withholding rewards. Because the behavior has not been rewarded regularly, the animal is prepared to have several unsuccessful trials before receiving the expected reward.

This is the meaning of the success proposition as derived from studying animal behavior. Applied to human behavior, particularly social behavior, it works in the same way, according to Homans's argument. If we again consider our example of the exchange of help for approval between Person and Other, it is the frequently occurring event, the experience of being rewarded with approval after having given help to another person, that leads Other to help Person when asked for help. And it is the experience of solving a problem at work after asking another person for help that leads Person to ask Other for help. Furthermore, it is the experience of receiving help more easily from other persons after having given approval for being helped in earlier instances that leads Person to give Other his approval in return for the help. In terms of the success proposition, Person is more likely to give approval in return for help the more often this has led to receiving help when he asked for it in earlier instances. In this way, the success proposition explains why Person and Other are apt to engage in an exchange of help and approval in the situation where Person has a problem at work. Both have had enough experiences in the past when such an exchange resulted in being mutually rewarded.

Because people strive to receive rewards and to avoid punishment, there is no reason why they should not embark on their exchange of help for approval. But it is only under the condition that they have had a positive experience of being rewarded in such an exchange that the success proposition would allow us to predict that both will undertake the exchange. If one of them has had no such experience or a negative experience, he would refuse to commit himself to the exchange. The less often Person has received help that really solved his problems and the less often Other has been rewarded with approval for giving help, the less likely it is that either will enter into the exchange. In such a situation we have a lot of mutual mistrust that keeps the rate of social exchange very low; whereas any increase in rewarding experiences from engaging in exchange will increase mutual trust and thus the likelihood of indulging in social exchange.

The Stimulus Proposition

The stimulus proposition reads as follows:

> If in the past the occurrence of a particular stimulus or set of stimuli has been the occasion on which a person's action has been rewarded, then the more similar the present stimuli are to the past ones, the more likely the person is to perform the action, or some similar action, now. (Homans, 1974: 22–23)

Look again at the example of the pigeon in a cage. The keys the pigeon has to peck in order to release the corn may have different forms and colors in different cages, and they may be located at different places. When pecking these different keys results in releasing the corn, the pigeon will learn to generalize the perception of the key. The key becomes a generalized stimulus that evokes the response of pecking within the animal, and that response is again reinforced by the release of the corn (the reward). The stimulus and the reward become connected in the animal's perception, resulting in the likelihood that it will peck the key whenever it is confronted with this stimulus because it arouses the expectation of being rewarded with corn. In addition, the animal learns to generalize the stimulus, abstracting from casual aspects and concentrating on those qualities that keys of different forms, colors, and location have in common. It discovers their similarity and learns to respond to similar stimuli (keys) in similar ways (pecking). However, the animal also learns to discriminate. Imagine that there are always two keys in a cage, one on the bottom, the other under the ceiling, and only pecking the one on the bottom releases the corn. Here the pigeon will learn to discriminate sharply between keys on the bottom and keys under the ceiling and will respond only to keys on the bottom by pecking them.

We can apply this example of pecking keys to the exchange between Person and Other. Both may have received rewards in exchange for their action with many different persons. Thus, they will generalize the stimulus from concrete persons to any person and will engage in social exchange with people whenever they need help or are asked for help. However, they may also have had very different experiences depending on the type of person they were confronted with. Here they will learn to discriminate and act favorably only toward persons who are similar to those with whom they have had rewarding encounters. Or Person may have learned that it is not rewarding to ask Other for help when he is under stress and looks unfriendly. Thus, he will ask Other for help only when he looks friendly and seems to have plenty of time.

We can summarize by stating that the stimulus proposition entails both stimulus generalization and stimulus discrimination; which of these predominates depends on whether it has been a wide variety of similar stimuli or only a very specific type of stimulus, which, when responded to, provided rewards.

The Value Proposition

The value proposition reads as follows:

> The more valuable to a person is the result of his action, the more likely he is to perform the action. (Homans, 1974: 25)

The behavior of the pigeon in our example is significantly affected by whether the animal is hungry or not. For the pigeon that is not hungry, the corn has no value. Value in this context has a similar meaning to the purchasing power of money. One hundred dollars had a high value in the past when it could be used to obtain many things, whereas the same amount is likely to buy fewer things and hence have a lesser value in the future. The same applies to the results of actions. Actions have a high value if they fulfill many needs, desires, wants, or preferences and/or those needs, desires, wants, or preferences to which a particular person gives a high priority. For the hungry pigeon, receiving something to eat is a result of pecking the key, which satisfies an urgent need at that moment: relieving hunger. The corn has a high value. It is different for the pigeon that is not hungry. The corn does not satisfy an urgent need in this case and has virtually no value at all.

Turning to the example of Person and Other, it makes a difference whether Person really has a problem and Other really likes receiving approval. Person will not feel rewarded by Other coming to help him if Person does not need this help. Indeed, Person may feel uncomfortable and even punished by Other's help, because this help makes him appear insecure in doing his job and decreases his status in the organization. Thus, Person will not ask Other for help and will even refuse offers of help when help has no value for him. Conversely, Other will not help Person if Person's offer of approval has no value for him. This is the case with someone who does not need or even does not like receiving approval from certain people or from people in general. If Other does not like Person, he will not appreciate receiving his approval. Person's approval has no value for Other, and he will not help him under these conditions.

Homans uses the term "value" to assess the results of actions that are more or less beneficial to a person by fulfilling his or her needs, desires, wants, and preferences. People assign these results a certain value on a scale ranging from extremely positive to extremely negative. Values can stand in instrumental relationships to one another. The corn has value for the pigeon because it is instrumental in relieving hunger, which is basically valued in itself. Other's help has value for Person because it is instrumental in allowing him to do his job, which in turn is instrumental in earning money, which is instrumental in acquiring many different things. Person's approval has value for Other because it is instrumental in enabling him to receive support for many different things. There are instrumental values, things that make us able to receive something else, and intrinsic values, things that we want to have for their own sake. Some values that become established for a person because of their instrumental value for other things may become divorced from their original instrumental connection and may acquire the character of an intrinsic value. Many people may have had the experience that being approved makes it easier to get along with other people, but over time they may feel rewarded by approval in itself. Approval is a value they will want to have for its own sake.

Converting a positive value is rewarding for a person, while converting a negative value is punishing. A negative value is an outcome of an action an individual wants to avoid. For example, Person does not want to be publicly blamed for being stupid by asking Other for help. The more he expects such a result from his action, the more he will refrain from this action.

There is a reverse relationship between positive and negative values. Withheld positive values have punishing effects on an individual and are felt in the same way as negative values. Conversely, negative values that have been avoided have rewarding effects and are hence equivalent to positive values. For this to hold true, however, a person must have expected the positive or negative value concerned as one alternative outcome depending on his or her choice of action in a certain situation. It is only when one is confronted with the "your money or your life" situation that the fact of being able to stay alive is felt in terms of having avoided an extreme punishment and is rewarding as such. Under normal circumstances, many people do not feel rewarded only by the fact of being alive.

On the matter of positive and negative values, rewards and punishments, we can ask, What is the effect of rewards and punishments on the continuation of social exchange? According to the value proposition, a person will continue exchange relationships that result in positively valued outcomes and discontinue relationships that result in negatively valued outcomes. Thus, there is a high stability in social interaction when both parties are pleased with valuable outcomes of their interaction and a low stability when at least one of them does not obtain valuable outcomes. If Other does not feel that he is receiving approval from Person or does not value Person's approval, he will not continue the exchange. The same is true of Person if he realizes that Other's help has no value for him because it does not solve his problems.

However, there are also situations that establish relationships of mutual punishment. Other may blame Person publicly for his inability to do his job on his own, thus leading Person to react by publicly blaming Other as arrogant, unreliable, and even unable to give valuable advice. Other may react to this assault by accusing Person of spreading untenable insults within the department. Person may react to his punishment by denouncing Other as someone who wants to dominate the department and tries to get everybody who does not subscribe to his claim of domination fired from their jobs. This is an interaction based on mutual punishment. The question now is, Why do people continue such punishing relationships? The reason is not that they like being punished, which would be contrary to the value proposition. It is rather that they enter into a spiral where they react to a punishment by another person in a way that is designed to counteract the punishment and cancel it out. Yet, this attempt to cancel out the punishment results in motivating one's opponent to reestablish the punishment, and so on. Person's reproachful reaction to Other's own reproach is an attempt to free himself from blame by projecting it on to Other, but all he achieves is a renewal of Other's blaming action. Both actors try to draw rewards from their interaction but paradoxically receive only punishments. Person punishes Other in order to reestablish a rewarding situation for himself, but Other reacts by punishing Person again in order to reestablish a rewarding situation in his turn, and so the spiral goes on.

There are two ways out of this situation: First, one of the two is more capable of upholding his blaming action, so the other has to give in and escape the situation in order to avoid further punishments, preferring to spend his time on more valuable interactions. Second, neither one is capable of winning the game, but at least one of them realizes the paradoxical effects of their encounter and leaves the situation in order to move on to more valuable exchanges. Both results would be in accordance with the value proposition. However, the preconditions allowing these solutions of the paradox to work are not always fulfilled. There often is a relative balance of capabilities to punish, and no one is farsighted enough to realize the paradoxical effects of his or her actions.

There is another situation of interaction from which seemingly neither party can draw valuable results. This is the situation where Person punishes Other in order to receive help. For example, Person may wear Other down with his repeated questions until Other gives in and comes to help Person solve his problem. Why then does Other help Person even though he has been punished by Person's questions? The reason may be that he just does not see any other chance of stopping Person's tiresome enquiries than finally solving his problem. Thus he is in a punishing situation and can overcome this situation only by helping Person. He stops being punished in this way, and this is what makes him feel rewarded after having solved Person's problem. Thus, the value proposition still explains Other's action. Having stopped Person's tiresome questions is most valuable for him.

However, in most cases it is not a question of having an action rewarded or punished by results of positive or negative value. Most actions are followed by rewards and punishments at the same time. Take only the rewards forgone by choosing one of a set of alternative courses of action. The rewards forgone are negative values and are perceived as punishments by the actor. Asking Other for help contributes to solving Person's problem, which is rewarding to Person but it also lowers his status in the department, which is punishing. Being approved for helping Person is rewarding for Other, but losing time in which to do his own work or pursue leisure activities is punishing for him. At least the time consumed by a rewarding activity stands for forgone rewards that might come from alternative activities. Every rewarding action is time consuming and rules out performing alternative rewarding activities, and this aspect is perceived as punishment. According to Homans, we use the term "costs" for all rewards forgone while committing ourselves to a specific rewarding action. For the economically rational actor, it is therefore not an absolute reward in itself that he or she seeks but, rather, as large a difference as possible between rewards and costs, which is the profit flowing from an action. In light of this argument we have to restate the value proposition as follows and may call it the profit proposition:

> The higher the profit (reward minus costs) to a person resulting from an action, the more likely he or she is to perform the action.

Person will be more apt to ask Other for help the more the reward of solving his problem outweighs the costs of lowering his status. Other will be more apt to help Person the more the reward of being approved outweighs the costs of losing time that could be used for alternative rewarding activities.

The Deprivation-Satiation Proposition

The deprivation-satiation proposition is:

> The more often in the recent past a person has received a particular reward, the less valuable any further unit of that reward becomes for him. (Homans, 1974: 29)

Referring again to the pigeon, it is natural that the animal will approach satiation the more it has been fed with corn after pecking the key. The time comes when any more corn would have no value for the pigeon, because it does not satisfy an urgently felt need any longer. On the other hand, the longer the time that has passed since the pigeon was last fed, the greater will be the deprivation of the animal with regard to the basic need of avoiding hunger. If the pigeon has been deprived of food for a long time, the value of any single grain of corn is all the greater. Thus, deprivation increases the likelihood of actions leading to its reduction; satiation decreases the likelihood of actions that would lead to even further satiation. The same holds true for social behavior, such as the interaction between Person and Other. The more Person has been helped in the past, the more he may have acquired the required skills and the less he will need any further help. The more Other has received approval for helping Person, the less he will need further approval. On the other hand, the more they have been deprived of help or approval as the case may be, the more valuable these rewards become for both of them.

However, there is a difference between help at work and approval. The first is a specific reward that leads to satiation inasmuch as Person can help himself. The second is a general reward like money that can be turned into many different specific rewards. This is the reason why we do not become satiated with rewards like approval as fast as is the case with rewards like help at work. Our specific needs, desires, wants, and preferences are almost infinite. We cannot become satiated with a generalized reward enabling us to realize all these different values as fast as with some specific reward.

The deprivation-satiation proposition is an instance of the principle of marginal utility that we know from neoclassical economics. For example, if we eat a series of apples, the first one has full value for us, because it is this apple alone that conveys the value, in full, of eating apples. Eating a second apple diminishes the apple's value to half of the first one, because now half of the value "eating apples" has been occupied by the first apple. Likewise, eating a third apple reduces its value to one-third, a fourth to one-fourth, a fifth to one-fifth, a tenth to one-tenth, and so on.

A Generalization: The Rationality Proposition

We learn from the deprivation-satiation proposition that the high frequency with which an action is rewarded does not make that action more likely under all circumstances. Inasmuch as frequent rewarding leads to satiation, the action concerned becomes less likely than before. The success proposition has to be qualified in the light of the deprivation-satiation proposition; it has to be limited to the condition that rewarding does not result in satiation. In other words, we have to distinguish between the probability an actor attributes to being rewarded for an action and the value of this reward for the actor. Frequent rewarding increases the probability an actor attributes to being rewarded for an action, but it decreases the value of any further unit of reward. And the likelihood of an action increases with the probability with which it is expected to be rewarded, and it decreases with the diminishing value of an expected unit of reward, which itself may be a function of frequency. Homans takes these considerations into account and formulates a more general proposition that is designed to sum up and replace the success, stimulus, and value propositions, whereas the deprivation-satiation proposition explains changes in the value of a reward resulting from rewarding itself. The rationality proposition is formulated according to the principle of rational choice as follows:

> In choosing between alternative actions, a person will choose that one for which, as perceived by him at the time, the value, V, of the result, multiplied by the probability, p, of obtaining the result, is greater. (Homans, 1974: 43)

Homans confuses his readers here because he now understands value not as the absolute value of a reward but as the relative outcome of an action expressed as reward minus costs, that is, profit. Relating the specific propositions borrowed from behavioral psychology to the rationality proposition, we can say that the success and stimulus propositions state conditions under which an actor's perception of the probability of a certain outcome of his or her action is influenced in the direction of assuming a higher probability. Frequent rewarding of an action and similarity of stimuli influence an actor to assume that the same action responding to similar stimuli is highly likely to result in the same rewards. Nevertheless, according to the rationality proposition, this will motivate the actor to perform this particular action only inasmuch as the expected outcome generates the highest profit.

The value and deprivation-satiation propositions state conditions under which an actor is motivated to strive for certain outcomes. There may be outcomes that are very likely but are uninteresting or dangerous for an actor. Thus, he or she will do nothing to achieve these outcomes. The condition under which a person strives for an outcome is, according to the value proposition, that an actor assigns a positive value to it. According to the deprivation-satiation proposition, the value of a reward is higher the more an actor is deprived of this reward and lower the more he or she is satiated with it. Briefly stated: the actor has to expect a higher profit from a certain action than from any alternative action in order to be motivated to perform this action. But he or she will not perform this action when the highly valued outcome is very unlikely, so that it is more profitable to turn to more likely outcomes with lower profit.

We can now formulate the rationality proposition as follows:

In choosing between alternative actions, a person will choose that alternative for which, as perceived by him or her at the time, the profit of the result multiplied by the probability of obtaining the result is greater.

In light of this, the likelihood of Person asking Other for help increases the higher the probability he assigns to Other's help in solving his problem and the more the reward of being helped outweighs the costs of having lowered his status, that is, the higher his profit is. The likelihood of Other helping Person increases the higher the probability he assigns to receiving approval from Person and the more the reward of being approved outweighs the costs of losing time for alternative activities, or again, the higher his profit is.

We can now qualify the four specific propositions in light of the rationality proposition:

The Success Proposition

1. For all actions a person takes, the more often a particular action is rewarded, the more likely the person is to perform that action, provided the product of the probability and the profit of the outcome is higher than it would be for any alternative action.

The Stimulus Proposition

2. If in the past the occurrence of a particular stimulus or set of stimuli has been the occasion on which a person's action has been rewarded, then the more similar the present stimuli are to the past ones, the more likely the person is to perform the action or some similar action now, provided the product of the probability and the profit of the outcome is higher than it would be for any alternative action.

The Value Proposition

3. The more valuable to a person the result of his or her action, the more likely the person is to perform the action, provided the product of the probability and the profit of the outcome is higher than it would be for any alternative action.

The Deprivation-Satiation Proposition

4. The more often in the recent past a person has received a particular reward, the less valuable any further unit of that reward becomes for the person and the less likely he or she is to perform the action resulting in this reward, provided the product of probability and profit of the outcome is lower than with one alternative action at least.

The Aggression-Approval Proposition

Under the heading of the aggression-approval proposition, Homans discusses what happens when the rewards or punishments received in exchange deviate from the expectations of the actors, either in a positive or a negative sense. He formulates the negative deviation in the first part of the proposition:

> When a person's action does not receive the reward he expected, or receives punishment he did not expect, he will be angry; the person becomes more likely to perform aggressive behavior, and the results of such behavior become more valuable to him. (Homans, 1974: 37)

The positive deviation is formulated in a second part:

> When a person's action receives the reward he expected, especially a greater reward than he expected, or does not receive punishment he expected, he will be pleased; he becomes more likely to perform approving behavior, and the results of such behavior become more valuable to him. (Homans, 1974: 39)

Looking at our example, Person may be angry and react with aggression when Other refuses to help him even though he thinks he has given him the appropriate approval on earlier occasions, so Other could expect to receive the appropriate approval. Person may blame Other for his selfishness and punish him insofar as Other does not like to be seen as a selfish person. The result for Person can be that his blaming of Other in itself eases his anger, because he feels rewarded by seeing Other punished in this way; or Other may try to avoid further pain from being insulted by Person and give in, thus helping Person, which restores the relationship to a balanced exchange of rewards. On the other hand, after having helped Person, Other may feel he has not received the appropriate approval, so he will be angry and react with aggression toward Person, blaming him for not being grateful. This may ease his pain; Other may feel rewarded seeing Person blamed as someone not worthy of receiving any help, or he may evoke Person's gratefulness in this way, restoring the relationship to a balanced exchange of rewards.

The same holds true for the positive deviation, according to the second part of the aggression-approval proposition. Receiving much more help from Other than the amount of help that would correspond to the approval he has given him on earlier occasions, Person feels pleased and tries to respond to Other's help by increasing his approval. Other, receiving enormous approval from Person for little help, feels pleased and forced to do better and improve his help. In this way, the balance of exchanged rewards is reestablished.

With this proposition Homans assumes a natural tendency toward balanced exchange relations. As soon as there is some imbalance, the processes of anger and aggression on the one hand and improvement on the other work in the direction of reestablishing a balance of exchanged rewards. The measure of balance the actors apply comes from the rewards they have received under similar circumstances in the past and from the rewards they see other people have received under similar circumstances. Any deviation from this standard calls for activities aiming at reestablishing balanced exchange. This is the standard of distributive justice; accordingly, the corresponding law was called the "law of distributive justice" in the first edition of *Social Behavior* (Homans, 1961: 75). It corresponds to Aristotle's rule formulated in his Nichomachean Ethics. The rule states a principle of proportionality: Everybody should have a share in products that is proportional to his or her merits.

What is interesting in Homans's treatment of this problem is his argument that people react to violations of the rule in such a way that the violation is overcome and the rule reestablished. In the second edition, he even avoids treating the phenomenon as a rule and states a corresponding law of social behavior instead: the angry and aggressive reaction of people to negative deviations from expectations of reward and the pleased, approving, and reward-improving reaction to positive deviations. He states a natural tendency toward balanced social exchange. It is not social control that contributes to reestablishing balance in cases of violations of the rule of distributive justice but the behavioral dispositions of the actors themselves. We have to keep this in mind until we come to a critique of Homans's theory.

Application and Critical Assessment

Now we will examine some of Homans's applications of his theory in order to assess its explanatory power.

Influence and Communication

Let us turn to an application of exchange theory. We take an example of Homans's (1961: 83–111; 1974: 115–38) interpretations of experimental results in the light of his theory, an experiment carried out by Harold B. Gerard (1954). This involves the calculation of rewards and costs, and therefore profit, by the participants in the experiment. The subject matter of the experiment is the working of influence. The investigator created groups of six people and had each group member read a case history of a labor-management dispute. Then he asked each one for his or her opinion about the outcome of the dispute, which had to be indicated on a seven-point scale running from "the union will be adamant" to "the union will give in immediately." Next, the investigator formed new three-person groups of three different kinds: subjects in agreement with one another, subjects in mild disagreement, and subjects in strong disagreement. Among these groups, the investigator made up two types: One type was made up of subjects he told they would find one another very congenial, the other of subjects he told they would not get on well together. Thus, we have six different groups.

Each group then met for a face-to-face discussion of the labor-management dispute. At the end of the discussion each group member was again asked to indicate his or her current opinion on the case. About a week later, each member was asked to represent his or her group in a discussion with a member of another group who was introduced as only fairly congenial. This was, however, a paid participant who had to represent an opinion that was, so far as possible, two steps removed from the subject's last opinion and in a direction that would pull the subject farther away from at least one other member of his or her group. The questions then were, How many members of the six different groups first changed their opinion toward someone in the group after discussing the case in the group? and, How many members of these groups changed their opinion toward the paid participant after discussing the case with him? The results are represented in tables 8.1 and 8.2.

Interpreting the results, Homans assumes three different rewards are involved in the experiment. Subjects feel the approval of the other group members in the high-attraction groups and see this as rewarding; they see consonance with other people as rewarding in itself; they see insisting on their opinion as rewarding in itself, because it emphasizes their personal integrity or autonomy. In light of this assumption, Homans interprets the action of members in the different groups in terms of rewards and costs, that is, profit, resulting from their action. The high-attraction/agree people

Table 8.1   Percentage of Subjects Changing Toward Someone in the Group

	Agree	Mildly Disagree	Strongly Disagree
High Attraction	0	12	44
Low Attraction	0	15	9

Table 8.2   Percentage of Subjects Changing Toward Paid Participant

	Agree	Mildly Disagree	Strongly Disagree
High Attraction	7	13	25
Low Attraction	20	38	8

achieved a high profit by not changing their opinion: they received approval
and consonance and did not lose integrity, because they were able to maintain their original opinions. The low-attraction/agree people did not make
as much profit but did achieve consonance and maintained integrity by not
changing their opinions. The low-attraction/strongly disagree people did not
get consonance but maintained integrity by not changing their opinions.
However, the high-attraction/strongly disagree people are interesting because
for them it was more profitable to change their opinions; in this way they
secured social approval, came into consonance with other people, yet had
the cost of losing integrity. Nevertheless, for 44 percent of them it was the
more profitable alternative. Another interesting group is the low-
attraction/mildly disagree group. They did not get very much integrity from
their original position because their opinion was not unique enough to be
far from other people. They were also receiving neither approval nor consonance. By changing their opinion toward someone in the group, they were
at least able to get some consonance. This is the explanation for why 15
percent changed their opinions. Look at table 8.2. It is remarkable that we
find 38 percent changing their opinions in this category. The change toward
someone in the low-attraction group implied the cost of agreeing with someone one did not like and meant more loss of integrity than changing away
from the group and toward someone who was at least fairly congenial; thus
it appeared more profitable for the 38 percent to change in this direction.

So much for Homans's interpretation of Gerard's experimental results
in the light of a reward-cost analysis. Let us now turn to an examination
of Homans's interpretation as a starting point from which to critically
appraise his theory. To begin with, it should be said that Homans's interpretations came post hoc and are more or less plausible. However, there is no
test of their truth; and the plausibility of the interpretations is not a test
of the theory's truth. On the other hand, the profit analysis draws our attention away from aspects of the experiment that seem to be important as soon
as we understand the discussion in its true sense as a dispute based on arguments. Certainly, there are economic aspects in every discussion, but these
aspects do not cover the whole phenomenon, particularly not the core of
communication itself. Some of the positions the participants occupy in the
discussion may indeed be motivated by their striving for profit. However,
interpreting the discussion as communication in the true sense gives some
different explanations of the positions of participants. Our subject here is
a controversial discourse based on arguments.

According to the rules of discourse, nobody can uphold his or her opinion against opposing positions without finding better reasons to defend that
opinion. The logical rule of exclusion of contradiction states that only one
of two opposing statements can be true. As long as discussants are engaged
in a discourse, they cannot uphold contradictory positions. They are forced

to discuss until they find out which of the contradictory positions is better sustained by reasons. On the other hand, as long as they are in agreement, there is no reason to change their opinions. This explains why nobody in the agreement group changed his or her opinion, neither the high-attraction nor the low-attraction ones. We do not have to look at calculations of rewards and costs in order to come to an explanation of these results. It is simply the participants following the rules of discourse that gives the explanation.

The same applies to the observation that the number of participants changing their opinion toward that of someone else in the group was greatest in the high-attraction/strongly disagree group. The rule of excluded contradiction exerts pressure either to sustain one's opinion with the better argument or to give up the opinion and accept the position that is sustained by better arguments. In this instance we can expect people whose arguments are not strong enough to change their opinions toward those discussants who have the better arguments to support their opinions and thus do not have to change. In this way we can explain why a good number of participants changed their opinions, whereas also a good number (more than half) did not do so. The latter had no reason to change because their opinion was confirmed in the discussion by the arguments found and by the other participants moving in their direction. In the mildly disagree groups there is less pressure to overcome contradictions, because the participants' opinions are not so far from each other, and they do not feel that they are wrong if the opinion of another member is right to the same extent as in the strongly disagree groups. Nevertheless, the pressure is stronger than in the agree groups. Therefore, we have a higher rate of change in these groups than in the agree groups and a lower rate than in the high-attraction/strongly disagree groups.

But how can we explain the rather low rate of change in the low-attraction/strongly disagree group? It is in this case that the rules of discourse apparently do not operate effectively. My explanation is that here a nondiscursive precondition for discourse is not fulfilled. In order to have a discourse people have to truly listen to each other and to trust in each other's purposes. They have to be confident that everybody is interested only in finding out the truth. Inasmuch as they do not trust each other, there is no reason for them to accept any opponent's arguments in a discussion. Coming together with someone who is characterized as a person I will not get on well with does not allow either of us to encounter the other on a very trusting basis. There is no disposition to truly accept the argument of the opponent as an argument one can trust. Therefore, there is no true discourse and correspondingly no pressure to solve contradictions.

Now we shall turn to the discussion with the paid participant. It is apparent that there is a certain minimal amount of change throughout all groups. To explain the results in terms of the rules of discourse we have to take into account that the paid participant in any case begins discussion in a two-point disagreement with the subject; the paid participant is prepared to sustain his or her position with arguments and is instructed not to give in during the discussion. We have here a rather strong discussant who was apparently often able to play out his or her discursive strength against the subject. Thus there is pressure in all groups to solve contradiction and either to sustain one's opinion by good arguments or to move in the direction of the position that is grounded by better arguments. This explains why even some people from the high-attraction/agree groups changed in the direction of the paid participant. The low-attraction/agree people felt even more pressure to solve the apparent inconsistency, and their original opinion was less firmly anchored in consensus, because it was a consensus not based on very much mutual trust. Therefore, they changed more than the high-attraction/agree people. For the two mildly disagree groups, the pressure to solve an apparent contradiction was even greater, because their opinion was not anchored in earlier consensus and therefore less firm, with the low-attraction people the least firm in their opinion. The latter did not agree with their group and did not trust the group; standing alone on an insecure basis, they were open to new arguments and prone to change toward someone who sustained his or her opinion with tenacity.

The high-attraction/strongly disagree people also felt relatively strong pressure to solve the contradiction and did not feel as confirmed in their position by their group as did the high-attraction/agree people; however, because of the strong disagreements they had already encountered they may also have been able to sustain their position against the paid participant with good arguments. This may explain why they did not change as much as the low-attraction/mildly disagree people. Nevertheless, the pressure to solve a contradiction is higher than in the high-attraction/mildly disagree group, which has at least an approximation to trusting consensus. The rather low rate of change in the low-attraction/strongly disagree group may be explained by the argument that these are people who established a very visible position and had to do so with good arguments. They were well prepared to confront the paid participant with their arguments and not to give in as easily as the members of most other groups.

Thus far we have arrived at an explanation of the experimental results by a theory of discourse that begins with the assumption that participants in a discussion are primarily oriented toward the rule that only one of two contradictory opinions can be true, and that the members of the different groups feel the pressure to solve this contradiction with different strength, depending on how much they trust each other and how far removed their opinions are from one another's. The pressure for person A to move toward the opinion of person B increases with the argumentative strength of person B and the insecurity of person A. Insecurity of people originally in agreement can result from a lack of trust underlying their consensus; on the other hand, people in strong disagreement in low-attraction groups develop argumentative strength to sustain their position.

Turning back to Homans's interpretation, we apparently do not need to move away from the primary feature of a discussion toward some underlying economic calculations in order to arrive at satisfying explanations. And it is the primary feature of discussion that is completely out of sight in Homans's economic theory. He does not make any attempt at addressing this dimension of the experimental situation that is indeed its primary feature. This is the reason why we have to be cautious with economic theory. Inasmuch as we see reality only in its perspective, we see nothing other than economic calculations of rewards and costs, and we do not see any dimension of social interaction that reaches well beyond economic calculation and exchange. Communication and discourse have their own rules that explain primarily the course of communicative and discursive action. We have no immediate access to these rules using the vocabulary of economic theory. There are economic processes involved in communication and discourse. Thus, we do not completely reject Homans's theory and interpretations of the discussion experiments. However, there is also a logic of communication and discourse that we do not understand correctly in terms of economic theory. It is this logic that lies outside its scope and calls for a theory appropriately formulated to cover communicative and discursive processes according to their own laws. This is why we have to limit the truth of economic theory to processes that are truly economic in character.

The limits of economic exchange theory with regard to understanding processes of communication and discourse become particularly apparent in Homans's (1961: 232–64, 1974: 241–68) discussion of distributive justice. One of his examples is the relative deprivation of the so-called ledger clerks comparing themselves with the cash posters in the Eastern Utilities Company (Homans, 1974: 243–48). The cash posters recorded customers' accounts. The ledger clerks communicated with customers and employees about the state of customers' accounts and recorded relevant changes to keep the accounts up to date. Their job implied more variety and responsibility, but they had to help with cash posting from time to time by order of the supervisor. They were in the more senior position because normally they had been promoted from cash poster to ledger clerk. Thus, their opinion was that they had higher investments, namely seniority, and higher costs — namely, having to do the more responsible job, which implied more concentration on work and less time for relaxation. However, the ledger clerks got the same pay as the cash posters. Because they saw themselves as having higher investments and higher costs, they felt they should get higher pay than the cash posters in order to have their different investments and costs remunerated with different pay. They felt they were unjustly treated by the company and complained about it. According to Homans, it was the principle of distributive justice that was violated by the company. The ledger clerks did not receive what they deserved in proportion to their investments and costs compared to the cash posters.

The interesting question now is, Where is the ledger clerks' complaint grounded? Is it just their personal and arbitrary expectation and their interest in making profit that have not been met? Certainly not, because they feel it is their right to complain. This right to complain makes the difference between the ledger clerks and the women in the address file. These women had the most monotonous and uninteresting job in the darkest corner of the building and got the lowest pay; nobody liked this job. But the women in the address file did not complain. The reason is that they didn't feel treated in an unjust way by the company compared to the other groups. They felt frustrated with the job, but they did not speak out publicly to demand that anything should be changed about their job, neither the circumstances of doing the job nor the pay. The example of the women in the address file demonstrates that it is not just frustration that leads to complaints but only frustration that is grounded in feelings of unjust treatment. And these feelings do not come by chance: they come only inasmuch as there is minimal agreement about the meaning of justice and injustice in the concrete case. The address file women do not attempt to complain because the prevailing opinion of all groups would not allow them to be seen as being treated in an unjust way by the company.

Homans runs into trouble dealing with this phenomenon in economic terms. He sees that both the ledger clerks and the address file women had higher costs from doing their job than the cash posters. For what reason then did the ledger clerks complain whereas the address file women did not? Homans's answer is that there are "costs that imply superiority and costs that imply nothing of the sort" (Homans, 1974: 247). The standard he is applying is the importance of the job. Costs for an important job justify higher demands; costs for an unimportant job do not. However, this is not an explanation in economic terms, because costs are no longer a criterion for the rewards one can expect. The criterion now is the importance of a job according to the prevailing values in a group, company, or society. The monotony of the address file workers' job is not in itself a cost for doing the job that is generally accepted as a reason for demanding higher pay than for work that is less monotonous. The measure of a just income distribution is not the investments and costs as subjectively incurred by the employees but the investments and costs according to the prevailing values in the company. Homans himself argues in this direction when he draws our attention to the fact that

> they agreed on most rankings, or, as some sociologists would put it, they shared most values. They all agreed, as would the rest of us, that a job with higher

pay was "better," on that count at least, than one with the lower. The more important dimensions were pay, seniority, chance for advancement, variety, responsibility, and autonomy. (Homans, 1974: 243)

What we witness here are not processes of economic calculation but processes of cultural legitimation; the latter simply cannot be understood in terms of economic theory. Whenever persons or groups are capable of proving against possible criticisms that they are treated unjustly in receiving smaller rewards than they deserve compared to other persons or groups, this does not depend on the subjectively incurred investments and costs but on the priority these investments and costs are assigned according to the prevailing values in a group, company, or society. The complaint that one is being treated unjustly is not merely an act triggered by immediate frustration, but results from frustration that can be reasonably legitimated as being derived from unjust treatment. It is an act of discourse that calls for justification by way of sustaining the complaint on generally accepted grounds. We cannot understand and explain these processes in terms of economic theory. What we need here is a vocabulary and theory designed to cover processes of communication and discourse.

Turning to Homans's agression-approval proposition, we can first say that this is a proposition that is not truly a part of economic theory, because it is not just subjectively incurred investments and costs that determine the expectations of rewards and the corresponding anger and aggressive behavior in case of their divergence but the measurement of investments and costs according to values generally presupposed in processes of discursive legitimation of claims for rewards. This qualification of the aggression-approval proposition is necessary even in the light of Homans's own argumentation dealing with cases of distributive injustice. And this qualification turns the proposition completely away from behavioral psychology and economic theory. It has to be reformulated in the following way:

> When a person's action does not receive the reward the person is entitled to expect according to his or her investments and costs in the light of the generally held values of a group, organization, or society, there is a good chance that his or her complaint about unjust treatment and demand for restitution of this violation of distributive justice will be accepted in discursive procedures.

It should be noted that the process of restitution here is not a natural process in which the angry person reacts by issuing punishment and thus restores long-term balance, as Homans put it. In complete contrast, this is now a process of cultural legitimation and justification of claims in procedures of discourse. Successful restitution here depends on coming to mutual agreement. Only inasmuch as there are processes of discourse institutionalized in society is there a chance of arriving at such a restitution by mutual agreement. Thus, we do not claim that factually existing relationships of investments and costs on the one hand and rewards on the other are always based on agreement. We claim only that inasmuch as people are able to ask for their legitimation it is only mutual agreement on generally accepted grounds that yields this legitimation. Economic transactions, power, and simply tradition have their effects on the factual compliance of people with regard to the distribution of rewards, but they do not provide legitimacy for this distribution. This is why we need a theory of processes of communication and discourse in order to understand and explain the phenomenon of distributive justice. And this is why economic theory fails in doing this job.

The second part of Homans's aggression-approval proposition has to be reformulated in a way that involves criticism of overpayment — it is not so much the likelihood of the overpaid person reacting by improving his or her investments and costs but the public pressure he or she feels to do so or to pay back the overpayment:

> When a person receives greater rewards than he or she is entitled to expect according to his or her investments and costs in light of the generally held values of a group, organization, or society, the person comes under pressure to improve his or her investments or costs or to pay back the amount overpaid the more rewards are discussed in the procedures of discourse.

The theory of discourse that underlies this reformulation of Homans's proposition of distributive justice can be formulated in the following two propositions:

1. The more people discuss ideas according to the procedure of discourse, which means that everybody is entitled to propose and to criticize ideas and everybody has to justify them by ideas accepted universally in earlier instances of discourse, the more they come to generalize the meaning of ideas.
2. The more people come to generalize their ideas in procedures of discourse and the more they measure actions and their regulations (institutions) against their underlying ideas, the stronger will be the pressure to change actions and their regulations (institutions) in the direction of a closer consistency with the ideas taken as measures for them.

These two propositions of discourse theory are not part of economic theory. Similar objections to those put forward against Homans's treatment of distributive justice can be made against the so-called relative deprivation theory of revolutions, which explains that protest and revolutions break out when expectations have gone up but are no longer met by the economic conditions (Davies, 1962). There is truth in this theory, but it has to be qualified in the same way as was pointed out in connection with Homans's discussion of distributive justice.

Conformity to Norms

Another field where it is a doubtful matter to found sociological explanation exclusively on the economic premises of exchange theory is the field of conformity to norms (Homans, 1961: 112–28; 1974: 94–114). According to Homans's understanding, Person indicates his expression of a norm when he complains that Other did not respond positively to his request for help. Other also acts in this way when he complains that Person did not give him approval after he had given him help. What leads both men to understand their expectations as a norm is, in Homans's view, the fact that on earlier occasions the exchange took place in the expected form. Thus, it is the frequency of past fulfillment that gives an expectation the quality of a norm. Norms are based on mutual rewarding, as is the case with the exchange between Person and Other. Expected reward is what leads Person to expect something of Other and what leads Other to conform to those expectations, and the other way around. Norms emerge from the survival of those exchanges that are mutually rewarding. In this way striving for profit in exchange relationships itself produces the norms of exchange.

Whenever there is deviation from expectations, the deprived person will react with punishment that will bring back the deviant person into mutually rewarding exchange, according to the aggression-approval proposition. Homans explains the self-correcting process of exchange using the example of controlling production rates in a work group. Groups of factory workers paid piece rates normally restrict their output to a certain limit, because they fear management will decrease the pay per item if the production rate increases too much. Thus, maintaining a certain output becomes a norm for the group. In economic terms and according to Olson's (1965) theory of collective action, which Homans cites in this case, the maintenance of a limited production rate is a collective good. Such a collective good needs everyone's contribution and is rewarding for everyone. Everyone has to keep up with the defined output, and everyone has the reward that management does not decrease the piece rate paid. However, the connection between contribution and reward grows looser and looser the greater the number of group members. In a group of five, the individual member's contribution is one-fifth, in a group of ten it is one-tenth, in a group of twenty, it is one-twentieth. Therefore, the larger the group, the more members can receive the collective reward without contributing individually. This is because the collective good cannot be withheld from those who did not contribute. The piece rate is the same for each member of the group. Homans sees five different categories of group members with regard to the question of their conformity to the output norm:

> These categories are: (1) those who find the results of conformity rewarding and conform from the beginning, (2) those who find the results of conformity rewarding, but do not themselves conform from the beginning, though they come to do so later, (3) those who do not find the results of conformity rewarding, but come to conform later, (4) those who do not find the results of conformity rewarding, never conform, but do not leave the group, and (5) those who never conform and who leave the group. (Homans, 1974: 101)

The first category are the true believers, the second are the freeloaders, the third are the skeptics, the fourth are the holdouts, while the fifth are the dropouts. As Homans points out, the true believers will react to the non-conformers by attacking and punishing them. For the nonconformers it then becomes rewarding to be able to avoid further punishment by conforming to the group norm. Those who do not conform may escape the true believers' punishment by leaving the group, or else they may be so strong and independent of the other group members' opinion that their attacks do not punish them really or that the true believers give up attacking them. The exchange between group members will result in a situation where the overwhelming majority of members mutually reward each other, with only one or a few occasional holdouts left. The relationship between the conformers and the holdouts nevertheless is not punishing in the long run, because the two coexist without taking notice of each other; otherwise, the holdouts will become either conformers or dropouts.

There is no doubt that group members calculate their conformity to the expectations of the other group members to a certain degree so that their participation in the group's activities becomes rewarding; and there is no doubt that the group members react to the behavior of the others in a way that makes their participation rewarding to them. However, is this the whole story of group norms and of conformity to them? The answer must be no. What we miss is the specific quality of group norms and of conformity to group norms that distinguishes them from economic goods and the exchange of economic goods. What is interesting here is the answer to the question, Why is it easier for one group to develop group norms and to achieve norm conformity than for another group to do so? Why are there groups that have to invest heavily in rewards and punishments in order to establish common norms and to make members conform to these norms? If Person and Other are friends, Person's asking Other for help would express a norm, and he could expect Other to help him without any offer of remuneration. Certainly, Other can expect Person to help him whenever he needs help. However, this is not because he expects appropriate remuneration for his help or because he has been helped before. He is expected to do so without any thought of being compensated for it. Helping only under this condition or with an eye to possible rewards violates the norm of selfless help in friendship. Offering approval for help and vice versa turns the relationship between Person and Other into a business relationship. Person's expectation of Other to help him is then no longer a common norm but a personal demand that can be turned into Other's corresponding behavior only by way of offering some reward. It is much more a norm of exchange that forces Person to remunerate Other appropriately for his help.

Friendship and economic exchange are governed by very different norms. It is not the individual calculation of profit that leads Other to expect or not to expect appropriate remuneration from Person for his help but his orientation to norms that define whether he is entitled to expect remuneration or not. A norm is not just an expectation of a person but an expectation to act in a certain situation in a certain way that is commonly held to be obligatory within a certain community (group, organization, or society) and upheld by this community even against deviations. When expecting conformity to a norm from Other, Person can rely on his and Other's group fellows' support in bringing Other into the line of the norm. He cannot rely on such support for his personal expectation. This is the difference between an arbitrary expectation and a norm.

Maintaining this distinction is important, because conformity to norms and fulfillment of arbitrary expectations have different preconditions. First, there is the difference of whether a group is able to establish a norm, that is, to come to shared mutual expectations, or not. Second, conformity to norms is expected from a person without conceding any remuneration for this. A person does not have to be rewarded for norm conformity, but he or she is punished for deviation from norms. However, this is not punishment by an individual person whose expectation has not been fulfilled. It is punishment by the group in order to maintain the binding character of the norm. And it is the binding character that distinguishes a norm from any arbitrary expectation.

The question now is, How do common norms of such a binding character emerge? The answer of Homans's economic theory is that a history of rewarding behavior that conforms to certain expectations turns these expectations into norms. We do not need to deny any influence of this process of rewarding on the development of norms. However, this is only part of the story. Making norms dependent on the rewarding effects of norm conformity implies a high velocity of change in norm-oriented behavior and a high tendency toward deviation, because the terms of profit change often from situation to situation and from person to person. Inasmuch as deviation occurs because people expect higher profit from deviation and changes in norms follow from this deviation, we can explain this by economic theory. However, though some norms change in this way there are many norms that do not change as quickly as we would expect from the change of the terms of profit for the actors involved. These are norms that are more deeply rooted in the community, and their enormous stability calls for a different explanation. The first root of these norms is the commitment of people to a group and the solidarity of this group. Being involved in mutual solidarity in a group having a feeling of "we" makes people much more likely to see the world in the same way and to expect the same behavior of people.

Solidarity is the root of consensus, and it is the consensus of people that turns world-views and expectations into norms. Whoever has a different view or acts in different ways steps outside the community, breaks its consensus, and violates its solidarity. Because the members share mutual solidarity, they react to any deviation from shared norms by supporting the victim and trying to bring the deviant member back into line or to close him or her out. Thus it is mutual solidarity that evokes reactions from a group to deviations, leading to the reestablishment of the binding character of its norms. For the majority of conformers, it is not the expectation of rewards that motivates them to conform but just their solidarity and consensus. These two qualities close out any alternative action from their minds. They just cannot conceive of the world and of appropriate action in a different way, because they simply do not know anything else. It is not something they prefer to something else on economic terms but something that is not compared with anything else. This is where the economic calculation of costs and benefits stops; it takes place only within the limits set by the common norms of the group.

Moreover, it is not only commitment, solidarity, and consensus that turn world-views and expectations into norms that close out alternatives; it is also consensus on a world-view and on norms that makes it much easier to come to consensual views and norms in concrete situations where both, a definition of the situation and a concrete normative regulation, have to be found. Specific views and norms become all the more easily established the more they conform to those that already exist and the more easily they can be incorporated into that existing body of common views and norms. It is not the expected profit from a regulation that decides on its acceptance but its closeness to an existing tradition, its connection with the common life-world of the group.

The nonconformers either do not know what the consensus is or do not believe in the consensus, or else they know but have had experiences outside group thought that bring alternative views and actions to light, and — most important — they no longer feel solidarity with the group. These actors are driven away from the group, either to share the solidarity of another group or to become marginal figures. They are freed from the group's view and normative definition of the situation and are therefore free to go beyond this normative frame. Whereas the conformers calculate profit only within the limits of the group norms, the nonconformers calculate profit beyond these norms. They are free to compare the rewards and costs of conforming and nonconforming behavior, to choose the most profitable way to act. The conformers are not free to do that; they simply cannot imagine doing it.

The nonconformers cannot always be brought back in line with the group norms simply by reestablishing blind solidarity. When solidarity fails, reason or rewards or punishment have to do their job. But they do it in ways very different from solidarity. Rewards are effective only as long as they make conforming truly more profitable than nonconforming. We cannot expect a high stability of conforming behavior from economic calculation, because the terms of profit change from situation to situation. The more people begin to calculate conformity or nonconformity, the more likely a change in norms will be. Punishment is effective only as long as the group has more power than the nonconformers in order to enforce conformity; we expect conflict and change here the more people apply power to enforce behavior. Justifying norms by reasons is effective only as long as the norms are indeed supported by generally accepted reasons; here we can expect a change in the norms in the process of attempts at justifying and criticizing them. The commitment of members to their group, the solidarity of the group, and the consensus coming from this solidarity turn world-views and expectations of behavior into stable, unquestioned norms. Inasmuch as commitment, solidarity, and consensus break up, norms are open to change.

This is where economic theory can partly provide explanations of change in norms. And certainly we do not always have fully realized commitment, solidarity, and consensus; it is often only partly realized. In the first instance, then, these conditions only explain the stabilization of norms in the majority of the group members. However, in the second instance, commitment, solidarity, and consensus of the majority of group members serve as a precondition for a stable reaction of the group to norm deviation, which itself is necessary to reestablish the binding character of a norm. In this way the nonconformers are brought back or excluded through rewards or punishments (or reasons) that are part of an economic explanation of norm compliance. Nevertheless, rewarding and punishing activities have to be rooted in the commitment, solidarity, and consensus of the majority of the group. Therefore, even in explaining the norm compliance of the nonconformers an explanation in economic terms is insufficient. We need a theory of commitment, solidarity, and consensus as foundations of the binding power of norms that is a theory in its own right and that cannot be reduced to economic propositions. Inasmuch as we try to explain the binding power of norms purely in economic terms, we stretch economic theory beyond the field for which it yields correct explanations.

We can formulate the following three interrelated propositions going beyond the limits of economic theory in terms of a theory of commitment, solidarity, and consensus:

1. The more people are committed to a community and the stronger the solidarity of that community, the more likely it is that these people will establish consensus and, accordingly, a common view of the world and common expectations that people will have to act in certain situations in certain ways, that is, norms.
2. The more people consensually bear common norms, the more they will arrive at common views and normative regulations according to their closeness to their traditionally existing common norms in actual situations.
3. The more people consensually share common norms, the more they will conform to norms out of mutual solidarity and the more they will react to norm deviations out of solidarity, bringing the deviators back in line with the norms by rewards, punishments, and reasons, and in this way, reestablishing the binding validity of the norms.

These are basic propositions of a theory of norm validity that are not part of economic theory.

Power

Another area where Homans's economic theory leads to doubtful interpretations is interaction that involves conflict and the application of power (Homans, 1974: 70–93). Because of his preoccupation with seeing social interaction as exchange, Homans conceives of power only as an ability to raise the price of the rewards one has to offer. Homans explains this conception of power in terms of Person and Other trading approval for help (Homans, 1974: 70–76). Suppose there is a "Third Man" who also offers Other approval for help. Thus, as Homans says, Other draws approval from two sources and reaches a point of satiation sooner, while he will have less time to do his own work, and this will now become more profitable for him. In this case Person has to offer warmer approval in order to continue to receive Other's help. Other now has a stronger position in the exchange with Person than before, and this will remain so as long as there is no alternative source of help for Person. Other is less interested in the exchange than Person compared to the situation where Other had no alternative source where he could obtain approval. In Homans's view, Other now has more power than Person because he is less interested in the exchange than his opposite number. The reason is that Other does not make as much profit from the exchange with Person as he would make from an alternative action. This forces Person to increase the reward he offers to a degree that would turn making the exchange into a more profitable action for Other than any alternative. In this case Other has more market power than Person. We do not need to decide whether Person or Other makes more profit from the exchange as Homans does in his confusing definition of power:

> When A's net reward — compared, that is, with his alternatives — in taking action that will reward B is less, at least as perceived by B, then B's net reward in taking action will reward A, and B as a result changes his behavior in a way favorable to A, then A has exerted power on B. (Homans, 1974: 83)

It is not that A makes less profit from the exchange than B that forces B to increase his reward, but the fact that A makes less profit from the exchange than from some alternative action. Person may make a high profit from the exchange because he is in extreme need of help to solve his problem at work. However, he may have many alternative sources of help. Other may make only a very small profit from the exchange because Person has a very low status, so that his approval is of little value in the department. However, Other may also be a low-status person and have no alternative sources of reward. In this situation Other makes little profit, and Person makes a high profit; nevertheless, Other is much more interested in the exchange than Person because Person would easily get help elsewhere, but Other would not so easily gain approval elsewhere. Thus, Other will have to increase the amount of his help so that it is more than any help from alternative sources. Here, contrary to Homans's definition, the person who makes little profit is much more forced to improve his or her offer than the person making a higher profit if the exchange is to be realized. Correcting Homans we can define market power in the following way:

> Market power is the ability of a party in exchange to force another party in that exchange to increase its offered rewards and therefore to incur higher costs compared to an earlier situation in order to realize the exchange.

Using this definition of market power we can formulate the following proposition:

> The fewer alternative sources of reward a person has, the greater the market power his or her partners of exchange can exert on him or her.

As we have learned, the fact that someone has more or less market power to exert on another person does not say anything about the amount of profit the parties make from the exchange. Indeed, the reverse relationship is not unusual in the economic area. For example, the Federal German postal service and railroad system have monopolized their services so that their customers have no alternative means of obtaining them. This gives the postal service and the railway system a great deal of market power, which the customers feel when they are forced to pay ever higher charges or fares for the use of those services. However, neither the Federal German Post Office nor the Federal German Railways in fact makes any profit; quite the reverse, for they have to fight with increasing losses.

Homans states a tendency toward the equalization of power in exchange relationships. Starting with the assumption that Person makes more profit (help) from the exchange than Other (approval), he says that Person is forced to increase his approval so that Other will have a higher profit. In this way the profit the two people make reaches a balance where both are equally interested in the exchange. Their respective power also comes into equilibrium, because at this point there is no further need on the part of Person to increase his approval, and Other has no further chance to exert pressure to obtain still higher profit.

Yet the above analysis is as confusing as Homans's understanding of power. It is not reaching the level of Person's profit that motivates Other to enter the exchange but only the fact that Person has increased his offer of approval up to a point where Other makes more profit from the exchange than from any alternative action. And this has nothing to do with equalizing their profits. Taking our example of the low status Other with no alternative means of earning even a very small profit and a low status Person with many alternatives that would bring a high profit, Other's improvement of his help in order to win approval from Person actually lowers Other's profit and further increases Person's profit. Thus Homans's statement about the equalization of profit and power in exchange relationships is simply false.

His confusion about power in exchange relationships goes so far that, according to his view, the person expecting less profit is always the more powerful person of the two, able to force the other party to improve his or her offer until a point is reached where both parties make equal profits. Because of this, no exchange that produces very unequal results for the two parties goes on. In Homans's view we cannot imagine any ongoing exchange in which one party always makes a large profit and the other party little profit. In this perspective we have no access to the peculiarities that distinguish power relationships from exchange relationships. In pure exchange both parties have alternatives and come together voluntarily because they derive most profit from just this exchange and not from any other. However, the two parties can make very different amounts of profit. In a power relationship the person who has no power does not voluntarily enter the relationship but is forced to do so by the powerful person; alternatively, in an existing relationship, the powerless person is prevented by the powerful one from leaving the relationship. Whereas the powerful person makes use of the powerless person on the basis of his or her free will, the latter has no freedom to decide whether to comply or not to comply. The powerless person has lost his or her freedom to the powerful person. Because the powerless person does not have the alternative of entering any other relationship or even having no relationship, the powerful person is capable of manipulating the situation for the powerless person so that the latter's only choice is between complying with the powerful person's demands and some alternative that would be even worse. The powerless person does not make any profit here. He or she has only the choice between a greater or smaller loss.

It is confusing to interpret the powerless person's choice of the smaller loss as rewarding as Homans does in order to keep this phenomenon in line with his economic proposition that people always choose the alternative with the highest profit. We are confused by this interpretation because it prevents us from seeing that in power relationships people can be forced to take actions that are not at all profitable for them. Homans ignores this aspect in dealing with what he calls coercive power. In his example, a man is held up by a bandit who confronts him with two alternatives that are both losses: "Your money or your life!" By choosing life and losing money, the man opts for the more profitable alternative, Homans says, because he is holding on to something that is rewarding in itself. Whichever way Homans turns this argument, however, there is no denying the fact that the man suffers a loss if the result of the encounter is measured against the situation before the bandit's appearance. Before, the man had life and money; now, he has only his life. The encounter with the bandit has robbed him of his freedom to act, because as an economically rational actor he would never have acted in this way. It was the power of the bandit that robbed him of his freedom and forced him to do things he would not have done voluntarily. He was forced to act in a way that was economically rational only under very restricted conditions: to incur a loss in order to avoid an even greater loss. The restriction of alternatives for action is imposed by the powerful person upon the powerless, and this is what calls for an explanation here.

The economic explanation of the man's choice of the smaller loss is not sufficient or even interesting in this case. The essential sequence of cause and effect is that the man decides to give away his money because his scope for action has been restricted to just two alternatives—losing his money or his life—because, in turn, the bandit has the capacity to exert power over him. The bandit has that power because he has a gun which he points at the man as he issues his ultimatum "Your money or your life!" Homans's preoccupation with economic theory prevents us from reaching this core of the power relationship and coming to a sufficient explanation of the facts. Homans turns into a relationship of social exchange what in reality is a conflict between two persons that is resolved not by negotiating profits but by enforcing one person's goal through applying power. The bandit has the goal of stealing the man's money, whereas the victim has the goal of keeping his money. The two are in conflict because both cannot attain their goals at the same time. In terms of the theory of games, they are engaged in a zero-sum game. Goal attainment for the bandit means failure for the man, and vice versa. Unless they give up their goals, they are in conflict with each other.

It is in a situation like this that economic theory does not tell us anything about the outcome and the respective action of the two protagonists. Because they are not willing to change their goals, they cannot calculate whether it may be more profitable to turn to some alternative action leading toward different goals. They do not calculate whether it is profitable to steal money or whether it is profitable to preserve every cent one has under all circumstances. The bandit's risk is that he will be arrested and lose his freedom. The victim's risk is that he will lose his life. As persons who are committed to their goals, they have no other choice than to use whatever means they have to force the opponent to move in a direction that allows each to attain his goal. A means available to the bandit is to raise his gun and say, "Your money or your life!" The man may react by striking the bandit's hand that is directing the gun at him, grabbing the gun, and turning it on the bandit. Here the outcome depends on who will be able to successfully direct a gun at the opponent. The person who attains his goal will be the one who succeeds in this struggle for power. Possession of the gun gives enough power to attain one's goal at the cost of the other person's goal attainment. If the bandit can keep the gun, he will have the power to get the money whether the man gives it to him on demand or whether he has to shoot him first.

This is how power works, and it works in a way that has its own character not covered by economic propositions. Homans's economic view of power prevents us from coming to an adequate explanation of its true character and the mechanisms by which it works. As we have seen, he does not correctly see the nature of power in exchange relations. The powerful person in an exchange relation is capable of dictating the terms of exchange so that he or she is better off than the (relatively) powerless person. The powerful person can increase his or her profit much more than the powerless person because that person has no alternative exchange transactions available. Moreover, there is no tendency here toward equalization of power, as Homans falsely states. Low-status Other with no alternative sources of approval can be forced to improve his help for Person while receiving only a very small amount of approval in return, whereas Person receives a great deal of help and therefore makes a large profit from the exchange. Nor is there any tendency for Other's very low profit to be raised.

This is what the theory of conflict and power tells us: Powerful Person is able to force powerless Other into an exchange that is very unfavorable for Other and not at all an exchange on equal terms. We can also formulate this insight in terms of relatively more or less powerful people. The more powerful persons are capable of forcing the less powerful into actions that are unfavorable to them, contrary to their goals, and lower their profit, actions that they would never perform were they free to choose from a wide range of alternatives. The more powerful people are also capable of dictating the type of interaction taking place between the two actors. For example, the more power an actor has, the more he or she will be able to force the opponent in a conflict to give up the straightforward realization of his or her goal and to enter negotiations according to the terms set by the more powerful actor. The bandit who directs the gun against the man saying "Your money or your life!" can force the man to accept the terms of trade he sets. Inasmuch as the man sees no chance of changing the unfavorable situation, he gives in and accepts the "bargain" offered. The bandit has his life in his hands, and handing over all his money is the price of winning it back. The man has the choice of one bitter alternative or the other.

On the other hand, two actors in conflict, for example, collective actors like a labor union and management, may come to a point where both of them see that aiming for full goal attainment may jeopardize the attainment of any goal at all. There may be the danger of a total loss instead of a total win. In this situation, they both feel forced to reduce their goals within a certain limit and to enter into negotiations about the terms of compromise. Management's goal may have been to accept a wage growth of only 2 percent and no reduction in regular weekly working hours. The union's goal may have been 5 percent wage growth and a reduction in regular weekly working from forty hours to thirty-five. After a long period of mutual threatening talk, management may offer 3.5 percent if the union gives up its demand for reduced regular working hours. This is the point where management gives up its conflict strategy and offers the other side the chance to enter into negotiations. If the union does not see a chance of fully realizing its goals and is not totally committed to those goals, it will move away from its conflict strategy too and negotiate for 3.5 percent *and* the reduction of the working week from forty hours to thirty-five hours. Now the two parties are close enough for a compromise that both can attain more easily than the realization of their original goals. This is the point where the actors move away from total conflict toward negotiation within the limits of the goals they set for themselves.

As we can see from this analysis of conflict and power, of exchange and power, and of negotiation and compromising as ways out of total conflict, economic theory does not sufficiently provide explanations of the working of power. Economic theory's propositions do not cover this field of social interaction. What we need to come to sufficient insights and explanations in this area is a theory of conflict and power in its own right; this theory cannot be built up in terms of economic theory. A general theory of action that aims at overcoming the outlined shortcomings of economic theory must incorporate the insights of conflict theory into its body of knowledge.

Exchange

The criticism so far directed against Homans's economic theory of social behavior as exchange does not deny this theory any explanatory power. What we have demonstrated is that its explanatory power is limited. This becomes apparent in Homans's attempts at dealing with discourse and distributive justice, norm conformity, and power. These are phenomena that are part of areas outside the realm of economic calculation and exchange. We have to acknowledge the fact that making profit is not the most basic element of human action to which every other element occurring in human life can be traced back. It is simply naive to believe this and no more than an expression of the predominance of economic thinking in our modern Western societies, particularly in American society. It is the rule of the economic ideology that makes us believe in economic theory's claim to explain the whole of our lives. As we have seen, there are at least three important areas of social interaction that are not covered by economic theory: discourse and argumentation, community and solidarity, conflict and power. Also essential are areas of human life reaching beyond interaction, like learning, personality development, and cultural symbolization.

However, though limited to the area of economic calculation and exchange, economic theory does provide us with insights that we cannot gain from other theories. Also, because discourse, communal association, and conflict also display economic aspects—though these are not the core of these forms of interaction—economic theory also partly provides explanations for phenomena in these primarily noneconomic areas, but only partly and not fully. This limitation of economic theory is what we have to insist on against unduly far-reaching claims from economic theorists.

For economic theory to be applicable to social interaction, human actors must be oriented primarily toward making profit, that is, to reaching an optimum of a set of different goals; this distinguishes the economic orientation from the political orientation toward totally realizing one single goal, the communal orientation toward conforming to the concrete norms of one's community, and the social-cultural orientation toward reaching consistency with general ideas. An economically oriented actor is flexible enough to look for those people who can contribute to increasing his or her profit. Inasmuch as other actors do the same, people will come together according to their ability to mutually increase their profit. Inasmuch as one actor has what another actor needs to increase his or her profit and the other actor has what the first actor needs, their needs are complementary. If Person needs help that Other can provide, while Other needs approval that Person can provide, it is profitable for both of them to enter an exchange of help and approval. Economically oriented actors will remain so as long as there is no alternative action promising more profit. Exchanging goods and services (rewards) is the natural interaction people will engage in who are looking for people to make a profit (Homans, 1974: 51–68). It is economic theory that provides the right propositions for the working of the exchange process:

1. The more profitable an exchange promises to be for an actor, the more likely he or she is to enter this exchange.
2. The more profitable an exchange has been in the past and promises to be in the future for an actor, the more likely he or she is to stay in this exchange relationship.
3. The more the terms of profitability change in exchange relationships, the higher will be the rate of change of the exchange relationships.
4. The more open a market is for new supply and new demand, the more rapidly the terms of profitability of exchange relationships will change and therefore the higher the rate of change of exchange relationships will be.

These propositions emphasize the dynamic change that characterizes an economic orientation, economic behavior, and economic exchange. This is the specific effect of economic markets on social behavior. The more economic calculation of behavior and processes of market exchange penetrate all areas of social life, the more these areas come under the pressure of rapid change:

5. The more economic behavior and exchange penetrate discourse, communal association, and conflict settlement, the higher the rate of change of ideas, communal association, and goal enforcement.

Interesting applications of economic theory to primarily noneconomic areas of social life concentrate on discovering the effects of markets, economic calculation, and exchange on social action in these areas. This, for example, is the line of argumentation in Anthony Downs's (1957) economic theory of democracy. Downs conceives of political decision making as a market and shows how economically rational actors, parties and voters, will act in exchange relations on the political market. He seeks, for example, to explain why there is a growing similarity between the programs of big political parties. His explanation is that parties as economic actors want to maximize votes, and to do that they cannot be totally committed to an unchangeable program. Rather than that, they have to subordinate the program to maximizing votes. Thus, inasmuch as the voting population is characterized by a broad middle class with similar preferences and big parties want to gain as many votes as they can, they have to offer programs that correspond to the preferences of this broad majority of the voting population. A political system that displays most the characteristics of a market of this kind will show the highest rate of change of political programs from election to election, not even allowing the chance to bind parties together in a thoroughly determined program. This lower degree of fixation of programs and higher rate of change in them is indeed a feature of the American political system, which displays much more the character of a political market than any European political system. We can explain this difference in economic terms as Downs does.

Another interesting application of economic theory is a negative one. It is concerned with the question of why people do not contribute to the production of collective goods from which they all benefit. This is what Olson (1965) seeks to explain by applying his theory of collective action. A collective good is one that cannot be distributed individually according to individual investments. Either it is produced and everybody profits from this, or it is not produced and nobody has a profit. Examples of such inseparable collective goods are clean air, clean water, regulated traffic, and social order. Everybody profits from social order because it makes people's actions more predictable. Olson shows that with an increase in the number of people in a social group, the number of people profiting from the provision of a collective good increases; however, the motivation for each person to contribute to the provision of the collective good decreases. The reason is that with the growing number of people required to contribute to the provision of the collective good, each person's part in contributing to it decreases steadily to approach zero in very large groups, for example, 1 out of 7 million in a city of that size. Contributing to social order by way of conforming to norms is very unlikely for a person in this situation. The person cannot expect any observable effect from his or her behavior, whether conforming or deviating behavior, on the provision of social order. Inasmuch as social order does not exist, the person cannot change this by conforming, or inasmuch as it does exist, he or she will also create no perceptible change by deviating. In the former case, the person has no profit at all, and in the latter case, he or she has the highest profit by taking the rewards of both personal deviation and collective order. Therefore, there is no reason for an economically rational actor to contribute to the provision of social order. This is the case as long as people are only individually and economically oriented and interact on the market.

In this way, we can demonstrate with economic theory why individual economic orientation and markets do not provide for the production of social order the greater the number of people involved in social interaction. Economic theory, however, does not tell us how social order can be produced, breaking the effects of economic orientation and markets. Here is the point where we have to consult theories of discourse, solidarity, and conflict settlement to come to satisfying answers. Only inasmuch as there are solidarity and tradition can we expect normative stabilization of social order; only inasmuch as there is centralization of power can we expect social order to be enforced against resistance; only inasmuch as centralized power and the enforcement of norms are anchored in the solidarity and consensus of most members of a group is it possible to resist forces of change; and only inasmuch as the norms of social order can be legitimized in discursive procedures will there be continuity of a legitimate order, however, a continuity that implies change in the direction of underlying general ideas.

Existing social orders normally are supported by a set of all these factors. Take the example of the totalitarian order in societies governed by what was termed real-world or "really existing" socialism. The immediate question is one of why so many people complained about the negative effects of this order but so few did anything to change it. A new order was a collective good many people wished to have, but only a few people did anything in this direction, because the effect of their contribution was nearly nothing. However, there was also the danger of creating chaos; thus, many people preferred to have at least some order, even a bad one, to the alternative of possible chaos. It was more profitable to muddle through under an existing order than to face chaos. Moreover, there was the large group of party and government officials who made a good profit from having certain privileges. This group actively resisted any change, because change would have endangered their profits. Furthermore, there was the group of active party leaders who had to fear losing control and power and therefore most actively resisted any attempts at change. The group of party leaders and of officials made up the core solidarity in society on which the order and its enforcement against deviation and resistance was founded. Finally, the dominating ideology of communism served as a basis for delegitimating any attempt at changing the system as a counterrevolutionary act bringing back the rule of ugly capitalism. Attempts at delegitimating the existing system were bound to argue for a true socialism or communism.

As we can see there was an overwhelming dominance of forces that contributed to the stability of the existing order in society under real-world socialism. This made change of that order very difficult, even though an overwhelming majority would have profited more from a new order. The breakdown of state socialism in the fall of 1989, therefore, was a surprise for most people. However, total loss of confidence in the ruling elite had broken the walls so that the people were now free to vote for a change of that order according to what seemed more profitable for them.

We can add the final qualification of economic theory. As demonstrated, this theory is the right one to explain processes of market exchange among economically oriented actors. However, the working of economic exchange itself cannot be explained completely in economic terms, because exchange involves and is dependent on features that are rooted in discourse, communal association, and conflict settlement through the application of power.

Actors involved in exchange normally have some ideas about the right terms of exchange. Unless they agree to terms of exchange that both parties and also a potential audience see as justified when measured against basic general ideas, one or both parties will consider the exchange unjust and try to get support for the restitution of that injustice. The more this is the case, the less people will be engaged in real exchange and the more they will debate the terms of exchange instead. It is very much a matter of discourse that penetrates exchange at this point, and only a theory of discourse can explain the workings of these aspects of social exchange to us. There is a growing pressure to make the terms of exchange consistent with the general idea of justice in exchange the more discourse penetrates exchange. Legitimacy of the terms of exchange can come only from such discursive processes. The most important ideas underlying exchange are the following: Everybody should enter exchange and make decisions to carry out the exchange voluntarily. Both parties in an exchange should have equal opportunities to engage in alternative exchange transactions. Both parties should have equal power in the exchange.

On the other hand, ongoing exchange normally displays the feature of a predictable order. We normally expect partners in exchange to be reliable and to abide by a concluded agreement. However, this feature of a collective order does not come from economic calculation itself. This order needs anchoring in the commitment to a market community in solidarity and consensus, and the enforcement of norms of exchange needs anchoring in the solidarity and consensus of the market community.

Finally, exchange very often implies conflict. Terms of exchange have to be enforced against resistance. This does not come from exchange itself but from the application of power that sets the limits for economic calculation. Either the more powerful party in the exchange is dominant, which explains its ability to enforce its terms of exchange against the less powerful party, or the enforcement of equal terms may imply the application of power against resisting parties. This will be possible only inasmuch as there is a centralized state power, which is itself anchored in solidarity and consensus and in procedures of discourse, applying ideas of justice to the enforcement of terms of exchange. We first need a theory of conflict and power to explain the enforcement of terms of exchange and then theories of solidarity and discourse in order to explain the enforcement of equal terms of exchange. This example demonstrates that economic theory does not cover all aspects of exchange completely. It is a theory with limited explanatory power; we have to be aware of this limitation in order to make good use of the theory.

NINE

A THEORY OF EXCHANGE AND POWER: PETER M. BLAU

AN ENORMOUS effort of extending exchange theory beyond its economic confines was undertaken by Peter M. Blau in his book *Exchange and Power in Social Life*, published in 1964. Blau is well aware of the limited explanatory power of a purely economic approach to social exchange. He supplements the economic approach by one that takes into account the fact that interpersonal social exchange is enmeshed in a complex network of macrostructures and the way in which it relates to processes of power and authority formation, normative control, cultural legitimation, and criticism.

Blau is one of the outstanding representatives of sociology at Columbia University in New York. In this context he has been exposed to the emphasis on the institutional structure of social life throughout his academic career, in accordance with the main thrust of Merton's empirical functionalism, though Blau did not join the functionalist camp. He has published highly acclaimed studies on bureaucracy (Blau, 1955/1963, 1956/1971), on exchange theory (Blau, 1964), on the occupational structure of American society (Blau and Duncan, 1967), and on the laws pertaining to typical structural settings (Blau, 1977). Here we deal with his extension of exchange theory.

Association, Attraction, and Exchange

Blau (1964: 12–114) starts his undertaking by citing social associations as the very core of social life and as the foremost and elementary subject matter of his sociological inquiry. He refers to Durkheim's (1895/1973) understanding of social facts as rooted in the association of people and to Simmel's (1908) approach to analyzing social association. Blau wants first to understand the processes of association and then to inquire into the more complex

257

social forces and structures emerging from these processes. He explicitly distinguishes this approach from any that is preoccupied with studying social action and its structuring in terms of underlying common values and norms. This structural approach established by Parsons in the tradition of Weber's sociology has thus been complemented by an approach that concentrates on the nature and processes of social association in their own right.

What is the basic nature of social association? That is, what are the forces bringing people together and setting them apart? Blau's first answer to that question is: mutual attraction. This is the proposition of attraction:

1. The more people are attracted to each other, the more they spend time together and are associated in common action.

There are many concrete reasons why people feel attracted to each other and therefore associate. However, they all have one quality in common, according to Blau: the rewards people extract from associating with others. Thus, we can state a proposition of rewards:

2. The more people receive rewards from associating with others, the more they feel attracted to these other people.

However, as we know from our discussion of Homans's propositions, every action and thus every association implies not only rewards but also costs, at least the costs of forgone rewards coming from alternative associations with someone else. There is also the effect that the value of a reward to a person decreases with every unit he or she receives, according to the principle of diminishing marginal utility. Blau is well aware that the costs incurred by an association play a part in actors' choices and that a principle of diminishing returns operates. He also speaks of expected rewards, which seems to entail that the actor takes into account the probability of receiving a reward. Summing up all these considerations, we can say Blau sees the probability of attraction growing in proportion with the amount of profit and the probability of the profit one person expects from associating with another. In order to predict the probability that an association will take place and be continued we could apply a proposition of profit that is parallel to Homans's rationality proposition:

3. The greater the product of profit and probability of receiving that profit people expect from associating with others, the more they feel attracted to these others.

We can correct the reward proposition to become the profit proposition (Blau, 1964: 101–3):

4. The higher the profit people expect from associating with others, the more they feel attracted to these others.

People associate because they expect rewards from this association, thus enhancing their profit. Association between people therefore is an exchange of rewards. This is the point of convergence between Blau and Homans:

> "Social Exchange," as the term is used here, refers to voluntary actions of individuals that are motivated by the returns they are expected to bring and typically do in fact bring from others. (Blau, 1964: 91)

If we take this view of social exchange literally, it implies that people do indeed calculate at least roughly the profit they expect from alternative relationships open to them, that they enter and continue exchange relations that are profitable and do not enter and do not continue those that are unprofitable, that people change from less profitable to more profitable relations, and that they always make their choice and are therefore permanently engaged in calculating profit. All this implies that there is a relatively high rate of change in exchange relations. Because Blau sees social exchange involved in a broad variety of social associations, it also follows that all these associations change at a high rate. We have to keep this in mind because paradoxically many of the forms of social exchange Blau discusses do not fit into this economic picture of social exchange but are much less open to change according to expected profit and much more restricted in character.

Rewards can be extrinsic and intrinsic in nature. The help, advice, approval, support, entertainment, interesting information, smiles, access to other people, warm reception, and pleasant conversation I receive from my partner in exchange are extrinsic rewards coming from the associations. An intrinsic reward is my feeling of being rewarded by the associations in and of themselves. I do not need any further reward to feel attracted to the person in this case. People who love each other, who are friends, or who are a couple normally enjoy spending time with each other whatever they concretely do. Their relationship is intrinsically rewarding for them. Many associations between people combine extrinsic and intrinsic rewards. Two lovers enjoy not only being together in the cinema but also watching an amusing film. Going to a party given by some friends may be intrinsically rewarding because I just want to be with them, but it may also provide some extrinsic rewards like enjoying a superb buffet and talking to some people who can further my career. Extrinsic and intrinsic rewards can be equally and unequally distributed between the partners in an exchange. Two lovers may feel intrinsically rewarded by the association with one another to the same degree. It may also be that the man feels intrinsically rewarded by the association with the woman, whereas the woman has a greater appreciation for the jewelry she gets from her lover.

Rewards given to another person call for some reciprocation. A person who has given help to another person without receiving anything in exchange feels an ingratitude on the part of that other person. Only inasmuch as the person giving help is intrinsically rewarded by the association will he or she continue the relationship with the other person. The alternative is for the second person to change his or her behavior and to reciprocate the help received by giving some extrinsic rewards to the helping person. A sign of gratitude is the least the helper would expect. A person who has refused to give the expected reward will see that he or she has to improve the rewards given to the helping person if the exchange and thus the rewards from the exchange are to continue. A tendency toward reciprocation is therefore part of the ongoing exchange itself. Exchange that does not meet this condition will simply be terminated by the disappointed partner.

This does not imply that there is always balance in an exchange. A person who feels rewarded just by the association with another person has to input a lot of external rewards into the exchange in order to make him- or herself attractive to the other person. In this way both get the rewards that draw them to the association. However, the first has to give much more than the second. The example immediately coming to mind and discussed by Blau several times is the boy who loves a girl and has to invest a lot in order to please and to attract her. The imbalance in their relationship forces the boy to invest more in order to have his effort reciprocated. The reciprocation takes place and the association is continued because the boy equalizes their originally unequal mutual attraction by improving the extrinsic rewards he offers and making himself attractive enough to have his investments reciprocated. Blau states that social exchange has a natural tendency toward reciprocation in this way that is only secondarily reinforced by a norm of reciprocity; he therefore opposes the position of Alvin Gouldner (1960), who formulated the principle of reciprocity:

> In contrast to Gouldner, however, it is held here that the norm of reciprocity merely reinforces and stabilizes tendencies inherent in the character of social exchange itself and that the fundamental starting mechanism of patterned social intercourse is found in the existential conditions of exchange, not in the norm of reciprocity. (Blau, 1964: 92)

However, Blau does not want to conceive of social exchange only in economic terms. He explicitly draws a line between social exchange and strictly economic exchange (see also Ekeh, 1974). What is expected is much less specified in social exchange than in economic exchange. Whereas in economic exchange goods, services, and the money paid for them are as precisely specified as possible, social exchange mostly entails unspecified obligations. Speaking of obligation in this context, Blau (1964: 88–112) reveals the normative dimension of social exchange. The examples he uses to demonstrate his point underscore the normatively regulated character of social exchange: Malinowski's (1922/1961) analysis of gift giving among the Kula Pacific islanders and Mauss's (1923–24, for translation, see 1967) analysis of gift giving at the Potlatch of the Kwakiutl and other Indian tribes. These are institutions, that is, normatively regulated forms of exchange. In Kula gift giving, the association is initiated by one party giving a gift to another party. This is accompanied by the expectation that the gift will be reciprocated by an equivalent counter-gift at some time. Yet it is left to the party having received the gift at what time and to what extent or indeed whether at all a counter-gift will be given to the party that has initiated the process. The gift giver may be disappointed and angry if he or she does not receive an equivalent counter-gift. But he or she has no right to coerce the party in exchange to conform to his or her expectations. However, not reciprocating the gift is seen as a sign of hostility and establishes hostility instead of the friendship that would have emerged from reciprocation. The receiver of the gift has the choice between friendship and hostility. There is nothing in-between.

Gift giving can be used in order to establish superiority and domination. The party that overwhelms other parties with gifts they never can reciprocate does not leave them any other choice than to accept the gift-giving party's superiority and be subordinate to its power. An extreme form of this type of gift giving was studied by Marcel Mauss among the Kwakiutl. The gift giver invites other members of the tribe to celebrate a feast and not only overwhelms them with gifts but also destroys large quantities of valuable possessions. The aim is to demonstrate the gift giver's wealth and superiority.

Gift giving and economic exchange start from two opposite positions. In economic exchange, one party wants to have something from the other party and has to motivate the other party by offering some equivalent. In gift giving, one party gives something away and can only vaguely expect reciprocation at an unspecified time and in an unspecified form and quantity. Gift giving is a form of association that entails exchange of rewards according to the principle of reciprocation. However, can we infer from this feature of gift giving that people enter this process because they expect to be rewarded? We know many instances where gift giving is nothing but conformity to a social norm. It is a common ritual to give gifts on certain special days: Christmas, Valentine's day, and birthdays. Many people do this without feeling any great affection and are doing no more than fulfilling a boring obligation. It is a societal institution anchored in a tradition reaching far back into societal history, and we follow this tradition just by way of habit. The question then is, Why should we analyze this habit in terms of an exchange of rewards that is guided by seeking rewards (profit) in association?

Blau says people associate because they attract each other, and they attract each other because they expect rewards (profit) from the association. However, gift giving, which is a major object of demonstration for Blau's exchange theory, does not fit in with this view of association. In gift giving, people fulfill a societal obligation, and the institution is the source of regularly occurring gift giving rather than the motivation that people seek rewarding associations. The appropriate place for such a view of association is the marketplace, with people free to make any choice of partners they want according to expected rewards. Rational choice presupposes that there is freedom of choice. However, the institution of gift giving is no such marketplace, and there is little room for making a choice. We do not choose our partners in gift giving freely, we do not choose the kind of gift freely, nor are we allowed to give it with the expectation of a reward. Thus, it makes no sense to apply principles of reward and profit in order to give an explanation for the association of gift giving. In doing so, Blau seems to be an unwilling victim of his decision to analyze social association in the first instance as an exchange of rewards. Here he falls short of his intention to go beyond the economic limits of Homans's exchange theory.

However, not all associations Blau discusses as social exchange are forms of gift giving. He also considers as social exchange forms of exchange that are similar to strictly economic exchange but do not involve exact transactions of goods and services and do not involve the use of money as the medium of exchange. A professor who is invited to contribute to a special issue of a journal and does so without receiving any money gives his or her article to the journal and receives the reputation of being published in that journal. Some invitations are not gift giving in the sense discussed above, with unspecified reciprocation, but involve immediate reciprocation. The American cocktail party is such an economic transaction. The host normally wants to have certain people participating to make the party attractive for the other participants and to be rewarded by being considered able to attract people who are interesting. In this way the host him- or herself becomes an attractive person, and the invited guests are offered the chance to meet attractive people. This is their reward. And they immediately reciprocate by accepting the invitation, because this makes the party attractive and therefore rewarding for the host. This is not gift giving with unspecified reciprocation but social exchange that resembles economic exchange. The only difference is that it does not involve money. It is an immediate exchange of services.

The exchange between two colleagues in which one asks for help and gives gratitude and/or approval or some help in another situation lies between economic exchange and gift giving. Here, to use Homans's terms, Person wants something and asks Other. However, Person does not normally offer a direct equivalent to the help he asks for. His reciprocation is left unspecified. Other does not give a gift spontaneously. He is asked for a gift and gives it with an unspecified expectation of reciprocation. Inasmuch as Other gives his help only if he can realistically expect Person's reciprocation, he turns gift giving toward the area of economic exchange. These examples show that social exchange varies from gift giving with completely unspecified reciprocation to exchange that is strictly economic in character.

A closer proximity to economic exchange gives more scope for the application of economic principles. The precondition is that there is a marketplace, and people are free to make their choices. Yet this does not mean that social exchange is completely guided by the profit principle in this case. Blau discusses three major elements involved in social exchange that work in the direction of restricting the scope of profit maximization either for both or at least for one of the parties in exchange. However, Blau does not come to realize fully the consequences of his discussion for limiting the profit proposition that constitutes the core of his view of social exchange. We will examine these more closely while reviewing Blau's discussion of the following three major elements of social exchange: (1) trust, trustworthiness, and commitment, (2) the norm of fair exchange, and (3) power.

Trust, Trustworthiness, and Commitment

According to Blau (1964: 91–97), social exchange needs trust and trustworthiness much more than strictly economic exchange to be kept in motion. In economic exchange, the terms for completing an exchange are much more specified, and no party enters exchange without being sure that it will be reciprocated within a specified period of time. Therefore, the success of the transaction is quite precisely predictable. This is much less the case with social exchange, which does not specify time and quantity of reciprocation, like gift giving. Here the donor gives something away without any negotiation regarding reciprocation. He or she has no other choice than to trust the other party that the gift will be reciprocated some time. The donor must trust in the gratitude and feeling of personal obligation of the other party, who will then be expected to demonstrate his or her trustworthiness by reciprocating appropriately. As Blau notes, the very process of social exchange contributes to producing reciprocation, gratitude, and a feeling of obligation, and hence also trustworthiness and trust. What Blau means is that the orientation of the parties toward maximization of profit makes them aware of the advantages they would have from appropriate reciprocation and the disadvantages resulting from inappropriate reciprocation. Any party not reciprocating in the appropriate way will no longer be chosen as a party of exchange, and thus it will destroy its chances of making any profit. The existence of a norm of reciprocity only reinforces in a secondary way the self-steering forces of profit seeking in social exchange.

This is how Blau sees trust and trustworthiness as major elements of social exchange but not of economic exchange. The interesting point is that he sees trustworthiness and trust emerging from profit seeking itself in social exchange. Blau is right that trust is needed much more in situations where the time and quantity of reciprocation is less specified than in immediate market exchange. However, economic exchange is not always as specified as Blau points out. It frequently involves concluding a contract for the delivery of goods or services at a time when the will-power needed to conclude such a contract presupposes a lot of trust by both parties in the willingness and capacity of the other party to deliver either the goods and services or the money at the time stipulated in the contract. Even buying some product or some service that is immediately delivered presupposes trust in the promises the seller makes about the quality of the product and his or her services for repairing it. If there is any difference between this trust required in economic exchange and trust in social exchange, it is only a difference of degree. However, social exchange like gift giving mostly takes place between people who are very close to each other, make up a community, and are committed to each other, so they naturally feel an obligation to conform to the expectations of their fellows. Therefore, reciprocating gifts is the normal event in social exchange.

Economic exchange, however, much more frequently involves associations between strangers. It is also a common historical experience that it has been very difficult to establish trustworthiness and correspondingly trust to the same degree to which economic exchange expanded and increasingly involved the association of strangers. As Max Weber (1920–1921a/1972a: 523–24; 1920–1921b/1972b) pointed out in his famous comparative historical studies of the development of the modern economic order, in the ancient Oriental cultures of China and India, economic exchange expanded as much as in the West, but with the crucial feature of universal mistrust. In distinction to this, it has been a unique feature in the West that trust in economic exchange has developed even though it expanded beyond the primordial ties of kinship. The reason, according to Weber, is the embeddedness of the Western economic order in the normative regulations and the community of Christianity, particularly in the area of the Protestant religion. The Christian, particularly Protestant, community and its interlinkage with expanding capitalism subjected economic exchange and activity to control by the norms of a comprehensive community. Therefore, the conditions emerged for making reliability and trustworthiness in economic exchange obligatory for the partners in exchange.

This historical comparison clearly shows that exchange does not of itself—or by virtue of the profit maximization of the parties involved— produce personal obligations, trustworthiness, and trust inasmuch as exchange expands beyond the limits of primordial ties. Only where the exchanging parties are members committed to a community with common obligatory norms will one party normally approach another to enter exchange and proceed with trust, and only under this condition will the other party normally prove to be trustworthy *without* difficult processes of adjustment by way of invoking sanctions. And what is most important, even the sanctioning process demonstrating the profitability of reciprocation to the deviant can occur in a concerted way only if a community exists to back up the sanctions. Otherwise, the violator will not be confronted with a unified line of sanctions but may be backed up by some other form of group, leading to complete confusion and quarrelling between conflicting parties.

We can summarize as follows: Blau's discussion of trust and trustworthiness is confusing. He is right that unspecified social exchange presupposes more trust than specified economic exchange. However, he misses the broad area of unspecified economic exchange requiring a lot of trust and trustworthiness. He does not realize that his examples of social exchange all take place *within* relatively close associations in which obligations imposed on the members of the community to conform to its norms are much more evident than in more open markets. His statement about the self-production of trustworthiness and trust by way of profit maximization in social exchange disregards the fact that social exchange mostly takes place within a community in which parties of exchange are obliged to conform to the rules of reciprocation. This is the precondition for entering exchange at all and for sanctions to be backed up and ordered by the community in such a way that it is indeed advantageous to conform and disadvantageous not to conform. Max Weber's comparative historical studies demonstrate that the expansion of economic exchange did not produce trustful exchange unless the communal ties and normative ordering expanded in the same way. Finally, we can say that expectations that reciprocation will be backed up by ordered sanctions of the community can only be normatively defined expectations that are anchored in that community.

This leads us to state that Blau does not attain the qualification of the economic view of exchange that would have been possible if he had followed his introduction of trustworthiness and trust to its logical conclusion. This logical conclusion can be formulated in the following proposition of trust:

5. The more profit seeking in exchange is controlled by communal ties and common norms defining the terms of reciprocation, the more trustworthiness and ordered sanctioning, and therefore trust as such, will emerge.

We can extend this line of reviewing Blau's analysis of social exchange and establish a much farther reaching limitation of the profit principle than Blau achieves by turning to his discussion of the commitment to an association (Blau, 1964: 100–106, 160–65). Blau admits that people are not permanently engaged in exploring alternative associations in order to make the best profit, for this would imply a permanent danger of existing relationships breaking down in favor of new ones that appear more profitable. He sees a tendency toward committing oneself to associations once they have been established and to stopping the exploration of potentially advantageous new alternatives. Only in an open situation does a person compare the alternatives available to him or her according to expected profit. As soon as an association has been established, the commitment to this association sets limits on further exploring:

> As long as these alternatives appear tempting, individuals are inclined to explore them, but once they decide on what they consider the best alternative, they are likely to become committed to an exchange partnership and stop further exploration, with the result that they may not be able to take advantage of better opportunities that do become available. (Blau, 1964: 101)

Here Blau clearly states the workings of a force of association that is obviously contrary to the economic image of man as a permanent seeker of profit. Instead, a person commits him- or herself to an association and stops further exploration of more profitable alternatives. This is what we know from many associations established between people. Once two people have fallen in love with each other they simply do not consider exploring alternatives; that would be the end of their love. However, this phenomenon is not confined to the special case of love; it is a feature of many associations, though admittedly in a less rigorous form. Marriage and friendship imply comparably firm commitments, and even partnership in business implies commitments between people that are not replaced by more attractive ones as easily and as frequently as could be expected from truly profit-seeking businesspeople.

How can one explain this phenomenon? True "devotees" of economic theory would say that maintaining an established association in many cases outweighs the costs of forgone alternatives, because looking for these alternatives and giving up economically satisfying relationships would imply much higher costs. There is no doubt that these economic reasons contribute to maintaining already established relationships. However, they do not tell us the whole story. They do not tell us why people refuse to take better alternatives into account, even in the face of such alternatives or why people stop calculating profit at all and would be deeply disappointed to see their partners and themselves comparing the profits expected from continuing a relationship or establishing a new one. Are there any noneconomic forces that set limits on profit seeking in social associations? This is indeed quite evidently the case. An individual who does not compare economically an established association with any alternative association gives the established association such a high preference that it is inevitably more profitable than any alternative.

What we then would like to know is why this preference has become so extraordinarily strong that nothing could stand against it. Here is the point where economic theory explicitly has no answer to give. It has to start with a given rank order of preferences. According to the economic theorist, we need a different theory in order to say anything about the formation of preferences. The theory that is relevant here is a theory of commitment formation. An association between people as such exerts binding effects on the associated partners. The more people are associated, the more they separate themselves from other people, just because their association takes time away from other associations.

Thus, the circle of interaction becomes more closed for people by the process of association itself. This closing effect of association separates the associated from others who naturally become outsiders. The associated begin to see each other as a unity in distinction to other people; they begin to share a common life-world and a common fate and to establish rites of association and a specific cult that gives their association an identity. They commemorate important events and dates of their association, for example, the day members first met and the day of official establishment of their association. These are processes of association that exert binding effects on the associated partners independent of whether the association gives more or less profit compared to alternative associations.

As we know, even very frustrated relationships are to a considerable degree held together by the binding effects of common fate, rites, and cults. Commemorating a wedding anniversary gives the most frustrating marriage a stability it would not have had without such binding powers internal to the association itself. Commitment to an association grows with the amount of time it consumes, the number of people it closes out, the exclusiveness of the common life-world and fate shared, the rites established for providing permanent renewal, and the cults celebrated, giving the association a special identity.

These forces of association deepen the commitment to an association. They close the mind of the association for considering potentially more profitable alternatives. It is this closing of the mind that does not allow any imagining of alternatives to arise. As a consolation for the economic theorist, we can say that this closing of the mind flowing from the commitment to an association gives the maintenance of the association the status of the preference that is high enough to always result in the highest profit. But this is not what interests us here. What are of interest are the processes that give the maintenance of an association such a high rank in the preference order of an individual.

Blau does not follow through to its full conclusion his statement about the preventive effects of the commitment to an association on any further calculation of profit coming from alternative associations. However, his statement can be completed in this direction, bringing the noneconomic forces on the stabilization of associations to a fuller expression than Blau himself achieves. We can first formulate the principle of preventing profit seeking in associations:

6. The stronger the commitment of the partners to an association, the less they calculate the profit taken from this association in comparison to alternative associations.

Then we can state the principle of closing a community:

7. The more exclusively people associate, that is, the more time they spend together, and the more they separate from other people, the more they form a closed community.

Next, we can state a principle of vitality of community life:

8. The more people live in a closed community, the more likely it is that they will share a common life-world and fate and celebrate common rites and cults; and the more they share a common life-world and fate and celebrate common rites and cults, the more vital their community life will be.

Finally, we can formulate the principle of commitment:

9. The more vital the life of a community, the more committed to that community its members will be.

Although Blau did formulate the principle of preventing profit seeking in associations, to come to a full understanding of the conditions that produce this effect we have to add the other three principles. Their formulation drives us farther away from economic reasoning than Blau's understanding of social association as an exchange of rewards seems to allow at first sight. We have to give the corresponding principle of reward and profit a limited validity. Profit seeking in association takes place only within the limits of existing commitments.

Fairness

A regulation of social exchange clearly stated by Blau (1964: 151–60, 228–31) is the regulation by common norms of fair exchange. This implies that it is not left to the individual's whims and willingness what to expect from an exchange and how to meet that expectation. Inasmuch as there are common norms defining fair exchange and people ask whether concrete expectations and reciprocations correspond to these common norms, they enter a discourse on right or wrong. And the outcome of such a discourse does not result from the laws of exchange. The more a discourse on the justification of expectations, quality of services, and reciprocations takes place, the more the laws of discursive reasoning instead of the laws of profit maximization define the terms of exchange. A party who offers a service has to do so according to common standards of the quality of that service; a party who reciprocates has to do so according to common standards of appropriate remuneration for the services provided. In the many cases where people come to divergent evaluations of the exchange, they enter a debate on the rights and wrongs of the services provided or the remuneration received. Here the criterion for coming to a mutually accepted result is not complementarity of profit expectations but the justifiability of claims according to universally valid norms of exchange. Socially, this justification holds true only inasmuch as there is agreement on the interpretation of the facts and their evaluation against the norms not only between the two parties but also in the wider public discourse. Social exchange and economic exchange are interwoven with such discursive processes, and the more that is the case, the more profit maximization takes place only within the limits of discursive justification of the terms of exchange according to common norms of fair exchange. We can therefore formulate a proposition of discursive control more explicitly than Blau does:

10. The more people engage in a discourse on the terms of exchange measured by common norms of fair exchange, the more the outcome of exchange corresponds to what can gain universal assent.

Power

A further force penetrating exchange relationships is most extensively discussed by Blau: power. Blau (1964: 115–42, 199–223) states the following conditions under which a person can escape the power of a partner in an exchange who delivers some rewards:

1. The person is able to reciprocate in an equivalent way.
2. The person turns to alternative sources of reward.
3. The person uses force to counteract the demands of the partner.
4. The person suppresses his or her needs for the rewards supplied by the partner in an exchange.

If the person has no chance to choose one of these alternative reactions to the rewards of the partner in exchange, he or she is open to the suppressive demands of any exchange partners who might acquire power over him or her. The first one of these alternative ways of escaping the power of an exchange partner, however, does not completely eliminate that power. The partner's power is equaled only by the power of the first person. In this case, both partners have power over each other. They will make more use of this power the less they mind being the object of the partner's power.

Coming to an analysis of the establishment of power, we turn to the constellation where none of the four ways of escape is open to a person. We can explain it using the example of a work group in which one man has much more skill than his colleagues. First, the reciprocation of the man's advice by gratitude and approval on the part of his colleagues gives him a higher status. Differentiation of status becomes established on the basis of shared appreciation of his skills and advice. However, he becomes satiated with approval. His colleagues cannot repay him; they have no alternative sources for his scarce advice; they cannot use force; and they are not able to do away with their need for advice altogether. This allows the skilled person to demand more of his colleagues than if they were equal to him. He may demand special services. This may lead back to reciprocation. However, if he is willing to command, he can use his power to command and direct the behavior of his colleagues at work. A leader is born. This leadership is established by turning power into commanding power that pushes the actions of those commanded in the direction set by the leader. In this sense, turning power into leadership does need the additional willingness of the powerful person really taking the lead. There are many people who have power but do not take the lead in order to turn power into directed group action.

Summarizing the considerations above, we can formulate a proposition of status differentiation:

11. The more a person can provide resources to other people in return for rewards, the higher his or her status as regarded by these other people.

The proposition of power differentiation reads as follows:

12. The more a person commands the resources for rewards needed by other people (either by possessing these resources or by using force) and the less these people command resources that the person needs him- or herself (again either by possessing these sources or by using force) and the less these people have alternative sources of reward and the more the person has such alternative resources and the more these people need the rewards relative to the person concerned, the more power the person has over the other people.

The conditions for turning power into commanding power of leadership are formulated in the proposition of leadership:

13. The more power a person has over other people and the more he or she is able to set goals for these people, the more the person will be able to command the actions of other people in a coordinated way and to take the lead.

A first consequence of the establishment of power and leadership is the enormous restriction of choices for the people subjected to the power of the leader. To begin with, they only have a choice between this association, which entails compliance with the commands of the person in power, and at least minimal satisfaction of needs on the one hand and no satisfaction of needs on the other. There is no marketplace in which they can exercise choice. The person in power can even physically force the people to associate and hence deny them any choice. The person in power can force people under his or her power to stay in the relationship and to act in ways that are completely frustrating for them—ways they would never freely choose for themselves. Thus, they do not have any chance to calculate the profit they could expect from alternative associations open to them. Their action is not guided by the principle of profit maximization but by the principle of compliance with superior power, and leads in directions that do not promise any profit to them. Many of Blau's considerations open our eyes to this restriction on profit-maximizing association; however, he does not explicitly restrict the scope of validity of the profit proposition and the corresponding view of association as guided by expected rewards.

Inasmuch as people want to decide their own fate, it is frustrating for them to be subjected to superior power. They will make attempts to resist or escape that power. Established power, therefore, is always confronted by attempts to overthrow it, by opposition, or by withdrawal from the relationship. Which, then, are the factors that produce the stabilization and destabilization of power relationships? Blau speaks of the advantages the leader has to supply for followers and those subject to his power, his or her contribution of benefit for them. In economic terms, the leader has to supply at least a little more profit than what the followers and subjects could expect by withdrawing from the relationship or opposing it. However, this economic strategy is often in danger of failing, because some people who are subjected to the power may calculate the costs of opposition and withdrawal lower than the costs of compliance even in the face of considerable benefits from the person in power. Such a tendency toward opposition becomes more likely the more people collectively share the frustration of being suppressed. This collective sharing of frustration is more likely the closer the suppressed live together, the more they can communicate about their situation, and the more they are able to formulate an oppositional ideology that gives them a common identity, to become organized, and to be coordinated and directed against the established power by oppositional leaders. We can formulate these insights in a proposition of opposition formation:

14. The more the exercise of power depends exclusively on the condition that the suppressed expect a higher profit from subjection than from opposition or withdrawal, the more the suppressed will move toward opposition inasmuch as they live closely together, communicate about their suppression, build an oppositional ideology, and become organized and directed against the established power by an oppositional leadership.

Because collective organization of the suppressed increases their power, the established power is in danger of being overthrown by the stronger collective power of the opposition. This is the proposition of collective power:

15. The more the suppressed can collectively organize, the more they will together acquire more power than the person or group in power who still has more power than each individual member of the suppressed and the more likely it is that the established power will be overthrown.

What, then, are the factors that stabilize established power? Here Blau (1964: 205–13) introduces Max Weber's (1922/1972c: 122–24) argument that only power rooted in legitimate authority based on a common belief in its legitimacy on the part of both the people in power and the people subjected to it can have a stable foundation. In accordance with Parsons's (1937/1968) view Blau sees the ultimate source of legitimate authority in its anchoring in the common norms and values of a society. Power that is rooted in or can be turned into legitimate authority receives the approval of the people subjected to it. Authority is a quality someone in a position of leadership has because people assign the incumbent of that position a right to command according to commonly shared norms and values. Conversely, the leader who exercises the power given to him or her in that position according to common norms and values, for example, norms of fair exchange between ruler and ruled, consequently receives the approval of his or her subjects who give his or her rule the legitimacy it needs. The exercise of power that is supported by the approval of the ruled can rely on the contribution of the ruled in approving of compliance with its commands and in disapproving of and punishing deviance, withdrawal, and resistance.

Summarizing these conditions, we can formulate a proposition of legitimate authority:

16. The more power is exercised in accordance with common norms and values, the more it will be rooted in legitimate authority and the more it will be supported by the approval of the ruled and their approval of compliance and disapproval and punishment of deviance, resistance, and withdrawal.

A proposition of stabilization of power can be formulated thus:

17. The more the exercise of power is rooted in legitimate authority, the more stable it will be.

Bringing these considerations of Blau's position to a conclusion, we can say that the establishment of power in a relationship turns this relationship away from an exchange in the strict sense, because the suppressed have no choice to make in a marketplace according to the principle: Which of several alternatives would be the most profitable exchange? On the other hand, the more the establishment of power is based on such considerations by the parties involved, the less stable it will be. This holds true even for the case where the people subjected to power are confined to calculating their relative gains from subjection, withdrawal, or opposition. Power relationships can be expected to be much more stable if they are rooted in legitimate authority based on common norms and values. Here, however, the people involved in the relationship do not act on the basis of calculated profits but on the basis of conformity to norms and values, which constrains the calculation of profit on both parts: that of the ruler and that of the ruled. Here the reason why an association lasts is not that it is mutually rewarding but that the two parties agree on the terms governing the exercise of power, which does not result from an exchange of rewards but from a discourse on the terms by which that power can legitimately be exercised. These are the consequences of Blau's considerations of legitimate authority, which we have to draw more precisely than he does himself with regard to legitimating the validity of the economic principles underlying his view of the exercise of power as social exchange.

In summarizing our considerations on commitment, power, and common values and norms we have to restrict the scope of validity of the profit proposition more rigorously than Blau does:

18. Inasmuch as actors' choices of alternative associations are not restricted by commitments to specific associations, binding values, or power relations, and actors are therefore free to make their choice, the following relationship holds true: The higher the profit people expect from associating with others, the more they feel attracted to these others.

Indirect Exchange

Blau himself draws our attention to the limited validity of the profit proposition for analyzing social exchange when he comes to the discussion of indirect exchange. According to Blau (1964: 255–63), this type of exchange includes more complex macrostructures than the more elementary exchange processes he was talking about in the first chapters of the book. Blau starts with an analysis of the "prisoner's dilemma": Two suspects who cannot communicate with each other are told by the district attorney that they have a choice either to confess or not to confess. Should one confess and the other not, the first will go free; the other who has not confessed will be sentenced to ten years in jail. Should both confess, both will be imprisoned for eight years. Should both refuse to confess, both will be imprisoned for only one year because of lack of evidence. In the latter case, they will receive the one year sentence for the lesser offense they are convicted of. Each suspect's individually most rational choice is to confess, because each has to fear the other's confession and thus ten years in prison. What they get is eight years, the second worst result. If they were able to communicate, they could agree to refuse to confess, therefore coming to a much better result than they are able to in isolation from each other.

Blau takes the example of unprofitable consequences of isolated rational choice to point to the need to control behavior by common norms and values in complex interdependent settings where face-to-face control does not work. Here, indirect exchange replaces direct exchange; the action of a person is no longer determined simply by the rewards he or she expects from a certain choice of action with regard to a certain other person and to that person alone. A wider community enters the situation and becomes the most important source of reward, and this community gives approval for behavior that conforms to its common norms and disapproval for behavior that does not conform. The businessperson who acts trustworthily receives the benefit of being approved and trusted in the wider market community. The doctor who restores the health of his or her patient with methods that must be applied against the will of the patient does so to get the approval of his or her professional community. Here, a social exchange takes place between two persons that is directed by the commitment of at least one of them to a wider community that gives approval or disapproval for conformity or nonconformity with its common norms.

Going beyond the analysis of social norms as mediators of indirect exchange, Blau (1964: 263–73) introduces common values as media of social transaction in complex settings. They differ from social norms in their level of generality. They do not prescribe concrete actions for certain situations as social norms do but provide general guidelines and standards for action. Blau distinguishes four types of common values guiding social transactions:

particularistic social values, universalistic social values, social values legitimating authority, and opposition ideals.

Particularistic values serve as media of social integration and solidarity. These are the values a community of people—such as a work group, an organization, a local community, an ethnic group, a social class, or a nation—hold in common. What is important for our analysis of association here is that people who share such particularistic group values associate independently of situational calculations of profit. They associate and enter social exchange because they share the values that give them a common identity and establish a stable preference of associating with their fellows rather than grouping together with any outsider. Joining one's fellows before joining anyone else is a stable first preference that determines action *before* profit calculation begins. Moreover, it is the solidarity and consensus of the group that provides for the stable approval or disapproval of conforming or nonconforming behavior. It is not the higher profitability of conforming behavior that bears the overwhelming weight of explanation here but the conditions that make it more profitable to conform: solidarity, consensus on particularistic values, commitment to the community, ordered rewarding of conforming behavior, and punishing of nonconforming behavior. Blau sees solidarity coming from sharing particularistic values. This relationship certainly holds true; however, an existing closeness among people furthers solidarity that itself gives rise to shared particularistic values. This is an important element of association that calls for an explanation different from the profit proposition.

Universalistic values serve as media of social exchange and differentiation. These are such values as standards of achievement, equality of opportunity, fairness in exchange, and trustworthiness. They guide the transaction of individuals in exchange according to universal cultural ideas. They provide a measure of what can be called true achievement that deserves appropriate approval and reciprocation or of equal conditions and fair exchange. Inasmuch as social exchange is guided by these universalistic measures, the way an exchange takes place depends on the ability of the parties in exchange to justify their terms of exchange before a wider public; in this respect it does not depend on the mutual expectation of profit. The motive of making profit in exchange is controlled by values that are applied to exchange in discursive procedures, and these discursive procedures differ from exchange in their character and in the results they produce.

Social values legitimating authority serve as media of organization. Inasmuch as there are social values that determine the right way of exercising authority and applying power, the transactions between people in power and people subjected to this power are not completely determined by the expected profits or by the strength of available power. In organizing collective action, profits are taken and power is applied according to values of proper leadership. These forces contribute to limiting the scope of validity of the profit and power principles.

Opposition ideals serve as media of social change and reorganization. The culture of a society entails ideas that very often reach beyond the confines of existing social institutions. In the light of these ideals, existing institutions are always full of defects and shortcomings. Insofar as an oppositional movement is capable of legitimating its critique and action by discursively applying these cultural ideals to the actual situation, it becomes a legitimate force of social change and societal reorganization. Here, discursive reasoning, not profit seeking or power, backs up the legitimacy of opposition and establishes it as a legitimate force of social change and reorganization. An opposition of this kind has much longer lasting effects on social change than an opposition that is based merely on the mobilization of countervailing power against the established power.

Critical Assessment

These are the cultural forces that subject profit seeking and the exercise of power to control that comes from the wider macrostructure of society. More explicitly than Blau, we have to be aware that every single social exchange that takes place in a society is intermingled with these macrostructural forces. Their controlling effect on social exchange holds true not only for what Blau calls indirect exchange but also for every type of social exchange. Put in another way, we can say that every single social exchange taking place in a society involves aspects of indirect exchange, that is, it involves not only the relationship between two exchanging parties but also their relationship to a group, organization, and society and to the wider structures of exchange, power, community, and culture. Therefore, Blau's analysis confirms our position—that an analysis of social exchange in purely economic terms is much too narrow in its explanatory power.

A further confirmation of this position comes from Blau's (1964: 273–80) conception of institutionalization, which involves processes relating to profit seeking, power, solidarity, and culture. People look for profitable patterns of behavior; however, this does not provide for stable patterns. What is needed is a certain degree of formalization of behavior, the anchoring of these formal procedures in the consensus and solidarity of a community, the legitimation by a tradition of cultural values, and its backing up by powerful groups in society. This is a complex view of institutionalization that would lead us far beyond economic exchange theory and toward a truly general theory of social action. Though Blau does not fully draw the consequences of this view to state the limits of economic theory even in the analysis of elementary social exchange, we can start from his analysis and try to go farther toward a more general theory of social action than he was able to go because he did not fully abandon his economic bias.

In contrast to Homans, Blau has, however, recognized from the beginning of his work the *sui generis* reality of social structure which implies that social structure also entails a set of laws of its own beyond the laws of economic exchange. In his later work he has paid much more attention to such *sui generis* laws of social structure, namely in his book *Inequality and Heterogeneity: A Primitive Theory of Social Structure*, published in 1977. In this book he looks at formal aspects of groups and intergroup relations like size and heterogeneity and then asks for consequences in other aspects of group and intergroup relations. He points out, for example, that the sheer size of the large group of whites and the small group of blacks in the United States makes it much more likely for whites to marry within their group than across, while blacks have a much greater chance of marrying across their group than within. As valuable as this book is in its rigorous concentration on formal aspects of social structure, one still very much misses their interconnection with substantial aspects of culture, consensus and dissensus, power and domination, markets and money. In a sense the book is more one dimensional than his earlier book *Exchange and Power in Social Life*.

PART FOUR

The Symbolics
of Social Action

THE DEVELOPMENT OF MORAL CONSCIOUSNESS: JEAN PIAGET

A MAJOR part of the individual's self is his or her moral consciousness, which tells the individual what is right and what is wrong. Mead's (1908, 1934) answer to the development of morality was the experimental method of trial and error, though this covers only the dynamic aspect of the permanent change of moral rules. With his emphasis on the extension of the individual's orientation to ever wider groups Mead also pointed to the social basis of moral generalization. However, he did not address as much the changing character of moral rules in the individual's development and the changing procedures of proving the social validity of moral rules and their binding determination of the individual's moral consciousness. With growing generalization and autonomy of the individual's moral consciousness, the character of moral rules and the structure of their social validation also change. This aspect in the development of moral consciousness was studied much more closely by the Swiss psychologist Jean Piaget than by George Herbert Mead. We therefore have to turn to Piaget to get a more complete understanding of the development of moral consciousness (Piaget, 1924/1963, 1932/1973, 1937/1950, 1945, 1947, 1950, 1974, 1975, 1980; for translation, see 1951, 1954, 1972, 1977, 1978, 1981, 1985).

Moral Respect

Piaget starts his famous study *The Moral Judgment of the Child* (Piaget, 1932/1973) with the statement that morality consists of a system of rules and it is the *respect* of the individual for these rules that is the essence of morality. The conformity to rules in general may have different sources. What characterizes moral rules is that conformity to them is rooted in the respect people have for them. People respect the authority of these rules.

The question then is: What are the sources of moral respect? Piaget's answer is that we have to distinguish two sources of moral respect that correspond to two stages in the moral development of the human individual: constraint and cooperation. The first is the basis of what he calls moral realism; the second is the basis of what he calls moral autonomy. These stages occur on the levels of moral practice and moral consciousness. Moral practice is the application of moral rules in actual conduct in a situation. Moral consciousness is our thinking about what is right and what is wrong. Piaget discovered in his empirical investigations that the moral consciousness of children lags behind their moral practice by about two years. He distinguishes four stages in the development of moral practice and three stages in the development of moral consciousness.

Moral Practice

The first stage of moral practice is the motorical and individual stage covering the first two years in the child's development. Here, the child learns to act according to ritualized schemes. Regulated conduct means motorical control of physical aspects of behavior like walking, cleanliness, and mastering other motorical schemes. At the age of two, the egocentric stage sets in, which lasts until the age of about five to six. This is the first stage at which rules not only have a physical nature but also acquire a moral quality. The stage is called egocentric because the child has now discovered his or her wants and tries to satisfy them. The child is not capable of cooperating with peers in play but does so for him- or herself. Rules of conduct are imposed by adults. The way to satisfy the egocentric wants is to imitate whatever behavior is demanded and submit to the external constraint of the adults.

At the age of seven to eight, cooperation between children sets in on a first stage. Now the children play coordinated games where they compete to win the game (e.g., marbles). This competition calls for attempts to apply mutual control and establish uniform rules of the game. However, there are considerable uncertainties about the rules. Asked separately, the children give very different answers about the rules of the game. It takes until the age of eleven to twelve to reach a fourth stage of codification of rules. Now the rules are applied in a predictable and unified way, and the children give the same answers about the rules of the game when questioned separately.

Moral Consciousness

Speaking about moral consciousness, Piaget distinguishes three stages: the motorical, the egocentric, and the cooperative stage.

The Motorical Stage

The motorical stage is a prestage before moral consciousness emerges. It lasts for the first three years in the child's development. There is no moral consciousness about right and wrong with regard to the schemes of motorical control the child learns at this age. There is a complementary relationship between the training in motorical control by adults and the pleasure the child feels in mastering the corresponding techniques.

The Egocentric Stage: Constraint and Moral Realism

At the age of three and lasting to the age of about nine, rules acquire a moral character for the child. They distinguish between right and wrong behavior. Deviating from these rules is not simply a failure to master a technique but a violation of strong normative expectations that calls forth disapproving reactions and punishment. The child's respect for the rules comes from his or her respect for the authority of adults who are in a position to impose sanctions in case of deviation from rules. The child learns from adults what is right and wrong and has to expect punishment when he or she does not conform. An external constraint imposed from above guarantees the binding power of the rules. The child's commitment to the rules is based on one-sided respect for adults. Because of the untouchable authority of the adults the rules themselves are considered sacred and everlasting.

A complementary relationship exists between the external constraint imposed by the adults and the egocentric orientation of the child to satisfying his or her wants. The child gets to know what he or she has to do in order to get things done as he or she wants. Adult control and the child's egocentrism mutually support each other.

Because of his or her egocentric orientation, the child has a very realistic attitude toward moral rules. They are commanding not in themselves but because their violation is followed by sanctions, by punishment. Asked why it is wrong not to allow his sister to play with his toys, a boy would answer that Mom said so and would put away his toys if he did not allow his sister to play with them. This realism in the child's attitude toward moral rules is complemented by a realism of objective consequences of action. It is not the intention or purpose of the action that decides on its moral character but the objective outcome that is observable. If the boy's sister has unintentionally broken a plate, it is as bad in the boy's view as the boy intentionally breaking the plate when he was angry. The actions are bad because they are sanctioned by Mom's warnings. The unintentional breaking of a rule with visible consequences is bad, whereas the intention to do so but without visible consequences is not. The child is capable only of knowing the right or wrong character of actions from their visible consequences and the reactions called forth by these consequences.

The child also tends to relate the strength of moral condemnation to the amount of damage caused by an action. Breaking two plates is morally worse than breaking one plate. A big lie is morally worse than a little lie. Thus, at this stage of moral development, there is no inner commitment to rules, no judgment of intention, but only external compliance because of fear of sanctions and judgment according to visible consequences in terms of damage and in terms of punishment. At this stage of moral development, morality is heteronomous in character, that is, imposed by a heteronomous power. Moral respect is the subordination to an external authority; moral consciousness is realistic in character: it is what Piaget calls moral realism.

The Cooperative Stage: Mutual Respect and Moral Autonomy

At the age of seven to eight, children begin to play coordinated games and to be concerned about the rules of their games. Cooperation about these matters begins to structure their relationship. It takes until the age of ten to twelve, though, before their moral consciousness has fully recognized this change from constraint to cooperation in moral practice and reaches a new level. The rules here are imposed by the group itself and on itself. These rules are no longer imposed by an external adult authority, and conformity no longer comes from external constraint. We now have a group of equals that makes rules, and abiding by the rules is no longer rooted in the one-sided respect for a superior authority but in the *mutual* respect of equals. Inasmuch as the child feels committed to the group, he or she will take the rules as binding. This is the case the more strongly the group is bound together in solidarity. The respect for the rules is based on mutual respect among peers. However, the consent to rules does not simply come from an *a priori* acceptance of the group's authority in this case. Because we have here a group of equals, consent to rules requires the voluntary agreement of the group's members. Rules have to be worked out and enacted with the cooperation of equals who participate autonomously with the same voice. This is why Piaget calls the morality emerging from these conditions cooperative and autonomous morality. It is based on the voluntary consent of autonomously cooperating individuals. A rule is no longer binding under these conditions because of the constraint that backs it up but because it can be justified in order to get the consent of each member of the group. Justification by reasonable grounds now becomes the way to make rules binding.

Rules are thus no longer sacred and untouchable but have to be worked out in processes of argumentation and consensus formation. The autonomous individual no longer accepts a rule as binding because it is based on superior authority and because of the sanctions applied to its violation but because the rule is seen as just *in itself*, on the basis of reasonable justifications given for the rule. Reason is the ground for the rule's validity. The very process of justification in working out rules also presents them as changeable on the basis of renewed mutual agreements. What is right and wrong is not predetermined once and for all and imposed by an external authority but continually worked out in a process of mutual consensus formation.

Now the meaning of the rule is the basis of its binding character. This also has consequences for the moral judgment of actions. Consistency of the action with the meaning of the rule is now the criterion for morally good or bad action. Intention and purpose are judged—no longer objective consequence. Only what is intentionally done can be approved or disapproved on moral grounds. One is now responsible only for what one has done intentionally; for example, it is bad to lie, regardless of the consequences. Justice is not simply what is rewarded by an authority, injustice not simply what is negatively sanctioned. With regard to the appropriate treatment of breaking rules, justice becomes retributive in character based on equality. Not strong punishment as such is right for violating rules, but an appropriate restitution of the former conditions and an appropriate reminder of the mutual sharing of the rules based on the idea of equal treatment. When a boy does not help his mother, he should himself see how it is to not get help when help is needed. With regard to the appropriate distribution of rewards, equity with consideration given to the specific circumstances becomes the principle of justice. There must be an equality of opportunity when rewards are distributed on the basis of achievement. Everybody has the same rights, and there must be a mutual respect of these rights. It is not right, for example, when the teacher gives one pupil special attention unless that pupil has some disadvantages for which the teacher is trying to compensate. That means in principle every pupil has a right to get the same attention from the teacher, but it is correct that the teacher cares especially for those who are disadvantaged for some reason.

As Piaget points out, there is a movement from constraint and moral realism to cooperation and moral autonomy in children's development at the age of about ten to twelve. This, however, is not a clear-cut transformation. The practice of cooperation begins at seven to eight when constraint and moral realism still dominate the moral consciousness of the child. And that constraint and moral realism does not disappear completely after the stage of cooperation and autonomy has been reached, nor does everybody reach the level of moral autonomy completely.

Summary

1. The more rules are made binding by external constraint, one-sided respect, and punishment, the more consciousness displays moral realism, relating

responsibility to the objective consequences of action and defining as right what is rewarded and as wrong what is punished by superior (adult) authority.

2. The more rules are made binding by cooperation, mutual respect, and justification by reasonable grounds and by voluntarily agreeing autonomous subjects, the more moral consciousness displays moral autonomy, relating responsibility to subjective intention and judging right and wrong with regard to the meaning of action based on the principles of retributive justice and equity.

Critical Assessment

Piaget (1932/1973) concludes his investigation into the stages of a child's moral development with an important criticism of Durkheim's (1925/1974) moral sociology. He argues that Durkheim does not sufficiently differentiate between the two very different social bases of morality pointed out by Piaget and conflates the two when he locates the source of morality in the moral authority of society over the individual and the corresponding attachment of the individual to the social group. In Durkheim's terms, discipline, attachment to groups, and autonomy of the will are the three elements of morality. However, what he calls autonomy of the will is rooted in teaching the individual the truth of moral science. Teachers have to act as priests of a secular morality. Nevertheless, this does not change the source of morality: it is still a superior authority instituted by society. Thus Durkheim does not really find out the social basis for developing moral autonomy. It is this aspect of moral development that has been pointed out most vigorously by Piaget: the transformation from structures of authority to structures composed of autonomous and equal individuals who cooperate in working out moral rules on the basis of mutual agreement with regard to the justification of rules by reasonable grounds.

However, Piaget's theory of moral development is biased to the dynamic aspect of moral discourse in a similar way to Mead's theory of the self's development in relation to society, though with more emphasis on discourse. Mead's theory gives special emphasis to the change and scope of the child's *association* in the movement from the significant to the generalized other. Piaget's major subject matter is the change of *procedures for justification* of moral rules from authority to discourse. However, while Mead draws our attention to the dynamics of an ever-changing self and an ever-changing society, Piaget concentrates on the *dynamics* of discourse. For Mead voluntary association is the basis for a mutually supportive and dynamic development of self and society. For Piaget, the discourse of autonomous equals is the basis for the dynamic change of moral rules, which are no longer sacred and untouchable but in permanent change according to the permanent renewal of agreement. What Piaget does not address so much is how even a group of equals contributes to *closing* the mind, or alternatively the moral consciousness of the individual is committed to the group and separates itself more from other groups to maintain a *close internal solidarity.* This is a group of equals, but not autonomous equals. However, inasmuch as moral rules are absolutely binding, there is at least some element of this closing character of groups in effect. This is what Durkheim teaches and what we cannot replace by the dynamics of moral discourse.

Piaget also misses the importance of the *conflict* between the individual and the group for sharpening the individual's ability to *question* and to criticize the dominating concepts of morality. Inasmuch as a *critical spirit* is part of moral autonomy—and there is no doubt that it is—the individual needs chances to oppose an external power. This is an important part of the individual's relation to authorities that has to be transmitted to his or her relationship to the group. Even a group of equals is an authority over the individual who needs chances to be in conflict with the group in order to develop a critical spirit.

Finally, moral development cannot reach beyond the spirit of the group as long as it remains bound to the concrete discourse within groups of peers. Inasmuch as there is a need for some development beyond these boundaries, the individual has to surpass them socially and to establish distance between him- or herself and any concrete group. The person has to *retreat* from any concrete group. This does not mean that he or she no longer engages in discourse; the discourse is an imaginary one between the figures of the centuries of development of human thought, leading up to an imaginary discourse on abstract positions and finally to pure contemplation. This is the way to complete *moral universalism and autonomy.* Inasmuch as moral consciousness ought to entail some element of such universality and autonomy, there must be some degree of such retreat from concrete groups. It is Habermas's theory of discourse that leads a step further toward this end. Another step has been contributed by Lawrence Kohlberg.

ELEVEN

SYMBOLIC INTERACTIONISM: HERBERT BLUMER

HERBERT BLUMER pushed forward the evolution of symbolic interactionism as a distinctive sociological paradigm by turning major elements of George Herbert Mead's thought into a programmatic statement. Besides George Herbert Mead, this program also includes elements drawn from pragmatists and early American sociologists such as John Dewey, William James, W. I. Thomas, Robert E. Park, Charles Horton Cooley, Florian Znaniecki, James Mark Baldwin, Robert Redfield, and Louis Wirth. Though its roots and even Blumer's introduction of the name in an article published in 1937 go back to the emergence of American sociology in the earlier decades of this century, symbolic interactionism became particularly prominent in the 1960s as one of the various reactions to the dominance of structural-functionalist sociology. The most programmatic statement of the growing approach was formulated by Blumer in the introduction to a collection of his essays published with the title of *Symbolic Interactionism: Perspective and Method* in 1969.

Meaning

Blumer (1969: 2) starts his outline of symbolic interactionism with three theses: (1) Human action always deals with the meaning of objects. (2) Meaning evolves from social interaction. (3) Meaning is defined in processes of interpretation.

In contrast to positivistic approaches, symbolic interactionism does not conceive of the relationship between the objects in the human actor's environment and the human being's action in a straightforward causal and deterministic way. There is no direct relationship between cause and effect in human action, so effects cannot be attributed automatically to certain causes. There is always the meaning of the objects involved that resides between object and action. When one man pushes another man aside in order to get through the gate of the football stadium and the other man stumbles backwards, this is just a physical process involving a causal deterministic relationship between the first man's push and the second man's stumble backwards. This will happen without any difference whenever the first man pushes someone of similar stature as the second in a similar situation. Here no meaning is involved, and the fact that the second man stumbles backwards is not action as we use the term since Max Weber gave it its famous definition as behavior that is meaningful.

However, the very physical process of pushing and stumbling backwards is nevertheless imbued with meaning as soon as the two actors recognize what they do. The first actor may have pushed the second accidentally because he stumbled. Then his action is also an effect of another cause and hence part of a complex causal chain. With the second actor's recognition that he has been pushed backwards by the first actor, meaning enters the scene. The second actor may recognize that the first actor's push was itself caused by accidental stumbling, or else that the first actor consciously intended to push the second backwards in order to enter the stadium, or indeed that the first actor recognizes the second as a fan of the opposing team and simply wanted to hurt him. Each one of these recognitions lends a specific meaning to the push given by the first man and turns the physical push into meaningful action.

As soon as this attribution of meaning to certain behaviors has occurred the process is determined not only by the physical laws of kinetics but also by the meaning both attribute to the action as it proceeds. If the second actor recognizes the first actor's push as unwillingly generated by some other cause, he may let the first actor pass without acting against him. If the second actor recognizes that the first man's push was a deliberate attempt to enter the stadium without a ticket, he may resist that action and try to capture the man as calmly as possible. If he recognizes the other person's push as an attack, he may counterattack. Going one stage farther, the first man's attribution of meaning to the second man's reaction will determine his own reaction. How the two act and react is thus largely determined by the meaning they assign to each other's actions. Their actions are symbols that convey a meaning to each of them. We can therefore say they are engaged in *symbolic interaction*. This is why we need a theory of symbolic interaction in order to understand and explain the course of social interaction.

Because meaning is an element in its own right in the determination of social interaction, we should know how meaning emerges. Blumer (1969: 3–4) discusses three theories of meaning: (1) Realism states that meaning is inherent in objects. (2) Psychologism states that meaning is attributed to objects on the basis of psychological processes. (3) Interactionism states that meaning results from social interaction. Objects to which actors are oriented can be of three different kinds: (1) physical objects like a chair, a tree, a mountain, a river, a push in its physical character; (2) social objects like other actors, their actions, groups, organizations, associations, institutions, and societies; and (3) abstract, cultural objects like gestures, words, phrases, and ideas.

Blumer rejects realism and psychologism as well and argues for an interactionist theory of meaning. According to this theory, the meaning of an object is neither inherent in the object nor a one-sided attribution determined by psychological processes on the part of an actor. The actor cannot simply decide by him- or herself how to recognize an object. Inasmuch as others react to a person's attribution of meaning to an object, their reaction will influence the person's continuation to attribute that meaning to it. Others' reactions confirm or disaffirm a person's meaning attributions. If the first actor has some experience with the reaction of others, he or she will anticipate their reaction in his or her meaning attributions. The actor's attribution is still oriented to theirs whether or not he or she conforms to them, and thus the actor's attribution is an outcome of the process of interaction in both the conformistic and the oppositional case.

Wherever interaction takes place, the meaning actors attribute to objects is shaped by the very process of interaction. The second man in our example may interpret the first man's push as an unfriendly attack and react by counterattacking. This may make the first man angry if he feels he was pushed unwillingly toward the second man, and he may get support from his friends surrounding him. Seeing the first man and his friends react in this way may force the second man to retreat from his first attribution of meaning and to apologize for misunderstanding the first man's action. Or he may get the support of his own friends and superimpose his interpretation on the first man and his friends, which would force them to retreat after being hurt by the second man. Alternatively the two groups may continue to struggle for a while until both retreat, being partly successful and partly unsuccessful in imposing their attribution of meaning on the other party. In each of these three cases, an attribution of meaning to the original action of pushing depends on the confirming and disaffirming reaction of the other party and the actor's ability to sustain his attribution. In all cases, meaning is shaped by interaction.

We also have to take into account Blumer's (1969: 5–6) third thesis. This states that meaning is not just imposed on the individual by external factors in a deterministic way. The emergence of meaning from social interaction does not imply that the individual has no choice but to accept meanings that have been established by society or by some dominating group. Meaning does not impose itself on the individual automatically but requires interpretation by him or her. Meaning is not just the first actor's attribution of meaning. The push is processed into a meaningful act by the second man's interpretation of its symbolic content. Without this interpretation, the push would remain a mere physical process. This is where the individual has the chance to determine his or her action and reaction according to his or her interpretation of other people's actions and reactions. The second man has the freedom to interpret the first man's push in different ways: as an accident, as an attempt to enter the stadium without paying for the game, or as an unfriendly attack. However, this freedom is not absolute. According to the second thesis, it is limited by the reactions of the others and by the actor's ability to again respond to these reactions. In a similar way, how a civil servant implements the law in a specific case is not completely determined by the law but depends largely on his or her interpretation of the law and the conclusion he or she draws with regard to that specific case. However, this does not mean that the civil servant is completely free in this process. Which interpretation will be successful depends on how successfully the person can fit in his or her interpretation with those of other people also involved in the interpretive process. Thus, the process of interpreting symbols is a permanent mutual fitting of interpretations in ongoing negotiations between actors.

After introducing these three premises, Blumer (1969: 6–20) goes on to present the message of symbolic interactionism in six basic ideas or "root images": (1) human society and group life; (2) social interaction; (3) objects; (4) the human being as an acting organism; (5) human action; and (6) the interlinkage of action.

Human Society and Group Life

The first root image, symbolic interactionism's view of society and groups, is directed against holistic, structuralist, and objectivist conceptions of society and group life that see them as objectively existing entities with qualities of their own and distinct from human action. In contradistinction to this view, symbolic interactionism conceives of society and groups as composed of human actors engaged in social interaction:

> The life of any human society consists necessarily of an ongoing process of fitting together the activities of its members. (Blumer, 1969: 7)

According to this view the structure or organization of groups and societies does not exist in itself but consists of what actually goes on in the actions of individuals. The structure of domination in an organization does not exist in itself; it is the ongoing interaction between actors. The authority of the director of a department over his or her subordinate assistants exists in the commands the director gives and the corresponding actions of the assistants. The structure of domination is not an entity that determines their mutual actions but an entity that is born out of those interactions. And how the actors act is worked out in the situation itself. The director of a marketing department may tell his or her computer assistant to introduce a new program designed to improve information about their clients within the next two months. The assistant may answer that improving the existing program would serve the same purpose and could be realized much more easily. The director may react skeptically and repeat the request for a completely new program. The assistant, however, may still resist by arguing that the costs of introducing a new program will be much higher. The director may still not be satisfied; however, the assistant may continue with the argument that it will take too long to introduce the new program and it will not be ready for the next sales period. After this arguing back and forth, the director may partly give in and be satisfied with improving the existing program within one month and then monitoring whether it will still be necessary to introduce a completely new program within a year.

The course of interaction between director and assistant represents the structure of domination in that department. This structure is very different from department to department and from situation to situation according to the contingencies of the process of interaction. This interaction proceeds in different directions according to the actions imputed by the participating actors. The process and outcome would have been very different if the assistant had not been able to negotiate intelligently and present an alternative that looked more attractive to the director. And it would have been different if the director had not been flexible enough to come to the insight that he or she would realize his or her goal more quickly with the assistant's plan, because insisting upon the first plan would cost more energy to overcome the resistance of the assistant and co-workers, would take more time, and could be counterproductive because of the resistance coming from co-workers.

In this way the structure of domination in the department is always a negotiated one, not a given quantity with no scope for change. Social order is always a negotiated order. This is what symbolic interactionism states in opposition to structuralist views of society, which assume a unidirectional relationship between a preestablished structure and corresponding actions determined by the objective structure. According to the latter view, the director and the assistant would just perform predetermined roles with, for example, one giving commands and the other carrying them out. Yet, whether the interaction proceeds in this direction or in the other direction outlined above depends on the actions of the two people in the situation and involves their ability to negotiate the course of action successfully. How the relationship of authority between them is worked out in the actual situation depends on how the director interprets his or her role of being responsible for the department and having the right to give commands and the role of assistant, how the assistant interprets his or her own role and the director's role, and how both interpret the symbolic expressions they exchange in their talk. The assistant can interpret the director's wish to introduce a new program as a strict command and may react by consenting to that command. Or the assistant could interpret the director's proposal as a search for a possible improvement of the existing program and may be motivated to present alternative solutions to the problem. If the two converge in their interpretations, negotiation will start. If they diverge, conflict arises and has to be settled according to their respective abilities to enforce their interpretations. According to these different possible interpretations of the director's talk, the interaction will proceed in different directions. Thus the very process of interpreting the meaning of symbolic expressions that are involved in every interaction works contrary to the structuralist view of society and introduces an element of contingency and negotiation into any social order.

Social Interaction

According to the outlined view of society, groups, and organizations, social interaction is the center of social life. The nature of social interaction is highlighted in the second root image presented by Blumer. He points out that human action is not just an outcome of static social factors like social status, norms, values, role demands, or requirements of social systems nor is it just an outcome of psychic factors like needs, motives, or attitudes. It is largely determined by the interaction with other people. This interaction is not only the location at which the effects of the social and psychic factors mentioned are realized in a straightforward way but also an arena that exerts its own unique effects on the actions of individuals. The director and the assistant in the example discussed above have a certain social status and play social roles that are linked in an authority relationship to one another; they also have certain needs, motives, and attitudes. However, what they really do in the situation of interaction depends largely on the ongoing process of reacting to each other's actions. The director may begin to act from his or her authority position and role as director; however, the reaction of the assistant pointing to alternative solutions of the problem raised can divert the director's view from that authority position. The two may engage in a competition to find the most feasible solution to the problem of improving information about clients in which the director may be beaten by the assistant contrary to his or her authority position, because the assistant is the better negotiator. Thus, the action of these two people does not result deterministically from their formal position in the process of interaction itself.

What does this process of interaction look like if we examine it more closely? In characterizing interaction Blumer relies on Mead's (1934) analysis of, first, the conversation of gestures that he calls nonsymbolic interaction and, second, symbolic interaction that involves the use of significant symbols. The conversation of gestures on the nonsymbolic level can be illustrated by a fight between two dogs. If one dog attacks, this either evokes a defensive reaction from the other dog in which it will move away or an offensive reaction in which it will attack the first dog. In this case there is a direct and instinctual or learned connection between stimulus and response but no interpretation of meaning in between. As Mead puts it, there can be no question about whether the attack has the same meaning for both animals. Because he couches his analysis in terms of behaviorism, he says the attack by the first dog does not evoke the same reaction in the second animal as it does in the first dog. The first animal does not experience for itself the same effect of its attack as the second animal expresses in its reaction.

The situation changes considerably with the use of vocal gestures. The vocal gesture of a bird is heard by other birds and by itself and evokes the same reaction in itself as in the other birds. For example, a warning call evokes the same urge to flee from danger in the warning bird as it does in its fellows that hear the signal, and all react in the same way. This vocal gesture is a significant symbol. It has a threefold relationship. It is the beginning of an action of the organism that articulates the significant symbol. That is, it announces a certain process of action by that organism. On the other hand, it evokes a reaction in the animal that hears the signal. And it evokes the same reaction in the first animal. In the case of the bird warning its fellows, the announced action is identical to the reaction, and this in turn is identical to the reaction of the others. However, an animal warning its enemy announces an attack, whereas the reaction of the enemy is fear and flight. The inner reaction of the first animal is the same because it also evokes the reaction of fear and flight in the animal itself. The warning signal has the same meaning for both, though the two do not act in the same way. The first continues to attack the second, which reacts with fear and flight. The meaning of the warning as a significant symbol is the reaction of the second animal, which is the same as that of the first animal.

The use of language is no different from the use of significant symbols. Language evolves from the vocal gesture, and its meaning can be understood in the same way. The man who asks his wife at dinner "Could you pass me the bread, please?" evokes the reaction in her to pass him the bread. His words announce his preparedness to receive the bread. But the words also evoke the reaction of passing bread in him. The words would evoke the same real reaction of passing bread within him if his wife had asked him for bread.

Mead tries to strictly conceive of meaning in terms of behaviorism. He calls his approach social behaviorism, because the behavior of actors engaged in interaction is his object of study and because he conceives of human identity and of meaning emerging from social interaction. However, the behavioristic language sets limits to his accomplishments. Is it the physical reaction of the woman that defines the meaning of her husband's words? And do these words evoke the same physical reaction in her husband? The man may imagine his wife's reaction when he speaks. Thus, there may be a convergence of his imagination of his wife's future reaction when he says the words. Only in this sense can we speak of the same reaction. However, in this case the reaction consists, on the one hand, of physically carrying out an action and on the other hand of an inner imagination of that action, but not really an identical reaction. The reaction would be identical only if we looked at different situations: first the man asks for bread, then the woman passes the bread.

Even more limits in conceiving of meaning in behavioristic terms emerge from its definition in terms of the reaction of others to spoken or written words. Our example of the husband and wife still fits into Mead's behavioristic model because it is a simple interconnection between a wish and its fulfillment. Likely commands and the carrying out of commands fit into this model. But what about more complex communications? Can they be reduced to a composition of simpler elements of stimulus and response? I don't think so. Look at the following example: The man may tell his wife: "I am going to have a power breakfast with your brother John this morning." She may respond by expressing a different thought: "Please remind him we're having dinner together on Friday." Does the woman's reaction define the meaning of her husband's words? Certainly not. We do not learn anything about what a "power breakfast" is from her reaction. We would not understand the man's words by looking at the woman's reaction. We would not learn that what the man means by the phrase "I am going to have a power breakfast with your brother John this morning" is that he intends to sit with John for at least an hour in a restaurant and talk business. We could learn this without an explanation from the husband only if we also participated in his meeting with John. Here the future action of the man defines the meaning of his words, not the reaction of his wife.

However, we can use words the meaning of which could not be discovered by our future actions. The man may tell his wife: "John and Robert had a power breakfast yesterday." Neither the woman's reaction nor her husband's future action tells us anything here about the meaning of the man's words. We would have to ask him, and he would explain the meaning to us in words we are familiar with: "A power breakfast is a meeting of people who eat breakfast together in a restaurant and talk business for at least an hour."

Because most of our talk proceeds along the lines of this example, Mead's theory of the emergence of meaning in interaction would be inadequate. However, we could say that a conversation about the meaning of terms would have to refer back to stimulus-response connections. Yet even this is sometimes neither possible nor necessary. Let us imagine that the woman does not understand her husband and asks him: "What is a power breakfast?" The man may tell her: "A power breakfast is a breakfast where people sit together to talk business in a restaurant for at least an hour." The woman may now answer: "Okay, I understand." However, their five-year-old son Tom, who witnessed this conversation, may ask: "Dad, what is business?" The man may answer: "Business is what Sam does in his store, selling all the things we need to live, like tomatoes, apples, potatoes, meat, noodles, and so on." Now Tom may be satisfied, saying: "Ah, that's business." Here the woman's reaction, Tom's reaction, and the action of the man tell us nothing about the meaning of the word "power breakfast," though the man had to go back to some more elementary words in his conversation with Tom. He first explains the meaning of "power breakfast" by referring to the more familiar words "talking about business while having breakfast," and then he explains the meaning of "business" by referring to an observable behavior of another person. It is now the observable behavior of someone they all know that explains the meaning of the word "business."

If we go back even further in the little boy's history, we may come across his experience of buying something at Sam's store. He may have gone into the store and said: "I would like to have two pounds of apples." Sam would have reacted by handing out two pounds of apples, saying: "There you go, boy, that's $2 please." Tom may have reacted by passing $2 to Sam. Here the reaction of the two to one another is the meaning of their words, and we are at the level of Mead's basic analysis of the emergence of meaning. However, there is a gap between this early experience and the later characterization of the complex interchange between Sam and Tom as "business" by Tom's father.

This gap is bridged not by a stimulus-response relationship but by linking an abstract word to a behavior or a complex interchange of behavior in some situation. Every word that refers to more than one single reaction to a stimulus has to be learned in this way. Even if Sam had said to Tom, "This is business, so please give me $2," this reaches beyond Tom's reaction of passing $2 to Sam, because passing $2 to Sam is not the meaning of the word "business." The term covers the whole of the interchange between the two: Tom's asking for two pounds of apples, Sam's handing them out and asking for $2, and Tom's passing the $2 to Sam. Here it is not any single reaction of one actor to another's stimulus that defines the meaning of a term but the whole complex of an interchange between two people. These people do learn the meaning of the term "business" in this interaction if someone associates the term with the complex of that interaction. But the meaning of the term is not the reaction of an actor to a stimulus. People have to understand the meaning of "business" by piecing it together from interconnected simpler relationships of stimulus and response. And this job of piecing together is not itself a reaction to a stimulus.

This is a new level of understanding meaning that bridges the gap between stimulus-response sets and abstract terms. This assembly of simpler elements of meaning to build up the meaning of more complex and abstract terms is an emergent quality of the evolution of meaning in social interaction. It cannot be reduced to stimulus-response sets of exchanging significant symbols.

We have to distinguish more clearly than Mead the level of communication with abstract terms from the conversation with significant symbols. Also, we have to conceive of this as an evolutionary process in which the earlier phases provide a basis for the later ones, but the development of the later ones necessitates the invention of new means of communication. The later phases evolve on the basis of the earlier ones by making use of their potential to invent something new in that we achieve more complex combinations of the earlier elements. However, this does not imply that the later phases can be completely reduced to the earlier ones. This is prohibited by the inventions peculiar to the later phases. Thus we can conceive of a development of meaning in three phases: (1) conversation of gestures; (2) conversation with simple significant symbols; and (3) communication with abstract terms.

Having examined Mead's analysis of the emergence of meaning in social interaction as it is used by Blumer (though Blumer passes by the deficiencies of Mead's social behaviorism), we can now return to analyzing the impact of meaning on the process of social interaction. According to Blumer, any interaction involves a first actor who makes an indication of his or her intentions to act in a certain way, an indication of a forthcoming action. This indication is a symbol that has a meaning conveyed to a second actor, who interprets the meaning of the symbol and reacts according to the meaning he or she has assigned to it. Also, the second actor's reaction first indicates the forthcoming action to the first actor and then he or she carries it out. Let us again take up the first example of a man entering the gate of a football stadium in order to examine this conception of symbolic interaction. The first man may arrive at the gate with the words: "Please let me through." The second interprets this as an indication of his forthcoming action of entering the stadium and reacts with the words: "Your ticket please." The first man interprets this as an indication that he will be stopped by the man at the gate, unless he shows him a ticket; because he has no ticket he says: "Let me in or I'll knock hell out of you!" The man at the door interprets this as an indication of an act of violence and will now calculate whether he is strong enough to stop the other man. If he is not strong enough, he will try to indicate the support of the police to the other man: "Stop, or I will call the police." By doing this he may now have impressed the other man with the strength available to back him up, and the other may retreat to the ticket office and buy a ticket. Before he will be prepared to do this, the man has to interpret the gateman's words as an indication that action really is forthcoming. If he does not believe the gateman's words, he will just push him away. Thus what he really does will depend on what the gateman says and on how he interprets those words.

Conveying and interpreting symbols is of great importance for determining the direction of an ongoing interaction. The gateman has to use the right words and make the right impression in order to stop the man who intends to enter the stadium. Interaction is always a process of fitting actions, and the use of symbols influences the course of this process. The interpretations of the symbols are themselves fitted to one another during that process. The gateman and the football fan talk and act until their interpretations fit. This means that their actions are coordinated. At the beginning, the interpretations of the gateman and the fan do not fit. The gateman may interpret the fan's words "Please let me pass" as the words of someone who has forgotten to show his ticket and answers: "Your ticket please." This, however, does not interpret the intention of the fan correctly, for he wants to get in without a ticket. It is not until the fan says "Let me in or I'll knock hell out of you!" that the gateman understands his intention correctly and is able to fit his interpretation of the fan's words to the fan's own interpretation. Likewise, the fan understands the gateman's intention only after he has referred to the police. Now the fan knows the gateman will stop him even if he has to call the police. His interpretation of the gateman's words fits with the gateman's own interpretation. According to their mutual understanding resulting from the fitting of interpretations, their actions become coordinated. The gateman stands his ground at the gate, and the fan goes to the ticket office. Should the gateman be unable to impress the fan and the fan reacts by striking him, the gateman has to revise his interpretation of the fan's intention, now knowing that his threat about calling the police does not frighten the fan. After that, his interpretation fits with the intention of the fan. That means the gateman has a correct interpretation of how the fan interprets his own words, can correctly predict the fan's actions, and can take the right actions to counter the fan's action in order to realize his goal: preventing the fan from entering the stadium without a ticket. Now he really will call the police.

Thus the process of fitting interpretations means that actors try to find out the correct interpretation of each other's interpretation of intentions (indicated actions) in order to successfully attain their goals. In this way they make plans, check their feasibility, and revise them in order to realize their goals by interpreting the plans of other actors and by adjusting their action to that of other actors. The process of fitting interpretations and lines of conduct is seen as a process of negotiation.

However, what does it mean to speak of the negotiation of interpretations? Symbolic interactionists are not very clear about that. In negotiations, two actors have conflicting goals and coordinate their actions through compromise in order to realize their goals at least partly. Let us take the communication between the director and the assistant. Their goals are in conflict inasmuch as the director wants to introduce a new program and the assistant wants to improve the existing program. Their interpretations of each other's roles and words may also be in conflict. The director understands their roles in an authoritative way and his or her articulated wish as a command. The assistant understands their roles in a participatory way and the director's words as an indication of a problem for which alternative solutions can be sought. The assistant may indicate that he or she and the other members of the team will not carefully carry out the director's commands unless they have a chance to participate in the decision and to find out the best solution collectively. The assistant implicitly offers a deal: "Let us participate in the decision and find a way of solving the problem. Then you will get a solution to your problem that may not be the same as you intended to have but will be carried out most carefully by us." The director may be induced to accept this offer and adjust his or her interpretation of their roles and of the command originally given to the assistant's interpretation: decision making by participation and articulation of wishes for which the best ways of realizing them have to be found collectively. In this way the director fits his or her interpretation of roles and wishes with that of the assistant. The assistant, who may first have had the opinion that they already have the best program and nothing should be changed, redefines his or her role in the sense that he or she cannot rely solely on carrying out existing programs and redefines the director's talk not as simply disturbing the normal processing of information with an established program but as a necessary indication of the need for permanently improving existing programs for information processing. The assistant has thus fitted his or her interpretation of roles and talk with that of the director's. Both have arrived at a compromise by way of negotiation. This is how negotiation over the meaning of roles and words proceeds.

Objects

The third root image Blumer deals with concerns the nature of objects. The basic statement here is that objects fill out the actors' environment, but they do not "play upon" the actors physically — neither physical objects nor social or abstract cultural objects do so. Their influence on actors is mediated through processes of interpretation of their meaning. A church is physically seen as a building like other buildings. What makes people keep quiet in the church is the sacred meaning attributed by their religion to that building. As meaning changes, so too does the influence of objects on people. A once admired sports star who has attracted the respect and deferential behavior of people may become the object of aggression after a series of defeats. To understand the action of people it is necessary to identify the world of meaningful objects that surrounds them. One has to know in which world they live from the point of view of meaning. Two people may live next door to one another but in very different worlds of meaning. One may be a salesman, the other, a musician. Every physical object surrounding them may have a different meaning for them; they live according to very different ideas and values. The world of the salesman and the world of the musician may have little in common. However, the world in which they live has not been made by themselves individually but in ongoing processes of social interaction.

The Human Being as an Acting Organism

The fourth root image sees the human being as an acting organism. That means that the human being does not just respond to others on the non-symbolic level in a way that is internally and externally determined by psychic dispositions and social facts. Human beings are able to actively intervene in the world that surrounds them. The human individual makes indications of his or her plan to others and interprets their indications from his or her perspective. Individuals are capable of locating their position in the world, which presupposes looking at themselves, knowing about themselves, and recognizing themselves as, for example, Californians or New Yorkers, men or women, white or black, Protestant or Catholic, salespersons or airline pilots. This means that humans have a self. Having a self has enormous consequences for the action of each human individual. Everything he or she does is processed through the self, through the concept the individual has of him- or herself. Whether the assistant in our example above—let us assume for a moment this is a man—carries out the director's command without questioning or whether he takes it as a starting point for presenting alternative solutions of the problem depends largely on his sense of self, that is, on how he sees himself, on what type of person he thinks he is. If he thinks he is a reliable person, he will carry out the command without question. If he thinks he is a bright, self-responsible person, he will feel forced to present alternatives in order to live up to his image of himself.

Having a self means being able to interact with oneself. The individual can be an object of his or her own action. He or she can observe and evaluate his or her action and change it according to that evaluation. This is the basis of the individual's self-control — control over his or her action — and its relation to other actors.

The individual's self emerges from interaction with others. Without such interaction no self could be formed. The individual interacts with others from early childhood — with people who have varying degrees of significance for the individual. People who are of central importance for the individual are significant others. They have a lasting influence on the formation of the self. The child's mother, father, brothers, sisters, friends, teachers at school, the adolescent's first love, a professor, and advisors are significant others who largely shape the self of the individual as he or she grows up. The interaction with these significant others is transformed into self-interaction. The individual talks to him- or herself in the role of the significant other. He or she takes the role of the other and looks at him- or herself from their viewpoint, talks to him- or herself in their words. The first stages in this development provide an overt expression of this transformation of social interaction into self-interaction. It is common with young children to play the roles of mother and father and to engage in self-talk between themselves and their parents. The young girl may say to herself: "I would like to play with Jeannie now," but continues to speak to herself in the role of her mother: "But you have to finish your homework first," says mother. "I would like to go outside to meet Jeannie now, because she is waiting for me," she says as herself again. However, she warns herself in the words of her mother: "But then don't forget to be home by five, so that you can finish your school work." "Don't worry, I'll be back in time," she says and continues in her mother's words: "That's a good girl." Then she goes outside.

This type of self-talk, in which the roles of child and mother are played simultaneously, is the first step toward building a self by transforming social interaction into self-interaction. We see here the origin of the double nature of the self. It is an interlinkage of the spontaneous disposition to act and attitudes that make the child a unique individual and the perception of that unique individual and the attitudes toward him or her arising from the perceptions and attitudes of others. The young girl's self is both: her wish to meet Jeannie and her mother's voice reminding her of her school work.

This is the interlinkage of the two parts of the self that Mead calls "I" and "me." The "I" is the spontaneous and unique part of the child; the "me" is mother's voice. The "I" and "me" are in permanent interaction with each other. The incorporation of the roles of a growing number of others leads the child to see and evaluate his or her actions from a multitude of viewpoints. The child learns to differentiate between attitudes that are held by a number or even all others and those that are held by only one or two others. By being repeatedly confronted with certain views and attitudes, the growing child learns to generalize these views and attitudes. Now when she speaks to herself, the girl does not speak in mother's words but in those of a concrete collectivity or "generalized other." She says: "We schoolchildren do our homework every day." Here she has generalized from a single significant other to the concrete collectivity of schoolchildren.

In Mead's terms, this is the first step toward the incorporation of the generalized other. A further step would be reached when the girl said to herself: "One does one's duties everyday." Here the abstract "one" represents an abstract community, the largest community the child can imagine. It includes everybody she knows. Mead explains the development of the orientation from the significant others to the generalized other with the difference between play and game. In playing the mother-child relationship, the girl takes only the role of a single significant other. All play is a sequence of such single relationships. The child does not integrate and generalize them. In a game such as baseball, children have to look at their play from the point of view of all their co-players and have to integrate their role into a coordinated set in order to coordinate their actions with each other. Otherwise, they would not be able to play the game of baseball. This is the first step in incorporating the generalized other. A further step will be reached when the players learn to look at their play from the viewpoint of the whole community of baseball players, which includes both teams and is represented by the umpire. Here the generalized other and the "me" thus generalized corresponds to the rules of the game, which may be represented in the principle of fairness.

To the extent that the individual's "me" develops toward the incorporation of the generalized other, this does not imply that the individual's "I" becomes irrelevant. It is still there, and the human self is still an interplay of the spontaneous and unique "I" and the self-perceiving, evaluating, and controlling "me."

Human Action

The next root image is concerned with human action. According to Blumer, human action is not just an outcome of some psychic or social factors that "play upon" the individual. In light of the foregoing analysis we have to take into account that it always implies an individual who has a self and is therefore capable of coordinating his or her action with a view to the actions of other actors. Every psychic or social influence is mediated through the work of the self. The individual has a "me" from the point of view that he or she evaluates not only his or her own actions but also those of other people. The more generalized the "me" has become, the more the individual can evaluate the pressure from concrete others from a more general moral point of view. Thus the person can make a choice of action in the interplay between his or her unique attitudes and spontaneous dispositions and his or her generalized moral viewpoint. The more the individual has developed uniqueness and a generalized morality, the more his or her action will be guided by reflection. In this way the individual reaches higher levels of sovereignty and is capable of mediating between spontaneous dispositions to act and the expectations of others. In Blumer's apparently more strategic terms, action does not mean carrying out preestablished roles and norms; it means taking these things into account and forging a line of conduct on the basis of interpreting them.

The Interlinkage of Action

The final root image deals with the interlinkage of action. According to Blumer, much of conventional sociology conceives of collective action and institutions as emergent entities in their own right without taking sufficient notice of how they are made by individual actors and their actions. They are emergent entities insofar as they link individual actions. Nevertheless, they are largely determined by the process of these individual actions. In Blumer's view, analyzing an acting collectivity means looking at the groups and individuals that compose this collectivity and are engaged in fitting their plans and actions with each other to form a coordinated action. An institution includes a set of norms. However, what an institution really is becomes concrete in the actions of individuals who interpret these norms from their point of view and coordinate their interpretations in processes of interaction. Institutions are a historical phenomenon. They have a history, which means that their norms did not fall from heaven according to systemic requirements but arose from the interactions of people. The norms thus generated form starting points for present and future interpretations that include their continuous change according to situational points of view and negotiations between actors.

Summary

1. Human action is oriented to the meaning of objects.
2. The meaning of objects evolves from social interaction.
3. The meaning of objects is defined in processes of interpretation.
4. The definition of meaning is the outcome of actors' mutually fitting their lines of conduct.
5. Meaning is not stable but varies from situation to situation according to the definitional process.
6. Human society and group life are composed of interactions of individuals.
7. Social interaction varies according to the situational processes of defining meaning.
8. Objects determine human action via the meaning they are attributed in definitional processes.

9. What an actor does is determined not simply by external objects but by the mediation of that influence through his or her self.
10. Human action is mediated through the individual's interaction with him- or herself.
11. Collective action and institutions result from interlinking individual actions.

Critical Assessment

We can learn most from Blumer's approach when it comes to the situational contingencies and variations of social action arising from its basic feature of involving the interactional interpretation of meaning. The basic message may read like this proposition:

> The more social action involves the interpretation of meaning, the less it will be predetermined by norms and the more it will vary according to the situational variation of mutually fitting interpretations in negotiations.

Blumer shows how contingent and negotiated social action is once we take into account its basic feature of interpreting meaning. What he really demonstrates is the contingent and negotiated character of communication. However, in doing so he completely drops the unique nature that differentiates communication from negotiation. We do not learn so much from Blumer about the conditions under which we understand each other. In his eyes, understanding is a casual outcome of a trial-and-error process leading to the "fit" of interpretations in strategic action. Yet, in reality, understanding is more than just the fitting of interpretations. It means arriving at a "shared world," and sharing a world is a different matter than fitting interpretations. People who "fit" interpretations try to reach specific goals individually in strategic action. People who try to come to a shared world approach each other in a different way: They want to reach a common understanding of something by tracing back their momentary divergence to commonly shared meanings on a deeper level. This nature of communication is completely out of sight in Blumer's perspective, not to mention how people reach rationally grounded interpretations of meaning. Blumer's approach allows us only to speak of the instrumental rationality of certain interpretations of symbols for the goal of an individual. How people can arrive at rationally grounded views reaching beyond individual instrumentality cannot be addressed in Blumer's terms. To answer this question requires a theory of discursive reasoning that binds the validity of views to their confirmation in a discourse in which everybody can make proposals, raise questions, and criticize proposals. These questions call for a theory of communicative action such as that developed by Jürgen Habermas, to which we will turn later on.

Blumer's symbolic interactionism has further deficiencies, however. It does not clearly formulate the laws that guide the process of negotiating meaning. To get more insight into this process we would have to consult explicit economic theories of negotiation. Blumer also fails to distinguish clearly between the situation of negotiation and the situation of conflict and domination, which is guided by different laws and can also influence processes of meaning interpretation. This knowledge is much better provided by conflict theory. Further, he does not sufficiently address the fact that many symbolic interactions are coordinated by self-evident norms of everyday life. This influence on the process of symbolic interaction has its unique laws too. Here we learn much more from phenomenological sociology.

Alternative Paths of Symbolic Interactionism: Manford Kuhn and Ralph H. Turner

There are alternative positions of symbolic interactionism to Blumer's that have laid much more emphasis on structural components and on strategic-conflictual components in interaction. Manford Kuhn (1964a, 1964b) has related symbolic interactionism with hard-nosed positivistic methodology looking for quantitative measures of the core variables introduced by Mead. Equipped with such a methodological approach he sees social reality in a causally deterministic way in contrast to Blumer's indeterminism; he conceives of the self much more as a constant set of measurable attitudes and of the situation of interaction as determined by external structures to which the individual has to adapt. Interaction is for him determined by the self-attitudes and the role-expectations directed at actors.

Ralph H. Turner (1962, 1968, 1976, 1978, 1979–1980) follows the other possible line in elaborating symbolic interactionism, the strategic-conflictual line. He extends Mead's idea of role taking by interpreting this process as an active undertaking that indeed very often implies role making. Instead of the conventional view of role theory, which sees actors forced to role conformity, Turner argues that much role behavior follows the norm of consistency, which requires actors to maintain a consistent line. However, this leaves the actor with many more role-making opportunities. In interaction, actors tentatively try out their role making and try to verify whether it allows them to maintain consistency. The same tendency of trying out consistent concepts holds true for individuals in establishing a self-concept. Turner specifies his general approach by formulating tendency propositions on various aspects of social role making: (1) the emergence and character of roles; (2) the role as an interactive framework; (3) roles in relation to actors; (4) roles in an organizational setting; (5) roles in a social setting; and (6) roles and the person. In general, Turner's approach is a promising version of symbolic interactionism that emphasizes the process of role making and formulates specific propositions on that process.

TWELVE

THE DRAMATURGY OF STRATEGIC COMMUNICATION: ERVING GOFFMAN

WHAT A person experiences, what he or she sees, how he or she reacts to it, what he or she does, and how he or she relates to other people is determined to a large degree by the frames applied by that person to experiences, observations, reactions, and relations to other people. The same is true for the other people who enter the situation and relate to the person in question. Neither party to the situation can frame its observations, experiences, actions, and relations independently of the frames applied by the other party to the situation. The framing of observations, experiences, actions, and relations is very much an outcome of the interaction between two or more parties engaged in the very process of framing situations including observations, experiences, actions, reactions, and relationships between people.

A frame applied by a person determines what is going on in a situation for that person. A frame is a means to observing and understanding what is going on. There are natural and social frames. An example of a natural frame is the cause-effect scheme that orders our understanding of natural phenomena. A social frame relates phenomena to the will of human beings and to their interactions. A person who receives something from another person may interpret that as a gift, and because of that framing of the situation, he or she will express thanks and will feel obliged to reciprocate the gift at an appropriate time: a birthday gift at the other person's birthday or a card on Valentine's day.

The framing of a situation means perceiving, interpreting, and understanding that situation and the actions and people involved in that situation in a certain way. This framing, too, determines very much how the person goes on to act and react in the situation and in future situations related to that situation. Framing is a process of perceiving, interpreting, understanding, and acting, of defining a situation in the light of symbolic systems of meaning, norms, aesthetic views, and cognitions. Investigating these processes means looking at the symbolic framing of action and the resulting order of action and interaction between people. What people perceive, how they understand what they have perceived, what they do, how they relate to each other, how they coordinate their perceptions and actions never occurs in a purely physical or physiological sense but is always framed by the symbolic systems applied by people to their situations of action and by the coordination of their framing activities.

The impact of such processes of framing on social action is the subject matter of Erving Goffman's famous contributions to sociology. His book on *Frame Analysis*, published in 1974, is an explicit expression of this approach to studying social action. His earlier and later publications are examples of studying processes of framing situations, actions, social relations, and personal identities, for example, *The Presentation of Self in Everyday Life* in 1959, *Asylums* in 1961, *Encounters* in 1961, *Stigma* in 1963, *Interaction Ritual* in 1967, *Strategic Interaction* in 1969, *Relations in Public* in 1971, *Gender Advertisements* in 1979 and *Forms of Talk* in 1981. The first four studies of this series, which reached from the late 1950s to the early 1960s, established Goffman's approach and reputation in the 1960s. This is why I include his contribution to sociology in the discussion of the discourse of sociological theory in that period of time, even though Goffman's later publications reach into the early 1980s. It was during that earlier period that his approach began to frame sociological discourse.

Frame Analysis

The framing of perception, understanding, action, and identity by symbolic systems is a common subject matter of any type of hermeneutical-interpretive and phenomenological approach to studying social action. What makes Goffman's (1974/1975) contribution to this paradigm a distinctive one is his framing of the process of framing itself. He does this very much in the sense of a dramaturgical staging of action, which gives special attention to the actor-audience relationship, and also very much in the sense of strategic action, which sees framing as a means of attaining specific goals. Because actors always need the cooperation of teammates, of an audience, and of the public in order to be successful in attaining their goals, they have to frame their performances in a way that motivates teammates, audience, and public to cooperate either in an active or in a passive way, by letting the actor go on in his or her chosen way. Impression management by way of framing one's actions and one's identity is of utmost importance for successful goal attainment in this perspective. This framing varies between sincere attempts at trustworthiness in one's actions and deception implying less sincere elements of framing in order to attain one's goals. The ability to define and to frame a situation in a way favorable to one's goals and personal identity decides one's success in strategic action. This ability, however, can be set in motion only if the external circumstances allow it; in other words, it will be set in motion according to the channeling effects of external circumstances. An important feature of these circumstances is the power available to an actor to impose his or her definition of the situation, which forces the less powerful actor to make the best of such a situation by escaping direct confrontations and by way of framings that allow the less powerful actor to satisfy at least his or her elementary needs. The more several actors have at least some power or are equal in power, the more the framing of situations will be a contest between actors and groups that bring the different techniques of framing situations fully into play in a way most favorable for their goals.

Goffman distinguishes between primary frames, modulations, and deceptions. All of these are involved in the framing of situations. Primary frames are used in the immediate framing of everyday actions. Two rival lovers of the same woman act toward each other within the primary frame of a fight. The staging of such a fight in a theater play is a modulation of that fight. It is a copy of the original fight put into another context, which changes its meaning. Within the primary frame, the audience watching the two rivals fighting each other with dangerous weapons would have to intervene or to call on the police to intervene. A man from a theater audience intervening in a fight on a stage would violate the rules of that game. He would break through the primary frame of the theater play, which assigns the audience a strictly passive role. Thus the modulation of the fight in the theater play is set between the parentheses of the primary frame of the theater play, which changes part of the fight's original meaning. A modulation is a copy of a primary frame applied to the framing of parts of action within another primary frame that gives the copy a meaning distinct from the original material.

There is a clear understanding of where playing the copy begins and where it ends, like the theater play's opening and concluding acts. Also, the actors and the audience know that a modulation is taking place. This is not the case with deception, which is also a copy of a primary frame set in motion within another primary frame but without knowledge of at least the audience or even — in cases of self-deception — the actor him- or herself. The steward on a plane who keeps cool in an emergency to avoid panic within the group of passengers applies a copy of cool appearance and action though he himself may be frightened. He conceals his real feeling and applies a copy of another feeling within the primary frame "emergency" in order to make the passengers react to his copied cool appearance and action and to remain cool themselves. "Emergency" is here the primary and "real" frame;

"cool appearance and action" is a deception copied from another primary frame and applied within the primary frame of "emergency." The latter determines the beginning and the end of applying the deception as a copied, not "real" frame. Though modulations and deceptions are copies of primary frames applied to situations that are defined by another primary frame, they are not complete repetitions of the original. Because of the application to another situation defined by another primary frame, the original material becomes transformed and acquires a new meaning. The fight between the two rival lovers in the theater play has another meaning for the actors and the audience than for the original rivals. The same is true for the cool appearance and action of the steward transmitted from an originally relaxed situation to the situation of an emergency.

Inasmuch as actions in situations interrelate primary frames, modulations, and deceptions, the individual action in such situations has to interrelate three levels of framing the action: the person, the role he or she plays according to the primary frame, and the role played according to the applied modulation and/or deception. In the theater play, the role of the actor, the figure played by the actor, and the person of the actor are interrelated with each other. Most situations of action involve several such levels of framing the action. Actors can communicate on each of these levels. The play of a fight between rival lovers can be communicated to the audience as such; however, the theater critics or even the actors may talk about the staging of that fight and even about how the identity of each actor's person frames his staging of the figure, and how the staging of the figure frames each actor's personal identity.

According to the frame perspective there is the action going on within the frame and the action going on outside that frame, which may be observed and even taken into account while acting within a certain frame. Very often action happening outside the actual frame is kept outside by enclosing the action within the frame physically, for example, by acting behind closed doors.

Frames guide action, but action may also break through frames. The man from the audience who intervenes in the rival lovers' fight breaks through the primary frame of the theater in order to re-transform the modulation of the rivals' fight to the status of a primary frame. The passenger who provokes the steward's loss of control breaks through the deception of keeping cool and may introduce panic as the new primary frame.

I have used "Frame Analysis" as described by Goffman to introduce his strategic-dramaturgical approach to the framing of situations of action because it provides the most general perspective for understanding his more specific studies of the same processes. This framing of our interpretation of some of his more specific studies will help us to understand the general theoretical message of these studies. To do this, and for further exemplification of his approach, we now turn to his studies on *The Presentation of Self in Everyday Life* (Goffman, 1959/1971a), *Asylums* (Goffman, 1961a/1968), and *Stigma* (Goffman, 1963).

The Presentation of Self in Everyday Life

In the dramaturgical view, as developed by Erving Goffman (1959/1971a), human action is a permanent staging of the individual actor. The actor plays a role in the presence of an audience. The actor is a performer. He or she gives a performance to the audience, and the audience reacts with applause (approval or disapproval). In this perspective, an exchange between actor and audience takes place in which a certain performance is exchanged for applause/approval.

What Goffman provides in his *Presentation of Self in Everyday Life* is a phenomenological description of different aspects of a performance. As the title of the book shows, the presentation of the actor's self in society is the crucial problem on which sociological interest is focused. We can ask what enables the individual to establish and maintain his or her identity as a person in the everyday performance of social roles. The interrelationship between self-realization on the one hand and carrying out of social role prescriptions on the other is the question here. Goffman describes different aspects of this interrelationship in a way that the presentation of self in roles becomes an object in itself with an internal logic for successful accomplishment. He enumerates several aspects of self-presentation in role performance to which we shall now turn our attention.

Aspects of Role Performance

Let us explain these aspects of role performance using the examples of teachers and students.

Sincere and Cynical Role Performance

A "teacher" is a social role defined by the socially prescribed norms of acting in the position of a teacher and the social expectations directed toward this position. Every occupant of the position of a teacher is confronted with the role-expectations regarding his or her position, and he or she has to meet these expectations in the concrete performance of the role. This is a performance on a stage. Students, colleagues, and the school board make up the audience for the performance. The "student" is a social role played by its incumbents in front of the audience of other students, teachers, and the school board. A teacher plays his or her role in a sincere way inasmuch as he or she believes in the part.

In this case, the teacher of a certain subject believes in the theoretical validity and practical utility of the books he or she assigns to be read and the knowledge of the discipline he or she represents. The teacher also believes in the capability of students to grasp and understand the complexities of the accumulated knowledge and methods of a discipline. And the teacher always discloses doubts when he or she has them regarding the theoretical validity and practical utility of knowledge and the capability of students. A sincere performer always says what he or she thinks is right, disregarding any consequences for him- or herself or other persons, including persons in the audience. A teacher who tells a student that he or she does not have the intellectual capabilities to succeed in learning the basic principles and methods if that teacher believes the student does not have these capabilities acts in a sincere way.

A teacher plays the role in a cynical way inasmuch as he or she does not believe in the part he or she plays. The teacher who has doubts regarding the theoretical validity and/or practical usefulness of the books assigned, the knowledge and methods taught, and the capabilities of students to grasp the complexities of the discipline, but does not disclose these doubts in order to keep students attracted to the subject, acts in a cynical way. The same applies to a teacher who does not tell a student that he or she thinks that student is unable to learn the principles and methods of the discipline in order to keep the student in class, because class size is a criterion of success in teaching. Between the two extremes lies the broad field of compromise between sincere and cynical performance. The teacher may disclose some doubts but not all of them and may relativize the doubts by saying that all academic disciplines have their theoretical and methodological problems and that all students have their problems in learning the principles of the discipline.

There is often a separation of sincere backstage talk and cynical front-stage talk at work. For example, the teacher may never disclose doubts about his or her discipline and the students to students in the classroom front-stage but will disclose those doubts to colleagues and to his or her spouse backstage. On the separated backstage, the teacher may even joke about this cynical performance front-stage: "I taught the students the x-method today. I don't think they will really understand what the method is about."

Front

The role performance of a teacher takes place on a stage that has a so-called front. A front defines the situation for the performance; it indicates which kind of role performance is taking place. A front can be differentiated into two basic aspects: social front and personal front. The social front is the setting in which a role performance takes place. The personal front is the appearance of the performer and his or her manners in performing the role. All these are expressive components of the role performance conveying an expressive meaning to the class. The social front, the setting of the teacher in the classroom, the arrangement of seats for the class, the lecturer's desk (sometimes similar to a pulpit in a church) all contribute to the expression of authority in knowledge. The equipment the teacher uses, like the blackboard and the overhead projector, indicate that he or she is an up-to-date teacher who uses modern equipment. The personal front of the teacher is, first, his or her appearance: title, sex, age, clothing, posture, speech patterns, facial expressions, and bodily gestures. Some of these are fixed permanently or over a span of time, such as sex, age, and title; others can be changed from situation to situation, such as clothing, speech patterns, and gestures. The appearance of a teacher is determined, for example, by title, membership in a famous department, and professional reputation. These are personal attributes that have been established before the teacher enters the classroom at a specific time and place and brings this appearance to the concrete situation of performance. Here, the teacher's manners come into play. This includes all the ways in which the teacher expresses him- or herself in front of the class: for example, maintains distance; acts formally, even bureaucratically; never allows digression from the strict carrying out of a pattern of role performances or, alternatively, bridges the teacher-student divide with some personal remarks; or encourages a relaxed atmosphere and even allows deviations from bureaucratic rules. This is the way the teacher fills out and defines the role he or she plays. Setting, appearance, and manners are all aspects of expression in role performance, and there is usually tension if they are not in consistency. For example, the teacher who is considered an authority but tells students that he or she has asked someone else the answer to a question would act inconsistently with his or her appearance, which could lower the teacher's reputation, thus leading to a new consistency.

The social front consists of the most generalized and standardized aspects of role performance, which the actor has to take as established patterns of role playing. The personal front is more open to personal invention.

Dramatic Realization

Dramatic realization means that an actor has to present his or her act in a way that highlights the importance of the action for the audience. A university professor who teaches only two courses a week and is able to put his or her own research into the lecture can achieve a dramatic realization more easily than a high-school teacher who has to teach many more hours a week can. Everything that highlights the uniqueness of the teaching contributes to dramatic realization. The more a teacher is able to bring in his or her personal achievements in advancing and transmitting knowledge, the more his or her performance stands out as something unique—a lecture that is different from all the available books and is imprinted by the teacher's character.

Idealization

An actor who tries to live up to the ideal and perfect performance of a role is inclined to an idealization of his or her role performance. In this case, the actor emphasizes those parts of role performance that fit in with the ideal picture of the role and hides those parts that do not fit into this picture. The teacher has to live up to the ideal of having comprehensive knowledge and competence. Every sign of lacking knowledge and competence endangers the teacher's authority in the class. Thus, he or she always has to demonstrate comprehensive knowledge and competence, for example, by referring to a lot of literature (name-dropping) and by assigning a lot of reading, which demonstrates a capability to teach complex and complicated matters. When professors officially report their sixty-hour working week, they also contribute to the idealization of scholarly work. On the other hand, they have to hide every instance of ignorance or incompetence. A teacher who cannot answer a student's question regarding the subject matter does not live up to the ideal definition of teacher.

Maintenance of Expressive Control

Let us define the opposite of maintenance of expressive control: An actor does not maintain expressive control, first, in cases of accidentally losing physical control, showing disrespect, and/or conveying incapacity; second, by showing too much or too little concern with an interaction; and third, in cases of inadequate dramaturgical direction.

In the first case, our teacher may stumble and fall in front of the class. This is an accident that puts him or her momentarily out of control and momentarily undermines his or her authority. But if the teacher has the right words at hand, perhaps a joke, he or she may gain some personal attraction because he or she becomes more human and less bureaucratic.

In the second case, our teacher may not listen to the question of a student or may not pay enough attention to this question. This can also undermine his or her authority. Too much involvement may make him or her nervous. The teacher may feel guilty in cases of imperfect transmission of knowledge. Not allowing any relaxation in the situation may also endanger the success of teaching.

In the third case, the teacher may not be adequately prepared and may lose control of the interaction whenever a student asks a difficult question. He or she may conduct an undergraduate class in the manner of a graduate seminar, without any attempt at breaking down the subject matter into pieces of knowledge that can be discussed step-by-step.

Misrepresentation

A misrepresentation occurs when an actor gives an expression in his or her role performance that does not correspond to facts of reality, for example, a blatant lie, a hidden secret, refusal to reveal inconvenient facts. The honest performer avoids application of such techniques; the dishonest performer does make use of them. The honest teacher acknowledges rightful complaints of students regarding the grading of their papers. He or she openly admits an error in grading a paper leading to a revision of the grading. A dishonest teacher never admits any error, even when he or she has made such errors, and conceals every fact that may lead to uncovering his or her error. Another case of misrepresentation is provided by the teacher who presents him- or herself to students as loyal and caring but in reality acts in disloyal and disregarding ways.

Mystification

Mystification is a way of placing a performer above normal actors by attributing to him or her exceptional qualities. A specific device of mystification is establishing social distance between actor and audience. The fact that students see their teachers only in the classroom and in their offices at work makes them pure scholars without any nonscholarly inclinations: dedicated to work, a hero of academic work who has no interests outside. Thus teachers are absolute authorities beyond any question.

Reality and Contrivance

Any role performance takes place between reality and contrivance; in the average case, there is no pure reality and no complete contrivance but a mixture of the two. Effective role performance and self-representation need this mixture. The honest, sincere, and serious performer also has to pay attention to his or her proper presentation just as much as a dishonest, insincere, and unserious performer does. The teacher who always tells students his or her doubts about the transmitted knowledge would confuse them completely. The teacher must sometimes conceal insecurities and errors in order to maintain authority and effective teaching. Yet this does not make the teacher a permanent liar. He or she can reveal doubts and errors in a way that does not undermine his or her authority. The perfect role performance is an act of balance between reality and contrivance.

Teams

A team is an ensemble of interrelated roles performed before an audience. The teacher and his or her colleagues are a team performing before the students. A basic criterion of their success is playing the role consistently. Teachers who contradict each other mutually undermine their authority, particularly in an undergraduate class. Two teachers engaged in mutual criticism in a graduate class, however, play roles of critical academics in a perfect way.

Regions

Regions are places in which the playing of a certain role performance typically takes place. The college campus is such a place for teaching. With its buildings and equipment for carrying out scientific work, it provokes respect for the teaching that takes place.

Discrepant Roles

Roles are termed discrepant when they do not conform to the established roles of a team but act as informants for other teams and/or the audience; examples are the confidence man, the spy, and the go-between. A teacher who tells students news from the teachers' committee meeting acts in a discrepant role. Teams have to establish control over the possibility of actors acting in discrepant roles.

Communication Out of Character

Teams who meet each other normally present themselves to each other in such a way that they are what they claim to be. They stay in character, play the official game, and speak the official language. However, the more they feel stress in doing so, the more they will make use of devices to indicate that they are not really what they seem to be in playing the official game. They communicate out of character. A team can speak backstage about the audience in a different way than they do on-stage. People can ridicule those to whom they spoke very seriously while they were present, after they have left the scene. This is a special, out-of-character treatment of absent persons. Teams can talk about staging in a much more critical sense when acting backstage than when acting on-stage; this is staging talk. Teams can communicate signs for better staging that are not perceivable to the audience; this is team collusion. Teams who interact officially can give signs to each other unofficially that open up new chances of coming together, which could not be done in official talk presented before an audience; this is realigning actions. For example, negotiations that do not come to results in the official language need such unofficial realignments in order to eventuate in successful agreements.

The Arts of Impression Management

A team needs dramaturgical loyalty, discipline, and overview of the situation in order to perform successfully. It needs defensive devices, for example, a control of access to the team, a separation of front-stage and backstage, and tact, also tact with regard to tact itself.

The teachers have to act loyally, with discipline, and with an overview of the whole situation. They have to control access, to separate front- and backstage, and to apply tact and tact regarding tact.

Asylums

Goffman's study on asylums (Goffman, 1961a/1968) is a demonstration of how the reframing of the social situation of a person who leaves his or her normal life-world and enters the new world of a total institution like a home for the aged, a mental hospital, a prison, an army barracks, or a convent leads to a reframing of the person's self, to the mortification of his or her earlier self, and to the establishment of a new self that is the organizing center of the person engaged in adjusting to this new environment. The power of the staff, the total enclosure of the inmates in the institution, the authoritarian organization of that institution, being cut off from any relationships to the external world, and the lack of any formal power on the inmates' part define the primary frame within which the inmates have to act in satisfying their needs, building and maintaining a personal identity, and attaining goals. Because the frame of the total institution is inescapable, everything the inmate does is primarily shaped by this frame. Whatever the inmate does, it will sustain his or her inmate status, for example, as a mental patient, and impose the inmate identity on him or her, replacing the earlier identity. Trying to maintain one's outside identity is interpreted as a deception by the staff and the other inmates. Adjusting to the new situation in order to satisfy basic needs gives the person an identity that is treated by the staff and other inmates as the typical inmate identity: unreliable, uncontrolled, and in need of external control. The framing of the person's identity by the institution, the staff and the other inmates succeeds over any attempts at maintaining the person's earlier identity.

Total Institutions

Goffman distinguishes five types of total institutions:

First, there are institutions established to care for persons felt to be both incapable and harmless; these are the homes for the blind, the aged, the orphaned, and the indigent. Second, there are places established to care for persons felt to be both incapable of looking after themselves and a threat to the community, albeit an unintended one: TB sanitaria, mental hospitals, and leprosaria. A third type of total institutions is organized to protect the community against what are felt to be intentional dangers to it, with the welfare of the persons thus sequestered not the immediate issue: jails, penitentiaries, P.O.W. camps, and concentration camps. Fourth, there are institutions purportedly established the better to pursue some worklike task and justifying themselves only on these instrumental grounds: army barracks, ships, boarding schools, work camps, colonial compounds, and large mansions from the point of view of those who live in the servants' quarters. Finally there are those establishments designed as retreats from the world even while often serving also as training stations for the religious: examples are abbeys, monasteries, convents, and other cloisters. (Goffman, 1961a/1968: 16)

In a total institution, a large number of people live a life separated from the outside world and minutely administered by an authoritative regime:

First, all aspects of life are conducted in the same place and under the same single authority. Second, each phase of the member's daily activity is carried on in the immediate company of a large batch of others, all of whom are treated alike and required to do the same thing together. Third, all phases of the day's activities are tightly scheduled, with one activity leading at a prearranged time into the next, the whole sequence of activities being imposed from above by a system of explicit formal rulings and a body of officials. Finally, the various enforced activities are brought together into a single rational plan purportedly designed to fulfill the official aims of the institution. (Goffman, 1961a/1968: 17)

The relationship between staff and inmates is shaped by this authoritative frame. Both see each other in a stereotyped way and express much hostility with regard to each other. The staff sees the inmates as "bitter, secretive, and untrustworthy," while the inmates see the staff as "condescending, highhanded, and mean." The staff feels "superior and righteous"; the inmates feel "inferior, weak, blameworthy, and guilty" (Goffman, 1961a/1968: 18).

The Mortification of the Inmate's Self

This is how staff and inmate frame their perceptions of each other and of themselves within the authoritative frame of the total institution itself. Goffman's analysis applies to all types of total institutions. The mental hospital may serve as a special case for illustration. Goffman demonstrates how the individual's self becomes mortified in the process of framing his or her actions and personal identity after entering the world of the total institution (Goffman, 1961a/1968: 119–55). In the case of mental patients, the transformation of the individual's self begins with certain events outside the hospital, which is the prepatient phase leading finally to the inpatient phase in the hospital. The prepatient phase usually begins with violations of rules for face-to-face interaction at home, at the workplace, or in semi-public or public places like churches, stores, streets, and parks. The person behaves in ways that other people do not tolerate as compatible with living together at the same place.

The first ones who make attempts at hospitalizing the person are often people who are close to him or her, such as members of the family and friends. This leads to a break in their relationships. The person feels left alone and cut off from his or her familiar relationships, which become transformed to acquire a new meaning. They are framed in a new way. The people with whom the person was once close become agents of an external power. Dropped by the community, the person is embittered and loses confidence in relatives and friends. He or she begins to see other people with growing mistrust. Everything that had contributed to establishing and maintaining the person's identity disappears, so that there is no longer any social support for continuing with that identity. The person falls into an ever-deeper crisis of how he or she is perceived by other people and how he or she perceives him- or herself.

When an individual enters a total institution like a mental hospital, he or she does so with a concept of self that already has been thrown into crisis because of losing confidence but is now stripped of the support by the arrangements the individual used to rely on. The individual was formerly able to establish and maintain a stable concept of him- or herself because of the stability of the arrangements in his or her home world. He or she now loses all these identity supports and undergoes a whole set of abasements, degradations, humiliations, and profanations of his or her self. Normally, an individual's self is seen as something sacred that cannot be touched; it is protected against humiliations. The mental patient's self becomes stripped of all that protection and therefore undergoes a process of transformation leading to its mortification and to the establishment of a new self, one that is accommodated to the world of the mental hospital. The individual is helplessly exposed to the framing of an inmate identity. He or she does not simply acquire a new social role but undergoes a change of identity. Various arrangements of the mental hospital exert their effects on this process:

- When the individual enters the mental hospital, a barrier between the inmate world and the outside world is established, which finally concludes the breakdown of support from a social environment within which the individual used to frame his or her identity.
- From the beginning, the admission procedures that entail obedience tests immediately subordinate the inmate to the staff's control.
- The recruit has to give away personal possessions and utilities that are basic parts of his or her self-image and public appearance. The person loses his or her identity equipment.

- The inmate has to engage in activities that are contrary to his or her conception of self, for example, the need to beg for water, cigarettes, and use of the phone, and being called by humiliating names.

Contaminative exposures continue this process of mortifying the inmate's self:

- uncovering of discreditable facts about one's life
- exposure to the public
- defiling of the body
- unclean living conditions
- forced physical contacts
- inspection of the body and of the bed
- censoring letters
- institutionally arranged confessions

There is disruption between the individual actor and his or her acts. Whatever the inmate does, it will be interpreted as motivated by intentions atttributed to his or her stereotyped inmate-self. The individual cannot escape the externally imposed image. A bad image produces bad acts independent of the character and intentions of those acts. This is what Goffman calls the looping effect. A special expression of this effect is generated by the close supervision of the inmate's daily activities. Whatever the person has done is recorded, and when that person tries to escape the negative image, he or she is simply confronted with the record of acts in support of the negative image. The inmate is under total regimentation and tyrannization. What a normal person in the normal world can do by him- or herself is denied to the inmate of a total institution. He or she must ask for the simplest things of everyday life, like going outside, going to the toilet, shaving, smoking, telephoning, mailing letters, and spending money.

The outcome of all these processes of humiliation is the total loss of self-determination. A main feature of the total institution's ordering of the inmates' life is the establishment of specific "house rules," granting privileges as rewards and withdrawing them as punishments.

Adjustments to the Total Institution

Once identity, appearance, manners, and behaviors have been framed by the total institution, the inmate cannot go on with his or her earlier frames. The inmate has to adjust to the new situation imposed by the total institution.

Strategies of Adjustment

Goffman (1961a/1968: 61–65) distinguishes five types of adjustment to the total institution, open to the inmate:

- Situational withdrawal: The inmate reduces his or her personal involvement in what is going on in the total institution to a minimum.
- Refusing to cooperate: The inmate does not subordinate to the rules of the total institution and opposes the staff's orders as often as possible.
- Colonization: The inmate derives advantage from accommodating to the system of the total institution; his or her conduct fits in with the system's order.
- Conversion: The inmate adopts the staff's view of the outside world, of the total institution, and of the inmates as his or her own view.
- Playing it cool: The inmate succeeds in adjusting to the privilege system and makes use of conversion, colonization, and loyalty to the inmate group according to the requirements of the situation for successful behavior, goal attainment, and identity management.

Adjustment and Institutional Ceremonies

A crucial role for the adjustment processes is played by institutional ceremonies like the Christmas celebration (Goffman, 1961a/1968: 89–105). They provide a mixture of establishing unity while maintaining the split between staff and inmates; they contribute to ordering the institutional life and are used for personal interests. Participating in the organization of such ceremonies with certain responsibilities is part of the privileges that, on the one hand, satisfy personal interests of the inmates and, on the other hand, contribute to the working of the system.

Primary and Secondary Adjustments

Goffman (1961a/1968: 171–266) goes on in his analysis of inmates' adjustment to the total institution by distinguishing primary and secondary adjustments. Primary adjustments are based on official means for coordinating behavior. These are the means officially applied by the leadership of the institution for evoking the cooperation of its members: providing for the welfare of the members, appealing to joint values, and applying incentives. These official means call for the primary adjustments of members to the institution. However, they by no means account for all forms of adjustment that play a vital role in any institution, particularly in total institutions. There are the unauthorized secondary adjustments, which comprise all the means that allow the members of the institution to make their lives livable within the institution. Because of its unofficial character, Goffman calls this area the underlife of a total institution. Such secondary adjustments can be contained ones, that is, they contribute not only to the furthering of personal interests but also to the working of the institution, because they secure the members' participation in institutional life. They can, however, also be disruptive, namely, when the activities called for work against the maintenance of institutional order and against the official goals of an organization. A first set of means for secondary adjustment can be called "make-do's." These are items of equipment, time schedules, rules of the system, work assignments, and social contacts with staff and people outside that are used by members for ends not officially authorized. They are exploited for the personal interests of members who are intelligent enough to take advantage of them.

A second set of secondary adjustments results from the intelligent use of places for personal ends. These can be forbidden, supervised, or free places.

Third is the interested use of the organization's facilities by its members for their personal ends, for example, storage places like safe-deposit boxes, cabinets, bureau drawers, and footlockers.

Fourth, the social structure of the institution provides for social relationships that can be used for personal interests: making use of others by way of private coercion, economic exchange, mutual help, private bonds, and patron relationships.

Secondary adjustments particularly are means that allow members of an organization to live in that organization but nevertheless to keep their distance, that is, not to be completely committed to its world-view and order and to keep alive an identity that does not completely merge with the conforming member of the institution but continues to be something different. As Goffman notes, the building up of a stable self needs two processes: inclusion in society and distance from society:

> Without something to belong to, we have no stable self, and yet total commitment and attachment to any social unit implies a kind of selflessness. Our sense of being a person can come from being drawn into a wider social unit; our sense of selfhood can arise through the little ways in which we resist the pull. Our status is backed by the solid buildings of the world, while our sense of personal identity often resides in the cracks. (Goffman, 1961a/1968: 280)

Stigma

Goffman's study on stigma (Goffman, 1963) looks at the framing of the identity of a stigmatized person as an outcome of the person's stigmatization by others and his or her strategies in dealing with that situation. The subtitle of the book calls this process "the management of spoiled identity."

Stigma is an attribute of a person that is considered in a society as a deviation from normality; it is the basis for not reaching fully the status of a normal member of society. Handicapped, delinquent, mentally ill, and minority people suffer from such an attribution of a stigma. The stigmatized person has much more difficulty than other people in successfully establishing an identity that other people and the person accept.

The identity of an individual can be differentiated into three aspects: the social identity, the personal identity, and the ego identity. The social identity of an individual results from his or her membership in a certain social group and is attributed to that individual from outside, from other people. The personal identity emerges from the individual's unique biography and is also attributed from outside. The ego identity is the subjective feeling and consciousness of a person about him- or herself, which includes dealing with his or her attributed social and personal identities.

Social Identity

Looking first at the level of social identity (Goffman, 1963: 1–40) we can say something on the origin of stigma: it results from a discrepancy between *virtual* and *actual* social identity. Virtual social identity is how a person should be according to the attributes generally ascribed to the members of certain social categories like American, middle-class, man, woman, white, black, Protestant, college graduate. Actual social identity is how a person is seen by others as someone who conforms or does not conform to the expectations based on his or her virtual social identity. One can deviate from such expectations because of tribal memberships of race, nation, and religion. In this case the members of these groups are considered by others as deviating from the standards that are claimed as binding for the larger group of which they form a subgroup. Blacks, Italians, or Catholics deviate, for example, from the standards of, say, a white, upper-class, Protestant New England person and are therefore likely to bear a stigma as second-class Americans. Here membership in a subgroup of Americans is the basis of being stigmatized. Other types of stigma result from individual deviations from standard expectations: abominations of the body like handicaps and blemishes of individual character like being treated as mentally ill or as a criminal.

A stigma can be known to everybody. People who are the bearers of such known stigmas make up the discredited people in society. Those who bear stigmas that are not known by others are the discreditable, who live on the borderline of being discredited.

Acceptance by other people, being included in normal life, having an accepted status in social life, and being treated as a fully responsible person becomes the major problem for the potentially or actually stigmatized person. How can he or she master that situation? Goffman distinguishes four different ways of coping with the situation:

1. The person can try to correct the attribute that is the basis of stigmatization.
2. The person can try to master particular activities that are prestigious in character and compensate for his or her other deficiencies: achievements in occupation and sports.
3. The person can try to make secondary gains. That means he or she takes advantage of being treated in a different way from other people, for example, by way of achieving on lower requirements than others.
4. The person can try to reassess the limitations of people who are seen as "normal," pointing out that these "normal" people also have many deficiencies, so that the stigmatized person's deficiencies can be relativized.

Stigma causes strain in social interaction on both parts, on the part of the stigmatized person and on the part of the other person. Neither person is sure about how he or she should approach the other; neither one knows what exactly the other thinks about him or her. Both very often feel uncomfortable while facing each other. For the stigmatized person, seeking association with his or her own and with "wise" people is one way to reduce strain, but it strengthens alienation from the people who are seen as "normal." His or her "own" are those who share the same fate; the "wise" are those who are used to living with the person—nurses and family members.

The major means for improving the status of stigmatized people in society and for normalizing their interaction with others is joining a social movement that aims at such improvements.

The process of stigmatization can set in for a person at different steps in his or her moral career, dependent on the time when the corresponding deficiency occurs or becomes publicly noticed:

- The stigma can be inborn and visible from the beginning of one's life.
- The stigma can be inborn but kept unnoticed through early protection by the family.
- The stigma can be experienced at a later stage of life (for example, being the victim of an accident leading to some handicap).
- The person may be socialized in an alien community and experience stigmatization when entering a new community because of his or her alien appearance.

In all these cases the individual's moral career oscillates between giving in and accepting a deficient status and fighting against it.

Personal Identity

Regarding the level of personal identity (Goffman, 1963: 41–104), an individual must deal with his or her biography in order to cope with the situation of possibly being stigmatized. Being stigmatized is also dependent on what a person conveys to others about his or her personal biography. Information control is the basic technical instrument of what Goffman calls stigma management. The potentially stigmatized person has to manage to participate successfully in social life and to establish an accepted personal identity.

First is the visibility of a potential stigma. The less it is visible, the more chances the individual has to participate in a normal way in social life and to establish a positive personal identity. The individual can also learn to "pass" for a "normal" person in actual situations. Techniques of information control help to manage the situation. The person can conceal discreditable facts about his or her person or cover what can be a source of discrediting reactions.

Ego Identity

On the level of ego identity (Goffman, 1963: 105–25), the stigmatized person always feels ambivalence about how to see him- or herself. How can he or she cope with the stigma? First, there is the level of cultural definitions of the situation. Professional presentations in the media—newspapers, radio, television—can provide models for individual persons. Such models may encourage acceptance of one's status, the overcoming of disabilities and inferior status, and protesting against stigmatization. Second, social alignments contribute to stabilizing the person's self-acceptance. These can be in-group alignments with people who share his or her fate or out-group alignments with people outside his or her own group.

Framing one's identity is finally a matter of a special politics of identity formation, of presenting oneself in a favorable way, of shaping how certain features of persons are publicly defined and evaluated. This is a political battle between groups that try to exert influence on this process of publicly defining what is "normal" and what is "deviant" (Goffman, 1963: 126–47).

Summary

Goffman draws our attention to the symbolic nature of social action and to the place and meaning in that action. What happens in the social world is to a large degree a matter of the symbolic definition of the situation, of the application of symbolic frames, of conveying meaning. However, Goffman presents the symbolic nature of social life in a specific way with an emphasis on a very specific feature. It is the *dynamics* of framing the situation of social action, of the staging of action, and of identity management that is the object of his investigation in the place of meaning in social action. This is a matter of relating actors to audiences, of evoking impressions.

Mastering the art of impression management is a precondition of mutual understanding, coordinating action, successful goal attainment, and identity formation. Goffman presents the human actor to us as someone who is placed in a situation where he or she is confronted with other people and then tries to achieve socially as someone who gets along with the expectations of other people and succeeds in achieving any kind of favorable ego identity. The actor does so in a way that allows him or her to get acceptance of or at least toleration of his or her role performance by other people and to do something for his or her personal interests, by performing the role either in a sincere way or in a cynical way, making use of any legal or illegal means of adjusting to the situation. The usual means for doing so is framing a situation to one's own advantage or, if one is in a disadvantaged position, to make the best of that situation by attempting to reframe the situation or by adjusting to a dominating frame and making secondary gains from that.

Goffman's actor calculates in a strategic and economically rational way the best symbolic means of managing both to get along with the expectations of his or her audience and to establish some favorable ego identity, whatever substance this ego identity may have. The actor uses appropriate means to favorably impress the audience and to serve his or her self-interest. Goffman describes the conditions under which the adjustment of social expectations and personal interests takes place in a most dynamic way. The world is full of primary and secondary adjustments, full of means for coping with any situation, for avoiding complete conformity with social expectations and maintaining personal differences in the roles one has to play. Even total institutions provide lots of opportunities for one to pass by controls and serve one's personal interests. The inmate's original self may have been mortified by the total institution; however, the institution cannot prevent the inmate from establishing an ego identity that escapes full commitment to the institution, keeps a distance, and makes use of privileges, make-do's, places, facilities, and social relationships for serving his or her personal needs and interests. Goffman's whole approach gives exemplifications of various kinds for one basic assumption:

> The more means of impression management a social situation provides for actors and the more intelligently they make use of these means, the more they will succeed in adjusting to any social expectation and any control without committing themselves completely to a social unit, while still being able to establish a distinctive ego identity and to serve their personal interests.

Critical Assessment

Goffman exemplifies his basic message with a mass of instances, situations, and means available to actors for adjusting to social situations. We learn from him in a very broadly demonstrated form what are the conditions under which the symbolic framing of actions provides for communication, coordination of actions, and the establishing of an ego identity *without* complete agreement, *without* shared ideas and values, *without* commitment, and *without* the thoroughgoing control of action by domination. This, however, is communication, coordination of action, and ego identity of a very special kind, namely, flexible types that vary from situation to situation, according to the best available means. There is no stable meaning in communication, no stable social action, and no stable ego identity. They change according to the situation. What Goffman teaches is the economics of symbolic impression management, but he does not spell out as much the conditions of firmly committing actors to common frames and norms through rituals confirming solidarity, of generalizing frames in discourse, of enforcing social order through domination. Goffman reduces the individual's self to an opportunistic agent of impression management and personal well-being. He does not spell out the conditions of finding an ego identity that maintains its meaning throughout any change of social situations by reflection, of stabilizing an ego identity through social inclusion and support, of acting out forcefully a unique ego identity against any social expectation rooted in a deep commitment to specific goals and a powerful capacity to perform in a successful way. Applied to these features of communication, coordination of actions, and establishing an ego identity, most of Goffman's analyses would give wrong explanations. Goffman's theory of symbolic framing, communication, and identity formation is a limited one; it is limited to the situationally changing aspects of these phenomena. To learn more about the other features of frames, communication, social coordination of action, and identity formation, we have to refer to theories concerned with discourse, commitment to social norms, domination, power, and personal performance capacity.

Bibliography

Alexander, Jeffrey C. 1982–1983. *Theoretical Logic in Sociology.* 4 vols. Berkeley: University of California Press.

Alexander, Jeffrey C. 1984. "The Parsons Revival in Germany." *Sociological Theory* 2: 394–412.

Alexander, Jeffrey C. (Ed.). 1985. *Neofunctionalism.* Beverly Hills, Calif.: Sage.

Alexander, Jeffrey C. 1987a. *Twenty Lectures: Sociological Theory Since World War II.* New York: Columbia University Press.

Alexander, Jeffrey C. 1987b. "The Centrality of the Classics." In Anthony Giddens and Jonathan H. Turner (Eds.), *Social Theory Today,* pp. 1–57. Cambridge: Polity Press.

Apel, Karl Otto. 1979. *Die Erklären-Verstehen-Kontroverse in transzendentalprag-matischer Sicht.* Frankfurt am Main: Suhrkamp.

Barber, Bernard. 1952/1978. *Science and the Social Order.* Westport, Conn.: Greenwood.

Barber, Bernard. 1957. *Social Stratification.* New York: Harcourt, Brace.

Barber, Bernard. 1963. "Some Problems in the Sociology of Professions." *Daedalus* 92, no. 2: 669–88.

Barber, Bernard. 1978. "Inequality and Occupational Prestige: Theory, Research, and Social Policy." *Sociological Inquiry* 48: 75–88.

Barber, Bernard. 1983. *The Logic and Limits of Trust.* New Brunswick, N.J.: Rutgers University Press.

Barthes, Roland. 1967. *Système de la mode.* Paris: Seuil. (Translation: 1983. *The Fashion System.* New York: Hill and Wang.)

Baum, Rainer C. 1976a. "Communication and Media." In J.J. Loubser, R.C. Baum, A. Effrat and V.M. Lidz (Eds.), *Explorations in General Theory in Social Science,* pp. 533–66. New York: Free Press.

Baum, Rainer C. 1976b. "On Societal Media Dynamics." In J.J. Loubser, R.C. Baum, A. Effrat, and V.M. Lidz (Eds.), *Explorations in General Theory in Social Science,* pp. 579–608. New York: Free Press.

Baum, Rainer C. 1981. *Holocaust and the German Elite: Genocide and National Suicide in Germany, 1871–1945*. Lanham, Md.: Rowman & Littlefield.

Bellah, Robert N. 1957. *Tokugawa Religion: The Values of Pre-Industrial Japan*. Glencoe, Ill.: Free Press.

Bellah, Robert N. 1970. *Beyond Belief: Essays on Religion in a Post-Traditional World*. New York: Harper & Row.

Bellah, Robert N. 1975. *The Broken Covenant: American Civil Religion in Time of Trial*. New York: Seabury Press.

Bellah, Robert N., R. Madsen, N.M. Sullivan, A. Swidler, and S. Tipton. 1985. *Habits of the Heart: Individualism and Commitment in American Life*. Berkeley: University of California Press.

Berger, Peter L., and Thomas Luckmann. 1966/1971. *The Social Construction of Reality*. Harmondsworth: Penguin.

Black, Max (Ed.). 1961. *The Social Theories of Talcott Parsons*. Englewood Cliffs, N.J.: Prentice-Hall.

Blau, Peter M. 1955/1963. *The Dynamics of Bureaucracy. A Study of Interpersonal Relations in Two Government Agencies*. Chicago: University of Chicago Press.

Blau, Peter M. 1956/1971. *Bureaucracy in Modern Society*. New York: Random House.

Blau, Peter M. 1964. *Exchange and Power in Social Life*. New York: Wiley.

Blau, Peter M. 1977. *Inequality and Heterogeneity: A Primitive Theory of Social Structure*. New York: Free Press.

Blau, Peter M., and Otis Dudley Duncan. 1967. *The American Occupational Structure*. New York: Wiley.

Bleicher, Joseph. 1980. *Contemporary Hermeneutics: Hermeneutics as Method, Philosophy and Critique*. London: Routledge and Kegan Paul.

Blumer, Herbert. 1969. *Symbolic Interactionism*. Englewood Cliffs, N.J.: Prentice Hall.

Bourricaud, François. 1977. *L'individualisme institutionel: Essai sur la sociologie de Talcott Parsons*. Paris: Presses Universitaires de France. (Translation: 1981. *The Sociology of Talcott Parsons*. Chicago: University of Chicago Press.)

Brown, Richard Harvey. 1987. *Society as a Text: Essays on Rhetoric, Reason, and Reality*. Chicago: University of Chicago Press.

Brown, Richard Harvey. 1989. *Social Science as Civic Discourse: Essays on the Invention, Legitimation, and Uses of Social Theory*. Chicago: University of Chicago Press.

Buckley, Walter. 1967. *Sociology and Modern Systems Theory*. Englewood Cliffs, N.J.: Prentice Hall.

Cicourel, Aaron V. 1964. *Method and Measurement in Sociology*. New York: Wiley.

Cicourel, Aaron V. 1973. *Cognitive Sociology*. New York: Free Press.

Cicourel, Aaron V. 1974. *Theory and Method in a Study of Argentine Fertility*. New York: Wiley.

Cloward, Richard A. 1959. "Illegitimate Means, Anomie, and Deviant Behavior." *American Sociological Review* 24: 164–76.

Cohen, Albert J., and James F. Short, Jr. 1958. "Research in Delinquent Subcultures." *Journal of Social Issues* 14: 20–37.

Colomy, Paul. 1985. "Uneven Structural Differentiation: Toward a Comparative Approach." In J.C. Alexander (Ed.), *Neofunctionalism*, pp. 131–56. Beverly Hills, Calif.: Sage.

Colomy, Paul. 1990a. "Uneven Differentiation and Incomplete Institutionalization: Political Change and Continuity in the Early American Nation." In J.C. Alexander and P. Colomy (Eds.), *Differentiation Theory and Social Change*, pp. 119-62. New York, Oxford: Columbia University Press.

Colomy, Paul. 1990b. "Strategic Groups and Political Differentiation in Antebellum United States." In J.C. Alexander and P. Colomy (Eds.), *Differentiation Theory and Social Change*, pp. 222-64. New York, Oxford: Columbia University Press.

Coser, Lewis A. 1956. *The Functions of Social Conflict.* New York: Free Press.

Coser, Lewis A. 1967. *Continuities in the Study of Social Conflict.* New York: Free Press.

Coser, Lewis A. 1971. *Masters of Sociological Thought: Ideas in Historical and Social Context.* New York: Harcourt Brace Jovanovich.

Dahrendorf, Ralf. 1958a/1965. *Homo Sociologicus.* Cologne/Opladen: Westdeutscher Verlag. (Translation: 1973. *Homo Sociologicus.* London: Routlege and Kegan Paul.)

Dahrendorf, Ralf. 1958b. "Out of Utopia: Toward a Reorientation of Sociological Analysis." *American Journal of Sociology* 64: 115-27.

Dahrendorf, Ralf. 1958c. "Toward a Theory of Social Conflict." *Journal of Conflict Resolution* 2: 170-83.

Dahrendorf, Ralf. 1959. *Class and Class Conflict in Industrial Society.* Stanford, Calif.: Stanford University Press.

Dahrendorf, Ralf. 1961. *Gesellschaft und Freiheit.* Munich: Piper.

Dahrendorf, Ralf. 1967. *Gesellschaft und Demokratie in Deutschland.* Munich: Piper. (Translation: 1979. *Society and Democracy in Germany.* Westport, Conn.: Greenwood Press.)

Darwin, Charles. 1888[6]. *The Origin of Species: By Means of Natural Selection.* London: Murray.

Darwin, Charles. 1977. *The Collected Papers*, 2 vols. Chicago: University of Chicago Press.

Davies, James D. 1962. "Toward a Theory of Revolution." *American Sociological Review* 27: 5-18.

Davis, Kingsley. 1949. *Human Society.* New York: Macmillan.

Davis, Kingsley, and Wilbert E. Moore. 1945. "Some Principles of Stratification." *American Sociological Review* 10: 242-49.

Dilthey, Wilhelm. 1883/1968[5] *Der Aufbau der geschichtlichen Welt in den Geisteswissenschaften.* In *Gesammelte Schriften.* Edited by Karlfried Gründer. Vol. 7. Stuttgart: Teubner. (Translation: 1976. *The Construction of the Historical World in the Human Studies.* In *Selected Writings.* Edited, translated and introduction by H.D. Rickman. Cambridge: Cambridge University Press.)

Dilthey, Wilhelm. 1924/1964. *Die geistige Welt. 1: Abhandlungen zur Grundlegung der Geisteswissenschaften.* In *Gesammelte Schriften.* Edited by Georg Misch. Vol. 5. Stuttgart: Teubner.

Douglas, Jack D. (Ed.). 1970. *Understanding Everyday Life.* Chicago: Aldine.

Douglas, Mary. 1966. *Purity and Danger: An Analysis of Concepts of Pollution and Taboo.* London: Routledge.

Douglas, Mary. 1973. *Natural Symbols.* Baltimore, Md.: Penguin Books.

Downs, Anthony. 1957. *An Economic Theory of Democracy.* New York: Harper & Row.

Durkheim, Emile. 1893/1973a. *De la division du travail social.* Paris: Presses Universitaires de France. (Translation: 1964. *The Division of Labor in Society.* Translated by G. Simpson. New York: Free Press.)

Durkheim, Emile. 1895/1973b. *Les règles de la méthode sociologique.* Paris: Presses Universitaires de France. (Translation: 1982. *The Rules of Sociological Method.* Edited by Steven Lukes. Translated by W.D. Halls. London: Macmillan.)

Durkheim, Emile. 1912/1968. *Les formes élémentaires de la vie religieuse.* Paris: Presses Universitaires de France. (Translation: 1976. *The Elementary Forms of Religious Life.* Translated by J.W. Swain. London: Allen & Unwin.)

Durkheim, Emile. 1925/1974b. *L'éducation morale.* Paris: Presses Universitaires de France. (Translation: 1961. *Moral Education.* Translated by E.K. Wilson and H. Schnurer. New York: Free Press.)

Eisenstadt, Shmuel N. 1963. *The Political Systems of Empires.* New York: Free Press.

Eisenstadt, Shmuel N. 1966. *Modernization: Protest and Change.* Englewood Cliffs, N.J.: Prentice Hall.

Eisenstadt, Shmuel N. 1973. *Tradition, Change and Modernity.* New York: Wiley.

Ekeh, Peter P. 1974. *Social Exchange Theory: The Two Traditions.* Cambridge, Mass.: Harvard University Press.

Etzioni, Amitai. 1961. *A Comparative Analysis of Complex Organizations: On Power, Involvement, and Their Correlates.* New York: Free Press.

Etzioni, Amitai. 1968. *The Active Society: A Theory of Society and Political Processes.* New York: Free Press.

Etzioni, Amitai. 1988. *The Moral Dimension: Toward a New Economics.* New York: Free Press.

Freud, Sigmund. 1923/1972. *Das Ich und das Es.* In *Gesammelte Werke.* Vol. 13. Frankfurt: S. Fischer. (Translation: 1927. *The Ego and the Id.* London: Institute of Psychoanalysis.)

Gadamer, Hans Georg. 1960. *Wahrheit und Methode.* Tübingen: Mohr Siebeck. (Translation: 1975. *Truth and Method.* London: Sheed and Ward.)

Garfinkel, Harold. 1967. *Studies in Ethnomethodology.* Englewood Cliffs, N.J.: Prentice Hall.

Garfinkel, Harold, Michael Lynch, and Eric Livingston. 1981. "The Work of Discovering Science Construed from Materials from the Optically Discovered Pulsar." *Philosophy of the Social Sciences* 11: 131–38.

Geertz, Clifford. 1973. *The Interpretation of Cultures.* New York: Basic Books.

Gerard, Harold B. 1954. "The Anchorage of Opinions in Face-to-Face Groups." *Human Relations* 7: 313–25.

Gerstein, Dean R. 1981. "Cultural Action and Heroin Addiction." *Sociological Inquiry* 51, no. 3/4: 355–70.

Giesen, Bernhard. 1980. *Makrosoziologie. Eine evolutionstheoretische Einführung.* Hamburg: Hoffmann und Campe.

Giesen, Bernhard. 1991. *Die Entdinglichung des Sozialen. Eine evolutionstheoretische Perspektive auf die Postmoderne.* Frankfurt am Main: Suhrkamp.

Goffman, Erving. 1959/1971a. *The Presentation of Self in Everyday Life.* Harmondsworth: Penguin Books.

Goffman, Erving. 1961a/1968. *Asylums.* Harmondsworth: Penguin Books.

Goffman, Erving. 1961b. *Encounters.* Indianapolis: Bobbs-Merrill.

Goffman, Erving. 1963. *Stigma.* Englewood Cliffs, N.J.: Prentice-Hall.

Goffman, Erving. 1967. *Interaction Ritual.* New York: Doubleday.

Goffman, Erving. 1969. *Strategic Interaction.* Philadelphia: University of Pennsylvania Press.

Goffman, Erving. 1971b. *Relations in Public.* New York: Basic Books.

Goffman, Erving. 1974/1975. *Frame Analysis.* Harmondsworth: Penguin Books.

Goffman, Erving. 1979. *Gender Advertisements.* Cambridge, Mass.: Harvard University Press.

Goffman, Erving. 1981. *Forms of Talk.* Philadelphia: University of Pennsylvania Press.

Gould, Mark. 1976. "Systems Analysis, Macrosociology and the Generalized Media of Social Action." In J.J. Loubser, R.C. Baum, A. Effrat and V.M. Lidz (Eds.), *Explorations in General Theory in Social Science,* pp. 470–506. New York: Free Press.

Gould, Mark. 1987. *Revolution in the Development of Capitalism: The Coming of the English Revolution.* Berkeley: University of California Press.

Gouldner, Alvin W. 1960. "The Norm of Reciprocity." *American Sociological Review* 25: 161–78.

Gouldner, Alvin W. 1963. *Modern Sociology: An Introduction to the Study of Human Interaction.* New York: Harcourt, Brace.

Gouldner, Alvin W. 1971. *The Coming Crises of Western Sociology.* London: Heinemann.

Gouldner, Alvin W. 1980. *The Two Marxisms.* New York: Seabury.

Grathoff, Richard (Ed.). 1973. *The Theory of Social Action: The Correspondence of Alfred Schutz and Talcott Parsons.* Bloomington: Indiana University Press.

Grathoff, Richard (Ed.). 1983. *Sozialität und Intersubjektivität. Phänomenologische Perspektiven im Umkreis von Aaron Gurwitsch und Alfred Schütz.* Munich: Fink.

Grathoff, Richard. 1989. *Milieu und Lebenswelt: Einführung in die phänomenologische Soziologie und die sozialphänomenologische Forschung.* Frankfurt am Main: Suhrkamp.

Habermas, Jürgen. 1981. *Theorie des kommunikativen Handelns.* 2 vols. Frankfurt am Main: Suhrkamp. (Translation: 1984, 1987. *The Theory of Communicative Action.* 2 vols. Boston: Beacon Press.)

Hayes, Adrian. 1985. "Causal and Interpretive Analysis in Sociology." *Sociological Theory* 3: 1–10.

Hegel, Georg Wilhelm Friedrich. 1821/1964-1971. *Grundlinien der Philosophie des Rechts.* In *Sämtliche Werke.* Edited by H. Glockner. Vol. 7, Stuttgart: Frommann Holzboog. (Translation: 1965. *Philosophy of Right.* Oxford: Clarendon Press.)

Heidegger, Martin. 1927/1949. *Sein und Zeit.* Tübingen: Mohr Siebeck. (Translation: 1978. *Being and Time.* Oxford: Basil Blackwell.)

Heritage, John. 1984. *Garfinkel and Ethnomethodology.* Cambridge: Polity Press.

Hobbes, Thomas. 1651/1966. *Leviathan.* In W. Molesworth (Ed.), *Collected English Works of Thomas Hobbes,* Vol. 3. Aalen, Germany: Scientia.

Holton, Robert J., and Bryan S. Turner. 1989. *Talcott Parsons on Economy and Society.* London: Routledge.

Homans, George C. 1950. *The Human Group.* New York: Harcourt, Brace.

Homans, George C. 1958. "Social Behavior as Exchange." *American Journal of Sociology* 63: 597–606.

Homans, George C. 1961. *Social Behavior: Its Elementary Forms.* New York: Harcourt, Brace.

Homans, George C. 1962. *Sentiments and Activities.* New York: Free Press.

Homans, George C. 1964. "Bringing Men Back In." *American Sociological Review* 29: 809–18.

Homans, George C. 1967. *The Nature of the Social Sciences.* New York: Harcourt Brace Jovanovich.

Homans, George C. 1974. *Social Behavior: Its Elementary Forms.* Rev. Ed. New York: Harcourt Brace Jovanovich.

Homans, George C. 1984. *Coming to My Senses: The Autobiography of a Sociologist.* New Brunswick, N.J.: Transaction Books.

Hondrich, Karl Otto. 1973. *Theorie der Herrschaft.* Frankfurt am Main: Suhrkamp.

Huaco, George. 1966. "The Functionalist Theory of Stratification: Two Decades of Controversy." *Inquiry* 9: 215–40.

Hume, David. 1739/1978. *A Treatise on Human Nature.* Edited by L.A. Selby-Bigge. Oxford: Clarendon Press.

Hume, David. 1777/1980. *Enquiries Concerning the Human Understanding and Concerning the Principles of Morals.* Edited by L.A. Selby-Bigge. Westport, Conn.: Greenwood Press.

Husserl, Edmund. 1900–1901/1928. *Logische Untersuchungen.* Halle: M. Niemeyer. (Translation: 1960. *Logical Investigations.* 2 vols. Washington: Humanities Press.)

Husserl, Edmund. 1950. *Cartesianische Meditationen.* In *Husserliana: Gesammelte Werke.* Edited by H.L. van Breda. Vol. 1. Den Haag: N. Nijhoff 1950–62. (Translation: 1970. *Cartesian Meditations.* The Hague: Nijhoff).

Jauss, Hans Robert. 1982. *Toward an Aesthetic of Reception.* Brighton: Harvester.

Jauss, Hans Robert. 1989. *Studien zum Epochenwandel der ästhetischen Moderne.* Frankfurt am Main: Suhrkamp.

Jensen, Stefan. 1980. *Talcott Parsons: Eine Einführung.* Stuttgart: Teubner.

Johnson, Harry M. 1973. "The Generalized Symbolic Media in Parsons' Theory." *Sociology and Social Research* 57: 208–21.

Johnson, Harry M. 1976. "The Mass Media, Ideology, and Community Standards." In J.J. Loubser, R.C. Baum, A. Effrat, and V.M. Lidz (Eds.), *Explorations in General Theory in Social Science,* pp. 609–38. New York: Free Press.

Kant, Immanuel. 1781/1964a. *Kritik der reinen Vernunft.* In *Werke in sechs Bänden.* Edited by Wilhelm Weischedel. Vol. 2. Frankfurt am Main: Insel Verlag. (Translation: 1952a. *Critique of Pure Reason.* In *Great Books of the Western World 42: Kant,* pp. 1–250. Chicago/London: Encyclopaedia Britannica.)

Kant, Immanuel. 1788/1964b. *Kritik der praktischen Vernunft.* In *Werke in sechs Bänden.* Edited by Wilhelm Weischedel. Vol. 4, pp. 103–302. Frankfurt am Main: Insel Verlag. (Translation: 1952b. *Critique of Practical Reason.* In *Great Books of the Western World. 42: Kant,* pp. 291–361. Chicago/London: Encyclopaedia Britannica.)

Kant, Immanuel. 1790/1964c. *Kritik der Urteilskraft.* In *Werke in sechs Bänden.* Edited by Wilhelm Weischedel. Vol. 5. Frankfurt am Main: Insel Verlag. (Translation: 1952c. *Critique of Judgment.* In *Great Books of the Western World. 42: Kant,* pp. 461–613. Chicago/London: Encyclopaedia Britannica.)

Kant, Immanuel. 1795/1964d. "Zum ewigen Frieden. Ein philosophischer Entwurf."
    In *Werke in sechs Bänden.* Edited by Wilhelm Weischedel. Vol. 6, pp. 193–251.
    Frankfurt am Main: Insel Verlag. (Translation: 1972. *Perpetual Peace: A Philo-
    sophical Essay.* New York/London: Garland.)
Knorr-Cetina, Karin D. 1981. *The Manufacture of Knowledge: An Essay on the Con-
    structionist and Contextual Nature of Science.* New York: Pergamon Press.
Kuhn, Manford. 1964a. "Major Trends in Symbolic Interaction Theory in the Past
    Twenty-Five Years." *Sociological Quarterly* 5: 61–84.
Kuhn, Manford. 1964b. "The Reference Group Reconsidered." *Sociological Quart-
    erly* 5: 6–21.
Lazarsfeld, Paul F., and Morris Rosenberg (Eds.). 1955. *The Language of Social
    Research.* Glencoe, Ill.: Free Press.
Lechner, Frank. 1984. "Ethnicity and Revitalization in the Modern World System."
    Sociological Focus 17: 243–56.
Lechner, Frank. 1985. "Modernity and Its Discontents." In J.C. Alexander (Ed.),
    Neofunctionalism, pp. 157–76. Beverly Hills, Calif.: Sage.
Lechner, Frank. 1989. "Cultural Aspects of the Modern World System." In W.H.
    Swatos (Ed.), *Religious Politics in Global Perspective,* pp. 11–28. New York:
    Greenwood Press.
Lenski, Gerhard A. 1966. *Power and Privilege: A Theory of Social Stratification.*
    New York: McGraw-Hill.
Lévi-Strauss, Claude. 1962. *La pensée sauvage.* Paris: Librairie Plon. (Translation:
    1966. *The Savage Mind.* Chicago: University of Chicago Press.)
Lidz, Charles W., and Victor M. Lidz. 1976. "Piaget's Psychology of Intelligence
    and the Theory of Action." In J.J. Loubser, R.C. Baum, A. Effrat, and V.M.
    Lidz (Eds.), *Explorations in General Theory in Social Science,* pp. 195–239. New
    York: Free Press.
Lipset, Seymour M. 1963. *The First New Nation: The United States in Historical
    and Comparative Perspective.* New York: Basic Books.
Loubser, Jan J., Rainer C. Baum, Andrew Effrat, and Victor M. Lidz (Eds.). 1976.
    *Explorations in General Theory in Social Science: Essays in Honor of Talcott
    Parsons.* New York: Free Press.
Luhmann, Niklas. 1982. "Autopoiesis, Handlung und kommunikative Verständigung."
    Zeitschrift für Soziologie 11: 366–79.
Malinowski, Bronislaw. 1922/1961. *Argonauts of the Western Pacific.* New York:
    Dutton.
Luhmann, Niklas. 1984. *Soziale Systeme. Grundriß einer allgemeinen Theorie.* Frank-
    furt am Main: Suhrkamp.
Malinowski, Bronislaw. 1926. *Anthropology.* In *Encyclopaedia Britannica.* First Supple-
    mentary Volume, pp. 131–39. London and New York: Encyclopaedia Britannica.
Malinowski, Bronislaw. 1948. *Magic, Science and Religion.* New York: Doubleday.
Matthes, Joachim. 1969. *Einführung in die Religionssoziologie.* 2 vols. Reinbek/
    Hamburg: Rowohlt.
Matthes, Joachim. 1983. "Religion als Thema komparativer Sozialforschung." *Sozi-
    ale Welt* 24, no. 1: 3–21.
Matthes, Joachim. 1985. "Zur transkulturellen Relativität erzählanalytischer Verfahren
    in der empirischen Sozialforschung." *Kölner Zeitschrift für Soziologie und Sozial-
    psychologie* 37: 310–26.

Mauss, Marcel. 1923–24. "Essai sur le don. Forme archaïque de l'échange." *L'année sociologique* 1: 30–186. (Translation: 1967. *The Gift.* New York: Norton.)

Mayhew, Leon. 1971. *Society: Institutions and Activity.* Glenview, Ill.: Scott, Foresman.

Mayo, Elton. 1945. *The Social Problems of an Industrial Civilization.* Cambridge, Mass.: Harvard University Press.

Mead, George Herbert. 1908. "The Philosophical Basis of Ethics." *International Journal of Ethics* 18: 311–23.

Mead, George Herbert. 1934. *Mind, Self, and Society.* Edited and introduction by Charles W. Morris. Chicago: University of Chicago Press.

Merton, Robert K. 1949/1968a. "Manifest and Latent Functions." In *Social Theory and Social Structure*, pp. 73–138. New York: Free Press.

Merton, Robert K. 1949/1968b. "Social Structure and Anomie." In *Social Theory and Social Structure*, pp. 185–214. New York: Free Press.

Merton, Robert K. 1949/1968c. "Continuities in the Theory of Social Structure and Anomie." In *Social Theory and Social Structure*, pp. 215–48. New York: Free Press.

Merton, Robert K. 1949/1968d. *Social Theory and Social Structure.* New York: Free Press.

Merton, Robert K. 1957. "The Role-Set: Problems in Sociological Theory." *British Journal of Sociology* 8: 106–20.

Merton, Robert K. 1968e. "The Matthew Effect in Science." *Science* 159, no. 3810: 56–63.

Miebach, Bernhard. 1984. *Strukturalistische Handlungstheorie: Zum Verhältnis soziologischer Theorie und empirischer Forschung im Werk Talcott Parsons'.* Opladen: Westdeutscher Verlag.

Miller, Walter B. 1958. "Lower Class Culture as a Generating Milieu of Gang Delinquency." *The Journal of Social Issues* 14: 5–19.

Mills, C. Wright. 1956. *The Power Elite.* Oxford: Oxford University Press.

Moore, Wilbert E. 1946. *Industrial Relations and the Social Order.* New York: Macmillan.

Münch, Richard. 1982. *Theorie des Handelns. Zur Rekonstruktion der Beiträge von Talcott Parsons, Emile Durkheim und Max Weber.* Frankfurt am Main: Suhrkamp. (Translation in two parts: 1987a. *Theory of Action: Towards a New Synthesis Going Beyond Parsons.* London: Routledge; 1988. *Understanding Modernity: Towards a New Perspective Going Beyond Durkheim and Weber.* London: Routledge.)

Münch, Richard. 1984. *Die Struktur der Moderne.* Frankfurt am Main: Suhrkamp.

Münch, Richard. 1986. *Die Kultur der Moderne.* 2 vols. Vol. 1: *Ihre Grundlagen und ihre Entwicklung in England und Amerika.* Vol. 2: *Ihre Entwicklung in Frankreich und Deutschland.* Frankfurt am Main: Suhrkamp.

Münch, Richard. 1987b. "Parsonian Theory Today: In Search of a New Synthesis." In Anthony Giddens and Jonathan H. Turner (Eds.), *Social Theory Today*, pp. 116–55. Cambridge, England: Polity Press.

Münch, Richard. 1991. *Dialektik der Kommunikationsgesellschaft.* Frankfurt am Main: Suhrkamp.

Övermann, Ulrich, T. Allert, E. Konau, and J. Krambeck. 1979. "Die Methodologie einer objektiven Hermeneutik und ihre allgemeine forschungslogische Bedeutung in den Sozialwissenschaften." In H.G. Soeffner (Ed.), *Interpretative Verfahren in den Sozial–und Textwissenschaften,* pp. 352–433. Stuttgart: Metzler.

Övermann, Ulrich. 1985. "Versozialwissenschaftlichung der Identitätsform und Verweigerung von Lebenspraxis." In B. Lutz (Ed.), *Soziologie und gesellschaftliche Entwicklung,* pp. 463–74. Frankfurt am Main: Campus.

Olson, Mancur, Jr. 1965. *The Logic of Collective Action: Public Goods and the Theory of Groups.* Cambridge, Mass.: Harvard University Press.

Parsons, Talcott. 1937/1968. *The Structure of Social Action.* New York: Free Press.

Parsons, Talcott. 1940/1954a. "An Analytical Approach to the Theory of Social Stratification." In Talcott Parsons, *Essays in Sociological Theory,* pp. 69–88. New York: Free Press.

Parsons, Talcott. 1951. *The Social System.* Glencoe, Ill.: Free Press.

Parsons, Talcott. 1954b. *Essays in Sociological Theory.* New York: Free Press.

Parsons, Talcott. 1959. "An Approach to Psychological Theory in Terms of the Theory of Action." In S. Koch (Ed.), *Psychology: A Study of a Science,* Vol. 3, pp. 612–711. New York: McGraw-Hill.

Parsons, Talcott. 1961a. "An Outline of the Social System." In T. Parsons, E.A. Shils, K.D. Naegele, and J.R. Pitts (Eds.), *Theories of Society,* pp. 30–79. New York: Free Press.

Parsons, Talcott. 1961b. "Introduction to Culture and the Social System." In T. Parsons, E.A. Shils, K.D. Naegele, and J.R. Pitts, *Theories of Society,* pp. 963–93. New York: Free Press.

Parsons, Talcott. 1964. *Social Structure and Personality.* New York: Free Press.

Parsons, Talcott. 1966. *Societies. Evolutionary and Comparative Perspectives.* Englewood Cliffs, N.J.: Prentice-Hall.

Parsons, Talcott. 1967. *Sociological Theory and Modern Society.* New York: Free Press.

Parsons, Talcott. 1969. *Politics and Social Structure.* New York: Free Press.

Parsons, Talcott. 1971. *The System of Modern Societies.* Englewood Cliffs, N.J.: Prentice-Hall.

Parsons, Talcott. 1977a. "Equality and Inequality in Modern Society, or Social Stratification Revisited." In Talcott Parsons, *Social Systems and the Evolution of Action Theory,* pp. 321–80. New York: Free Press.

Parsons, Talcott. 1977b. *Social Systems and the Evolution of Action Theory.* New York: Free Press.

Parsons, Talcott. 1978. *Action Theory and the Human Condition.* New York: Free Press.

Parsons, Talcott, Robert F. Bales, and Edward A. Shils. 1953. *Working Papers in the Theory of Action.* Glencoe, Ill.: Free Press.

Parsons, Talcott, and Robert F. Bales. 1955. *Family, Socialization and Interaction Process.* New York: Free Press.

Parsons, Talcott, and Gerald M. Platt. 1973. *The American University.* Cambridge, Mass.: Harvard University Press.

Parsons, Talcott, and Edward A. Shils (Eds.). 1951a. *Toward a General Theory of Action.* Cambridge, Mass.: Harvard University Press.

Parsons, Talcott, and Edward A. Shils. 1951b. "Values, Motives, and Systems of Action." In Talcott Parsons and Edward A. Shils (Eds.), *Toward a General Theory of Action,* pp. 45–275. Cambridge, Mass.: Harvard University Press.

Parsons, Talcott, and Neil J. Smelser. 1956. *Economy and Society*. New York: Free Press.

Piaget, Jean. 1924/1963. *Le jugement et le raisonnement chez l'enfant*. Neuchatel: Delachaux & Niestlé. (Translation: 1972. *Judgement and Reasoning in the Child*. Totowa, N.J.: Littlefield & Adams.)

Piaget, Jean. 1932/1973. *Le jugement moral chez l'enfant*. Paris: Presses Universitaires de France. (Translation: 1977. *The Moral Judgement of the Child*. Harmondsworth: Penguin Books.)

Piaget, Jean. 1937/1950. *La construction du réel chez l'enfant*. Neuchâtel: Delachaux & Niestlé. (Translation: 1954. *The Construction of Reality in the Child*. New York: Basic Books.)

Piaget, Jean. 1945. *La formation du symbole chez l'enfant: imitation jeu et rêve, image et représentation*. Neuchatel: Delachaux & Niestlé. (Translation: 1951. *Play, Dreams, and Imitation in Childhood*. New York: Norton.)

Piaget, Jean. 1947. *La psychologie de l'intelligence*. Paris: Colin. (Translation: 1981. *Psychology of Intelligence*. Totowa, N.J.: Littlefield & Adams.)

Piaget, Jean. 1950. *Introduction a l'épistemologie genetique*. Paris: Presses Universitaires de France.

Piaget, Jean. 1974. *Recherches sur la contradiction*. Paris: Presses Universitaires de France.

Piaget, Jean. 1975. *L'équilibration des structures cognitives: Problème central du developpement*. Paris: Presses Universitaires de France. (Translations: 1978. *The Development of Thought: Equilibration of Cognitive Structures*. Oxford: B. Blackwell; 1985. *The Equilibration of Cognitive Structures*. Chicago: University of Chicago Press.)

Piaget, Jean. 1980. *Adaptation and Intelligence*. Chicago: University of Chicago Press.

Pollner, Melvin. 1987. *Mundane Reasoning: Reality in Everyday and Sociological Discourse*. Cambridge: Cambridge University Press.

Popper, Karl R. 1963. *Conjectures and Refutations: The Growth of Scientific Knowledge*. London: Routledge.

Popper, Karl R. 1972. *Objective Knowledge: An Evolutionary Approach*. Oxford: Clarendon Press.

Psathas, George (Ed.). 1973. *Phenomenological Sociology: Issues and Applications*. New York: Wiley.

Psathas, George. (Ed.). 1979. *Everyday Language: Studies in Ethnomethodology*. New York: Irvington.

Radcliffe-Brown, Alfred R. 1922. *The Andaman Islanders*. London: Macmillan.

Radcliffe-Brown, Alfred R. 1935. "On the Concept of Function in Social Science." *American Anthropologist* 37: 394–402.

Radcliffe-Brown, Alfred R. 1952. *Structure and Function in Primitive Society*. New York: Macmillan.

Ricoeur, Paul. 1971. "The Model of a Text: Meaningful Action Considered as a Text." *Social Research* 38: 529–62.

Robertson, Roland. 1980. "Aspects of Identity and Authority in Sociological Theory." In R. Robertson and B. Holzner (Eds.), *Identity and Authority*, pp. 218–65. Oxford: Blackwell.

Robertson, Roland. 1990. "Mapping the Global Condition: Globalization as the Central Concept." *Theory, Culture and Society* 7: 15–30.

Roethlisberger, Fritz J., and W.J. Dickson. 1939. *Management and the Worker*. Cambridge, Mass.: Harvard University Press.

Sacks, Harvey. 1963. "Sociological Description." *Berkeley Journal of Sociology* 8: 1–17.

Sacks, Harvey. 1972a. "An Initial Investigation of the Usability of Conversational Data for Doing." In D. Sudnow (Ed.), *Studies in Social Interaction*, pp. 31–74. New York: Free Press.

Sacks, Harvey. 1972b. "Notes on Police Assessment of Moral Character." In D. Sudnow (Ed.), *Studies in Social Interaction*, pp. 280–93. New York: Free Press.

Sacks, Harvey, Emanuel Schegloff, and Gail Jefferson. 1974. "A Simplest Systematics for the Analysis of Turn Taking in Conversation." *Language* 50: 696–735.

Sahlins, Marshall. 1976. *Culture and Practical Reason*. Chicago: University of Chicago Press.

Sartre, Jean Paul. 1943. *L'être et le néant*. Paris: Gallimard. (Translation: 1966. *Being and Nothingness: An Essay on Phenomenological Ontology*. Edited by Hazel E. Barnes. New York: Pocket Books.)

Saurwein, Karl-Heinz. 1988. *Ökonomie und soziologische Theoriekonstruktion*. Opladen: Westdeutscher Verlag.

Schegloff, Emanuel. 1968. "Sequencing in Conversational Openings." *American Anthropologist* 70: 1075–95.

Schegloff, Emanuel. 1980. "Preliminaries to Preliminaries: 'Can I Ask You A Question?'" *Sociological Inquiry* 50: 104–52.

Schegloff, Emanuel. 1987. "Between Macro and Micro: Context and Other Connections." In Jeffrey C. Alexander, Bernhard Giesen, Richard Münch, and Neil J. Smelser (Eds.), *The Micro-Macro Link*, pp. 207–34. Berkeley: University of California Press.

Schegloff, Emanuel, and Harvey Sacks. 1973. "Opening up Closings." *Semiotica VIII*, pp. 289–327.

Schegloff, Emanuel, Gail Jefferson, and Harvey Sacks. 1977. "The Preference for Self-Correction in the Organization of Repair in Conversation." *Language* 53: 361–82.

Schluchter, Wolfgang. 1979. *Die Entwicklung des okzidentalen Rationalismus. Eine Analyse von Max Webers Gesellschaftsgeschichte*. Tübingen: Mohr Siebeck. (Translation: 1981. *The Rise of Western Rationalism*. Berkeley: University of California Press.)

Schluchter, Wolfgang. 1988. *Religion und Lebensführung*. 2 vols. Frankfurt am Main: Suhrkamp. (Translation: 1989. *Rationalism, Religion, and Domination: A Weberian Perspective*. Berkeley: University of California Press.)

Schmid, Michael. 1982. *Theorien sozialen Wandels*. Opladen: Westdeutscher Verlag.

Schütze, Fritz. 1975. *Sprache soziologisch gesehen*. 2 vols. Munich: Fink.

Schütze, Fritz, W. Meinefeld, W. Springer, and Ansgar Weymann. 1973. "Grundlagentheoretische Voraussetzungen methodisch kontrollierten Fremdverstehens." In Arbeitsgruppe Bielefelder Soziologen (Ed.), *Alltagswissen, soziale Interaktion und gesellschaftliche Wirklichkeit*. 2 vols., pp. 433–95. Reinbek/Hamburg: Rowohlt.

Schutz, Alfred. 1932. *Der sinnhafte Aufbau der sozialen Welt*. Vienna: Springer. (Translation: 1967. *The Phenomenology of the Social World*. Evanston, Ill.: Northwestern University Press.)

Schutz, Alfred. 1962. *Collected Papers I: The Problem of Social Reality*. The Hague: Nijhoff.

Schutz, Alfred. 1964. *Collected Papers II: Studies in Social Theory.* The Hague: Nijhoff.

Schutz, Alfred. 1966. *Collected Papers III: Studies in Phenomenological Philosophy.* The Hague: Nijhoff.

Schutz, Alfred and Thomas Luckmann. 1973. *The Structure of the Life World.* Evanston, Ill.: Northwestern University Press.

Schwanenberg, Enno. 1970. *Soziales Handeln — Die Theorie und ihr Problem.* Bern: Huber.

Schwanenberg, Enno. 1971. "The Two Problems of Order in Parsons' Theory: An Analysis from Within." *Social Forces* 49: 569–81.

Sciulli, David. 1984. "Talcott Parsons' Analytical Critique of Marxism's Concept of Alienation." *American Journal of Sociology* 90: 514–40.

Sciulli, David. 1986. "Voluntaristic Action as a Distinct Concept: Theoretical Foundations of Societal Constitutionalism." *American Sociological Review* 51: 743–66.

Sciulli, David. 1988. "Foundations of Societal Constitutionalism: Principles from the Concepts of Communicative Action and Procedural Legality." *British Journal of Sociology* 39: 377–407.

Sciulli, David. 1989. "Analytical Limits of Communicative Action: Two Requirements of Habermas' Critical Theory and of Societal Constitutionalism." *Current Perspectives in Social Theory* 9: 55–90.

Sciulli, David, and Dean Gerstein. 1985. "Social Theory and Talcott Parsons in the 1980s." *Annual Review of Sociology* 11: 369–87.

Shils, Edward. 1972. "The Intellectuals and the Powers: Some Perspectives for Comparative Analysis." In *"The Intellectuals and the Powers" and Other Essays,* pp. 3–22. Chicago: University of Chicago Press.

Shils, Edward. 1975. *Center and Periphery.* Chicago, Ill.: University of Chicago Press.

Sica, Alan. 1986. "Hermeneutics and Axiology: The Ethical Contents and Interpretation." In Mark L. Wardell and Stephen P. Turner (Eds.), *Sociological Theory in Transition,* pp. 142–57. Boston: Allen and Unwin.

Simmel, Georg. 1908. *Soziologie. Untersuchungen über die Formen der Vergesellschaftung.* Berlin: Duncker & Humblot.

Skinner, Burhus F. 1938. *The Behavior of Organisms.* New York: Appleton-Century-Crofts.

Skinner, Burhus F. 1953. *Science and Human Behavior.* New York: Macmillan.

Smelser, Neil J. 1959. *Social Change in the Industrial Revolution.* Chicago: University of Chicago Press.

Smelser, Neil J. 1962. *Theory of Collective Behavior.* New York: Free Press.

Smith, Adam. 1759/1966. *The Theory of Moral Sentiments.* New York: Bonn.

Soeffner, Hans-Georg. 1989. *Auslegung des Alltags — Der Alltag der Auslegung.* Frankfurt am Main: Suhrkamp.

Soeffner, Hans-Georg. 1992. *Die Ordnung der Rituale.* Frankfurt am Main: Suhrkamp.

Sorokin, Pitirim A. 1927. *Social Mobility.* New York: Harper.

Sorokin, Pitirim A. 1928. *Contemporary Sociological Theories.* New York: Harper.

Sorokin, Pitirim A. 1937–1941. *Social and Cultural Dynamics.* 4 vols. New York: American Book Co.

Sorokin, Pitirim A. 1956. *Fads and Foibles in Modern Sociology and Related Sciences.* Chicago: Regnery.

Spencer, Herbert. 1972. *On Social Evolution. Selected Writings.* Edited by J.D.Y. Peel. Chicago: University of Chicago Press.

Sutherland, Edwin H. 1939. *Principles of Criminology.* Philadelphia: Lippincott.

Sykes, Gresham M., and David Matza. 1957. "Techniques of Neutralization: A Theory of Delinquency." *American Sociological Review* 22: 664–70.

Sztompka, Piotr. 1974. *System and Function: Toward a Theory of Society.* New York: Academic.

Sztompka, Piotr. 1986. *Robert K. Merton: An Intellectual Profile.* London: Macmillan.

Tilly, Charles. 1978. *From Mobilization to Revolution.* Reading, Mass.: Addison-Wesley.

Tiryakian, Edward A. 1962. *Sociologism and Existentialism.* Englewood Cliffs, N.J.: Prentice-Hall.

Tiryakian, Edward A. 1975. "Neither Marx nor Durkheim . . . Perhaps Weber." *American Journal of Sociology* 81: 1–33.

Tiryakian, Edward A. 1977. "Durkheim and Husserl: A Comparison of the Spirit of Positivism and the Spirit of Phenomenology." In J. Bien (Ed.), *Phenomenology and the Social Sciences,* pp. 20–43. The Hague: Nijhoff.

Tiryakian, Edward A. 1978. "Emile Durkheim." In T. Bottomore and R. Nisbet (Eds.), *A History of Sociological Analysis,* pp. 187–236. New York: Basic Books.

Tiryakian, Edward A. 1983. "Puritan American in the Modern World: Mission Impossible?" *Sociological Analysis* 43: 351–67.

Tönnies, Ferdinand. 1887/1963. *Gemeinschaft und Gesellschaft.* Darmstadt: Wissenschaftliche Buchgesellschaft. (Translation: 1963. *Community and Society.* New York: Harper & Row.)

Tumin, Melvin M. 1953. "Some Principles of Stratification: A Critical Analysis." *American Sociological Review* 18: 387–94.

Turner, Jonathan H. 1986. *The Structure of Sociological Theory.* Chicago: Dorsey.

Turner, Ralph H. 1962. "Role-Taking: Process versus Conformity." In Arnold Rose (Ed.), *Human Behavior and Social Processes,* pp. 22–40. Boston: Houghton Mifflin.

Turner, Ralph H. 1968. "Social Roles: Sociological Aspects." In *International Encyclopedia of the Social Sciences,* Vol. 14/15, pp. 552–57. Edited by David L. Sills. New York: Macmillan & Free Press.

Turner, Ralph H. 1976. "The Real Self: From Institution to Impulse." *American Journal of Sociology* 81: 989–1016.

Turner, Ralph H. 1978. "The Role and the Person." *American Journal of Sociology* 84: 1–23.

Turner, Ralph H. 1979–1980. "A Strategy for Developing an Integrated Role Theory." *Humboldt Journal of Social Relations* 7: 123–39.

Veblen, Thorstein. 1928. *The Theory of the Leisure Class.* New York: Vanguard Press.

Wagner, Gerhard. 1991. "Parsons, Hobbes und das Problem sozialer Ordnung. Eine theoriegeschichtliche Notiz in systematischer Absicht." *Zeitschrift für Soziologie* 20: 115–23.

Weber, Max. 1920–1921a/1972a. *Gesammelte Aufsätze zur Religionssoziologie.* Vol. 1. Tübingen: Mohr Siebeck. (Translations in two parts: 1976. *The Protestant Ethic and the Spirit of Capitalism.* Translated by Talcott Parsons. New York: Scribner's, 1964. *The Religion of China. Confucianism and Taoism.* Translated and edited by H.H. Gerth and D. Martindale. New York: Free Press.)

Weber, Max. 1920–1921b/1972b. *Gesammelte Aufsätze zur Religionssoziologie.* Vol. 2. Tübingen: Mohr Siebeck. (Translation: 1967. *The Religion of India: The Sociology of Hinduism and Buddhism.* Translated and edited by H.H. Gerth and D. Martindale. New York: Free Press.)

Weber, Max. 1922/1972c. *Wirtschaft und Gesellschaft.* Tübingen: Mohr Siebeck. (Translation: 1968. *Economy and Society.* 3 vols. Edited by G. Roth and C. Wittich. New York: Bedminster Press.)

Wenzel, Harald. 1991. *Die Ordnung des Handelns. Talcott Parsons' Theorie des allgemeinen Handlungssystems.* Frankfurt am Main: Suhrkamp.

Wieder, Lawrence D. 1973. *Language and Social Reality.* The Hague: Mouton.

Wrong, Denis. 1961. "The Oversocialized Conception of Man." *American Sociological Review* 26: 183–93.

Yinger, Milton J. 1960. "Contraculture and Subculture." *American Sociological Review* 25: 625–35.

Zimmerman, Don H. 1970. "The Practicalities of Rule Use." In J.D. Douglas (Ed.), *Understanding Everyday Life*, pp. 221–38. Chicago: Aldine.

Zimmerman, Don H., and Melvin Pollner. 1970. "The Everyday World as a Phenomenon." In J.D. Douglas (Ed.), *Understanding Everyday Life*, pp. 80–103. Chicago: Aldine.

Alexander, Jeffrey C., 116–18
Apel, Karl Otto, 167
Aristotle, 232

Baldwin, James M., 288
Bales, Robert F., 34–36, 88
Barber, Bernard, 117
Barthes, Roland, 167
Baum, Rainer C., 116–17
Becker, Gary S., 10
Bellah, Robert N., 117
Bentham, Jeremy, 10
Berger, Peter L., x, 144, 148–50,
    152–57, 159, 163, 166, 169–71
Black, Max, 116
Blau, Peter M., x, 257–60, 262–69,
    271–77
Bleicher, Joseph, 167
Blumer, Herbert, x, 288–91, 293–94,
    297, 299, 302–5
Bourricaud, François, 116
Brown, Richard H., 167
Buchanan, James M., 10
Buckley, Walter, 118

Calvin, Johannes, 96–97
Cicourel, Aaron V., 186

Cloward, Richard A., 132
Cohen, Albert J., ix, 138–40, 143
Coleman, James S., 10
Collins, Randall, 199
Colomy, Paul, 117
Comte, Auguste, 10, 122
Cooley, Charles H., 288
Coser, Lewis A., x, 189–200

Dahrendorf, Ralf, x, 189, 199,
    201–13
Darwin, Charles, 8, 91
Davies, James D., 241
Davis, Kingsley, 101–2
Dewey, John, 288
Dickson, William J., 130
Dilthey, Wilhelm, 165–66
Douglas, Jack, 171
Douglas, Mary, 167
Downs, Anthony, 253–54
Duncan, Otis Dudley, 257
Durkheim, Emile, 4, 80, 88, 91–92,
    114–15, 121–24, 131, 149–50,
    156, 174, 211, 257, 286–87

Effrat, Andrew, 116–17
Eisenstadt, Shmuel N., 117

Ekeh, Peter P., 260
Etzioni, Amitai, 118

Freud, Sigmund, 14, 29, 80, 88, 115
Friedman, Milton, 10

Gadamer, Hans Georg, 166–67
Garfinkel, Harold, x, 170–71, 173,
    176–86
Geertz, Clifford, 167
Gerard, Harold B., 232, 234
Gerstein, Dean R., 117
Giesen, Bernhard, 118
Goffman, Erving, x, 170, 306–10,
    316–17, 319–26
Gould, Mark, 117
Gouldner, Alvin W., 213, 260
Grathoff, Richard, 167, 171

Habermas, Jürgen, 12, 84, 92, 118,
    148, 167, 171, 287, 304
Hayes, Adrian, 169
Hegel, Georg Wilhelm Friedrich, 12
Heidegger, Martin, 165–66
Heritage, John, 186
Hobbes, Thomas, 8, 9, 12, 15
Holton, Robert J., 116
Homans, George C., x, 3, 217–25,
    227, 229, 231–34, 237–42,
    246–50, 252–53, 258–59, 262,
    277
Hondrich, Karl Otto, 210
Huaco, George, 101
Hume, David, 9–10
Husserl, Edmund, 145–47, 165

James, William, 288
Jauss, Hans Robert, 167
Jefferson, Gail, 186
Jensen, Stefan, 118
Johnson, Harry M., 117

Kant, Immanuel, 4, 12–13, 84–85, 87
Knorr-Cetina, Karin D., 186
Kohlberg, Lawrence, 80, 116, 287
Kuhn, Manford, 305

Lazarsfeld, Paul F., 119
Lechner, Frank, 117
Lenski, Gerhard A., 102
Lévi-Strauss, Claude, 167
Lidz, Charles W., 72, 88, 116–17
Lidz, Victor M., 72, 88, 116–17
Lipset, Seymour M., 100
Livingston, Eric, 186
Locke, John, 10
Loubser, Jan J., 116–17
Luckmann, Thomas, x, 144, 148–50,
    152–57, 159, 163, 166, 169–71
Luhmann, Niklas, 15, 92, 99, 118, 167
Luther, Martin, 96
Lynch, Michael, 186

Madsen, Richard, 117
Malinowski, Bronislaw, 121–23,
    125–28, 261
Marshall, Thomas H., 4, 91
Matthes, Joachim, 171
Matza, David, x, 138, 142–43
Mauss, Marcel, 261
Mayhew, Leon, 117
Mayo, Elton, 130
Mead, George Herbert, 80, 115–16,
    281, 286, 288, 294–97, 302, 305
Meinefeld, Werner, 166
Merton, Robert K., ix, 119, 125–37
Miebach, Bernhard, 118
Mill, John Stuart, 10
Miller, Walter B., ix, 138, 140–42
Mills, C. Wright, 213
Moore, Wilbert E., 101–2
Münch, Richard, ix, 42, 116, 118

Oevermann, Ulrich, 171
Olds, James, 88, 115
Olson, Mancur, Jr., 241, 254

Pareto, Vilfredo, 4, 91
Park, Robert E., 288
Parsons, Talcott, ix, 3–4, 7, 13–24,
    26, 29–31, 34–6, 39–40, 45, 47,
    50, 53, 56, 59, 72, 77, 79–80, 82,
    84–85, 88, 90–93, 95, 98–103,
    114–19, 130, 202–3, 217, 258, 272

Piaget, Jean, x, 80, 115–17, 281–82, 284–87
Platt, Gerald M., 72, 88
Pollner, Melvin, 178, 186
Popper, Karl R., 74, 92
Psathas, George, 171

Radcliffe-Brown, Alfred R., 121, 123–26
Redfield, Robert, 288
Ricoeur, Paul, 167
Robertson, Roland, 117
Roethlisberger, Fritz J., 130
Rosenberg, Morris, 119

Sacks, Harvey, 186
Sahlins, Marshall, 167
Saint-Simon, Claude-Henri de, 10
Sartre, Jean Paul, 31
Saurwein, Karl-Heinz, 118
Schäffle, Albert, 122
Schegloff, Emanuel A., 186
Schluchter, Wolfgang, 118
Schmid, Michael, 118
Schütze, Fritz, 166, 171
Schutz, Alfred, 145–48, 165–66
Schwanenberg, Enno, 118
Sciulli, David, 117
Shils, Edward A., 16–19, 23–24, 29–30, 34–36, 72, 115, 117
Short, James F., Jr., x, 138–40, 143
Sica, Alan, 167
Simmel, Georg, 4, 116, 189–91, 257
Skinner, Burhus F., 221
Smelser, Neil J., 45, 47, 117
Smith, Adam, 9–10
Soeffner, Hans-Georg, 171
Sombart, Werner, 3

Sorokin, Pitirim A., 3
Spencer, Herbert, 91–2, 122
Springer, Werner, 166
Sullivan, William M., 117
Sutherland, Edwin H., 132
Swidler, Ann, 117
Sykes, Gresham M., x, 138, 142–43
Sztompka, Piotr, 137

Thomas, William I., 288
Tilly, Charles, 204
Tipton, Stephen, 117
Tiryakian, Edward A., 117
Tönnies, Ferdinand, 34
Tumin, Melvin M., 101
Turner, Brian S., 116
Turner, Jonathan H., 200
Turner, Ralph H., 305

Veblen, Thorstein, 130

Wagner, Gerhard, 15
Weber, Max, 3–4, 74–76, 79, 81, 91–92, 97, 115, 167, 207, 258, 264–65, 272, 289
Wenzel, Harald, 118
Weymann, Ansgar, 166
Wieder, Lawrence D., 186
Winch, Peter, 167
Wirth, Louis, 288
Worms, René, 122
Wrong, Dennis, 115

Yinger, Milton J., x, 138, 142–43

Zimmerman, Don H., 178, 186
Znaniecki, Florian, 288

Subject Index

Accounting, of social reality, 181–83
  methods of, 180
  process of, 173, 175–76
Accounts, 173–76, 179–82, 185
Achievement, 34
Acting organism, 300
Acting out of conflict, 196–98
Action, theory of, 16
Actions, 7, 10, 15–17, 42, 302–3
  choice of, 302
  collective, 254
  communicative, 12
  concrete, 13
  contingency of, 42
  ends for, 42
  generalizing scope for, 44
  idealistic explanations of, 10
  interlinkage of, 303
  means for, 42
  motivation of, 87
  nonrational elements of, 15
  opening scope for, 42
  positivistic explanations of, 7
  social, 182, 304
  specifying scope for, 44
  strategic, 7
Action space, 42

Action subsystems, interrelating, 77
Action systems, 72, 84–85, 87,
    109–10
  subsystems of, 72–82
Action theory, 3, 16, 103, 117
Actors, 310
Adaptation, 35–37, 40, 42
  to cultural structure, 130
Adaptive upgrading, 88, 91–92
Ad-hocing, 183
Adjustments, 320
  primary, 320
  secondary, 320–21
Adolescence, 90
Adulthood, 90
Affect, 75
Affective neutrality, 33
Affectivity, 32
Agency, 14–15
  human, 100
Agents, 15
Aggression, 231
Aggression-approval proposition,
    231–32, 239–41
A-G-I-L scheme, 34, 37, 40–1
Agreement, 5, 286
Aims, redefinition of, 81

Anomie, 5, 130
Application of culture, 79
Approval, 49, 220–21
Arguments, 11, 234–36
Ascription, 33
Associations, 115, 257–63, 266–68, 273
   voluntary, 100
Asylums, 316–21
Attachment, 89–90
Attraction, 257–63
Audience, 310
Authoritarianism, 9, 100–101
Authority, 207, 272, 275, 286
   legitimate, 208, 272
   superordinate, 9
   roles, 203
Autonomy
   individual, 14
   moral, 282, 284–85
   of the will, 286

Behavior
   inborn determination of, 8
   patterns of, 120–21
   recurrent, 121
Behavioral psychology, 221, 239
Behavioral system, 76, 80–81
Behaviorism, 294–95
Boundaries, 25
   of the system, 22
Boundary maintenance, 23–24
Britain, 99
Buddhism, 94

Capitalism, 97–98, 264
   rational, 98
   spirit of, 97
Categorical imperative, 12
Cause and effect, 124
Cause and function, 122
Change, 16, 23, 201, 203, 205
Checks and balances, 100
China, 94
Choice, 31
Christianity, 96, 264
Citizenship, 94, 98–100
   rights of, 52

Civilization, state of, 9
Civil religion, 15
Civil rights, 179, 183
Class conflict, 102
Class differentiation, 102
Cohesion, 20, 194
Collective goals, 71
Collective good, 241, 254
Collectivity, 303
Collectivity-orientation, 32
Commitments, 244–46, 263, 266–68
   to values, 62
Common Law, 184, 186, 195
Common practices, 136, 149
Common-sense reality, 175
Common values, 177
Communal association, 21–22
Communication, 6, 21–22, 25, 55,
      115, 179, 232, 234, 237, 239,
      295, 297, 299, 304, 326
   strategic, 306
   universal contexts of, 185
Communication out of character, 315
Community, 20, 34, 244, 264–65, 268
Community system, 52, 59, 67, 69
Competition, 5–6, 195
Complementarity of actions and
      expectations, 18
Compromise, 251
Conditions, 7, 10
Conflict, 49, 137, 189, 194, 201, 205,
      208, 250–51, 287
   acting out, 196–98
   disruptive effects of, 199
   external, 193–97
   intensity of, 190–92, 197–98
   internal, 192–93
   latent, manifest, 204, 206
   nonrealistic, 190
   origination of, 203–5
   realistic, 190
   severity and intensity of, 205
Conflict and change, 205–10
Conflict settlement, 195, 199, 202
Conflict theory, 197, 200, 209–10,
      250
   of social roles, 213

Conflict view of society, 201
Conformers, 245
Conformism, 115
Conformity, 18, 52, 131, 242–43, 245
Confucianism, 94
Consciousness, 145, 165
  moral, 281–82, 284
Consensus, 11, 15, 20, 236, 244,
    245–46
  formation of, 77, 285
Conspicuous consumption, 129–30
Constraint, 212, 283
  external, 282–83
Contraculture, 142
Contradictions, 235–36
  exclusion of, 234
Conversation, 166, 296
  of gestures, 294
Cooperation, 5, 282, 284–85
Costs, 227, 233, 237–40
Criticism, 77
Cultural pattern, consistency of, 25
Cultural structure, adaptation to, 130
Cultural systems, 17, 24–25, 74, 77,
    79–80
Cultural values, and economic
    resources, 66
Culture
  application of, 79
  process of selecting, 79
  testing of, 80
Cybernetic hierarchy of conditions
    and controls, 39–40

Darwinism, 91–92
Deceit, 5
Defensive reactions, and deviance,
    29–30
Definitions of the situation, 74
Deflation, 48, 50, 54, 57
Delinquency, 140, 142–43
  contraculture and, 142
  gang, 140–41
  lower-class culture and, 140–42
  subcultures of, 138–40
Delinquent behavior, 139
Delinquent subcultures, 139

Deprivation, 18, 21, 50, 228
  relative, 237
Deprivations, mutual application of,
    22
Deprivation-satiation proposition,
    227–30
Developmental logic, 74
Deviance, 30
Deviant behavior, 132, 138
Deviation from norms, 243
Deviations, 5, 18, 120, 243–44
Differentiation, 88, 91–92
  functional, 99
  systemic, 99
Diffuseness, 32
Discourse, 15, 179, 234, 237, 239,
    269, 286
  rules of, 235
  theory of, 240
Discursive procedures, 12
Discursive reasoning, 276
Disorder, 5–6
Dispositions, spontaneous, 303
Dominating culture, 138
Domination, 201, 206–8
Double contingency, 18–19, 22
Dramatic realization, 312–13
Dynamics and growth, 108, 110–11

Economic action, legitimation and
    cultural shaping of, 65
Economic activity, 71
  control over, 69
Economic calculation, 237, 239, 252
  of costs and benefits, 244
  of cultural thought, 65
Economic consumption, 65
Economic production, 65
Economic subsystem, 48
Economic system, 47, 63, 69–70
  normative regulation of, 69
Economic theory, 237, 239–40, 243,
    245–46, 252–55
  of democracy, 253
Economic transactions, 137, 262
Economy, 48, 100
  steering, 71

Education, universal, 97
Ego, 88, 90
Ego identity, 88, 90, 324, 326
Egypt, 93
Empires, intermediate historic, 93
Empirical functionalism, 119
Empirical ordering, 84
Ends, 7, 37, 42
Enlightenment, 97–98
Epistemology, 181
Equality, 285
Ethnomethodology, 173, 185–86
Everyday life, 149–53, 155, 169, 310
    structure of, 144
Evolution, 7
    socio-cultural, 90–92, 99, 113, 116
Exchange, 5–6, 21, 47, 222–23, 226,
        241, 246–48, 252–56, 257, 260,
        264, 269
    barter, 220
    balanced, 231–32
    economic, 220, 243, 253, 260–65,
        269, 277
    fair, 275
    of goods and services, 47
    of gratifications, 18, 21
    of gratifications and deprivations,
        115
    indirect, 274–76
    social, 5, 217–21, 225, 232, 257,
        259–65, 268–69, 273, 276
Exchange theory, 217, 257, 262, 276
    application of, 232–41
Existential philosophy, 165
Expectations, 4, 18, 243–44
    mutual, 18
Experience, ordering of, 80
Expressive control, maintenance of, 313

Fairness, 268–69
    principle of, 302
Feeling of belonging, 52
Force, 5, 9, 49
Four-function paradigm, 34–38, 116
Four-function scheme, 40, 45, 116
Frame analysis, 307–10
Frames, 306, 308–9, 324

Framing, 306–8, 316–17, 324, 326
Fraud, 5, 9
Freedom, 31, 212–13, 249
Free will, 249
Friend/enemy scheme, 10
Friendship, 243
Front, 311–12
Frustration, 238–39
Functional analysis, 122, 125, 131
    application of, 129–37
    paradigm for, 128–29
Functional contributions, interchange
    of, 59
Functional explanations, 128, 132, 134
    of institutional practices, 122
    of social practices, 123
Functional indispensability, 127–28
Functional prerequisite, 135
Functional unity, 125–27
Functionalism, 121–25, 201
    analytical, 3, 117
    postulates of, 125–28
Functionally specialized systems, 99
Functions, 35–40, 42, 45, 107,
    109–10, 112–13

Geisteswissenschaften, 165
General ideas, 44
Generalization of mutual attach-
    ment, 89
Generalized media of interchange, 45
Generalized other, 302
Generalizing scope for action, 44
Generally valid ideas, 10
Gift giving, 261–63
Goal attainment, 35–37, 40, 44, 49
Goals, 44
God, covenant with, 97
Government, 98
Grand theory, 130
Gratifications, 21
Greece, 96
Greek city states, 95
Group of equals, 287
Groups, 291
    informal, 129
Growth, 113

Habitualization, 157
Health, 84
Hermeneutic circle, 166
Hermeneutic interpretation, 166
Hermeneutics, 165–67, 171
Hierarchy of conditioning, 39
Hierarchy of controls, 39
History, universal, 91
Hobbesian problem of order, 8–10
Homo sociologicus, 211
Human action, 302–3
Human agency, 100
Human being, as acting organism,
    300–302
Human condition, 82, 110–12
    interrelating substems of, 85–87
    subsystems of, 82–85
Human rights, 179, 182
Human society and group life,
    291–93
Humanities, 165

I, 301
Id, 88, 90
Idealism, 10, 13, 92, 104–5
Idealistic dilemma, 12
Idealization, 313
Ideas, 10, 37, 42, 44
    radical, 100
    with universal validity, 98
Identification, 89–90
Identity, 23, 25, 193, 310, 318
    ego, 324
    personal, 323–24
    social, 322–23
Illegitimate means, 132
Impression management, arts of,
    315–16
Incentives, 47
Inclusion, 88, 90, 92
Indexical accounts, 177
Indexical expressions, 177
Indexicality, 177–79, 183
India, 94
Individual, the, 23
Individuality, 212–13
Inflation, 48, 50, 54, 57

Influence, 53–5, 232
Innovation, 131
Instinct of sympathy, 9
Instincts, 10
Institutionalization, 25–27, 77, 115,
    131, 156–59
    of value patterns, 59
Institutionalized pattern of behavior,
    120–21
Institutional ceremonies, 320
Institutional structure, 119, 121
Institutions, 120, 122, 136, 157, 303
    adjustments to, 319–21
    total, 316–19
Integration, 35–38, 40, 44, 52, 275
    external, 195
    internal, 192–93
    social, 275
Intellectuals, 162–63
Intelligence, 76
Interaction, 4, 18, 21, 294
    as exchange, 218–21
    extended, 89
Interactionism, 305
Interchange of functional contribu-
    tions, 59
Interest groups, 204, 206
Interests, convergence of, 136
Internalization, 25, 27–28, 79, 115, 131
    of culture, 79
Interpenetration, 13, 27–29, 59, 107,
    109, 111
Interpretation, 298–99
Intersubjectively shared typifications,
    146
Intersubjectively shared world, 147
Intersubjectivity, 165–66
Inter-role conflict, 212
Investments, 237–40
Islam, 94
Israel, 95–96

Judgmental dopes, 182, 185
Justice, 285
    distributive, 232, 238
Justification, 269, 286
    discursive, 269

rational, 20
rational, of ideas, 11
Justification of claims, 239
Justification of decisions, 63

Kantian problem of order, 12–13
Kinship, 264

Language, 154–55, 294
Latent pattern maintenance, 36–38,
   40, 44, 55
Learning, direction of, 81
Legitimation, 30, 136, 159–63, 169,
   209
   cultural, 239
   for political authority, 63
Liberalism, 9
Life-worlds, 11, 52, 136, 145, 147–49,
   165, 167, 244, 266
Lineage system, 124
Love, 89
Lower-class cultures, 140–41
Loyalty demands, 59

Market exchange, 220
Market power, 247–48
Markets, 8, 210
Mastering the wilderness, 100
Me, 301
Meaning, 6, 41–2, 55, 84, 144, 146,
   166–67, 169, 176, 179, 288–91,
   295–96, 300, 324, 326
   interpretation of, 305
   objective, 146
   subjective, 146
   understanding, 297
Meanings, commonly shared, 304
Means, 7, 37, 42, 45
Mediation, 108, 110–11
Mesopotamian empires, 93
Middle range, theory of, 130
Misrepresentation, 314
Modernity, project of, 101
Modernization, 10
Molding, 80
Money, 47–48, 220, 228
Monopolization of physical force, 20

Moral authority, 20
Moral consciousness, 282–85
Moral practice, 282
Moral realism, 282–84
Moral respect, 281–82, 284
Morality, 284, 286
Mother–child interaction, 88
Motives, 146
Movements, fundamentalist, 100
Mystification, 314

Natural selection, 7
Natural state, 9
Nature, meaning and cultivation of,
   87
Need-dispositions, 23
Negotiating between contradictory
   demands, 100
Negotiations, 251, 291, 293, 299,
   303–4
Neofunctionalism, 117
Network of interlocking systems, 98
Neutralization, techniques of, 142
Nonconformers, 244
Nonconformity, 245
Norm, universal, 179
Norms, 22, 37, 42, 44, 120, 274
   for action, 44
   categorical, 13
   common, 264, 268, 274
   concrete, 11
   conformity to, 241–46
   hypothetical, 13
   legitimation of, 59
   self-evident, 11
   shared, 20
   and values, 272, 274
Norms of exchange, 241, 269, 272
Norm-compliance, 245
Norm-deviation, 245

Objective reality, 173–77, 181
Objectivity of knowledge, 165
Objects, 299–300
Operant learning, 221
Opposition ideals, 276
Order, 5–6, 9, 13, 16

accidental, 8-9
and change, 16
compulsory, 8-9
concrete action and, 13
conformistic, 11
cultural problem of, 30
Hobbesian problem of, 8
ideal, 11
institutional, 159
internal problem of, 30
Kantian problem of, 12-13, 115
legal, 12
motivational problem of, 30
natural, 85
negotiated, 292
normative, 11-13, 15
positivistic explanation of, 7
problems of, 15, 30, 106, 114
social, 4, 6, 149, 184-85, 154-55
totalitarian, 255
voluntaristic, 14-15
Order of action, 85
Orders, factual, 7, 15
Organic life, 87
Organic system, 84, 87

Particularism, 33
Pattern variables, 30-34, 36-38
Performance, 310-312
Performance capacity, 76
Performer, 310
Personal dispositions, 80
Personal identity, 316, 323-24
Personality development, 88-90,
    112-13, 115
Personality system, 17, 23-24, 25,
    76, 79-81
Phenomenological reduction, 145,
    152, 165
Phenomenological sociology, 144,
    147, 149, 171
Phenomenology, 145, 165-66, 171,
    185
Physical force, 19, 50
Physico-chemical system, 84, 87
Political decisions, 64
Political decision making, 67

Political leadership, 68
Political machines, 134-37
Political power, 50-51
Political responsibility, 67
Political systems, 49, 63, 67, 70
Polity, 100
Position, 211
Positivism, 9, 103-4
Post-adolescence, 90
Postmodernity, 101
Power, 5, 136-37, 189, 206, 246-52,
    257, 269-73
    collective, 272
    struggle for, 5, 250
Power differentiation, 270
Power game, 198
Power struggle, 208, 210
Practices, recurrent, 121
Predestination, theory of, 96
Preferences, 218
Pre-understanding (Vorverständnis),
    166
Primordial groups, 10
Prisoner's dilemma, 274
Production, 108-9, 111
Professional-client relationship, 34
Profit, 227, 229, 233-34, 245,
    247-48, 250, 252-54, 258-59,
    266
    calculation of, 273
    maximization of, 210, 263-65,
    269, 271
Profit proposition, 227
Protestantism, 96
Punishment, 218-19, 226-27, 239
Puritan sects, 96

Qualitative studies, 147
Quasi-groups, 203-4, 206
Quest for meaning, 84

Rational adaptation, 7
Rational choice, 262
Rationality proposition, 228-30
Reality and contrivance, 314
Reasons, 245
Rebellion, 131

Reciprocation, 260–63, 265, 270
Reciprocity, principle of, 260
Reference group(s), 133, 212–13
Reflexivity, 179–80
Reformation, 96–97
Regimes, authoritarian, 101
Reification, 159
Reincarnation, 94
Relativism, 181
Religion, 100
Renaissance, 96
Resocialization, 164
Resources, 69–71
Respect, mutual, 284
Retreatism, 131
Retribution, 94
Revolution
    cultural, 98, 100
    democratic, 98
    industrial, 98
Reward(s), 218–20, 227–29, 233,
    258–60
Reward–cost analysis, 234
Rites, religious, 122
Ritualism, 131
Role conflict, internal, 212
Role constraint, 210–13
Role expectations, 212–13
Role interpretation, 81
Role performance, 325
    cynical, 310–11
    sincere, 310–11
Role-set, 133–34
Roles, 211, 310
    discrepant, 314
    social, 22, 159, 211–13
Roman Empire, 94, 96
Rules, 284
    moral, 283, 286
Rulers and ruled, 203, 207–8

Sanctioning power, 19, 212–13
    central, 8
Sanctions, 211
    negative, 19, 50
    positive, 19

Sedimentation, 158
Self, 300–301, 310, 317–19, 325
    mortification of, 317–19
    presentation of, 310–16
Self-control, 301
Self-interaction, 301
Self-maintenance, 23
Self-orientation, 31
Self-talk, 301
Significant other, 301
Significant symbol, 294
Social behavior, 222, 232, 252
Social behaviorism, 295, 297
Social causes, 123
Social change, 204
Social conflict, 189–90, 197
Social construction of reality, 146,
    148
    actors', 147
Social contract, 9
Social control, 67
Social fact(s), 121, 150
Social functions, 123
Social identity, 322–23
Social interaction, 30, 75, 153–54,
    218–19, 222, 252, 289, 293–99
Social knowledge, change of, 81
Social life
    institutional structure of, 119–21
    regular patterns of, 144
Social mobility, 210
Social order, 4
    examples of, 4–6
    maintenance of, 6–16
Social reality, 149, 176–78, 183–86
Social regulation, 209–10
    of conflict, 210
Social stratification, 101–3, 114
Social structure, 130
    maintenance of, 209
Social system(s), 17–23, 25, 80–81,
    107–9, 116
    interrelating subsystems, 58–72
    subsystems of, 45–58
Social-cultural system, 55, 59, 63, 65
Socialism, "really existing," 255

Socialization, 26, 28–29, 88, 112–13, 115, 163–64, 169
Societal community, 92, 98–9
Society, 34, 155–64, 291
    functionalist view of, 201–3
    opportunity structure of, 131
Societies
    archaic, 93
    developing, 10
    modern, 95, 98
    non-Western, 100–101
    primitive, 93
    seedbed, 95
Socio-cultural evolution, 90–103, 113–14
Sociological language, 181
Sociological methods, 181
Sociological phenomenology, 169–70
Sociological theory, ix
    synthesis in, 114
Solidarity, 6, 20, 94, 124, 194, 244–46, 275, 287
    structure of, 92
Specification of values, 63
Specificity, 32
Specifying scope for action, 44
Stage, 310–11
Staging, 310
Standards of learning, 81
Status-differentiation, 270
Steering economy, 71
Stigma, 321–24
    management of, 324
Stigmatization, 323–24
Stimulus proposition, 221, 223–24, 229–30
Stratification
    functionalist theory of, 102
    social, 101, 103, 114
Structural change, 204–6
Structural functionalism, 101, 121
Structuralism, 92, 123
Structure, 167
Structure of domination, 292
Structures, objective and subjective, 148

Subculture(s), 138, 142
Subsystems of human condition, 82
Success proposition, 221–23, 228–30
Superego, 29, 88, 90
Supreme Court, U.S., 185
Symbolic complexity, 42
Symbolic constructions, 74
Symbolic interaction, 289
Symbolic interactionism, 148, 288, 291, 305
Symbols, 42, 55–56, 298
    interpretation of, 298
    universal, 56–58
Sympathy, instinct of, 9
Systems of action, 72
    theory of, 16
Systems theory, 3, 107

Teams, 314–15
Telic system, 82, 85, 87
Text(s), 166–67
Theory of middle range, 130
Tradition, 11, 158
Traditionalism, 100
Transcendental ordering, 82
Trust, 5, 223, 235–36, 263–68
Trustworthiness, 263–68
Typificatory schemes, 153

Understanding, 165–67
United States, 99
Universal functionalism, 127
Universal morality, 12
Universally valid knowledge, 182
Universalism, 33
    moral, 287
Utilitarian dilemma, 9
Utilitarianism, 9, 91
Utility, marginal, 258

Validity
    criteria of, 74
    universal, 186
Value commitments, 56–58
Value consensus, 15
Value generalization, 88, 92

Value proposition(s), 221, 224–27, 229–30
Value system, 102
Values, 224–26, 229, 238
  common, 274
  particularistic, 275

specification of, 63
universal, 20
universalistic, 275
Verstehen, 165
Violence, 198
Voluntarism, 14, 105–7, 115